LINCOLN BIBLE INSTITUTE

W9-CBA-520

JAMES A. GARFIELD.

HIRAM COLLEGE

.....AND......

Western Reserve Eclectic Institute

FIFTY YEARS OF HISTORY

1850-1900

By F. M. GREEN, A. M., LL. D.

WITH

An Introduction by PROF. E. B. WAKEFIELD

THE O. S. HUBBELL PRINTING CO.
CLEVELAND, OHIO
1901

Copyright 1901,
by
F. M. GREEN.

286.6
G 79
c.2

6372

DEDICATION

To the many thousands who constitute
the goodly Fellowship
of
Hiram College
and
The Western Reserve Eclectic Institute,
this
VOLUME

of interesting facts and memories is dedicated by one,
who, familiar with their history for fifty years,
has brought into order these chronicles.

PREFACE.

There are some things which can be stated in a Preface or Introduction better than in the body of a book. Some personal explanations can be made which would be altogether out of place anywhere else. In the preface the author of a volume or treatise mounts his throne and asserts his dictum. It should be known to all that the author whose name appears on the title page of this volume was not the first in the Hiram fellowship to gather material, to outline its use, and to enter upon the writing of a Hiram history. Mainly to the Faculty of Hiram College, and especially to Professor A. C. Pierson who was selected by them, is the credit due for the idea which has been expanded into the present volume. To the great sorrow of a large circle of friends and co-laborers in behalf of Hiram College and higher education, Prof. Pierson died suddenly at the begnning of his work, leaving for another hand to do what it was hoped he would be able to perform. He had gathered considerable material and had outlined his plan of work, and had written a little more than one chapter. Substantially he completed the first chapter of the history, and with slight change that chapter stands as he wrote it and as a memoral of high personal regard and of the high esteem in which he was held by his associates in the Faculty and the students and friends of Hiram College. In his foreview of "University and its Sons," Dr. John Eaton, himself an eminent educator, says: "How often do both the faculty and students of a generation fail to gain the inspiration justly theirs, by reason of the lack of knowledge of the sacrifices and triumphs of those who have gone before them. How many fail to bestow their wealth in aid of this instruction, and how many sons fail to take advantage of it because they, or those advising them, do not know what those receiving it have thereby gained to themselves, or what they have contributed to the uplifting of mankind and the advancement of civilization." To furnish this knowledge of what Hiram College has accomplished in fifty years in material equipment, and in "the uplift of mankind" is the purpose of this history. The power of a college is not in what it promises to do but in what it does, and this cannot be estimated until many years of deeds have been accomplished. Compared with Harvard with its 265 years of history; Yale with its 201; Princeton with its 155; and Columbia with its 147, Hiram is but a youth; and yet the fifty years of its history now past have proven to be in many respects, within the most wonderful semi-centennial period since the birth of Jesus Christ. Hiram has a past that is worth the study of the friends of education both higher and lower. To give that history accurately and impartially, and to make it pleasantly readable has been the steady purpose of the author. In its preparation he has examined every page of the records of the Board of Trustees for fifty years; its fifty annual catalogues; the records of its Faculty meetings for forty years; a large number of private letters and other communications; and much history of contemporary institutions. Acknowledgment is made for aid rendered in material and valuable suggestion to the Faculty of the College, to individual members of its Board of Trustees, to intimate personal friends, to Dr. William T. Harris of the United States Bureau of Education, to members of the Faculty of the University of Michigan, and to Dr. Charles F. Thwing, President of Western Reserve University for his valuable discussion "College Administration," and to all others who for little or much have been willing helpers.

The book is in its nature a memorial, and the personal element is one of its main characteristics, and to deal with these persons and their work without exaggeration giving to each one his proper estimate and setting, without distinction or invidious comparison has been the desire and effort of the author. In many respects the author has had a great advantage in that he had personal and often intimate knowledge of the Institution for fifty years, and of the men and women who from its first Board of Trustees, its first Faculty, and its first body of students have shone in its heavens. With nearly all he was personally acquainted and with some had an intimate personal and professional relationship. From the student body of the College many have arisen who in various positions as business men, preachers, lawyers, educators, statesmen and chief executives of State and Nation have ranked among the best. In memory of these and for the pleasure and profit of those of their humbler companions who yet remain and to the many who will be interested in their history in the years, perhaps ages to come; this history of prophecies fulfilled, of struggles met, of victories won, of ambitions yet unrealized, has been prepared with ever-increasing interest by one who owes much to the Institution and its gifted teachers for what he has been, is, and hopes to be.

F. M. GREEN.

Kent, O., March 11, 1901.

INTRODUCTION.

The founding of a successful school is an event of great significance. Such an institution becomes a sort of second home to a great body of young people, a place where the family group enlarges and the horizon of life expands. Of measureless value is such a place, if it fulfilled its mission. To build a house is not to make a home. That comes of the close and tender associations, the comedies and tragedies, the toils and tears of the long years. There is a momentum strange and powerful in the character of such a place. A thousand subtle influences bear in upon the life that follows after, and change at length becomes almost impossible.

The institution at Hiram was fortunate in its beginning. No possible selfish speculation, no merely individual interest had aught to do with its planting. It was not dropped from the hand of some wealthy benefactor that it might create for itself a mission or call to itself patronage. It came in answer to a demand. It was pushed into being by a people who were rich only in faith and aspiration because they felt there was imperative need of it.

It may be said that Hiram was never built to imitate, or to compete with, any other institution. Methods of education approved by experience it has ever been ready to adopt, but it has had from the first its own distinctive field and purpose. Whether it keeps pace with the fads or fashions of other colleges it little notes or cares. It has its own ideals; it strives to keep them highest and best; and it seeks to send out students who in the front ranks of life's real service can endure hardness equal to any others.

The institution has been fortunate in its history. Well founded before the civil war, she sent her sons to stand on almost every hard-fought battlefield, and gave the momentum of her life to the saving of her country.

In all the changing tides, the storms and stress of religious and social life, Hiram has at once been true to its own highest conception of duty, and to the charge committed by the men and women by whom it was founded. There never has been a time in the history of the institution when it could have been accused justly as narrow and illiberal on the one hand, or unstable and unsound on the other. The institution has always felt that all truth was not yet found, but it has accepted certain facts beside the law of gravitation as fixed.

It has varied somewhat in its expression, it has from the first been courteous and tolerant, but the college has always been religous.

It has been *reverent* What a story it would tell if the old chapel could repeat the prayers that have been breathed within it in a succession of fifty years! Here manhood has held profound respect, and God has been unceasingly adored. It has had the *spirit of service*. It has taught that it is ignoble to take more from the world than one gives; that the world-lifters are immeasurably better than the world-burdeners, no matter how much tinsel the latter wear. It has been a *place of faith*. There has always been accepted a sublimer hope than that man is the child of a clod and doomed to return. If ever it ceases to hold for man the unwavering inspiration of a divine origin, a divine communion, and an immortal life, the college that has been will cease to be.

What a wealth of history these fifty years have made on Hiram Hill! Only fragments of it can be told, but these well indicate the kind of life that has been lived. The institution has called to itself earnest and wholesome lives, and furthermore it has developed them. The "Hiram fellowship" is not selfish, it does not forbid others, and yet it remains to a vast company as the choicest and happiest that ever life affords.

As a whole the history of this college is singularly clear and open. In the days of its poverty and hard limitations some faithful workers were too poorly sustained and requited, but intentional injustice has been done to no one. There is no skeleton in the closet here; and so far as the reputation of the college is concerned, the historian might write in utter abandon of all that has occurred.

Finally, the college has been fortunate in its historian. No man lives who at once knows so well the whole history of Hiram College, and holds so largely the culture and the balance of the good writer, as the author of this volume. For nearly half a century, since 1853, he has been associated with the institution as student, lecturing visitor, or trustee. He has breathed its air and known its workers in all the years. He has no narrow perspective. As a true son of Hiram he has done good work out in the wide world. He has preached ably far and near; as a missionary secretary he has known the length and breadth of the land; he has stood in halls of legislation; and he has written, and written well, more than can here be told.

But best of all his works, as we believe, is this present volume; for in it he preserves a story that should not be lost, and he tells it as no other could.

With a loyal affection, and in clear and good conscience, he has written the historic truth.

While other histories discourse of more renowned events and cover far wider fields, none of them strike deeper root into the soil of human experience. Here is the story of a group of workers who put their bare hearts against the most serious problems of life, who felt the darkness and found the brightness, and furnished in their own lives examples of the noblest aspiration and achievement.

To write this volume has been to the author a labor of love. It would be hard to give to any writer and his work a higher commendation.

Hiram, O.   E. B. WAKEFIELD.

TABLE OF CONTENTS.

CHAPTER I.

CHAPTER II.

CONTENTS.

CHAPTER III.

THE ECLECTIC INSTITUTE—THE GARFIELD ADMINISTRATION—1857-1863.

CHAPTER IV.

THE ECLECTIC INSTITUTE—ITS LATER LIFE AND CLOSE—1863-1867.

CONTENTS.

CHAPTER V.

CHAPTER VI.

CONTENTS.

CHAPTER VII.

HIRAM COLLEGE—A CRISIS AND HOW IT WAS MET—1883-1888.

CHAPTER VIII.

HIRAM COLLEGE—ADMINISTRATION OF E. V. ZOLLARS—1888-1900.

CONTENTS.

APPENDIX.

History of Hiram College.

CHAPTER I.

THE INCEPTION AND FOUNDING OF THE ECLECTIC.

1849-50.

In the year 1849 the religious body known as Disciples of Christ, or simply Christians, was very active on the Western Reserve. The distinctive principles of the movement which they followed and which was styled by them the "Reformation" were a return to the primitive Christianity of the Apostolic Age, the setting aside of church creeds and traditionary theology, and the use of the Holy Scriptures alone as authority in matters of faith and practice. Realizing the value of education to this movement Alexander Campbell, one of its principal leaders, had founded Bethany college among the hills of the Pan Handle in what is now West Virginia in 1840.* This institution, the only one among the Disciples, had already enjoyed nine years of

Preliminary.

---

*The Institution was opened for the reception of College Students October 21st, 1841.

prosperous life, and its influence had no doubt kindled longings for similar undertakings in other places. But Bethany was hard to reach in those days of primitive travel, and, besides, very few people, among any of the religious bodies—or outside of them for that matter—could afford to send their children to distant schools or colleges. Possibly the situation of the institution on the slavery side of the Ohio may have supplemented the physical obstacles to its access with sentiments likely to arise in a community where New England ancestry and tradition were so pronounced.

Be this as it may, the Disciples in north-eastern Ohio wanted a school of their own and they wanted it in an environment congenial both to their tastes and their pocket-books. Time and place were very favorable to such a measure. The Western Reserve had proven a rich soil for the growth of the principles of the Reformation. The evangelistic labors of Walter Scott, Calvin Smith and other pioneer preachers had resulted in numerous churches whose flourishing membership seemed a promising constituency to which to appeal for financial aid. Moreover as the reformatory movement was a popular one, many men of much natural ability but without the poise and polish of education had entered the ranks of the ministry, and leading Disciples felt the force of occasional thrusts from denominational opponents against a body that permitted men to preach who had not graduated from some theological school, or from any school at all. However the general interests of education probably had more weight than the absence of merely theological training, seeing that the Disciples had brushed away creeds and insisted on a face to face study of the Bible.

It was a time, too, of general educational awakening all over the country. There was a rustling in the air, a

going among the mulberry trees whose direction could not
be mistaken, and which was calling people away from
clearing the woods and building homes to the mental and
moral welfare of their children. The Ohio public school
system, as it exists now, was just beginning to advance to
something definite and orderly, but the high school had
not yet thrown its shadow across the old fashioned academy, several of which, more or less under religious control, flourished on the Reserve. Hudson and Oberlin
colleges had both been founded on the Reserve and most
all the leading religious denominations had colleges in
various parts of the state. Then, too, the enginery of
that great inventive and literary period that occupies the
latter half of this century had gotten well under way and
men were beginning to feel the jar of its mighty pulsa-
tions.

Just where and how long the first impulses were stir-
ring that gave rise to the Eclectic Institute, it is hard to
tell. All records and notes of primary meetings held to
originate it have perished or become
scattered beyond recall. All that can
be said accurately is that A. S. Hayden, Wm. Hayden,
Isaac Errett, and other pioneer preachers and representative men among the Disciples had been exchanging views
upon the matter for several years prior to 1849.

In those days of imperfect and precarious postal service, and absence of the religious convention system of
later times the yearly meeting of the Disciples was an institution of great importance. This
institution originated on the Reserve
and was peculiar to the Reformation.
It was the legitimate successor of the annual meetings
of the Mahoning Association of Baptist Churches
that flourished on the Reserve in the decade between

Early Impulses.

The Yearly
Meeting.

1820-1830.   *This   Association   was   dissolved   in   the
latter year at Austintown, Ohio, but the yearly meeting
was continued by the reformers and was for many years
the principal means of gathering preachers and people
into a sort of convention for preaching the gospel and re-
porting and discussing the progress of the church.   It
was the religious occasion of the whole year.   Coming in
the warm weather and in the season of good roads it was
accessible from all parts of the country and was attended
by great crowds of people.   It had none of the objection-
able features of the old fashioned camp-meeting and was
in no way its descendant.   It generally began on Friday
afternoon with services in the church of the local congregation where the meeting was held.   On Sunday the services were held in the woods or groves, the weather per-
mitting and consisted of a morning and an afternoon
sermon, the communion service preceding the latter.
The people who came for miles† were lodged with the
brethren, houses and even barns generally being filled to
overflowing.   On Monday forenoon the meeting broke
up.   The majority of the preachers and representative
church members from over broad districts were generally

---

*The Association referred to was held in Austintown in August,
1830.   It was held in the first meeting-house erected by the Disciples
on the Western Reserve.   The motion to dissolve the Association was
made by John Henry, who said:—"We want nothing here which the
word of the Lord will not sanction."   It was an "advisory" association—not legislative.   The motion carried with great enthusiasm, and
the assembly was manifestly in favor of demolition.   Mr. Alexander
Campbell then proposed that the brethren meet annually, hereafter,
for preaching the gospel, for mutual edification, and for hearing reports of the progress of the cause of Christ.   This was unanimously
approved.   Thus ended the Association and thus began the yearly
meeting system which still remains in force in some parts of the
Western Reserve.

†Many had come as far as forty or fifty miles to this (the meeting
at Austintown in 1830) feast of love.—*Hist. of W. Reserve*, p. 297.

to be found at the yearly meeting so that in addition to its primary function of presenting the plea of the Disciples to large congregations, it afforded ample opportunity for that personal exchange of views and opinions denied by the primitive condition of the country throughout most of the year.

In June 1849, there was a yearly meeting held with the church at Russell, Geauga Co., which is an important one in the history of the Eclectic Institute. Presumably consequent upon some informal discussion of the question of the school, Mr. A. L. Soule, one of the leading members of the Russell church, suggested that the matter be stated publicly, and that a call be made for all who were interested to meet at his house on Monday morning, June 12th, 1849, at eight o'clock. A. Bentley, William Hayden, A. L. Soule, Myron Soule, Benjamin Soule, Anson Matthews, Zeb Rudolph, A. S. Hayden, W. A. Lillie, Alanson Baldwin, E. Williams, F. Williams, E. B. Violl, M. J. Streator, W. A. Belding, A. B. Green,* together with many others, met at Mr. Soule's house. The meeting was entirely informal and views were freely expressed. Mr. A. L. Soule was made chairman of the meeting and Mr. A. S. Hayden secretary. The feeling was entirely in favor of the school and a resolution was passed to take steps toward founding it immediately. The secretary was instructed to prepare an address to the

*Among the men who helped to lay the foundation for the Eclectic Institute none bore a more exalted character, intellectually and morally, than Almon B. Green. He was a great preacher and teacher of men. In personal presence he was imposing and impressive. He was about six feet in height, of light complexion and sandy hair, and dark eyes which were full of expression. The verdict of his contemporaries was unanimous as to his greatness as a preacher and goodness as a man. He was born in Litchfield, Connecticut, January 12, 1808, and died in Cleveland, Ohio, March 31, 1886.

churches on the subject and invite them to send delegates to discuss it at a future meeting. This meeting at Russell was undoubtedly the first definite step toward founding the Institute.

The Delegate Meetings. Mr. Hayden performed his duty faithfully and the result was a delegate meeting held in connection with the yearly meeting at North Bloomfield, in the following August, 1849. The object of this meeting—to secure a fuller expression of the people's views—was easily attained. There was high enthusiasm in favor of the school and a vigorous demand for another meeting to mature plans for it.

Bloomfield.

Delegates assembled again at Ravenna, October 3d, 1849. Dr. J. P. Robison, of Bedford, was chosen chairman of this meeting and Mr. A. S. Hayden again chosen secretary. The lines of discussion were drawn somewhat more sharply than at Bloomfield. That the school should be established had been practically settled, but where and of what kind remained to be decided. Concerning these points Mr. Hayden says:

Ravenna.

"The delegates discussed various questions, one of which was the grade or rank of the contemplated institution. Two classes of views were represented. Some proposed the founding of a college asserting our ability to create an institution of that grade; others were in favor of establishing a school of high grade but not to clothe it as first with collegiate powers. The latter views prevailed and the sense of the convention was expressed nearly unanimously in a resolution to that effect. The meeting appointed five of its members a delegation to visit all places that solicited the location of the school, to investigate and compare the ground of their respective claims

THE ECLECTIC INSTITUTE: ERECTED IN 1850.

and to report at the next delegate meeting, when the question of location was to be decided." Of this visiting delegation Mr. Hayden has preserved the names of but four: Aaron Davis, Zeb Rudolph, B. F. Perky and Wm. Richards. Seven towns petitioned for the school—North Bloomfield, Newton Falls, Hiram, Shalersville, Aurora, Russell, and Bedford.

To all these towns the delegation went in the latter part of the fall of 1849. There is a tradition of its visit to Hiram which says that B. F. Perky was greatly pleased with the beauty and healthfulness of the location, and that he actually pointed out as a site for the building the identical one afterward fixed upon. Other tradition has it that Hiram was commended to the delegation by the numerous springs of water that gushed out around the hill; and another exceedingly comical one relates that while the men were spying out the land the township doctor drove by whose lank form, thin visage, and starveling horse seemed to indicate no superfluous amount of public patronage. "Gracious!" exclaimed one of the visitors, "a township that can't afford sickness enough to keep a doctor better than that is just the place to put the school in." Whatever truth may be in such stories it is safe to infer, from subsequent events, that the visiting delegation did nothing prejudicial to the interests of any of the contending towns but reported their respect-ive claims clearly and left them to be discussed and de-cided on their merits.

The meeting that received this report was held in the Disciple church in Aurora, November 7th, 1849. It was, from some points of view, the

Aurora.   most important of the four delegate meetings, as it was, by far, the most spirited and conten-tious. The probable decision of the location of the school awakened great interest and the meeting was well attended. Thirty-one churches were represented by as many delegates.* Besides these a large number of interested visitors came from various localities. The weather preceding the meeting was fair, though the night of the seventh of November set in rainy and stormy, very much in keeping with the character of the proceedings themselves.

The report of the visiting delegation was discussed throughout most of the day, and the discussion arose at times to a point where Christian forbearance was stretched to a dangerous tension. It was determined to decide the location by ballot, and the balloting went on far into the night. Rival claims went up and down in the balance and it seemed likely that the meeting would break up without coming to a decision. Four of the delegates, wearied with the prolonged contest, went home before the final vote was taken. The delegates from Hiram, Mr. Carnot Mason and Mr. Hartwell Ryder, became persuaded for some reason or other that Hiram's chances were becoming hopeless, and after the twelfth ballot had been taken, Mr. Mason, who all along had lamented the acrimonious spirit of the proceedings, rose and in a very short but dignified Christian speech announced that Hiram would withdraw. This decision was met with vigorous disapproval so that Mr. Mason finally consented to con-

---

*It is difficult, if not quite impossible now to enumerate each of these churches and the name of its delegate, for the records of the meeting are lost. The following partial list rests upon the memory of some of the delegates and can hardly pretend to perfect accuracy: Bloomfield, C. Brown; Ravenna, F. Williams; Bazetta, A. Davis; Norton, A. B. Green; Euclid, A. S. Hayden; Russell, A. L. Soule; Shalersville, Eldredge; Bedford, J. P. Robison; Munson, J. G. Coleman; Mantua, Darwin Atwater; Solon, W. Richards; Aurora, A.V. Jewett; Garrettsville, Zeb Rudolph; Hiram, Carnot Mason; Wadsworth, Almon Brown.

tinue Hiram in the contest. The struggle had now nar-
rowed down to Russell and Hiram, and on the very next
ballot, the thirteenth, the decision was made in favor of
Hiram by a vote of seventeen to ten. Speaking of this
incident, more than thirty years afterward at the Hiram
College reunion of 1880, Mr. Hayden said:

"When the delegate convention of thirty-one members from thirty-one churches met in Aurora, November
7th, 1849, to decide the question of the location of the
Western Reserve Eclectic Institute, and when the advocates of the contesting locations, in a very Chicago style,
were pushing their claims, a speech delivered by Carnot
Mason was in my judgment, then and now, the means of
influencing the vote that gave the institution to Hiram."*

However true Mr. Hayden's judgment may be, it
must not be forgotten that Hiram did not enter the contest without substantial claims. These were, aside from
healthfulness of location, which might have been claimed
equally truly by other places—seclusion from large towns
and cities—a condition then deemed very desirable for
the life of students†—"a vigorous church that would
furnish the desired religious environment, and last but

---

*The three men to whose exertions the selection of Hiram was
principally due were Alvah Udall, Esq., Carnot Mason and Pelatiah
Allyn, Jr. That is, they roused up the people of Hiram and put the
town into such shape that it became a formidable contestant. Mr.
Udall seems first to have agitated the question.—*Hinsdale. Historical
Discourse on Hiram Church.* Note p. 40.

†"Let us expose our children to the virus of pestilence; let them
fall by the touch of the Asiatic scourge rather than expose them to
the moral effluvia that poison the great pathways of public travel."—
Announcement of First Session of Western Reserve Eclectic Institute,
p. 12.

"Put your seminary on your own domain. Be owners of the soil
on which you dwell, and let the tenure of every lease and deed depend
on the express condition that nothing detrimental to the morals and
studies of youth be allowed on the premises."—*Bishop Philander
Chase, in Hist. of Higher Education in O.* p. 93.

not least a contingent subscription of four thousand dollars—no mean inducement to the trustees of a school that was not expected at its founding to cost more than twice or thrice that sum.''*

The meeting at Aurora adjourned to convene in Hiram on the 20th of December, 1849. This was the last of the delegate meetings and was especially marked by two procedures; the selection of the incorporators of the Eclectic and the drafting of its charter. The twelve men who incorporated the institute were by the provisions of the charter to constitute a provisional board of trustees until seven thouand dollars of the capital stock of the corporation should be subscribed when they were to call a meeting of the stockholders who were to elect a permanent board. The names of these men are all found in the charter. The committee that drafted this important instrument consisted of Isaac Errett, Charles Brown and A. S. Hayden. They were assisted by Judge King, of Warren. The charter they prepared met the approval of the board with a few slight alterations. The clause referring to the facts and precepts of the Holy Scriptures as a basis for the teaching of literature and science, especially moral science, was inserted on the motion of William Hayden. The name of the school, "Western Reserve Eclectic Institute," was suggested by Isaac Errett.† The charter received the sanction of the Ohio Legislature, March 1st, 1850.

As no trouble was expected in getting the charter the corporators anticipated its arrival and met in Hiram the day after their selection to organize—December 21st,

---

*Hinsdale.—Garfield and Education, p. 16.

†Then pastor of the church at North Bloomfield.

The First Meetings of the Corporators.

1849.   Carnot Mason was elected president, Zeb Rudolph, secretary; Symonds Ryder, treasurer; and William Hayden was appointed a solicitor for funds.   A building committee was also appointed.   This committee was Pelatiah Allyn, Jr., Zeb Rudolph, Carnot Mason, Jason Ryder and Alvah Udall.   The first two of these men were practical carpenters and afterward rendered substantial aid on the Institute building.   The natural business ability of Esq. Alvah Udall as he was called placed him at the head of this committee and the rapidity with which the edifice was planned and completed was largely due to his untiring energy.   This meeting also adopted a seal for the institution the design of which was—a vignette, a dove with an olive branch in its beak, its wings half raised, resting on the open Bible, with the motto, "Let there be light."

On the 12th of February the corporators met again, adopted a plan for the building, and empowered the building committee to make a contract with Thomas F. Young for the north part of his farm containing about fifty-four acres* for the use of the Institution.   Although not a member of the building committee one of the most active men in negotiating this business was Mr. Aaron Davis, one of the incorporators and one of the five who had composed the delegation sent by the Ravenna meeting to view the proposed locations of the school.   Mr. Young was not desirous to sell his land and had about discouraged even Esq. Udall himself.   But Mr. Davis, like the importunate widow, persevered until finally successful.   This piece of land was afterward surveyed by the county surveyor and laid out into lots and the plat of the

---

*The records at Ravenna show fifty-six and a fraction.

survey recorded. These lots were mostly all sold, a plat of something over seven acres being reserved in which the building was erected. This plat is now the college campus, and is second in beauty and attractiveness to none in the state.

The extreme northern part of the farm bought by the building committee contained a valuable stone quarry. Here the stone was procured for the foundation of the first building and the erection of later buildings owes much to the same source.

First Meeting
Under the
Charter.

On the 7th day of May, 1850, the Board met under the following charter. It legalized its proceedings of the previous two meetings by adopting them.

AN ACT TO INCORPORATE

THE WESTERN RESERVE ECLECTIC INSTITUTE.

Sec. 1. *Be it enacted by the General Assembly of the State of Ohio*, That George Pow, Samuel Church, Aaron Davis, Isaac Errett, Carnot Mason, Zeb Rudolph,

The Charter.

Symonds Ryder, J. A. Ford, Kimball Porter, William Hayden, Frederick Williams, A. S. Hayden, and such other persons as may hereafter become associated with them, be and they are hereby created a body corporate and politic, by the name and style of the "Western Reserve Eclectic Institute" to be located in the township of Hiram, in the county of Portage, and by that name they shall have perpetual succession, and possess all the incidental powers and privileges of similar corporations; provided the capital stock of said corporation shall not exceed fifty thousand dollars to be divided into shares of twenty-five dollars each and used for no other purpose than the instruction

of youth of both sexes in the various branches of literature and science, especially of moral science, as based on
the facts and precepts of the Holy Scriptures.

Sec. 2.   That said corporation shall be capable in
law of receiving, acquiring, and holding either by gift,
grant, purchase, devise or otherwise, any real or personal
estate, and of improving, selling, or otherwise disposing
of the same for the benefit of said Institution.

Sec. 3.   That the corporate concerns of said Institute
be managed by a board of trustees consisting of not
less than nine or more than twelve members, to be chosen
as hereinafter specified, one of whom shall be elected
President, any five of whom shall form a quorum for doing
business; they shall have power to fill all vacancies which
may occur in their own board by death, resignation or
refusal to serve, which appointments shall be valid until
the next annual election; said board of trustees shall have
power to appoint a treasurer, secretary, and such other
officers and agents as they may deem necessary and prescribe their duties; employ such professors and teachers,
allow them such compensation, and continue them such
length of time as they may judge proper, regulate the
government and the admission of the students of said Institute; expel any disorderly student, require satisfactory
bonds of any of their officers or agents for the faithful
discharge of their respective trusts, prescribe the mode of
obtaining subscriptions to the capital stock and the terms
and conditions of payment thereof, and all other measures
necessary for the establishment and efficient management
of said Institute.

Sec. 4.   All deeds and other instruments of writing
that may be required to carry into effect any contract
made by the board of trustees shall be executed by the
President and sealed with the corporate seal which may be
adopted by said corporation.

Sec. 5.   That the corporators named in the first section of this act, or so many of them as may choose to act shall have power to open books for the subscription of the capital stock of said corporation, and exercise all the power conferred upon the board of trustees, until they shall have obtained subscriptions to the amount of seven thousand dollars, when it shall be their duty to call a meeting of the stockholders at some convenient place in the town of Hiram, notice of which meeting shall be given to said stockholders at least ten days previous to said meeting.   At such called meeting, the stockholders shall proceed to elect not less than nine nor more than twelve suitable persons to constitute the first board of trustees, one-third of whom shall be designated by the ballots electing, as holding said trust for one year, one-third for two years, and one-third for three years from the date of their next annual election; each stockholder being entitled at all elections, one vote in person or by proxy, for every share of stock owned by him; provided that no stockholder shall have more than four votes for one hundred dollars, six votes for two hundred dollars, seven votes for three hundred dollars, and eight votes for four hundred dollars or more; provided also that no stockholder shall be entitled to vote at any annual election, on stock which has not been paid up according to the requirements of the board of trustees.

Sec. 6.   That the annual meeting of the stockholders for the election of a board of trustees or such portion thereof as may be vacant shall be held in the township of Hiram on the last Tuesday of June in each and every year, or such other day as the board of trustees may appoint of which they shall give due notice to the stockholders; but a failure to elect on said day, shall not work a dissolution of the corporation, but the trustees then in office may call a meeting for that purpose at any future day, and hold their offices until others are appointed in their places, and in case the stockholders still shall fail to meet, then the remaining trustees shall elect the number of new trustees necessary to fill up the board and continue to do so from year to year until the stockholders shall again meet and resume the exercise of their power.

Sec. 7.   The board of trustees shall have power to make such by-laws for the efficient management of the Institution as they may deem necessary and prescribe the mode of transferring the shares of said capital stock.

Dated March 1st, 1850.

BENJAMIN F. LEITER,
Speaker of the House of Representatives.

CHARLES C. CONVERS,
Speaker of the Senate.

As subscriptions were slow in being made the Board, at this meeting proceeded to strengthen the force of solicitors.   It   ordered   a   circular   to be   prepared   giving general information regarding the plan of the school, and appointed Isaac Errett and A. S. Hayden a committee to negotiate for a Principal.   Mr. Zeb Rudolph resigned the office of secretary and Dr. Lyman W. Trask was elected to succeed him.   The Doctor was one of the most faithful and efficient secretaries that ever served the Board of Trustees and when he died in 1862, after holding the office twelve years, a resolution passed by that body bore testimony to the efficient manner in which he had discharged his duties.

In the mean time the building committee had been hard at work.   December, 1849, had not ended when Esq. Udall made a long journey to Rootstown to conduct ne-

The First
Building.

gotiations for the brick and stone-work of the building with Mr. W. A. Holcomb, a stone-mason of that township. Mr Holcomb came up to Hiram in January, 1850, driving in a sleigh over the round-about route by way of Ravenna and Garrettsville. He stayed over night and met the building committee at the home of Esq. Udall. On the next day, after looking over the ground, he returned home to figure on the building. The result was that he came back to Hiram about April 1st, 1850, bringing with him twenty-one workmen, a man and wife to do the cooking, and two cows. He put up a shanty near a spring on the east side of the north and south center road near the present home of Mr. Lester Bennett. Here he made his headquarters and boarded his hands.*

The plan of the building adopted by the Board at the meeting of February 12th, 185C, had been presented by a Mr. Sweet of Farmington, but Mr. Hayden says the drawings followed by Mr. Holcomb were from the pencil of an architect, J. N. Skinner. Whatever this may mean, it is certain that the old Eclectic building was in its form and arrangements similar to that of the Western Reserve Seminary still standing (1900) in the village of West Farmington, but a much finer building. Mr. Holcomb was to oversee all the brick and stone-work, receiving for his services $2.25 per day. The workmen were paid $1.25 per day. Most of the wood-work was done by Pelatiah Allyn and Zeb Rudolph. The brick were burned expressly for the purpose down on the banks of the creek on the farm of Esq. Udall. The workmen engaged in this part of the service were under the direct supervision of the Squire himself. It

---

*The spring referred to is hardly known to present day Hiram students, as it lies west of the walk and is covered with a large stone. Mr. Bennett however pipes water from it to his house.

is almost needless to say that no better brick ever went into a building. It, no doubt, sounds odd to this generation to read in the old records, "resolved the building be made of brick;" but such a thing was not then a matter of course. Several of the prominent academies on the Reserve could boast of nothing but frame, and outside of the towns brick houses were not common. The question of a frame building had been suggested in the Board, but Mr. Carnot Mason, the president, urged a building that would give tone and dignity to the whole enterprise.

The summer of 1850 was exceptionally fine. Only one slight interruption occurred to interfere with Mr. Holcomb's progress. Simultaneously with the work he was doing at Hiram, a large brick building for a factory was going up at Kent. The promoters of this enterprise by offering twenty-five cents more per day for brick-layers created dissatisfation among Mr. Holcomb's workmen, and for a short time a real strike seemed imminent. The wisdom and sagacity of Esq. Udall came to the rescue and a compromise was affected that proved entirely satisfactory. Autumn brought with it a large crop of apples, and the orchard on the Institute land was loaded with the fruit. The building stood just on the south edge of this orchard and, as October drew to a close, the high dome that crowned it began to tower into the view of the surrounding country—the cynosure of all eyes.   Judge H. C. White thus records his first impressions of it.

"I first entered Hiram in December, 1850. My approach was from the west, and my first glimpse of the new building was just at the close of a clear, crisp winter day. I had ridden all the way from Cleveland in a sleigh, and as we rose over the shoulder of the hill out of the Cuyahoga valley, on the road from Mantua, the last rays of the sun were flashed back from the new cupola on the 'old Eclectic.'* The scattering village was strung along the highway we traveled and as the lofty Institute north of the village burst upon us, village and all seemed transfigured in the glow of the setting sun. If ever you saw an old 'Webster's Spelling Book' of that date, you will remember that the frontispiece was the picture of an impossible Temple of Fame set upon a steep and rugged mountain side with a youth struggling up toward the high portal. That 'Speller' had been my last text-book and there before me was the counterpart and realization of that picture."

Many a country boy who saw the building then for the first time, and who came to visit it again long after he had seen

"The vision of the world, and the wonder that would be"

was surprised and grieved to see how its magnificent proportions had dwindled in the intervening years. It was a great building for that day. Mr. Hayden described it in extravagant terms, deeming it no violation of taste to draw his imagery from the effort of the great Solomon himself.

"The edifice is three stories high;† the first story of freestone of a beautiful reddish color. The next two are high stories of brick. The material of its perfect walls is unsurpassed in beauty and durability. The height of the walls from the ground to the eaves is forty-one feet; to the ridge, fifty feet. The cupola is nineteen feet high, surmounted by a dome twelve feet in diameter and seven and one-half feet elevation. The building is put up on a beautiful and tasteful model more neat and elegant than

---

*The dome remained for a long time unpainted and its bright tin always flashed back the rays of the setting sun. General Garfield said he felt exceedingly sorry when the first coat of paint was put on.

†Mr. Hayden calls the basement a story.

showy. It presents a front from the extremity of
the wings of eighty-four feet, with a rear extension of
sixty-four feet; the wings are twenty-two by twenty-four
feet; of the same height as the main walls, and set
back three feet from the front end of it, relieving the
prospect from a continuous unbroken front.   Like the
temple on Mt. Moriah, one large eastern entrance leads
into its spacious rooms.''

Mr. Hayden was right in much of his eulogy.* Good
material and good work were both put into the building.
The walls with the exception of a few slight cracks, made
by the weight of another wall on top of them—part of
the addition of 1886—now remain, after fifty years, as
smooth as when they received the last stroke of Mr. Holcomb's trowel.

The Hiram that saw this imposing structure rise in
its midst was a mere country cross roads.   At or near the
immediate center stood about a dozen houses.   The
dwelling of Thomas F. Young con-
Hiram in 1850.   taining the post office stood on the
northwest corner.   On the southwest corner stood the
frame Disciple church burned in 1856.   On the corner east
of the church—the south-east corner—was the old stone
school house known later in Hiram parlance as "the
Jug.''   On the northeast corner were a small house and
barn belonging to a Mr. Fitch.   There were two blacksmith
shops just west of the cross-roads.   A Methodist church
occupied the site of the present Y. M. C. A. building.
North and west of the Methodist church was the plat of
land purchased for the Institute.   In the north and east
part of this plat was the orchard already referred to—a
favorite place in after years for holding Commencements.

---

*Announcement of the first session of the Eclectic, p. 13.

Two or three trees belonging to this old orchard are still standing (1900) just west of Bowler Hall. A little north and extending west from the orchard was the stone quarry. A rail fence ran just south of the orchard separating it from a piece of cultivated land. The very first work ever done toward the Institute building was to remove this fence in order that Ozias Allyn to whom Mr. Holcomb had given the contract might begin digging the foundation. There were no stores at the "Center." as it was called. To buy even a pound of nails required a trip to Garrettsville, if not to the remoter towns of Shalersville or Ravenna.* A weekly mail straggled through the village coming, sometimes by way of the east and west center road from Warren or Cleveland, at other times on the north and south roads from Parkman and points beyond. Mr. T. F. Young, who had been appointed postmaster by Postmaster General Meigs in 1816, and continued in the office till his death in 1852 distributed this mail not only to residents of the township but to many who came from points far beyond the "Rapids," north, and over the line of Freedom, south. There was no hotel— this hospitable service being rendered by the household of Mr. Young whenever it became necessary.

The coming of the school, aside from the social changes to be spoken of later, worked some curious physical changes that appear in the various transformations through which some of the original houses of the village of 1850 have passed. The stone school house was abandoned in 1858 and became the wagon shop of Levi Bishop. A few years ago, its present owner converted it into an ice-house. The Fitch house was modeled and remodeled

---

*Shalersville at this time was one of the most flourishing towns in the county and contained a store claimed to rival any in Ravenna.

and finally became a good sized boarding-house long known in the history of Hiram as "Ingleside." It is now known as the "Murray" house. Fitch's barn was moved a few rods to the north and made over into a dwelling house. Students whose name is legion roomed in it from time to time and it was dignified by the name of "Sunnyside." One of the college professors made it his home for several years and it finally became the office of the village doctor which purpose it still serves. One of the two blacksmith shops was long known to later generations of students as the home of old Granny Diehl. It stood as late as hallowe'en night in 1895 when it was burned down. The old Methodist church, on the disbanding of the congregation, became the property of the township and after being used for a long time for a town hall was removed to its present site in the western part of the village and made into a livery stable where,

"Stamp of foot and neigh of hackney horse
Have taken the place of sermons, hymns and prayers."

CHAPTER II.

The first session and first term of the WESTERN RE-
SERVE ECLECTIC INSTITUTE began Wednesday, November

The Beginning. 27th, 1850. It was a day which had been
ardently wished for by those who had
been prominent in the inception and founding of the Institution, and by those who were to be its first patrons.

The building, in the erection of which Jason Ryder,
Carnot Mason, Alvah Udall, Zeb Rudolph, and Pelatiah

The Building. Allyn, Jr., had given of their time, their
money, and their intelligence as a build-
ing commitee, was not yet completed; but "a full suite of
rooms was ready for the reception of students."

The building as it finally stood complete, is enthusiastically described as follows: "The edifice is three stories
high; the first story of free stone, of a beautiful reddish
color. The next two are high stories of brick. The material of its perfect walls is unsurpassed in beauty and durability. The height of the walls from the ground to the
eaves is 41 feet; to the ridge, 50 feet. The cupola is 19 feet
high, surmounted by a dome 12 feet in diameter, and of
seven and one-half feet elevation. The building is put up
on a beautiful and tasteful model, more neat and elegant
than showy. It presents a front from the extremity of the
wings of 84 feet, with a rear extension of 64 feet. The

wings are 22 by 24 feet, of the same height as the main walls
of the edifice, and set back three feet from the front end of it,
relieving the prospect from a continuous and unbroken front.
Like the temple on Mount Moriah, one large eastern entrance
leads into its spacious rooms. Passing the first door, you are
in the large reception hall, designed for the loose garments,
etc., of the pupils. The south wing at your left hand is the
Primary Department. At the other end of the hall in the
north wing is a capacious recitation room. Directly across
the hall, opposite the front door, is another, opening into
the principal school room, seated with five rows of double
desks. Here the whole school assemble at 8 o'clock A. M.
and after one hour spent in examination of sacred history,
and in music, they repair to the studies of the day."*

The site of the building and the scenery surrounding
may be recalled by a few descriptive sentences: "The site
commands a very extensive horizon, surrounding a varied and richly adorned
scenery, embracing a vast extent of well-
improved farm lands, lying in valleys and on upland slopes.
Several villages can be seen, and innumerable forest covered hills, rising one above another and fading away in the
dim distance."* Hiram scenery certainly deserved some
words of praise. "Seeing is believing; and with all the
changes that time has wrought, the landscape is still the
same. The woodlands have become fewer and smaller in
area, while the fields have expanded; but then, as now, verdure clothed the hills and the valleys in the spring-time,
while the chestnuts yellowed, the oaks and ashes browned,
the sassafras and the pepperidge reddened, and the maples
burst into scarlet and gold, as they have done in the autumn

The
Situation.

*First Announcement and Catalogue.

for fifty succeeding years. The whippoorwill sang in the woodside at evening then as he sings now."*

The opening day of the new school was in the nature of a thanksgiving service. Before the first classes were organized a meeting of the trustees, friends of the institution from abroad, and of the citizens of Hiram, was held in the old meeting-house, where the principles and objects of the school were ably and enthusiastically presented by William Hayden, Almon B. Green, J. Harrison Jones, and others. The speakers proclaimed it the completion of long cherished purposes, and the realization of many anxieties and hopes concerning "this child of much consultation, prayer and hope." In prophetic words it was declared, that "this hill would yet become a Minerva, a center and source of light, of literature, and of refinement. From this place would go forth men of ample moral and mental growth, to fill stations of honor and usefulness in all departments of social life. The churches would send young men to gain here the skill and power to plead the gospel, and to lift up the cause of human redemption."†

After the exercises at the meeting-house, the prospective students to the number of eighty-four, the little band of selected teachers, consisting of Amos Sutton Hayden, Thomas Munnell, and Mrs. Phoebe Drake, the trustees, prominent preachers among the Disciples, and a large number of the friends of the school, and citizens generally, repaired to the new building, where further preliminary exercises were held "attendant on the nativity of the Eclectic Institute." Before the classes were formed addresses were made by A. S. Hayden, Thomas Munnell, J. H. Jones, and Isaac Errett.

*Address of B. A. Hinsdale, June 22, 1900.
†Early History of the Disciples in the Western Reserve, p. 265.

In view of the great energy and good taste of the building committee in the erection of the building, the following resolution was offered by J. H. Jones and very enthusiastically adopted by the whole assembly: "Resolved, That we consider the edifice here erected and now nearly completed, as admirably adapted to the purposes for which it is designed, as it regards alike its capacity, its beautiful and convenient model, and its tasteful and elegant style; and also as evincing the eminent architectural skill of the builders, and the very great energy of the building committee."*

The first teachers of the Eclectic Institute were A. S. Hayden, at that time a distinguished preacher among the

Organizing the School.

Disciples, a man of good ability, of unblemished character, of scholarly instincts, of musical taste, and, perhaps, the best fitted for the leading place in the new school of any of his contemporaries; Thomas Munnell, a graduate of Bethany College, a scholarly man, a competent teacher, a good public speaker, and a cultivated gentleman; and Mrs. Phoebe Drake, who possessed considerable experience as a teacher and was well qualified to take charge of the Primary Department.

A committee, which had been appointed for the purpose, had outlined a provisional "course of study," and it

Course of Study.

had been adopted. The school was divided into three departments, a Primary, a Higher, and a Highest, with the following branches assigned to each: *Primary*—Spelling, Reading, Writing, Arithmetic, Modern Geography, Grammar (begun), Composition (begun), and Modern History. *Higher*—English Grammar, Ancient Geography, Logic and

---

*First Catalogue.

Rhetoric, Natural Philosophy, Bookkeeping, Uranography (astronomy), Natural History, Physiology, Moral Science and Evidences.

Highest—Latin Grammar, Greek Grammar, Greek Reader, Arithmetic, Algebra, Higher Mathematics, Chemistry and Ancient History, Sacred History and Vocal Music; this latter to be taught to the whole school.

As this schedule was only provisional and temporary, it was soon superceded by a more pretentious—

"Course of Study."

The following, requiring three years for its completion, has been adopted, as it realizes the designs of this institution:

FIRST YEAR.

Arithmetic ....Ray
Geography .... Mitchell
Grammar .... Wells
Philosophy .... Parker
Modern History .... Goodrich
Ancient Geography .... Mitchell
Sacred History .... The Bible
Elocution .... McGuffey
Latin .... Andrew's Latin Lessons, and Caesar
Algebra .... Ray
Watts on the Mind........................ Emerson

SECOND YEAR.

English Analysis .... Green
Ancient and Modern History...................Willard
Physiology .... Cutter
Rhetoric .... Jamieson

Greek (begun) .... Kuhner
Virgil and Sallust............................ Anthon
Astronomy .... Mattison's Burrit's
Algebra .... Bourdon
Geometry .... Davies
Sacred History (Con.)................................
French ....Collot's Series
Drawing and Painting........ ....
Music ....
Bookkeeping .... Crittenden

THIRD YEAR.

Trigonometry .... Davies
Mensuration .... Davies
Surveying .... Davies
Conic Sections ....Coffin
Mental Philosophy............................. Upham
Moral Philosophy............................. Wayland
Political Economy............................ Wayland
Logic .... Whately
Cicero and Horace............................ Anthon
Xenophon ....
Herodotus ....
Greek Testament and Septuagint......................
Chemistry .... Gray
Botany .... Wood
Geology .... St. John
Agricultural Chemistry .... Johnston
Butler's Analogy ....
Evidences of Christianity .... Paley

In choosing this course of instruction the demands of
the age have been kept in view. Any student not wishing
to remain three years may take those studies having refer-

ence to the occupation he chooses to follow. Our motto
is not, *"How Much,* but *How Well."**

This "eclectic" course was not followed very rigidly,
or systematically; but classes were organized as they were
called for, and it became necessary to enlarge the teaching
force.

The name "Western Reserve Eclectic Institute" was
suggested by Isaac Errett and readily adopted as a fitting
description of the scope and character of the new school.

The Name. A thing is called "eclectic" that claims
the right of freely choosing from all
sources. The original "eclectics" were Greek philosophers
who sought to construct a whole from the various and in-
congruous parts of different systems. In regard to the
Eclectic Institute the theory no doubt was that the school
should not be bound by any system already adopted or by
a stereotyped college curriculum; but that its Principal and
Faculty should be free to choose the best of all systems as
they might be given the wisdom to see it. The Eclectic
Institute took no one school for its model. It did not adopt
wholesale, the ideas of schools east or west. It sought to
choose the good from all, and aimed to furnish instruction
and educational discipline such as its patrons and the times
demanded.

The attendance of the school increased so rapidly that
new teachers were demanded, and the teaching force was
increased before the end of the first term, by the addition
Early Teachers. of Charles D. Wilber and Miss Almeda
A. Booth. Norman Dunshee was added
soon after, and Laura A. Clark was associated with Mrs.
Drake in the Primary Department. During the seven
years ending with Mr. A. S. Hayden's administration in

*First Catalogue.

June, 1857, the following persons were published as teachers. Some of them remained only a brief period; others remained after they were chosen, until the end of and some beyond, the Hayden administration: A. S. Hayden, Thomas Munnell, Norman Dunshee, Charles D. Wilber, Almeda Ann Booth, Mrs. Phoebe M. Drake, Laura A. Clark, Calista O. Carlton, Amaziah Hull, James A. Garfield, Harriet E. Wood, Harriet Warren, S. L. Hillier, J. B. Crane, Mrs. Charlotte R. Crane, Miss Sarah Udall, Julia J. Smith, J. H. Rhodes, G. C. Reed, Hannah S. Morton, Jennie A. Chapin, Platt R. Spencer, J. W. Lusk, H. W. Everest, and Mary Atwater. At one time the sons and daughters of P. R. Spencer were associated with him in the Department of Drawing, Painting and Penmanship.

Some of these passed over into succeeding administrations of the Institution, but the most of them completed their work in Hiram during the first seven years. Several of them reached a high eminence as teachers, and in character and life are worthy of the high honor in which they have always been held by those who knew them best. Their names are worthy of more than a passing notice.

The birthplace of AMOS SUTTON HAYDEN was Youngstown, Ohio. He was born September 17, 1813. He died at Collamer, Ohio, September 11, 1880. He was the youngest child in a family of eight children, **A. S. Hayden.** seven of whom were sons. His father, Samuel Hayden, came from Pennsylvania to Ohio in 1804. His children were reared on the farm and inured to the hardships and privations of a pioneer family's life. Amidst such surroundings as existed in eastern Ohio in that early day, the boyhood of A. S. Hayden was spent. He was of slight frame and of a delicate physical organization, with an eager mind and a moral tone which were the controlling influences in his life. It was soon manifest that he pos-

sessed the temper and disposition of the student rather than
that of the mechanic or farm laborer.   Language and literature were more congenial to his taste than mathematics.
He was a great lover of books, especially religious books.
He never graduated from any college, and yet, he was a
good student, and by private study, became a fair scholar.

He became a Christian under the preaching of Walter
Scott, March 20, 1828; and in 1832 he began to preach,
being in his nineteenth year.   For forty-eight years he remained a faithful preacher of the Word of God.

March 1, 1850, the Charter for the Western Reserve
Eclectic Institute was granted by "The General Assembly
of the state of Ohio;" and at the fourth meeting of the
Board of Trustees, held in Hiram July 17, 1850, a committee, of which Isaac Errett was chairman, reported in part as
follows:—"The Committee to whom was referred the duty
of negotiating with some person to be Principal of the Institute, report,—that they have had correspondence with
several individuals on the subject; among whom were Dr.
R. Richardson of Bethany, Va., Robert Milligan of Washington, Pa., and Samuel Church of Pittsburgh, Pa., without, as yet, making any definite arrangement with any
person."

This report received "full discussion and consideration;" and it was finally, *"Resolved,* That A. S. Hayden be
appointed Principal of the Institute."

Mr. Hayden accepted the position unanimously tendered, and held the place until June, 1857.

After his connection with Hiram ceased, he was chosen
Principal of the "McNeely Normal School," at Hopedale,
Ohio, where he remained one year laboring in the double
capacity of Principal of the school and preacher for the
church.   He resigned in August, 1859, and returned to
Collamer, where, with the exception of short periods spent

at Eureka, Illinois, and in Hiram, he continued to reside
until his death September 11, 1880.

He was thirty-seven years old when he became Principal of the Western Reserve Eclectic Institute at Hiram.
He led the "foremost files" of the thousands of young
men and women who have made up its student list.   He
did much, perhaps more than any other, to lay the foundation of the school, honestly and solidly on the rock of
Christian truth and enterprise.   The genial and inspiring
enthusiasm for what is true, for God and for man, and
the invincible prowess, and steady progress which have
manifested themselves, in the career of the Institution, over
all obstacles for fifty years, were very largely the result
of his wise and persevering labor.   Others helped, and
without them, he could have done nothing; but his was the
one name that was always spoken in connection with the
"Old Eclectic."   In the progress of the years other names
grew out of the earlier "Hiram fellowship" which over-
topped his; but, after all, their glory in large degree, was
but the result of his loving watchfulness and faithfulness
toward them, when they were the "little ones" of Hiram,
and he the center of all eyes.   And so, the honest features
of the old Principal, teacher, pastor, preacher, and friend,
should be held in grateful and lasting remembrance.

Associated with Mr. Hayden at the beginning of the
school, was THOMAS MUNNELL.   He was the graduate, the
scholar of the trio, which was chosen to
teach the first classes.   On Tuesday,
November 26, 1850, the Board of Trustees adopted the following resolution: "That Thomas Munnell be appointed a
teacher in the Institute."

Thomas Munnell.

One of the traditions that has come down from the
first day of the first session of the first term of the Institute,

is that Thomas Munnell heard the first lesson ever recited within the walls of the old building.

His Department embraced the teaching of Ancient Languages; and History, ancient and modern.

In June, 1850, he had graduated from Bethany College as one of the "honor men" of his class. Prof. B. A. Hinsdale, speaking of him, says: "Thomas Munnell was a graduate of Bethany College, a scholarly man, a competent teacher, a good public speaker, and a cultivated gentleman. He came from beyond the Ohio river, and brought to Hiram some flavor of southern manners and personal cultivation. I never recited to him, but a friend who did says he was a good drill-master, perhaps better than his colleagues. He was here at two different times, but did not remain long at either one."*

When Mr. Munnell left Hiram in 1853 the Board of Trustees placed on record a resolution, thanking him "for the fidelity and ability with which his duties had been discharged."

In his address on Almeda A. Booth delivered at Hiram June 22, 1876, James A. Garfield related the following incident: "I came to the Eclectic in the fall of 1851, and a few days after the beginning of the term, I saw a class of three reciting in mathematics—geometry, I think. They sat on one of the red benches, in the center aisle of the lower chapel. I had never seen a geometry; and, regarding both teacher and class with a feeling of reverential awe, from the intellectual height to which they had climbed, I studied their faces so closely that I seem to see them now as distinctly as I saw them then. And it has been my good fortune, since that time, to claim them all as intimate friends. The teacher was Thomas Munnell; and the members of his

---

*Hiram Address, June, 1900.

class were William B. Hazen, George A. Baker, and Almeda A. Booth."*

In regard to Mr. Garfield's early student life at Hiram, Mr. Munnell is on record:

"Mt. Sterling, Ky., December 23, 1881.

F. M. Green: *Dear Sir*—In compliance with your request, I send you the following fact concerning Garfield as a student. I belonged to the first Faculty of Hiram College—the Eclectic Institute then—and in November, 1850, heard the first lesson ever recited within its walls, and, therefore, knew the general impression made by the noble student when he first appeared upon the campus, and, especially in the professors' rooms.

When he arrived he had studied a little of Latin grammar, but had done nothing in the way of translating. I had no class to suit him in elementary Latin, one being behind him, and another far in advance. He resolved at once to overtake the advanced class, provided I would hear his recitation after class hours, which I readily agreed to do. Teachers all know that an average lesson for an ordinary student, beginning Cæsar's Commentaries, is half a page, while carrying on the usual number of other studies; but, on no occasion did Garfield come in to said recitations without *three pages of* Cæsar, or six ordinary lessons, and then could go on further if I had time to hear him. His method of getting a start, as he afterwards told me, was resolute and determined. He went to a secluded place in the college with his Cæsar, dictionary, and grammar, and undertook to translate the first paragraph of half a dozen lines by writing down every Latin word, and under it every definition of that word, till he found the one that made the best sense, and when he had fairly made out,

---

*Address, Almeda A. Booth, Page 17.

'*All Gaul is divided into three parts,*' he thought his triumph had begun; and when he had completed the whole paragraph, he said, he 'just knew that he knew it.'

This was in line with all his after studies, for he always sought a conscious victory over every difficulty.

Truly yours,

Thomas Munnell."*

After Mr. Munnell left Hiram he was Principal of academies at Williamsburg, New York, Mount Sterling, Ky., and New Castle, Ky. He served, also, as pastor and preacher for several churches among which was the historic Church of Christ at the corner of 8th and Walnut streets, Cincinnati, Ohio. Quite early he gave his attention to organized missionary work, among the Disciples of Christ. He was for several years the Corresponding Secretary of the "Kentucky Christian Missionary Society," and did much to bring organized missionary work to the front in that state. In 1869 he was elected Corresponding Secretary of the "American Christian Missionary Society," and served continuously in that office, until 1878, a period of nine years. For this society he was a tireless worker; and, to him, perhaps, more than to any other man, is due the present usefulness of that society. He was distinguished for high intellectual and moral qualities. He was emphatically a good man, and his intellectual equipment was of the best quality. From the time of his graduation in 1850 until his death, his life was devoted to teaching and preaching. He was not an orator, but he was a plain, practical, instructive, and entertaining preacher. He had a tough bony frame, and a sharp, black eye, and was well organized for great mental and physical exertion. He, also, wielded

*Life of Garfield, by F. M. Green, p. 99.

a trenchant pen, and was always a formidable opponent to any "knight of the quill," who attempted to dispute either his positions or plans. He was born in Ohio county, West Virginia, February 8, 1823, and died in Alma, Illinois, in 1898. His work was well done, and his life, at last well-closed.

November 26, 1850, the Board of Trustees, resolved, "That Mrs. PHOEBE M. DRAKE be appointed Principal of the Primary Department." She accepted the position and had charge of the Primary Department for about one year. But little biographical material concerning her has been preserved. She came to the position with "much experience as a teacher, and was well qualified to preside over the Department to which she was chosen." She was a good and faithful woman, and a teacher whose name is worthy of remembrance. Following her in the Primary Department were Laura A. Clark, Calista O. Carlton, Harriet E. Wood, Sarah Udall, and Mary Atwater.

Mrs. Phoebe M. Drake.

Of these SARAH UDALL remained the longest and left the deepest impression on the Department. Her life history was brief but interesting. She was born in Susquehanna County, Pennsylvania, in 1815, and died in Warren, Ohio, in 1858. While she was yet a child her parents removed to Jefferson, Ohio, making the journey of four hundred miles through the wilderness with a span of horses and a wagon. Soon after coming to Jefferson she became a member of the family of Hon. Joshua R. Giddings though she was never legally adopted by him. But Mr. Giddings and his wife were to her father and mother, and the Giddings homestead was always her home. She attended school at Jefferson and at the Female Seminary then located at Willoughby.

Sarah Udall.

She began her work of teaching, at the age of fifteen, in a district school in Jefferson. As her ability became known, her services were sought for in many places and she availed herself of every advantage, teaching in different parts of Ohio, and in Pennsylvania, thus widening her experience and enlarging her circle of influence. There are letters preserved by the Giddings family which prove the high esteem in which she was held by them. Her letters to Mr. Giddings during the exciting anti-slavery days, are beautifully written, and show that she was well informed in political affairs. They are full of affectionate encouragement to that grand man who stood almost alone in Congress strenuously contending for his faith. Under date of June 30, 1848, she wrote to him: "I was truly rejoiced at the bold spirit you manifested. I am rejoiced that there is one, at least, who dares, on the floor of Congress, to let his voice be heard in the cause of right and justice. * * * I cannot but hope that the time is near when there shall not be one soul from the great lakes to the gulf but shall be free."

In 1847 she came to Hiram and taught the center school. When the Western Reserve Eclectic Institute opened she entered as a student; and from 1853 to 1856 she was Principal of the Primary Department. She was married in April, 1857, to J. H. Goodale of Warren, Ohio. She died in 1858 and her body was buried at Jefferson, near the home of her childhood.*

Thomas Munnell and CHARLES D. WILBER became teachers in Hiram about the same time, Mr. Munnell being chosen first. In the record of the Board of Trustees, held

Charles D. Wilber. on Friday, May 30, 1851, it was "*Resolved*, that Charles D. Wilber be appointed teacher of the Natural Sciences." The records of

*Letter of A. L. Arner, M. D., Jefferson, O.

the Institute do not contain much concerning him; but when he was chosen to teach the "Natural Sciences" he was introduced as "a young gentleman of fine attainments and approved didactic ability." His health was not rugged and within about one year he resigned his position as teacher and left Hiram. In view of his ability and faithfulness, the Board of Trustees June 23, 1853, expressed a resolution of thanks to him, "for the fidelity and ability with which his duties had been discharged." From Hiram he went to Williams College and then to the West where he became well known as a geologist. It is probable that to him Hiram owes a debt of love for first suggesting to Mr. A. S. Hayden the name of Miss Almeda A. Booth as a teacher for the young "Eclectic." He was a very enthusiastic and popular teacher of science. "An experienced teacher who knew him well says his methods were more in accord with what we call modern teaching that those of any of his colleagues." Perhaps it is not material to know where he obtained his early education; but he went to Williamstown, Mass., with "Kai Gar," as he called Garfield, in 1854, and graduated in the same class two years later. "After a life of some ups and downs, he died December 20, 1891, at Aurora, Ilinois, in his 63d year."

At the seventh meeting of the Board of Trustees of the Western Reserve Eclectic Institute held October 14, 1851, it was "*Resolved, that* NORMAN DUNSHEE be ap-

Norman Dunshee. pointed teacher of Mathematics and Modern Languages in the Institute." This was Mr. Dunshee's introduction to Hiram and the beginning of his honorable relation to Hiram as one of its ablest teachers. Norman Dunshee was born in Bedford, Cuyahoga County, Ohio, January 24, 1821. He was prepared for college at the Twinsburg Institute, Twinsburg,

Ohio, conducted by Rev. Samuel Bissell. He graduated at
Western Reserve College, Hudson, Ohio, in 1845. He
afterwards studied theology at Hudson during the years
1847-49. He taught in the Twinsburg Institute from 1849
to 1851. He began his work in Hiram in 1851 and continued until 1859. From Hiram he went to Kansas where
he was county superintendent of public instruction from
1867 to 1869. He was Professor of Mathematics in Oskaloosa College, Oskaloosa, Iowa, from 1870 to 1877. He
then became Professor of ancient languages in Drake University, Des Moines, Iowa, in 1881. This position he held
to the time of his death in 1890. In character he was an
excellent man; "and by far the first scholar in the early
Hiram group, and, all things considered, perhaps the most
learned man who ever taught on the Hill. Students could
learn in his class-room, and many did learn, but he was not
an inspiring teacher. Even Homer sometimes nodded, and
Dunshee also nodded while teaching Homer. He also
preached, but, unlike Hayden and Munnell, was primarily
a teacher.*

His body is buried in the cemetery at Des Moines,
Iowa, and lies not far from that of Harvey W. Everest,
another of Hiram's best teachers.

ALMEDA ANN BOOTH came to Hiram in 1851. On
May 30 of that year the Board of Trustees "appointed her
a teacher in the English Department." To her, more than
Almeda A. Booth.   to any other person, is due the consist-
ency and permanence of the Western Re-
serve Eclectic Institute. With the exception of one year
spent in Oberlin College, she was in Hiram from the spring
term of 1851 until Commencement 1866—in all forty-three
terms. Though she was appointed to teach in the English

---

* "The Eclectic Institute," by B. A. Hinsdale, p. 11.

ALMEDA A. BOOTH.

Department, she soon became Principal of the Ladies' Department. Her power over students was very great, and "it is no exaggeration to say that in Northern Ohio no lady teacher has surpassed Miss Booth, taking into account length of service, number of pupils taught, uniform success, and strength of personal influence. She was in Hiram during nearly the whole of the Eclectic period, and for several years gave the shifting corps of teachers such continuity and permanence as it had. First and last more Eclectic history gathers about Almeda Booth than about any other person in the school."*

Few women of nobler character, purer life, or better mental equipment, have ever lived. She was born in Nelson, Ohio, August 15, 1823, and died in Cleveland, Ohio, December 15, 1875. During all of her term of service at Hiram the light of her soul illuminated the classroom, and the social walks of the students. It is difficult to institute a comparison between her and others of her generation. She had a distinct individuality and an almost divine personality. No one who ever came in contact with her can forget her. Even-tempered, an empress in her power to control, a conqueror of every will that seemed to her to stand in the way of true progress, she was undisputed mistress of all who came within the sphere of her influence. Her early pupils regarded her with almost as much reverence as the devout Romanist does the Virgin Mary. Her sweet, Christian spirit made more fragrant by the sorrows of her life, permeated with its richness, the history of Hiram school and social life, for a full quarter of a century. Mr. Garfield, who was associated with her so long, and knew her so well, in his address June 22, 1876, at Hiram shows such a sympathetic insight into her life and

---

*B. A. Hinsdale.

character, as to make his estimate particularly valuable to those who would know her as she was known.

The lesson and legacy of her life, left to her friends and to Hiram, are felicitously expressed by her appreciative biographer: Her life was so largely and so inseparably a part of our own, that it is not easy for any of us, least of all for me, to take a sufficiently distant standpoint from which to measure its proportions. We shall never forget her sturdy well-formed figure; her head that would have appeared colossal but for its symmetry of proportions; the strongly marked features of her plain, rugged face, not moulded according to the artist's lines of beauty, but so lighted up with intelligence and kindliness as to appear positively beautiful to those who knew her well.

The basis of her character, the controlling force which developed and formed it, was strength—extraordinary intellectual power. Blessed with a vigorous constitution and robust bodily health, her capacity for close, continuous, and effective mental work was remarkable.

.It is hardly possible for one person to know the quality and strength of another's mind more thoroughly than I knew hers. From long association in her studies, and comparing her with all the students I have known, here and elsewhere, I do not hesitate to say, that I have never known one who grasped with greater power, and handled with more ease and thoroughness, all the studies of the college course. I doubt if in all these respects I have ever known one who was her equal. She caught an author's meaning with remarkable quickness and clearness; and, mastering the difficulties of construction, she detected, with almost unerring certainty, the most delicate shades of thought.

She abhorred all shams in scholarship, and would be content with nothing short of the whole meaning. When crowded with work, it was not unusual for her to sit by her lamp, unconscious of the hours, till far past midnight.

Her powers were well balanced. When I first knew her, it was supposed that her mind was specially adapted to mathematical study. A little later, it was thought she had found her fittest work in the field of the natural sciences; later still, one would have said she had found her highest possibilities in the languages.

Her mind was many-sided, strong, compact, symmetrical. It was this symmetry and balance of qualities that gave her such admirable judgment, and enabled her to concentrate all her powers upon any work she attempted.

To this general statement concerning her faculties there was, however, one marked exception. While she enjoyed, and in some degree appreciated, the harmonies of music, she was almost wholly deficient in the faculty of musical expression. After her return from college, she determined to ascertain by actual test to what extent, if at all, this defect could be overcome. With a patience and courage I have never seen equalled in such a case, she persisted for six months in the attempt to master the technical mysteries of instrumental music, and even attempted one vocal piece. But she found that the struggle was nearly fruitless; the music in her soul would not come forth at her bidding. A few of her friends will remember, that, for many years, to mention "The Suwanee River" was the signal for a little good-natured merriment at her expense, and a reminder of her heroic attempt at vocal and instrumental music.

The tone of her mind was habitually logical and serious, not specially inclined to what is technically known as wit; but she had the heartiest appreciation of genuine humor, such as glows on the pages of Cervantes and Dickens. Clifton Bennett and Levi Brown will never forget how keenly she enjoyed the quaint drollery with which they once presented, at a public lyceum, a scene from "Don Quixote;" and I am sure there are three persons here to-day who will never forget how nearly she was once suffocated with laughter over a mock presentation speech by Harry Rhodes.

Though possessed of very great intellectual powers, or, as the arrogance of our sex accustoms us to say, "having a mind of masculine strength," it was not at all masculine in the opprobrious sense in which that term is frequently applied to women. She was a most womanly woman, with a spirit of gentle and childlike sweetness, with no self-consciousness of superiority, and not the least trace of arrogance.

Though possessing these great powers, she was not unmindful of those elegant accomplishments, the love of which seems native to the mind of woman.

In her earlier years she was sometimes criticised as caring too little for the graces of dress and manner; and there was some justice in the criticism. The possession of great powers, no doubt, carries with it a contempt for mere external show. In her early life Miss Booth dressed neatly, though with the utmost plainness, and applied herself to the work of gaining the more enduring ornaments of mind and heart. In her first years at Hiram she had devoted all her powers to teaching and mastering the difficulties of the higher studies, and had given but little time to what are called the more elegant accomplishments. But she was not deficient in appreciation of all that really adorns and beautifies a thorough culture. After her return from Oberlin she paid more attention to the "mint, anise, and cummin" of life. During the last fifteen years of her life, few ladies dressed with more severe or elegant taste. As a means of personal culture, she read the history of art, devoted much time to drawing and painting, and acquired considerable skill with the pencil and brush.

She did not enjoy miscellaneous society. Great crowds were her abhorrence. But in a small circle of congenial friends she was a delighted and a delightful companion.

Her religious character affords an additional illustration of her remarkable combination of strength and gentleness. At an early age she became a member of the Methodist Episcopal Church, and continued in faithful and consistent relations with that organization until she united with the Disciples, soon after she came to Hiram.

I venture to assert, that in native powers of mind, in thoroughness and breadth of scholarship, in womanly sweetness of spirit, and in the quantity and quality of effective, unselfish work done, she has not been excelled by any American woman. What she accomplished with her great powers, thoroughly trained and subordinated to the principles of a Christian life, has been briefly stated.

She did not find it necessary to make war upon society in order to capture a field for the exercise of her great qualities. Though urging upon women the necessity of the largest and most thorough culture, and demanding for them the amplest means for acquiring it, she did not waste her years in bewailing the subjection of her sex, but employed them in making herself a great and beneficent power. She did far more to honor and exalt woman's place in society than the thousands of her contemporaries who struggle more earnestly for the barren sceptre of power than for fitness to wield it.

She might have adorned the highest walks of literature, and doubtless might thus have won a noisy fame. But it may be doubted whether in any other pursuit she could have conferred greater or more lasting benefits upon her fellow-creatures, than by the life she so faithfully and successfully devoted to the training and culture of youth. With no greed of power or gain, she found her chief reward in blessing others.

I do not know of any man or woman, who, at fifty-one years of age, had done more or better work. I have not been able to ascertain precisely how long she taught before she came to Hiram; but it was certainly not less than fifteen terms. She taught forty-two terms here, twenty-one terms in the Union School at Cuyahoga Falls, and, finally, two years in private classes; in all, nearly twenty-eight years of faithful and most successful teaching, to which she devoted the wealth of her great faculties and admirable scholarship.

How rich and how full was the measure of gratitude poured out to her, from many thousands of loving hearts! And to-day, from every station of life, and from every quarter of our country, are heard the voices of those who rise up to call her blessed, and to pay their tearful tribute of gratitude to her memory.

On my own behalf, I take this occasion to say, that for her generous and powerful aid, so often and so efficiently rendered, for her quick and never-failing sympathy, and for her intelligent, unselfish, and unswerving friendship,

I owe her a debt of gratitude and affection, for the payment of which the longest term of life would have been too short.

To this institution she has left the honorable record of a long and faithful service, and the rich legacy of a pure and noble life. I have shown that she lived three lives. One of these, the second, in all its richness and fulness, she gave to Hiram. More than half of all her teaching was done here, where she taught much longer than any other person has taught; and no one has done work of better quality.

She has here reared a monument which the envious years cannot wholly destroy. As long as the love of learning shall here survive; as long as the light of this college shall be kept burning; as long as there are hearts to hold and cherish the memory of its past; as long as high qualities of mind and heart are honored and loved among men and women,—so long will the name of Almeda A. Booth be here remembered, and honored, and loved.*

Other Teachers. Other teachers of more or less merit, but who remained for brief periods during this administration, and are worthy of mention, are Amaziah Hull, who afterwards became Professor of Languages in Oskaloosa College; S. L. Hillier, who went to New York to practice law; James A. Garfield, H. W. Everest, and J. H. Rhodes, who became distinguished as teachers; and J. B. Crane.

Provision was made for teaching Music, Drawing, and Penmanship. J. W. Lusk and the Spencers, father and sons, were for many years employed as teachers of penmanship.

When the Western Reserve Eclectic Institute was first opened for students in November 1850, the Trustees had not waited to finish the building and the opening day found

*Life and Character of Almeda A. Booth.

The Accommodations for Students. it in a state of incompleteness. The first sessions were held in the lower story. The large upper room so long used as a chapel, and now used for the library, was not finished before 1851. The two wings and the large room in the west extension were, at first, the only ones used. The Primary Department was in the south wing. The large room back of the entrance hall served as a chapel. For this reason, it was known throughout the entire history of the original building as the "Lower Chapel." For sometime after the opening of the school its class room exercises were disturbed by the sound of hammer and saw in the upper story of the building.

The accommodations for students in the matters of boarding and lodging were also very limited. The suddenness with which the Eclectic sprang into life on Hiram **Boarding and Lodging.** Hill took the quiet rural community with no little surprise. Outside the ranks of the Disciples there were not many people who had given any attention to the school movement. As prominent a citizen as Esquire Udall had not even heard of it until about time for the delegate convention at Aurora to meet. The entire change took place in less than a year. In the midst of their unpretentious homes the big building arose with Aladdin-like celerity, a flood of young people came pouring in from the surrounding country, and from distant points, and the community suddenly found itself face to face with a demand to throw open its private doors for their reception and comfort. The strain on the people's resources was not slight but they met it generally with hearty good will. They were glad to have the school in their midst and to have their children brought into the circle of its associations—a little proud, no doubt, of the distinction it would give the town. The village proper was, of course, not adequate to this sudden demand. There was not a farmhouse within a mile without boarders. Some of them were full. As many as eighteen were at one time domiciled at George Udall's down at the foot of the east hill where Mr. Frank Udall now lives. Many students boarded at Esquire Udall's, the house east of George Udall's on the hill. Others boarded up at the Packer farm —now Mr. Ford's. Judge H. C. White found a home at Mr. Orrin Hutchinson's up west of the cemetery on the north side of the road, while the old Beaman house down in the hollow below the east hill, was the home of a student who afterward became president of Hiram College.*

The local patronage was large. Both young men and young women walked from points on the diagonal road to Garrettsville south-east from the present home of Mason Tilden. Some came from the old red brick house on that road—the Wheeler home. Some from Raymond's, Young's, and Mason's on the south center road almost as far away as the present railroad station. Others from far north over the Geauga Co. line. As might be expected this sudden influx of students required no end of planning and devising in order to extend the accommodations of houses whose builders saw no such vision as this. An old student tells of a small room at George Udall's which had a sort of shelf or offset around three sides of it so that a bedstead could not be set up. But two legs of the bedstead were sawed off and then placed on the offset while the remaining two reached the floor. At the same house the shelves of a pantry were torn out to accommodate a bed, and the pantry dispensed with or moved to another part of the house. Three, sometimes four students, occupied

---

*Burke A. Hinsdale.

one room—often a small one—yet they contrived to study
hard and to maintain a good standing in the work of the
school.   Boarding was about $1.25 per week—good, sub-
stantial, about what may be found in the average farm
home on the Western Reserve today.   There was abundance of boiled dinners, soup, vegetables and good bread—
while for tea there was a lighter meal of bread and butter
and cookies, cheese and maple syrup.   There was pie
often enough, but none of the indigestible knick-knacks
that now-a-days so often set a student's stomach at variance
with his brains.

At the close of the spring session in 1851, the Board
passed a resolution to thank the citizens of Hiram for the
accommodating disposition shown in furnishing boarding
to the students of the Institute.   As the number of students
increased the problem of furnishing them comfortable
quarters became a serious one and in 1852 the Board considered the advisability of erecting a boarding hall.   This
scheme, however, was laid aside and a new building committee was empowered to contract a loan of three thousand
dollars to be used in putting up boarding houses furnished
with such conveniences as might be thought necessary.   Both
Board and Building Committee assumed mutual and individual responsibility for this loan.   The houses were built
in 1852 but do not seem to have been a paying venture.
The rents on them steadily declined for several years and
they were finally sold, but on exactly what terms cannot
now be determined.   The history of the management of
boarding halls and dormitories by the authorities of a school
is not an encouraging one generally, and shows that such
things are better in the hands of private enterprise.   The
houses built by the committee are all standing in Hiram at
the present date.

They are the two on Peckham Avenue and now occupied, one by Mr. William Oliver and one by Mrs. E. P. Warren. The one on the south-west corner of West and North Campus Street resided in at present by Mr. H. B. Cox; the old Carroll house immediately south of it now falling to pieces, and the little white house just west of Mr. Bower's large barn—the home of Mrs. Nora Quinn. This last house is well known in Hiram history as "Tiffany Hall." Another over sanguine venture of the Board may be mentioned in this connection. This was the purchase of the Higley farm, as it was called. This body of land occupied the whole east slope of Hiram hill, running for a half mile east on the east and west center road and as far north on the north and south road as the present farm of Lester Bennett. The south half of this farm was plotted and laid out into lots, but none were ever sold except three or four on the north center road now in the midst of the village proper. The rest of the land was finally disposed of in lots to suit purchasers. Had this scheme worked out a large part of the village would have occupied the east slope of the hill—a poor exchange probably for the peach and apple orchards that now cover it.

On the 6th of May, 1851, the first public exercises of the students of the Eclectic were held. They consisted of three divisions, one given in the morning, one in the after-

First Public noon and one in the evening. The first
Exercises. two divisions were given in Mr. John Buckingham's orchard almost half a mile north of the Institute building on the north and south center road. This orchard has been entirely destroyed. It stood just a little south of the old Packer farm, but on the opposite side of the road. The last division was given in the church at the center. Between the two first divisions a lunch was served on board

tables under the trees.   The teachers and students marched
from the building down the north hill and beyond to the
scene of the performance.   Tradition says that Emily Ford
was marshal of the day.   The exercises whose number would
terrify a modern audience were extremely crude and show
how close to the primitive district school were the first sessions of the Eclectic.

The immediate influences of the planting of the Eclectic Institute at Hiram were of a three-fold character.   First,
upon the Disciples at large—the "Brotherhood," second,
upon the village, and last, upon the Hi-
ram Church.   The school at once became popular.   In the year 1850 and 51
there were three hundred and thirteen different students
in attendance.   In 1853-4 this number had arisen to five
hundred and twenty-nine.   Seven states and countries
were represented the first year; fourteen in 1853-4.*   But

The School's
Influence.

*The following table of attendance during the whole life of the
Eclectic, was compiled by Professor B. S. Dean, in 1894, for the
HIRAM COLLEGE ADVANCE:

TABLE OF ATTENDANCE.

Year.	1st Term.	2d Term.	3d Term.	Total by Terms.	Total dif. Students.
1850-51	102	147	60	309	*313
1851-52	181	233	89	503	410
1852-53	211	226	205	642	529
1853-54	166	236	188	590	523
1854-55	262	201	138	601	445
1855-56	235	215	177	631	494
1856-57	[Term records missing].				440
1857-58	260	175	230	665	487
1858-59	302	194	200	696	502
1859-60	263	155	217	635	462
1860-61	260	153	182	595	427
1861-62	209	65	115	389	315
1862-63	185	107	140	392	296
1863-64	236	171	145	552	389
1864-65	159	125	118	402	306
1865-66	214	148	157	519	352
1866-67	156	106	105	366	250

*Includes four terms.

this does not indicate that, especially outside of the Western Reserve, the school, all at once, became a great figure before the Disciples. Its patronage, at first, was largely local. Its students were mainly from Portage, Summit, Trumbull, Geauga, Cuyahoga, Medina, Ashtabula, and Wayne Counties. The religious character of the school, probably exercised some influence in determining its patronage, but this was not the only influence. It was a school of higher grade and was a long step upward from the ordinary district school. Its first students were mainly from Disciple families or communities where the Disciples of Christ were most numerous.

It was announced that "the course of instruction is designed to embrace whatever is adapted to the developing and training of those under its care for the useful and practical duties of life. The chief attention will be directed to the attainment of sound literature and useful science." It was also declared that "the Bible is the foundation of all the morality in the world. It contains all moral power for the improvement and refinement of the human race. Its counsels are eternal wisdom. Its morality is perfect. It cannot, therefore, be hazardous to lay the Bible as the moral basis of the ECLECTIC INSTITUTE." The Bible was to be taken as the foundation of education, and as a classic taken into the institution. Every student was expected to devote a part of each day in the study of the details of human history as found in the Bible. But it was explicitly stated "that nothing is to be taught in this Seminary under color of these Biblical lessons, or otherwise, partaking in the least degree of sectarian character." Nor was it to be, in any sense, a Theological School, though it would seek to develop and strengthen the intellectual powers in subordination and subserviency to the moral faculties. Its aim was to make men and women of the youth committed to its trust; good men and good women, and "leave it to the finger of providence to point out to them the path of usefulness."

These frank statements concerning the scope and purpose of the school, had a good effect over a large territory, and soon its horizon extended and its influence greatly increased. Alexander Campbell, then President of Bethany College, gave his endorsement to the enterprise in these felicitous words: "Such institutions, well conducted, are streams that make the wilderness and solitary place glad, and contribute to the cause of human redemption."*

The planting of the school brought to Hiram new classes of people, who, in turn, helped to establish a new order of things. "What had been a mere cross-roads became a small village." The effect upon the church at Hiram was immediate. What had been a very homogeneous congregation became very heterogenious,—"a variety of general culture, critical acumen, and æsthetic taste." Some of the members of the church as then constituted, never appreciated what the school did for them or for the church. They thought of what it had cost them in money and trouble, and failed to look at the compensations. When the school was given to Hiram, after the contest over its location had been settled in her favor "there went with the act certain responsibilities, peculiar, heavy, solemn." All that has given the name "Hiram" power for a half of a century, flowed from that act.

The Church of Hiram has some prominent characteristics. "One of the most prominent is stability, permanence. Since 1835, she has kept steadily on the even tenor

*Millennial Harbinger, 1850, p. 473.

The Church of Hiram.

of her way. She has either steadily grown, or she has firmly held her ground." She has been a conservative church. "Having steadfastly set her face as though she would go to Jerusalem, she has never swerved from the 'old paths.' Hiram has never been a hatching or a moulting ground for isms and 'new-fangled notions.' Her members, as a class, have not been of those who are tossed to and fro and carried about with every wind of doctrine. Millerism, abolitionism, come-outer-ism, spiritualism, etc., have not disturbed her peace. She grew in anti-slavery faith as the Nation grew, no faster and no slower; and when the shock of arms came, she supported the National Government, almost to a man." These two qualities, stability and conservatism, have borne invaluable fruit. "Hiram has never been torn by factions contending about points of doctrine and questions of order. There have been no exscinding resolutions, no secessions, no convulsing cases of discipline. Conservatism has not excluded great tolerance and liberality. All along there has been a practical recognition of the line separating faith and opinion. The brethren have never been *sound* above what is written. It has never entered their heads that it would be a good thing to tear the Church to pieces over the 'organ question.' Nor have they had any scruples as to the rightness of co-operative religious enterprise. Born of a movement that began in co-operation, they have never proclaimed themselves spiritual bastards." This historic Church vindicates in a very large degree the grand "movement" of which it is a part. Here is a Church that for sixty-five years "has gone on her way without Articles or Rules of Order, converting the people, building herself up in faith and love, supporting the gospel at home and abroad, meteing out discipline, and assisting in benevolent enterprise. Her story is an answer, clear and convincing, to those who, in the beginning, said that the principles of the Campbells would lead to doctrinal latitudinarianism and ecclesiastical disorder. Whatever else the story may be worth, it shows that a Christian congregation can stand on the Bible alone, without a 'constitution,' holding fast the form of sound words and maintaining the unity of the Spirit in the bonds of peace."*

Of families which came to Hiram at the beginning of the school, there were some who became identified with its

Firm Friends of the School. fortunes, and were its firmest friends to the end of their lives. Their homes were the homes of the students and their kindness to them cannot be forgotten by a very large circle of the early Hiram fellowship.

ZEB RUDOLPH moved from his farm near Garrettsville about 1850 and built the house west of the church where Miss Rena Young now lives. Here he lived until

Zeb Rudolph. he moved to his much finer residence, now Mrs. Wheeler's, down the hill on the north side of the east road next to Prof. Wakefield's. Delightful reminiscences of a winter spent in "Uncle Zeb's" family are at hand. "Uncle Zeb had that winter besides his own family of seven persons, including the hired girl, eleven boarders. We were packed in like sardines, and, I think the same conditions prevailed in every other house in town and out of town. The board was $1.50 per week and very good as the Hiram women were most of them good cooks and Aunt Arabella (Mrs. Rudolph) was the peer of any of them. We burned tallow candles at night. * * * * * I was greatly impressed with the wisdom

---

*Historical Discourse, by B. A. Hinsdale, 1876.

and learning of this household. Uncle Zeb read Greek and Hebrew and was in appearance a very wise man. His daughter read Latin and Greek and French. Clarinda Hardman who was one of my three room-mates wrote poetry. Mr. Dunshee, one of the faculty, who was my cousin, boarded in the house. He had graduated at Hudson College and was so important in the family that he had a seven by nine bedroom to himself."*

C. L. P. RENO, known to many of the students as Uncle Perry, and to most of the townspeople simply as "Brother Reno" moved with his wife from Sharon, Pa., about 1853

C. L. P. Reno. and lived in the large white house on the east road where Professor Wakefield lives now. Their home, generally filled with students, always had an open door, and the social gatherings there from time to time, were one of the greatest sources of pleasure both to the church people and the school. Mr. Reno was for many years an elder of the Hiram church, and it was in the early '90's before his tottering form, his earnest inquiring face, and his bald head with its thin fringe of gray locks, ceased to appear every Lord's day at the church services. He died November 21, 1890, and his wife, February 15, 1896.

JAMES RATCHFORD NEWCOMB came to Hiram from Wadsworth in 1856. He bought the Harris property on the east and west center road just west of the present home

James R. Newcomb. of Mr. Richard Hank, where his daughter, Mrs. J. C. Ellis, still lives. Mr. Newcomb was a man of great taste and loved to ornament his grounds. He piped water from a large spring in one of his back fields, and no description of Hiram village would be complete that did not mention his

---

*Recollections of **Mrs. B. A. Hinsdale.**

J. A. Garfield 1866 — A. S. Hayden — H. W. Everest — C. W. Heywood — A. J. Thomson — J. M. Atwater

PRINCIPALS OF THE ECLECTIC.

beautiful circular fountain, often adorned with miniature boats. Sometimes students, on moonlight nights, would gather on the edge of the big stone basin under the circle of evergreen trees and sing Hiram songs, a practice still frequently indulged in.

TIMOTHY J. NEWCOMB—a distant relative of James —came from Freedom some time in the later 50's. He bought the farm on the south-east corner of the two center roads. Afterward he moved into the house

Timothy
Newcomb.

now occupied by Mr. Dyson south of the church. He was one of the pioneer preachers among the Disciples and well known on the Western Reserve. There were several children in the family all of whom were at sometime students of the Institution, unless it were an invalid daughter Stata who grew to womanhood, and became an artist. Part of the house now occupied by Mr. Harry Leach was once her studio. When Stata Newcomb died she left a small fund to Hiram College to be used for the benefit of students who might be situated like herself.

THUEL NORTON came to Hiram with his large family from the south part of the township. He lived where Mr. Dudley's fine house now stands, then,

Thuel Norton.

later, in the house now the home of Miss Eunice Ballard. The names of his children and grandchildren, appear in various catalogues of the school.

HOLLAND BROWN came to Hiram in 1853, and lived in the house which Miss Eunice Ballard now occupies. Here his daughter, Mrs. Jessie Brown Pounds,

Holland Brown.

was born August 31, 1861. Mrs. Pounds occupies a high place among the Disciples of Christ, at the present time, as a poet and prose author.

JOHN BUCKINGHAM came from Howland in the spring

of 1851. He bought a farm of John Young north of the
village. The next year he built the large house, still stand-

John
Buckingham.

ing, on the west side of the north and
south road near the watering trough.
This house was considered a very pre-
tentious one in that day and, even before its completion,
called forth a flattering notice in the second catalogue of the
school, as one designed, "for friends and visitors to the
school who may wish entertainment." Among the roomers
at Mr. Buckingham's in 1853 was a son of Judge Jeremiah
S. Black, an eminent jurist of Pennsylvania, one of the
Judges of its Supreme Court from 1851 to 1857, and afterwards a member of the Cabinet of President James Bu-
chanan, at first as Attorney General, and later as Secretary
of State. The son was Chauncey F. Black, who afterward became Governor of Pennsylvania.

There were other families that had much to do in providing for the life of the school in its opening years; but
of them no chronicles have been left within reach.

Mr. Orrin Brown built a hotel where Miller Hall now
stands.* This hotel afterward passed into the possession

The
Hiram House.

and charge of Mr. R. W. Merriam and
his family. The old Hiram House is
full of associations to many old students.
In the period of the Eclectic Institute social gatherings
of almost all kinds, whether commencements, socials, dinners, or anything that called for what is popularly known as

Social
Gatherings.

"refreshments," were shared in, and
aided, more or less, by the residents of
the village. For many years after the
College period began, the annual banquet which the Senior

---

*The first hotel in Hiram was kept by John Fletcher Bennett,
near the foot of the first hill to the east of town.

Class gave to the undergraduates, was furnished by the ladies of the various families in the village. Lines were not drawn so strictly then as they are now. Many of the townspeople attended the banquet, and, generally, the entire Faculty. This has all ceased with the modern period of improvement, and the expense of the banquet becomes the care of the Seniors, while the attendance is restricted to the Class-Professor and the members of the lower classes. The growth and expansion of the school under College conditions tended to do away with the freedom and unconventionality of the earlier period.

Of all the voluntary student activities that have originated in connection with Hiram, during the period of the Eclectic Institute, or since Hiram College **The Rise of the Literary Societies.** was established, and have become permanent features of the Institution, none have been of greater strength to the school and of culture to its students than the Literary Societies. The oldest ones now existing took their rise in the early days of the Eclectic Institute, and have continued to develop, with varying fortunes until the present time, when they stand the equal of any similar organizations connected with the Colleges of Ohio. These are the Olive Branch, the Delphic, and the Hesperian Societies.

"The history of Literary Societies in Hiram may be divided into three periods: The Ancient, the Mediaeval, and the Modern. The Ancient period begins with the Institution and closes with the organization **Different Periods.** of the Delphic in the winter of 1853-4; the Mediaeval period extends from the close of the Ancient to the organization of the Institution as a college in 1867; the Modern period reaches from the close of the Mediaeval to the present day. The first was a period of experiment and failure; the second, a period of experiment and success; the third, a period of experiment and uncertainty, with certain conclusions and a definite policy appearing very clearly toward the close."*

Before the Eclectic Institute was founded the Literary Society as a means of culture had ceased to be an experiment; and when the wheels of the new school were fairly in motion, this means of culture was called in as an auxiliary.

The Eclectic.   "The Eclectic" was the first society organized in Hiram; and among its leading members were Corydon E. Fuller and James A. Garfield.† The exact date of its organization has not been preserved, but Mr. Orris Atwater, who was a member of the school during the first term, says: "It dates back to the first fall term." It had a short but honorable life, "and gathered up into its membership the most brilliant and promising male students. It has the credit of giving the first Public Lyceum given in the history of Hiram."

On Wednesday evening, September 1, 1852, a few members of the Eclectic met in the recitation room of Prof.

The   Norman Dunshee, and organized by
Philomathean.   choosing Symonds Ryder, Jr., President, and Corydon E. Fuller, Secretary. At that meeting were James A. Garfield, Symonds Ryder, Jr., Corydon E. Fuller, John Harnit, Philip Burns, William D. Harrah and Ellis Ballou. Perhaps there were others. Addresses were made by several of those present, and it was finally unanimously agreed, "That we mutually agree to secede from the Eclectic Lyceum, and form ourselves into a new society."

*This division into Periods was made by Mr. B. A. Hinsdale, in an address at the Delphic Reunion, in 1875.

†See Reminiscences of Garfield, by C. E. Fuller, p. 41.

On Monday evening, September 6, 1852, the new society was organized and called "The Philomathean." But the birth of the Philomathean was the death of the Eclectic. It was a strong society from the beginning. In its first membership were Henry B. Boynton, Ellis Ballou, Philip Burns, John Encell, C. C. Foote, Corydon E. Fuller, Ceylon C. Fuller, William A. Faddis, James A. Garfield, John W. Horner, John Harnit, William D. Harrah, Salem P. Merrifield, Symonds Ryder, Jr., J. Carroll Stark, and Charles D. Wilber; and a little later, the names of Orris Clapp Atwater, Harvey W. Everest, Walter S. Hayden, Joseph King, Sterling McBride, O. P. Miller, and Leonard Southmayd appear on the lists. The most brilliant period in the history of this society was the winter of 1853-4. Its meetings were public and all who cared to do so attended. Such subjects as Secular History, Church History, Prophecy, Phrenology, Geology, and Logic and Rhetoric, were discussed in twenty-minute lectures, by James A. Garfield, H. W. Everest, O. P. Miller, Philip Burns, Norman Dunshee, and Amaziah Hull.

The Philomathean Society made a deep impression on a great many minds. Orris C. Atwater considered it "the most brilliant society ever gathered on the Hill." Henry M. James says: "It was supported by what seemed to me in those days, a very remarkable body of men."

B. A. Hinsdale says: "The impression made upon my own mind was quite as deep. Night after night I climbed the east hill, sometimes in rain and darkness, to hear those wonderful debates and lectures."* The society was short-lived and in about two years it ran its course. Its standard of ability kept its membership small, and when the old

---

*I was in school in the winter of 1853-4, and my enthusiasm over the work of the Philomathean Society was at fever heat.   F. M. Green.

members began to leave, some for college and some for practical work, "the society reeled under the blow."

Other societies were organized during these early years of Hiram, but they were too ephemeral and too weak to make much of an impression or to live long. It is hardly possible to even get their names. Some of them have been preserved, such as "The Websterian," "The Demosthenian," "The Junto," "The Washingtonian," "The Meritorian," "The Philozetian," and "The Independent." These societies did not all exist at the same time, but followed each other in quick succession, were born and died. None of these early societies "had any property basis, either furniture or library." An entry in the minutes of the Philomathean shows what property it was customary for a society to have in those days: "On motion, the Secretary was instructed to purchase a blank book; and the Marshal five candlesticks, two pairs of snuffers, and five pounds of candles." And this was about all the equipment that any society had, in Hiram, previous to the organization of the Delphic.

Other Societies.

The Olive Branch Literary Society was organized under that name January 8, 1853. There had been an organization known simply as the "Ladies' Literary Society," which had given the year before "The first Public Lyceum ever given by the ladies in the history of the Eclectic." The origin of the name "Olive Branch" is given as follows: "There were in the Society—(the Ladies' Literary Society) —at this time—(1853-4)—twelve members and when the term was nearly half finished, preparations were made for another "Public Lyceum." Up to this time the Society had not had a printed programme. After much discussion it was decided to take a step in advance and send our pro-

The Olive Branch.

gramme to the printer.   It was made ready, when someone suggested that it would make a better appearance if the Society had a more pretentious name.   We sat around the stove in the north-east corner of this room (the "Chapel") one cold winter day discussing the question of name, when Mary Hubbell said: "Girls, let us call our Society the Olive Branch."   What suggested the name to her I cannot tell, but probably it was the journal of that name, published by N. P. Willis, in Boston.   On calling the house to order, a motion was made to this effect, 'That this society hereafter be known as THE OLIVE BRANCH.'   It was seconded and carried without a dissenting voice."*

On January 19, 1854, the Society rendered its first programme under its new name.   The Order of Exercises consisted of music, a colloquy on "Evil Speaking," and essays and recitations on "The Aboriginal Inhabitants of America," "The Divinity and Destiny of Genius," "Astronomy," "China," "A Leaf from Memory," "The Dark Ages," "Ambition," "Faith," "Poetry—Its Influence," "Arabia," "Land of Palestine," and "Immortality," by Adelle A. Luse, Sarah S. Lanphear, Ellen H. Wood, Mary L. Hubbell, A. A. Booth, N. E. McIlrath, Sarah A. Soule, Mary Atwater, Sarah Bailey, B. E. Fisk, Mary E. Turner, and W. A. Hayden.

The colloquy on "Evil Speaking" was written by Miss Booth and the twelve members of the Society took a part in it and the young ladies signed a paper "pledging themselves not to speak evil of each other."   Of the young ladies who participated in that first programme not more than three or four remain to this present and those who do remain are bearing the white blossoms of age.

The "Olive Branch," though nearly a half century old,

*Mrs. B. A. Hinsdale, Reunion Address, 1877.

is fresh and vigorous as at the beginning. It is, as it always has been, an adornment and a constant helper to the literary and social life of Hiram.

Up to 1877 its membership included 549 names, to which have been added since 475, making a total of 1,024. And in the felicitous lines of Mrs. E. E. C. Glazier in her poem read in 1877 at the reunion of the society, this brief sketch of a noble society may be closed:—

> "And may our Tree from off the earth
> Its fruitage never cease;
> Forever and forever wave
> The Olive Branch of peace!"

The Delphic Literary Society, or "Delphic Lyceum," as it was chartered May 10, 1862, was organized November 24, 1854. As it gathered up many of the most brilliant essayists and strong debaters from the societies that had preceded it, difficulty was encountered in finding for it an appropriate name. It was proposed to call the new society the Philomathean, but this proposition was opposed and abandoned. The name, "The Delphic," was proposed by Mr. Thomas Munnell and this name was adopted. "Of course, it was borrowed from Delphi, the city of the greatest oracle in Greece." Among its charter members, or those who organized the Society, were W. H. Coddington, John M. Faddis, J. J. Harrison, R. A. Gaines, Thomas Farley, R. J. Hathaway, O. F. Hoskins, H. J. Morgan, Henry Parmly, Robert Moffett, B. F. Wood, J. H. Rhodes, H. Y. Russell, A. B. Way, and Augustus H. Pettibone.

Robert Moffett, who since then has reached a high and honorable place as a preacher among the Disciples, was its first President. From the beginning, the Delphic was a strong, intelligent, and vigorous society. During the first term of its existence it came before the public with a "Public Lyceum." Mr. Munnell presided, and the exercises occupied the afternoon and evening. There was the usual programme of exercises. The interest of the occasion centered in the discussion, *"Resolved,* That the present circumstances of Europe furnish reasons to expect an essential amelioration of human affairs." This proposition was affirmed by Robert Moffett and Augustus H. Pettibone, and denied by B. F. Wood and J. H. Rhodes. The programme as rendered made a profound impression on many that heard it and was accepted as a prophecy of its future strength and usefulness. Its later history has proved worthy of this beginning.

For two years after its organization "The Delphic" had no property beyond "the necessary candlesticks, snuffers, and the inevitable budget box;" but it was the first society to fit up a room for its meetings, and the first to own a library. To J. H. Rhodes belongs the credit for the proposition "to paper and furnish a room in a tasteful manner." It is said: That he greatly bewildered some of the members by saying "it was customary for literary societies in colleges to have elegantly furnished rooms and valuable libraries." His proposition was accepted and a tax of one dollar *per capita* was laid on the members, which with the receipts from a Public Lyceum, furnished the necessary means. *The new quarters were fitted up, and though "plain and tasteful, they seemed quite gorgeous in contrast to the dreariness of the Lower Chapel." The foundation of the Delphic library was laid in the year 1857. At the close of a term four or five dollars remained in the treasury and some one moved that the money be expended for books. Three

---

*In the present Physical Apparatus Room, on North side first floor.

books were purchased, one of these "Pulpit Portraits; or Pen Pictures of Distinguished American Divines," by John Ross Dix. This was the small beginning that has greatly increased to the present handsome and valuable library of the Society. Its growth has been slow since then, but continuous and sure. Mr. O. C. Atwater says in a recent communication, "The last thing I recollect sharing in Delphic matters was in the appointment of a committee to select and purchase our first bill of books. They were directed to consult the teachers as to their selection. Several important steps were taken—the founding of a library, the gaining of an evening at Commencement for Society exercises, with a charge at the door, and the seeking of the best wisdom, the school afforded, in the choice of books. Few libraries have less trash in them than the Hiram Society Libraries. These steps in accumulating and preserving property are all of Delphic origin.

Up to, and including 1875, its membership contained the names of 515 persons, to which have been added since 506, making a total of 1,031, at the close of the century.

And those now living of its oldest and earliest membership, say to its youngest membership:
"Then here's to our boyhood, its gold and its gray!
The stars of its winter, the dews of its May!
And when we have done with our life-lasting toys,
Dear Father, take care of thy children, THE BOYS;"
For over the place the old man's galley crossed,
The boasting Present in the Past is lost.*

*The Delphic Emblem, which hangs in their Hall, was painted by Miss Emma Johnson (Mrs. Dean) in the Spring of 1867. It is based upon a small design that used to be printed in the Eclectic Catalogues, over the list of Delphic members. The original design was drawn by Miss Kate Stark (Mrs. A. Wilcox) in consultation with Mrs. Garfield. The present Hesperian Emblem was painted by Miss Stata Newcomb soon after the Delphic Emblem.

The Hesperian Literary Society, or Hesperian Lyceum, as it was chartered May 3, 1862, was organized August 22, 1855. Of its earliest membership not many names have been preserved, but here are some who were, probably, present at its organization: John Hurd, W. H. Turner, A. B. Curtiss, E. B. Monroe, Ambrose Mason, Frank H. Mason, Basil G. Hank, James Mason, C. Harris, Edward Allen, and Dudley Beaman.

The Hesperian.

The foremost men in the Society at the beginning were John Hurd "grave, deliberate, and decorous," and William H. Turner, "intense, pointed and positive." Its equipment in property and furniture was meager in the extreme. Its earliest condition was not unlike that of its chief competitor, the Delphic. "The gloom of the place of meeting, which was a room too large, by far, was only aggravated by a prodigal display in one corner, of four or five candles. An unvarnished box, 'brown with the umber of human contact,' was the repository of dull conundrums, local hits, and pointless wit, whence during the evening the Secretary was wont to draw forth things, both "new and old." This was the far-famed "budget-box," which it required considerable debate in after years to abolish. I recall nothing remarkable in the exercises of the Society, during this period.[*] The chronicles of the Society and its traditions reveal the fact that it passed through several "wars of revolution" before its evolution into the strong, energetic, radical, and intense Society, "curbed and reined by the conserving force of parliamentary law and usage," that it afterwards became. During its earliest years "the accessions to its membership were from a fair average of the students of the Institute; not always profound in scholarship, nor brilliant in orator-

[*]Judge H. C. White, in Historical Address, 1876.

ical display, they yet became infused with one virtue on becoming members, a deep and hearty Society spirit."*
Among the propositions debated as early as 1858 was,
"Roman Catholicism is dangerous to the American Republic, and ought not to be tolerated by its laws."

During the spring term of 1859, "the Hesperian hall
was neatly painted and decorated, and adorned with a picture of the star of Hesper, done in oil, and presented to the
Society by Miss Kate Stark, a member of the Olive Branch.
At this time and afterward, the interchange of civilities between the Olive Branch and Hesperian was quite frequent;
the societies often calling upon each other, during their respective sessions."

In the autumn of 1859 the Hesperian Society made its
first great effort to found a library. With the societies, as
with the school, the "library question" was a great question.

The
Library Question.

In the month of November, 1853, there
was not a single library or book that belonged to the Institution, either directly
or indirectly, with the possible exception of the Bible, in the
chapel. In the winter of 1854-5, a library for the Western
Reserve Eclectic Institute was, with due ceremony, inaugurated, with "brief speeches by Principal Hayden, Mr. Munnell, and probably Mr. Dunshee, appropriate to the occasion." In 1858, not more than eighteen volumes comprised
what was called the Delphic Library. About the same time
that the Delphic Library was established, "the Hesperian
Society began to collect funds for the purchase of books."
Its course was somewhat different from that followed by
the Delphics. Instead of using money, more or less, that
might be in its treasury from time to time, in the purchase
of a few books, it allowed time to elapse, and a larger fund

*Judge H. C. White, 1876.

was collected, before any books were purchased.   And when the new Hesperian Library was installed in the Library room, "it was decidedly an event, owing to the number and choice quality of the books that were displayed when the library was opened."

One of the great controversies relating to the Hesperian library, and one which, for a time, threatened the dissolution of the Society, was over the question of allowing the Delphic Society equal privileges in the use of their books. Amzi Atwater offered the motion that created the storm. He was supported by H. D. Carlton, H. S. Glazier, E. B. Monroe, Sutton Newcomb, and others; while the opposition was led by "Jack" Dille, supported by P. C. Reed, J. W. Nelson, B. G. Hank and others.   Only a few members were among the doubtful ones and subject to persuasion.   The argument in favor of the proposition was based on the ground—First, for friendly relations with our rival; second, if we grant them the use of our library they will return the favor; third, that thus we shall have access to a wider selection of books, and the societies will not need to duplicate important works.   The opposition warmly maintained: First, we were independent of them and wished no connection, and we would neither grant nor ask favors; second, too much use of the books would wear them out; third, the many slights and insults received from the Delphic Society should be against the proposition.   The debate continued for weeks and finally resulted in the refusal to grant the use of the library to the Delphics, by a majority of one or two votes. The matter was reconsidered at a subsequent term and the more liberal policy adopted; and the two society libraries have been of mutual value ever since.

Up to and including 1876, its aggregate membership had included 456 persons, to which have been added since,

and including 1900, 531, making a total of 987. A few of
those who constituted the first membership of the Hesperian
Society are yet living, and of its experiences each one says:

"I see the shadow of my former self gliding from childhood up to man's estate;" and they are glad to let some of
its sunbeams fall along the life-path of their younger brethren, in whose "bright lexicon of youth there's no such word
as fail."

The historian of the Delphic Society in 1875 placed on
record some observations which are very interesting a quarter of a century later. He said: "Fruit-
ful as the ancient period had been in lessons of experience, some things remained
to be learned. They are these:

**Value of
Society History.**

1—There is room in Hiram for only three literary societies—two for Gentlemen and one for Ladies.

2—The Gentlemen's societies must be co-ordinate.

3—The proper place for the younger pupils is the Rhetorical Class, where they can be under the eye of an instructor. Such, no doubt, will be the policy of the college in the
future.

Experience has also taught another thing: The two
Gentlemen's societies are never equal in ability for any long
time; first one leads and then the other. A society becomes
strong; it becomes particular about its members; the younger students are drawn towards the other. As a result the
stronger society is not recruited, and as its old members
leave, it becomes weak, while the weaker becomes strong.
Then the same process begins again, only the societies have
exchanged places. How many times in twenty years have I
seen this law assert itself!"*

*Historical Address, 1875, by B. A. Hinsdale.

The following reminiscence from Mrs. B. A. Hinsdale will fittingly close the Eclectic period of society history:

It was at the beginning of the Winter term of 1852-3 that I first came to Hiram. There was in existence at that time a society called simply the Ladies' Literary Society. I attended its first session for the term. It met that night in the "Primary," now Prof. Colton's room. I was greatly impressed with its ability, and I think now, as I look back to it with my enthusiasm subdued by the judgment of mature years, that it really had much literary strength. Miss Booth was the controlling power. The Miss Carltons and Clarks were members. Among the younger members were Lucretia Rudolph, Mary Mason, Mary Atwater, Parintha Dean, and others whose names I have forgotten. * * * * * One feature of the exercises was conversation. The theme one evening was the "Life and Character of Margaret Fuller." Miss Booth was greatly interested in the career of this noble woman, and as this was shortly after the publication of her "Memoirs" by Horace Greeley, the story of her wonderful life, so sadly terminated, was fresh in many minds. Miss Booth had this book, which she took pains that the different members of the Society should read. This Society had given a Public Lyceum the term before—the first Public Lyceum ever given by the ladies in the history of the Eclectic. The fame of this performance had sounded all over these hills, and far away into the valleys. Its echoes had not yet died away when I came. From this one and that one, I gathered thoughts, expressions, and incidents it had scattered so that I could write its history to-day better than the history of which I was myself a part. It had published a paper called the "Eclectic Star," and the Eclectic Society, composed of gentlemen, of course, treated it in this manner in a paper of their own:

> "Twinkle, twinkle, little star,
>   How I wonder what you are;
> Up above the world so high,
>   Like a pumpkin in the sky!"

An incident occurred at this Lyceum which shows the authority of Miss Booth over the young ladies. Some one reported that Mr. Dunshee had said, "Women have no souls." This report was made the text of an article called "Mahommedanism in Hiram." The editor of the paper began to read this piece, which had been smuggled into its pages. The audience had listened long enough to perceive the direction of the thought, when Miss Booth arose from her seat, took the paper from the young lady's hand, saying, "This article has never been submitted to the inspection of the proper authority. Its reading can proceed no further."

In the spring of 1853, this Society gave its second Public Lyceum. I have forgotten almost the whole programme, but Miss Atwater's subject was "The World's Fair," Miss Lucretia Rudolph's, "Europe in the 16th Century." There was a written discussion about the utility of studying Greek and Latin. Miss Jennie A. Gardner affirmed that it was best to pursue these studies; Miss Mary E. Turner denied. For the latter young lady this was a great undertaking; but after much anxiety and mental strain her room-mate, Miss Wealtha Ann Hayden, said her paper would do if it ended with a few good sentences in addition, and as she wielded a readier pen she kindly furnished them. Whether Miss Gardner ever found this out or not, I cannot say. I can remember only one word in the whole performance, and that is "amaranthine."

The financial condition of Hiram College, from the opening days of the Eclectic Institute to the close of its half-century of history, has always been a cause for more or less solicitude to those who have been depended upon to raise and invest the money needed for all purposes. The first Board of Trustees banked quite largely on the faith they had in their enterprise and on those whom they believed would stand by them, instead of a good bank account. They often builded by faith instead of by sight. With about half of the money subscribed, necessary to buy the land and erect the building, they went on and pushed the enterprise through its first stages, and opened the school. It was a courageous

Financial Affairs.

FRANCIS MARION GREEN.

thing to do, but courageous men were behind it. The Western Reserve Eclectic Institute was in the hearts of many, though their hands had not yet been trained to large liberality. It was a stock corporation, with the power of perpetual succession given to its stockholders and Board of Trustees; with a minimum stock of seven and a maximum of fifty thousand dollars, as provided by the charter. This stock was divided into shares of twenty-five dollars each. It was not until the fall of 1851 that the minimum stock was subscribed and then the subscriptions fell more than three thousand dollars short of the debt that had been incurred. The actual cash received into the treasury fell more than two thousand dollars short of the subscriptions. Numerous solicitors were appointed, but funds came in but slowly and in small amounts. In 1852 the Building Committee reported that its debt was about five thousand dollars. In the meantime the Board had contracted a new debt of three thousand dollars to build boarding-houses, and subsequently it bought the Higley farm for about two thousand more. Toward the close of the period of establishment the debt, notwithstanding the sale of the boarding houses and part of the farm, was more than five thousand four hundred dollars. It is not necessary to enumerate the various plans which were proposed for raising the money, and which in many cases came to nothing. The entire debt was not paid during the lifetime of the Eclectic Institute, and many times its burden almost crushed the life out of the school.

During the entire lifetime of the school until it became a college, it depended for its current expenses upon the liberality of its patronage. It had no endowment and if any wills had matured they had not yet become available for income. The salaries of its teachers were paid by the receipts from tuition; and notwithstanding the number of

students this source of income was inadequate.   The tuition
was very low.   In the first sessions it was:

Elements of English $3.00
Higher English 4.00
Higher Mathematics and Languages 5.00

In the second year an advance of fifty cents per term
was made in all these branches, and a small incidental fee
charged.   But the average tuition throughout the seventeen years of its existence was only a little more than $5.50
per term.   No official record exists of what was paid to the
teachers at first, but it can be said that the amount paid them
was very small.   There is a tradition that Miss Booth received two dollars per week.

In 1853 an arrangement of salaries was made as
follows:

Principal $700
Teacher of Languages 450
Teacher of Mathematics 450
Teacher of Natural Science 400
Teacher of English Department 300
Assistant Teacher in English Department......... 250
Teacher in Primary Department 150

The next year these salaries were slightly increased.
But even these small amounts were not received with any
degree of regularity, and embarrassing debts were often
the result.   In 1855 there was a deficit of over seven hundred dollars, and this burden fell generally on the teachers.
Consoling resolutions were frequently passed by the Board
of Trustees in favor of the teachers, of which the following
is a specimen: "Resolved, that a note to Norman Dunshee
for $75.45, dated June 18, 1857, for balance due him at that
time on salary as teacher, be paid as soon as funds can be

had from the treasury." It is no wonder, therefore, that the Faculty page in the catalogues of the Eclectic show so many changes, and yet, it is a source of no little gratification to know that most of the prominent teachers remained for many years with the institution and gave it a large part of the very best of their life and work. These teachers were animated by the same spirit, manifested by Mr. Garfield in 1857, when in a letter to a friend, he says of his return to Hiram: "I have determined to do so, partly to hold it up, and I am determined that it shall move for one year." And the work that he did during his first term as Principal is a characteristic specimen of the work done by these poorly paid but consecrated teachers during the period of the "Old Eclectic." He says: "We have raised over four hundred dollars to build a fence round the Eclectic grounds. We have remodeled the government, published rules, published a new catalogue, and have now, the fourth week, 250 students—no primary—as orderly as clock-work, and all hard at work. Our teachers are Dunshee, Everest, Rhodes and Almeda. I teach seven classes and take the entire charge of the school and its correspondence besides. I have the most advanced classes in the school and deliver the most of the morning lectures."

Mr. A. Teachout, who has been officially connected with the college since 1867, and whose friendship for the school has never been lukewarm or cold, in a report made as President of the Board of Trustees in 1890, has this to say concerning financial affairs: "In that regard I have to say, that we are, as we always have been, struggling with poverty. But we still manage to wear good clothes. If any doubt that, look over this building from basement to garret. Then, take a walk over to the Boarding Halls, and, I think, you will say with me, that if any of the largely en-

dowed colleges can make any better showing in Club rooms,
Library, Museum, and Society Halls, as well as Boarding
Halls, let them show up and we will compare notes. But
while we have these elegant new buildings, they would be
almost valueless in this place, if the school should go down
as it has sometimes in its history. Therefore, the strictest
economy in the running expenses should be observed, and,
what endowment we have, to produce income, should not be
allowed to diminish, no matter what the emergency, but
rather a strong effort should be made to increase it."

To the credit of the Institution it may be said that during the entire period of its history, or for fifty years, no
scandals have ever clouded its financial transactions, no de-
falcations in solicitors or agents have ever occurred, and no
serious mistakes have ever been made in investing its funds.
And while, occasionally, its creditors have been compelled
to wait a little longer than was agreeable for what was justly
due them, in the end, the Institution has paid dollar for dollar of its obligations, or made with the parties concerned, a
satisfactory adjustment.

Perhaps the most flourishing libraries of Hiram College are those belonging to the Literary societies, but the
College Library proper has attained a good degree, and

The Libraries
of the
College.

"greatly increased" since its small beginning in the early days of the Eclectic Institute. As it never has had any official
patronage, no official records can be
found concerning its foundation; but Mr. B. A. Hinsdale
has furnished the following personal recollections:

"When I first went to Hiram in the month of November, 1853, there was not a single library or book that belonged to the Institution, either directly or indirectly, with
the possible exception of the Bible in the chapel. There

was a room between the two staircases looking out to the eastward that was called the 'Library' but it was empty so far as books were concerned. This continued to be the state of things until the following year, that is, the winter of 1854-55.

When I returned to Hiram in the fall of 1854, my attention was called to a few shelves of books in Esquire Udall's bookstore. These I was told were to constitute the new library, which now I heard of for the first time. In the course of that term it was announced from the chapel that the library would be duly inaugurated at a time fixed, and at this time the books were brought to the chapel, piled up on the breastwork in front of the stand, and the dedication exercises went forward. I do not know how many volumes there were, but doubt if there were to exceed 100, although there may have been. Brief speeches were made by Principal Hayden, Mr. Munnell, and probably Mr. Dunshee, appropriate to the occasion. The books were then carried to a bookcase with glass doors that stood in the southwest corner of the Lower Chapel. At stated times, perhaps once a week, this bookcase was opened, and books were drawn by those who wished to draw them.

As to the manner in which these books were provided. It was stated at the time that during the term or terms previous to the inauguration of the new library, a musical society or class had been organized, the members of which paid tuition fees, with the understanding that the proceeds were to be applied to the purchase of books for the use of the school. I was not in school at the time that this society flourished, and probably should not have been a member of it if I had been, but I understood that the instruction was given by Principal Hayden and by Mr. Gideon L. Applegate, who was a student of musical talents prominent in

Hiram circles in those years. One set of books that was purchased with these funds, was the British Essayist, the American edition, bound in black cloth, some of which, I suppose are still found in the library. I think if the fly leaves of some of these volumes are examined, the word "Atheneum" will be found written in Principal Hayden's hand. If so, I suppose the meaning to be that this was the name of the musical society. Still other books were given by individual donors. I may add that it was by the way of the volumes just described that I first became acquainted with British essayists, to the reading of which I was at one time much devoted.

This library grew slowly owing to lack of funds. Books were given by teachers, by students, and occasionally by outside friends. I remember, too, that literary exercises were occasionally given for the purpose of raising money for the library. What is more, the government documents that have been contributed to the Institution so freely since General Garfield's first year in Congress always found their way to the shelves of this library. Its growth, however, has been very slow, for I do not suppose the Board of Trustees has ever voted a dollar for the purchase of books. All things considered, there is reason for surprise that this library has attained its present size and usefulness."

The College library at present numbers 1,538 volumes; the Delphic 1,410; the Hesperian 1,121; the Olive Branch 415; all others, 4,322; making a total of 8,806 volumes. These books have generally been well selected and are of more than ordinary value. The volumes unclassified above include catalogued Public Documents, and the libraries of the Y. M. C. A., Student Volunteer Band, Natural History Society, and the Medical Association.

No history of Hiram College would be complete without some reference to its early commencements. In many respects they were unique. They were not, as in colleges and universities, the occasion for confer-

Early Commencements. ring degrees upon graduates for in that sense, there were no graduates and there were no degrees. They were occasions, rather, when friends of the Institution came from near and from far, to spend a good day, to take their children back to their homes, to give encouragement to the hard working teachers, to get a good dinner, and to hear and see such literary wonders and development as the annual programmes chrystalized and advertized. But little of detail has come down to the present concerning these events. Of the first commencement Mrs. Lucretia R. Garfield, in a letter to Prof. A. C. Pierson, dated April 28, 1900, writes: "The first

Mrs. Garfield's Letter. commencement exercises were held under the apple trees of an old orchard which reached over the north-east corner of the Eclectic grounds. A stage was built around one of the largest trees, and decorated with whatever we were able to get from the scant flower gardens of that time. Seats for the audience were improvised in the usual way—boards resting on chairs and blocks. No admission was charged, as the chief purpose was to call together as many people as possible to show what we were doing. I do not think the audience was large, still a good many came. I do not remember, but I think the music must have been only vocal, as I think there was no music teacher or an instrument those first two terms*

---

*The first reference to instrumental music, in connection with the school, is found in a resolution passed by the Board of Trustees, October 14, 1851. "Resolved, that when lessons shall be given in instrumental music, the Melodean shall be the instrument used for that purpose."

June 20, 1855, another resolution was adopted by the Board: "That the person who has charge of the Seminary property be empowered to sell the Melodean for what it will bring."

It was a perfect day, bright and cool, and had you not given the date, 'May,' I should have said it was a perfect day in June, and we were all in that state of exaltation which belongs to the beginnings of new enterprises. The women of this community loaded a long table with appetizing viands, and opened their houses in the largest hospitality their accommodations would permit. This public table became a burden when it grew evident that many came merely for the 'loaves and fishes;' and it was abandoned. The memories of those days, almost half a century away, seem to belong to another world when the enthusiasms and ambitions filled heart and soul. The details of the Commencement exercises are entirely lost to me. I could not have told you that I took any part in them, and don't remember the subject of my poor little essay, nor anything about the 'Colloquy.' Like a woman I have a rather vivid recollection of the dress I wore—that's all."

Not many of the programmes of those early Commencements have been preserved, but on such as have been brought down to the present the names of Lucretia Rudolph, Mary L. Root, Elizabeth A. Woodward, Mary Atwater, Eliza E. Clapp, Mary E. Turner, Mary M. Buckingham, Sarah A. Harrison, W. W. Hayden, C. P. Bowler, O. C. Atwater, John M. Atwater, H. O. Newcomb, Alanson Wilcox, B. A. Hinsdale, W. L. Hayden, H. M. James, and many others, are written large.

Commencement Programme, 1857. The last Commencement programme under Mr. A. S. Hayden's administration presented the following:

Order of Exercises

FORENOON

MUSIC

1 ESSAY,   -   -   -   -   -   /   The Unseen
ELIZA KNOWLTON, *Eagleville*

2 ESSAY,   -   -   -   -   -   -   -   China
ELIZABETH A. WOODWARD, *Lordstown*

3 ESSAY,   -   -   -   -   -   -   Petra
SARAH RUDOLPH, *Garrettsville*

4 ESSAY,   -   -   -   -   -   -   Fine Arts
MERINDA A. STARK, *Garrettsville*
MUSIC

5 ESSAY,   -   -   -   -   Female Poets of America
FRANK H. ROBINSON, *Ravenna*

6 POEM,   -   -   -   -   -   A Dream of Youth
SYLVIA HAVEN, *Shalersville*

7 ESSAY,   -   -   -   -   -   -   Bubbles
MARY M. BUCKINGHAM, *Hiram*

8 ESSAY,   -   -   -   -   -   Bayard Taylor
MARY ATWATER, *Mantua*
MUSIC

9 ESSAY,   -   -   -   -   -   -   Gumption
SARAH A. HARRISON, *Painesville*

10 ESSAY,   -   -   -   -   The Eloquence of Ruins
ELIZA E. CLAPP, *Hiram*

11 DISCUSSION,   -   -   -   -   -   -   -
Has the Bonaparte Family been a Blessing to France?
AFF.—H. L. MOORE, *Mantua*
NEG.—P. C. REED, *Auburn*
MUSIC
AFTERNOON.

MUSIC

1 LATIN SALUTATORY,   -   -   -   -   -
W. W. HAYDEN, *Deerfield*

2 ORATION,   -   -   -   Ruins in Central America
C. P. BOWLER, *Auburn*

3 ORATION,   -   -   -   The South and Migration
O. C. ATWATER, *Mantua*

4 ORATION,   -   -   -   A Representative Man
W. H. TURNER, *Troy*
MUSIC

5 ORATION,   -   -   -   Progress of Mind in America
H. O. NEWCOMB, *Hiram*

6 ORATION,   -   -   -   -   -   Water
A. WILCOX, *Hinckley*

7 ORATION,   -   -   -   The Commercial Equator
W. L. HAYDEN, *Deerfield*

8 ORATION,   -   -   -   -   Chivalry
                J. M. ATWATER, *Mantua*
9 COLLOQUY,   THE JEWESS,   (from Ivanhoe)
                PERSONÆ COLLOQII

King Richard, O. C. Atwater	Rebecca, Delia L. Turner
Ivanhoe, A. B. Mathews	Herald, B. H. Bostwick
Grand Master, H. M. James	1st Witness, H. Woods
Sir Albert Malvoisin,	2d Witness, S. P. Wolcott
J. M. Atwater	Higg, (a peasant), P. J. Squier
Sir Brian Guilbert, H. H. Mack	Physician, H. C. White
Robin Hood, I. W. Ludlow	

Squires and Guards

10 ORATION,   -   -   -   -   -   -
            Unity of Purpose—with the Valedictory Address
            H. M. JAMES, *Troy*
                MUSIC

Hiram College has always been fortunate in the selection of its Board of Trustees. With scarcely any exceptions the men selected to manage its business affairs have
Board of Trustees. been men successful in their own business, of high character, and of commanding influence in the Church or community of which they were a part. This is eminently true of its first provisional Board chosen in 1849, the most of whom passed over and became the Trustees under the charter of the Eclectic Institute.

CARNOT MASON was long and favorably known as one of the leading citizens of Hiram. No man was more faithful or more useful in the founding and support of the school.
Carnot Mason. He did much at the meeting held in Aurora November 7, 1849, to settle the question of the location of the Western Reserve Eclectic Institute. He was firm but not contentious in his disposition. He was a member of the Building Committee and insisted on putting up a good building, for the reason that it would give character and rank to the school. He was President of the Board of Trustees from 1849 to 1856. He was an active, devoted Christian and faithful in all his rela-

tions in life. He was born in Vermont December 16, 1804, and died January 31, 1856.

SYMONDS RYDER had in him the Pilgrim blood and the Puritan firmness. He was the lineal descendant of a Ryder who came over in the Mayflower. In character he was as sturdy as the oak. He was a man of sound judgment and maintained an inflexible character for candor and righteousness. He was a man of peace and cared strictly for his own affairs, and not interfering with others; yet the affairs of others sought him out, and often asked his skillful hand in their adjustment. When he became a member of the church of Hiram in 1828 "he was the most important accession that the Hiram Church has ever had, so far as local results are concerned." His judicious counsels were always appreciated by the Board of Trustees. He was the Treasurer of the Board from 1849 to 1860 and "in his hands every penny was accounted for." He was born November 20, 1792, at Hartford, Vermont, the same town which was the birthplace of Carnot Mason, and died August 1, 1870.

Symonds Ryder.

ISAAC ERRETT was "a full-orbed man." The elements were wisely proportioned and mixed in him. During his life he was recognized as a man of extraordinary power and of surpassing fulness of mental equipment. His father was born in Ireland, his mother in England. He was one of the best friends Hiram ever had. He was one of the wisest and most capable of its first Board of Trustees. At his suggestion the name, Western Reserve Eclectic Institute, was adopted. In personal appearance he was striking and prepossessing. He was simple and direct in his speech; his language was chaste and copious from his vocabulary of Anglo-Saxon words. He was born in New York City January 2, 1820, and died December 19, 1888.

Isaac Errett.

WILLIAM HAYDEN was the incarnation on the Western Reserve of the religious principles of the Disciples of Christ. To his foresight, decision, influence and tremendous energy,

William Hayden.

is due, probably more than to any other person the origin and foundation of the Western Reserve Eclectic Institute. Years before the enterprise was announced he discovered the coming need, and conversed upon it with persons who were in his intimate counsels. After his death in 1863, his associates in the Board of Trustees placed on record: "To him this Institution owes its existence and present prosperity." He was the first "solicitor" or financial agent of the new school; and one of its trustees at the time of his death. He was born in Pennsylvania June 30, 1799, and died April 7, 1863.

ZEB RUDOLPH was a man of rare qualities physically, mentally, morally, and to the end of his long life he sustained a blameless reputation. He was a pillar of truth,

Zeb Rudolph.

justice and honor wherever he appeared. In the earliest counsels of the Eclectic he was wise in judgment and efficient in action. He was the first Secretary of the Board, and a member of the Building Committee, and a workman in the construction of the building. He was loved and venerated by all who knew him in his mature years. He was born in Maryland in 1803, and died October 20, 1897.

FREDERICK WILLIAMS, though a native of Massachusetts, was long a prominent citizen of Portage County, Ohio. He was actively identified with church and educa-

Frederick Williams.

tional affairs for many years. He was one of the first Board of Trustees of the Eclectic Institute and remained a member of that body until 1863. On his retirement his associates said: "We lose one from our number whose earnest interest and zeal commend his example as worthy of imitation by each."

On Tuesday, November 9, 1858, he offered the first resolution, and which was unanimously adopted, that resulted several years later, in changing the name and character of the Western Reserve Eclectic Institute to Hiram College. He was also appointed on a committee consisting, besides himself, of Zeb Rudolph and James A. Garfield, "to inquire into the expediency of providing for, and introducing measures to commence a theological class."

He was born in Warwick, Massachusetts, March 2, 1799, and died at Ravenna, Ohio, January 10, 1888.

AARON DAVIS was one of the first Board of Trustees, and a man of decided influence in that body. He was one of the first agents employed by the Trustees to solicit funds for the new institution; and was asked "to spend as much time as shall be in his power, in Trumbull County, Ohio." He was a man of excellent judgment and keen business sagacity, all of which he used, for the time being, in the interest of the school of which he was one of the incorporators. He was the leading member of the committee of five which was appointed at the delegate meeting in Ravenna, Wednesday, October 3, 1849, "to visit all places which solicited the location of the school, to investigate and compare the grounds of their respective claims, and report at the next delegate meeting, when the question of location was to be decided." He always stood high in the esteem of his neighbors and friends in the church and community.

He was born April 23, 1809, in Washington County, Pa., and died in Cortland, Ohio, March 6, 1895, at the age of 86 years.

JOHN ANSON FORD was the Burton member of the first Board of Trustees of the Western Reserve Eclectic Institute. The Fords were the pioneers in Burton, the founders

John Anson Ford.

of its society, and leaders in all its benevolent and educational enterprises. He came with his parents from Connecticut into Ohio in 1807. He was a farmer who quietly and successfully pursued "his chosen avocation till a competence enabled him to retire partially from active work." His associates recognized in him, a man firm in purpose, benevolent in his impulses and practice, a thoughtful man, candid and wise. Such a character could not have other than great influence over his fellow men.

He was born in Connecticut September 18, 1798, and died at Wilmington, Illinois, June 23, 1878.

WILLIAM W. RICHARDS was one of Hiram's earliest friends and business managers. At the age of twenty-four he came from the State of New York and settled in Solon,

William W. Richards.

Ohio, where for many years he was a successful farmer. He was a valuable citizen. In personal appearance he was tall and manly. He was kind-hearted and just in his business transactions. As a Christian he was held to be a pillar in the church, in which he held a useful membership for many years.

He was born in Columbia New York, August 14, 1809, and died at Newburgh, Ohio, September 25, 1871.

GEORGE KING was a member of the first Board of Trustees. His home was in Chardon. He came from Connecticut when he was eighteen years old. The family

George King.

came the long journey with teams of oxen and horses. The leading qualities of his character were "strength of will, energy, moral integrity, and individual perseverance." He was slow to touch new things, but when he decided he was firm and unyielding. He was always a good counselor and his memory is fondly cherished where he lived so long.

He was born in Suffield, Connecticut, October 20, 1793, and died at Chardon, O., June 8, 1862.

AMBROSE LATIN SOULE was a man of extraordinary personality. In every way he was a remarkable man. Physically he was full six feet three inches in height, and

Ambrose Latin Soule.

finely proportioned. His countenance was mild and pleasant, yet clean and clear-cut. He was by nature a leader of men, and "never so much at ease as when in the management of great business." He was hospitable and social, genial and gentlemanly, and yet never forgot to be the dignified man. He was a sincere Christian, and as benevolent and enterprising for the promotion of the cause of true religion and humanity as for temporal concerns. "The first meeting ever held to consult on the founding of the Eclectic Institute was at the instance and at the residence of A. L. Soule. It was at a yearly meeting in Russell in 1849. Mr. Soule was, himself, chairman of the meeting; and, here, in the parlor of Latin Soule's mansion, the purpose took definite form, and from that time proceeded to the completion of the cherished purpose."

He was born in Dutchess County, New York, May 24, 1801, and died at Muir, Michigan, June 24, 1857.

JEFFERSON HARRISON JONES is the only one yet living of the honorable and remarkable body of men who formed the first Board of Trustees, provisional and permanent, of

Jefferson Harrison Jones.

the Western Reserve Eclectic Institute. He was then a young man of 36 years of age and in the full vigor of a splendid physical, mental and moral equipment. At the beginning he was a sincere friend to the new enterprise, and to this day he has never faltered in his interest. For 67 years he has been a minister of the Word of God. At present, he is living in the serene glow of his long and useful life, at Mount Union, Ohio.

He was born in Trumbull County, Ohio, June 15, 1813.

SAMUEL CHURCH was one of the incorporators of the Eclectic Institute. He was from Pittsburgh, Pa., a business man as well as a preacher. His parents were from

Samuel Church.

Ireland and came into Lancaster County, Pennsylvania, in 1796. He was a man of unusual business ability and became wealthy. His life was full of benefactions. He bore the principal expenses for the education of William Baxter, at Bethany College. He was a Christian, in business, in education, in living— everywhere. He was born in Lancaster, Pa., February 5, 1800, and died at the Astor House, New York City, December 7, 1857.

KIMBALL PORTER was a business man of large experience in Wooster, Ohio. For many years he was an elder in

Kimball Porter.

the Church of Christ in that city. In 1849 he was chosen as one of the incorporators of the Eclectic Institute. He was a good man and beloved by all who knew him.

He was born July 4, 1803, in Lee, Massachusetts, and died June 27, 1863, at Iowa City, Iowa.

GEORGE POW was born in England, and came to America with his parents when he was twenty-one years of age, and settled on a farm near Albany, New York. He after-

George Pow.

wards came to Mahoning County, Ohio, where he lived the remainder of his life. As a man he was respected by all who knew him. Though a farmer, "he was a reader, a scholar by self-culture, and a linguist of no mean attainments." He was a man of great firmness, clear thought, superior judgment, candid and conscientious. The oldest record that has been preserved of the delegate meeting held in Hiram December 20, 1849, is that which announced him as one of the Board of Trustees "to carry out the wishes of the delegates" in that meeting.

He was born in England December 6, 1800, and died March 14, 1871.

These represent "the men who did for Hiram something first, that it might be afterward able to do more for itself." The Board of Trustees, thus personated, were a harmonious body of men. So far as the records show, their action on all matters of importance was unanimous. It could not well have been otherwise, for they were all working for the same end, and controlled by the same great principle.

During the period of A. S. Hayden's administration, or from July 15, 1850, to June 17, 1857, Carnot Mason held the office of President of the Board of Trustees for six years and Alvah Udall for one year. These two men held that office for the entire lifetime of the Eclectic. Mr. Udall held the office longer than any other person; his service beginning in 1856 and ending in 1880. In that position he never had a superior and it is doubtful whether he ever will be surpassed in all the qualities necessary for the office.

Presidents of the Board of Trustees.

The financial agents, or solicitors as they were generally called, were quite numerous during this period. William Hayden was the first one chosen. Afterwards Horace Dutchin, Calvin Smith, J. H. Jones, Aaron Davis, Deacon Chapin, S. R. Willard, Symonds Ryder, Charles Brown, J. A. Ford,

Financial Agents.

A. B. Green, Frederick Williams, Brown Penniman and Warren A. Belding were chosen for the same purpose, and often several of them were operating at the same time. They had the usual fortune of such agents—a varying success. It cannot now be told which was the most valuable. It is probable that Mr. Belding secured more cash and pledges than any other. He was in the field longer than any other agent, and had rare qualifications for such work. No serious attempt, if any, was made during this period for an endowment fund. What was raised was needed for current expenses, and a debt created at the beginning of the Institution, was not satisfied during the time of the Western Reserve Eclectic Institute.

Symonds Ryder was Treasurer of the Board of Trustees from his first election in 1849 until 1860, and no

Treasurer.

man ever was more faithful in the discharge of the duties of a like trust.

In many respects Mr. Hayden's administration had been eminently successful. He had been very fortunate in the choice of teachers associated with him in class room and management. His honorable char-

Close of the First Administration.

acter had deeply impressed itself upon the school and its patrons. His wide acquaintance as preacher and educator had greatly enlarged the horizon of the Institution. But it soon became apparent that his growth in the qualities of leadership was not increasing with the growth and widening influence and patronage of the school. Dissatisfaction was expressed by many of its oldest, best and most intimate friends. In some cases the teachers who had entered the class rooms of the Eclectic Institute unknown except to a very limited number had passed their Principal in scholarship and in administrative ability. Miss Booth, one of the

Miss Booth's Judgment. greatest teachers the school ever had, in a letter to a friend, April 13, 1855, said: "I cannot see very clearly what fate has in store for the Eclectic, but surely it will be a great oversight to allow it to remain in its present position."* In a letter to Mr. Garfield while a student at Williams College, in February, 1856, Miss Booth said: "Brother Hayden thinks you are morally bound to come back here, but I think the moral obligation resting upon him is quite as strong to give up the management to you if you do come. I know you can never endure to work under him, for it is ten times as irksome to me as it was before I went away. James, would you risk to come here and see what you can do with the school? It certainly is a good location, and I know you would succeed, if you were not embarrassed by dictation or management."*

Others expressed themselves in an equally radical way. Mr. Hayden could not help seeing the trend of things and wisely on May 20, 1857, offered "his resignation as Principal of the Institute, to take effect at the end of the present term," to the Board of Trustees, "which was read, considered and accepted." The Board of Trustees on motion of Dr. M. Jewett, "Resolved, that the thanks of the Trustees of the Western Reserve Eclectic Institute, be tendered to A. S. Hayden for the faithful and efficient manner in which he has fulfilled the arduous duties while acting as Principal of the Institute." June 18, 1857, closed Mr. Hayden's relation to the Institution as Principal. In his farewell words he said in part: "The Institution was founded in the year 1850, and is now completing seven full years of its history. Since the day it was opened it has progressed

Mr. Hayden's Farewell.

*Reminiscences of Garfield, by C. E. Fuller, p. 186; p. 217.

steadily and rapidly in numbers and public favor. The number of students for the last few years has been from two hundred to two hundred and fifty in constant attendance. They are drawn from half the counties of this state, from thirteen or fourteen of the other states, and from Canada." * * * "It is a leading object of the Institute to impart thorough instruction in the elementary branches of an English education. It is determined, therefore, to bestow constant and careful attention upon this department. Yet this is not a mere English or Normal school. Few colleges in the west cultivate more successfully the study of the Classics, including Hebrew, French and German, than does this Collegiate Seminary. It encourages no hothouse scholarship. It would secure the inestimable advantages of a correct education by a due and proportionate attention to all its departments."

"A distinguishing feature of the Eclectic Institute is the morning lecture on Sacred History. This is found to be not only highly engaging and instructive, but likewise so **Morning Lectures.** to impress the students with correct moral principle, under the weight and sanction of Divine authority, as to result in the happiest consequences of good order and upright behavior." * * * * "At the close of this session terminates my connection with the Eclectic Institute. I retire from these responsible duties with gratifying recollections of all the principal events of its history. I cherish the kindest personal regards, and warmest attachments of friendsnip towards all the teachers and aids who have co-labored in raising the Institution to its present enviable position in the confidence of the public. For seven years I have watched with anxious solicitude the establishment of the great principles of order and morality, which, it is trusted, are yet to carry it to a higher po-

sition of far greater influence. Other important duties in the Kingdom of God press upon me. And having filled up the full measure of time anticipated by myself in accepting the appointment; without the abatement of jot or tittle of my anxious interest for its prosperity; with entire harmony of feelings towards the present, experienced and very able Board of Instructors, I commend the Institution to the discriminating and generous public. I am happy to assure the friends of the Institution that it is to continue under the management of the present highly accomplished Board of Teachers, so fully acquainted with its spirit, and the wishes of its numerous patrons. Every department is fully provided for. They have appointed J. A. Garfield, Chairman of the Board, through whom the correspondence of the Institute may be conducted. To God be all
Benediction. the praise for all the good it has wrought; and may the riches of His grace in Jesus Christ our Lord fall upon it like the dews on the mountains of Zion, that it may prove an exhaustless fountain of truth and goodness among men."

In 1861 Mr. Hayden was elected to the Board of Trustees and served in that office until the Institution became a College in 1867. From this time he ceased to be an active participant, either as counselor
A Trustee. or administrator, for the school, whose interests had commanded the best of his heart and life during all the years of its inception, poverty, peril and progress. And, whatever credit may be given to others who followed him, for the success of the Institution whose foundation he helped to lay, his name cannot be, and will not be forgotten.

CHAPTER III.

THE ECLECTIC INSTITUTE—THE GARFIELD ADMINISTRATION—1857-1863.

History, it has been said, has its foreground and its background, and it is principally in the management of its perspective that one artist differs from another. Some events must be represented on a large scale, others diminished. The great majority will be lost in the dimness of the horizon, and a general idea of their joint effect will be given by a few slight touches. Such must be the case, in a degree, concerning the period in the history of Hiram College, now to be considered.

When Mr. Hayden offered his resignation May 20, 1857, and it had been accepted by the Board of Trustees, "It was resolved, that the present teachers of the Institution be constituted a Board of Education, to conduct the educational concerns of the school, subject to the counsel and advice of the Board." This board of instruction which consisted of James A. Garfield, Norman Dunshee, H. W. Everest, J. H. Rhodes, and Almeda A. Booth, made Mr. Garfield its chairman, and he was so published in the catalogue of 1856-57. By this action he became Principal in fact though not in name. The next year he became Principal in name as well. From this time onward until 1866 his name appears annually in the catalogues, either as Principal or advisory Principal and Lecturer, with the exception of the year 1864. After his service as Principal and Teacher ceased, he became a member of the Board of Trustees and remained such until his death in 1881.

Mr. Garfield came to Hiram in 1851, and entered as a student in the Western Reserve Eclectic Institute August 25 of that year.   From that time until he removed his fam-

The Hiram History of Garfield. ily to Mentor in 1877, Hiram was his home. Great as the temptation is to reach out into his life as soldier, states-

man and President of the United States, the history here given must be mainly that in which Hiram is the center. When he came to Hiram in 1851 he lacked a few months of

His Personal Appearance. being twenty years of age. He was strong, broad shouldered and substantial, with a large head and bushy, light brown

hair.   His features were plain but manly and sensible.   For so young a man his character was strongly marked by unflinching principle and "illimitable common sense."   He had in him the instincts of a gentleman, though his manners were not polished or elegant.   He was always polite and

His Courtesy. courteous but his politeness and courtesy were matters of principle and not of pol-

icy.   He was moved in his intercourse with men, not by the rules and regulations of the drawing-room, or exquisite society, but by the rules that are fundamental to a true Christian character.   There was a genial kindly look in his blue eyes, which every one felt who came in contact with him, and yet a certain dignity which always commanded respect; but on occasion his mild blue eyes "blazed like battle lanterns lit."   During two terms at Hiram he was

Janitor. janitor of the building; and he made the fires, swept the floors and rang the bell

and Mr. Corydon E. Fuller, one of his most intimate

friends, says: "My first distinct recollection of him, was within a day or two after the opening of the term August 25, 1851, as he stood in the hall grasping the bellrope to signal the change of classes; his clothing was of material then known as Kentucky jeans, and his arms to the elbows were protected by sleeves of calico."

His first term at the Eclectic closed November 14, 1851, and so rapid had been his progress, that at the "public exercises" with which the term closed, Mr. Garfield pronounced the valedictory oration.* Only the first

Valedictory Oration.

and last paragraphs of this oration are here given: *"Fellow Students,* the time has at length arrived when our connection with this institution and with each other, as seekers of knowledge, is about to terminate, at least for a season. It is fitting that we take a retrospective view, and consider for a few moments that series of events which is now about to close." * * * "In all the various relations we have sustained to each other there has been hardly a jarring note to interrupt the harmony of our intercourse. We part. Never again shall we all meet on these mundane shores. We go and soon are scattered o'er the earth. Death does his work and we sink down into his dark domains. Shall we there rest while endless ages roll? Shall morning never dawn upon that dreamless sleep? Religion holds the lamp at Death's dark threshold and lights the passage through its gloomy shades. We'll pass its dusky portals—eternity bursts in upon our view—and there around the throne of God we'll meet to part no more."

In the winter of 1852 he taught his last district school. This was in Warrensville, O. Looking forward to his re-

---

*The oration entire may be found in "Reminiscences of James A. Garfield," by C. E. Fuller, pp. 36-38.

His Last District School.

turn to Hiram in the spring he wrote to a friend: "Now won't we have a time there next spring? We'll study, clash, combat and discuss, make 'student's offerings' and engage in all the other soul-stirring operations of a student's life." In the same letter written February 14, 1852, he moralized as follows: "Oh! that I possessed the power to scatter the firebrand of ambition among the youth of the rising generation, and let them see the greatness of the age in which they live, and the destiny to which mankind are rushing, together with the part which they are destined to act in the great drama of human existence. But, if I cannot inspire them with that spirit, I intend to keep it predominant in my own breast, and let it spur me forward to action. But let us remember that knowledge is only an increase of power and is only good when directed to good ends. Though a man have all knowledge and have not the love of God in his heart, he will fall short of true excellence."*

The spring term at Hiram opened March 22, 1852, with about forty students, among whom was Mr. Garfield. April 2nd following he was taken down very sick with the measles. Writing of that event and giving his impressions of the sick student,

The Spring Term, 1852.

Mr. Fuller said: "You will think I am writing at rather an unseasonable hour, but I am watching by the sick bed of James A. Garfield. He is here, some twenty miles from home and very sick with the measles. Still, he is getting along very well, and we think is now near the worst. I know you would like him and if you come here you will be sure to get acquainted, for he thinks as much of me as I do of him. He is really a noble fellow;

---

*Letter to Corydon E. Fuller.

talented far above the generality of young men, of sound principles, he must, if he lives, make a man in the world, and one whose influence will be felt."* Notwithstanding the interruption caused by his sickness Mr. Garfield made great progress in his studies. His wonderful endurance enabled him to work almost unceasingly, and what has been described as "the amazing progress" of his class was due in a large measure to him. It has been noted that his lessons for April 30, 1852, were as follows: "Three pages of Sallust, one of Virgil, five of Geometry, five of Algebra. and one of Latin Grammar;" and during the first four weeks of the term the class read, "seventy-two pages of Sallust, and learned seventy-five pages of Legendre's Geometry and Bourbon's Algebra, besides grammar, and a review of Virgil." No wonder a member of the class said: "We were all very proud of our work."

In these days when every school devotes special attention to instrumental music, it will appear astonishing that in such an institution as the Eclectic, with an attendance of

Music
in the Eclectic.

a large number of ladies during the school year, there was not a piano in Hiram. Probably not more than one or two were brought to Hiram during the seven years preceding Mr. Garfield's administration. The only musical instrument used in the school was a Melodeon, upon which a few of the ladies took lessons. Mr. Garfield was very fond of music. He had a deep rich voice and a heart that overflowed with melody. As often as he had opportunity, and permission was granted, he would visit the Raymond boarding house to hear the Soule girls, Sarah and Julia, and Hattie Storer, play and sing, "Lillie Dale," "Don't you re-

*Corydon E. Fuller to his mother.

member sweet Alice, Ben Bolt?" "Blue Juniata" and other popular songs of that day.

Early in May, 1852, a strolling lecturer named Joseph Treat came to Hiram. He was a miniature edition of the Robert G. Ingersoll style of philosopher. He had read a

Mr. Garfield as a Debater.

few infidel works, and felt himself amply equipped to "defy the armies of the living God." With rare audacity he entered Hiram and delivered a series of his lectures. At the close of each lecture he would challenge any one in the audience to answer him, but for several evenings no one accepted the challenge. But one night Prof. Thomas Munnell was prevailed upon to answer him. His effort was hardly satisfactory, for Mr. Munnell though conscientious, cultured, earnest, honest, reverent and sincere, was not the man to deal with a braggart, "who could swagger and amuse the unthinking and raise a laugh at the holiest principles of truth without compunction and without a blush." Mr. Garfield was, finally, prevailed upon to reply to Treat. The opportunity soon came and many of the students and others were present, all expecting the encounter. It is not known that Mr. Treat had any intimation of what was to come. He had been able to raise a laugh at the expense of the courteous Munnell, and felt that he had gained a victory. He made a most venomous attack on the Bible, and charged all who believed in it with the grossest credulity. He charged that the translations of the Scriptures were not reliable. The Bible was written in Hebrew and Greek, and had been translated to suit the notions of designing and dishonest priests, and was wholly unreliable either as history or revelation. He closed with his usual challenge to anyone to answer his indictment.

Mr. Garfield arose and said that he had
Reply to the listened with great attention to the gen-
Infidel Treat. tleman's speech. He hardly knew what
to say in answer but he would like to ask him a question:
"Would he be so kind as to tell the audience what was the
present participle of the verb *to be* in Greek, or in other
words, the Greek word to correspond with the English word
'being.' Mr. Treat made no answer, and the question
was repeated, and he was challenged to answer, but the
poor man did not know." Mr. Garfield then turned to the
audience and asked them what they thought of a man traveling over the country criticising the work of the world's
great scholars, when he did not know the first thing the
school-boy learned in his Greek grammar. He did not re-
proach the gentleman because he had no knowledge of
Greek, but because he sought to overthrow the Christian
faith and dethrone the Christian's God, while passing himself off under false colors—pretending to knowledge he
did not possess; he sought to destroy, but proposed no substitute for the Christian religion; to rob us of the faith we
learned in cradle hymns and at our mother's knee, and leave
us without a chart or guide, to sail upon an unknown sea. He
then uttered an impassioned eulogy upon the Bible as the
source of civilization, the creed of the mightiest nations, the
accepted moral guide of all the grandest men in history, and
the only light through a dark world to eternal light, and life
and peace. The speech was like an electric shock. He soon
had the audience with him and the applause was generous
and hearty. He spoke with a readiness, power and eloquence that astonished even those who had expected much.
Since that day, few if any, perambulating infidel lecturers
have visited Hiram.*

*Reminiscences of J. A. Garfield, by C. E. Fuller, pp. 51-54.

Mr. Garfield always respected his Hiram teachers. These were A. S. Hayden the Principal, Norman Dunshee, Thomas Munnell and Amaziah Hull. It is probable that

His Hiram Teachers. he recited more to Dunshee than to all the rest of his teachers. To some of his class-mates he owed a "higher debt intellec-tually" than to any of his teachers. This was especially true of Miss Booth, whose "generous and powerful aid, quick and never-failing sympathy, and intelligent, unselfish and unswerving friendship" were always acknowledged by him as among the most valuable aids he received in his remark-able intellectual ascent. But there was in him, in almost prodigal abundance, the material from which his majestic character was constructed. The help of teachers, school-mates and admiring friends was the stimulus of the great intellectual and moral forces of his nature, to their best and most comprehensive action. He was not jealous of what others had done, or perhaps, could do. He was always generous in his emulations, though "his eye never wandered from the 'other fellow' in the class who might master the problem first." "He was a vast elemental force, and noth-ing was so essential to him as room and opportunity;" and for a time Hiram gave him the room and furnished his op-portunity.

It was not possible to hold him long simply as a scholar in the classroom and in the catalogue of 1853-4 he was announced as "Teacher in the English Department and

Garfield a Teacher. of the Ancient Languages." During the two years which followed, before he left Hiram for Williams College, he taught arithmetic, grammar, algebra, penmanship, geometry, and classes in classics. "He handled large classes in the English studies with conspicuous power. He took captive

LINCOLN BIBLE INSTITUTE

the members of his classes. He won the students as a body." No one of the 110 persons who made up his great arithmetic class in the winter of 1853-4 can forget it.

The spring term of the Eclectic in 1852 closed June 25. and the fall term of the same year opened August 23, 1852. During the vacation Philip Burns, Corydon E. Fuller, and James A. Garfield, of the non-resident students, remained in Hiram. Mr. A. S. Kilby was building a house near the Eclectic, and Mr. John Buckingham one on the north. Mr. Garfield engaged to work for Mr. Kilby for seventy-five cents a day and board, and Mr. Fuller made a similar contract with Mr. Buckingham at the same price. The two young men spent most of their nights together, sometimes at Mr. Kilby's and then at Mr. Buckingham's. Neither of them regarded it a hardship to work at the same trade that Jesus worked at with his father in Nazareth. They were both strong and vigorous, young, healthy and hopeful and they spent no time regretting that they had not plenty of money which they had not earned. But carpenter work was not the only work he could do, for later, August 20, 1853, Mr. Garfield, Miss Booth and Mr. Fuller spent the day at paper hanging for Principal Hayden, and on that job Mr. Garfield was the foreman, and brought the work to a successful conclusion.

Garfield the Carpenter.

In the early days of the Disciples of Christ on the Western Reserve, or seventy-five years ago it was not a difficult thing for a young man to enter the ranks of the Disciple ministry. If he was a Christian, had fair natural gifts of body and mind, knew the alphabet of the Gospel of Christ, was willing to study, and had a desire to preach he was encouraged to preach. Very few of the early Disciple preachers were

Garfield the Preacher.

ever "ordained" to the ministry, in the modern ecclesiastical sense of that term. Hence in the commonly accepted sense, he was never a preacher or minister; but this could also be said of hundreds of other preachers among the Disciples, at that time, before and since. He did, however, "preach the word." He did hold "revival" or protracted meetings and often with great success. In Hiram in 1858 where he did the most of his preaching there were 34 additions, in Newburgh, the same year 20 additions, and more or less wherever he preached. He did baptize people on the confession of their faith. He married people and oftentimes he stood by the caskets of the dead, and at their graves and uttered words of comfort to the living and of committal for the dead. In short he did, on occasion, everything that is required of a minister of the Gospel.

First Sermon in Hiram.

His first sermon in Hiram was in the winter of 1853-54. His subject was, "The first and second comings of Christ," and in illustration he sketched in a vivid way the first and second comings of Napoleon Bonaparte to France.* For a number of years, five at least, he preached somewhere nearly every Sunday. In a number of churches he preached "one half his time" for several years. At the great "yearly meetings" at Bedford and elsewhere he was always a favorite preacher. Indeed, he did not cease entirely to preach until after his election to Congress in 1863. On September 2, 1853, with a friend, he went from Hiram to attend the yearly meeting at Euclid. On the Sunday following Alexander Campbell preached on the theme, "What think ye of Christ?" It was said of that sermon, "It was worth a

---

*I heard the sermon referred to, and though 47 years have passed since, it is as vivid before me as a thing of yesterday.
    —*F. M. Green.*

journey of a thousand miles." The pulpit took a strong hold on his mind, and in some of his letters to intimate friends, the foundation is laid for the belief that he would make preaching his chief work in life. But as he increased in years and experience he seemed to realize that he did not have "the inward vocation for the work." No doubt he would have achieved high distinction as a preacher, but "his genius drew him to the State by its very bent, as anyone who has followed his history can see." At the same time that he left the pulpit he left the classroom. His preaching and teaching had been of great value to others and a source, also, of great strength to himself, both as a man and a public servant.

After his return to Hiram from Williams College in 1856 he began the study of law, and in 1859 he entered his name as a student-at-law in the office of Williamson and

Garfield the Lawyer. Riddle of Cleveland, and in about two years he was admitted to the bar by the Supreme Court of Ohio, upon the recommendation of Hon. Thomas Key and Hon. Richard Harrison, who subjected Mr. Garfield to a just, but thorough and searching examination, and in their report to the Court they spoke of his mastery of the law as unusual and phenomenal. In the sense of ordinary practice of law, Mr. Garfield never "practiced law." He did very little, if anything, in the lower courts. In his study of the law, he was as in everything else, determined to be with the first. In the confidence of a letter to an intimate friend July 30, 1854, and just after his arrival at Williams' College, he wrote: "I almost feel that there are but two tracks before me—to stand at least *among* the first or *die*. I believe I can do it if granted a fair trial." It has been said, and the statement has not been disputed, "that he was the first and

THE HIRAM CHURCH: ERECTED IN 1844; BURNED IN 1856.

THE HIRAM CHURCH: ERECTED IN 1856; BURNED MAY 25, 1897.

the only man born in America, who made his first plea as a lawyer, before the Supreme Court of the United States."*

His First Legal Plea. Mr. A. G. Riddle in speaking of the event said: "It was a splendid sight. The young lawyer, not ten days admitted, making the first legal plea of his life before the most august tribunal of justice in the nation, and upon a question involving the civil rights and liberties of men for whom he had no personal regard, and whom he had never seen; men, too, the like of whom, so far as their political sentiments were concerned, he had fought with a soldier's bravery from Middle Creek to Chicamauga."

The chapel lectures, or "morning lectures" as they were called, were an interesting feature of Hiram during the years of the Eclectic Institute. These usually followed the

The Chapel Lecture. Scripture reading, singing and prayer, by which the daily sessions of the school were introduced. During the administration of Mr. Hayden these lectures were mostly a study of the Bible—its facts and the literature of its various books. When Mr. Garfield took charge of the school the form and character of the morning lecture were somewhat changed, but they were in entire harmony with his own method, pursued before he went to Williams. His first lecture in the Institute was in the winter of 1853-54. His subject was, "Historical Elements of the English Language."

His chapel lectures were a great source of instruction and influence. "Of these he gave many hundreds, ranging over education, teaching, books, methods of study and read-

---

*While visiting at his house in Mentor, in February, 1881, just before he left for Washington, I asked him if the statement was true; for I desired to insert it in the story of his life which I was soon to write. He said he knew of no exception to it—that he thought it was literally true.—*F. M. Green.*

ing, physical geography, geology, history, the Bible, morals, current topics and life questions. These lectures were full of fresh facts, new thoughts, striking illustrations, and were warm with the glow of his own life."* "He generally spoke from notes that he had carefully prepared, and that he carefully preserved. If these notes should be brought forth from their hiding place and published, men would be astonished at the sweep of his thought, the versatility of his mind, and the fertility of his resources." His method of teaching combined "the technical question, the general question, the topic, and the teacher's own discussion of the question in hand." He strove to awaken the student's faculties, and he rarely ever failed to energize or vitalize him. "He stimulated thought, created the habit of observation and reflection, aroused courage, widened the field of mental vision, and furnished inspiration in unlimited measures."

Where to go when he should leave Hiram was a difficult question for Mr. Garfield to answer, but after carefully considering the question, he decided in favor of Williams College. June 26, 1854, he wrote to a friend: "The last link is broken, and I have snapped the last arrow upon the grave of my fathers. The scenes of our dear Eclectic are over and she is left covered with glory. I can never go to Bethany. Next Thursday I start for the Old Bay State. Within ten days I shall be at Williamstown, Mass., where I may remain two years. Again I am to stand alone among strangers and in a strange land." July 11, 1854, he arrived at Williamstown, and in the afternoon of that day met President Hopkins, passed his examination in mathematics, Greek and Latin, and was allowed to enter

From Hiram to Williamstown.

---

*I have six of his Lectures on Geology, taken down in outline at the time they were delivered and preserved. They seem to me wonderful now.—*F. M. Green.*

the coming junior year. He remained two years in Williamstown and graduated August 6, 1856, receiving one of
the honors of his class. Out of a class of 45 only six received graduating honors. Of himself he writes May 15,
1856: "I am one of the six, and received the Metaphysical
Honor, which is considered second only to the Valedictory,
which last is always awarded to one who has been here the
full time, other things being nearly equal." Of the result
on Commencement Day it was written, "that his was the
great oration of the day."

It is impossible to enter more fully into the details of
this wonderful personal history and deal justly with other
matters which belong in this chapter. It must suffice to
sum up some of the characteristics of this
Back in Hiram.
man whose name and fame have covered
Hiram with glory. He was modest and self-possessed,
without vanity or self-consciousness and free from affecta-
tion. His intellections were clear, vigorous and easy in all
directions. He had a great desire to conquer, to prove superior to every difficulty, to excel all competitors, and finally,
to conquer and surpass himself; and over all he shed the
glory of a happy disposition, full of hope and manly courage. He called out the demonstrativeness and affections
of men in a way almost unprecedented. His heart none
but the most utterly obdurate could resist. He was full of
unshed goodness, gentleness and tenderness. His proportions never grew less to those who became acquainted with
him, for as they grew he grew too; "and they never had
occasion to measure him over again." "He always discussed large subjects in a large way." He excelled almost
all men in comprehensive generalizations; and also in the patient, untiring labor with which he would hunt down special
facts. He treasured up knowledge of all kinds, "for," he

would say, "you never know how soon you will need it."
He conscientiously performed every duty assigned him at
home or abroad, in field or in shop, in school room or pulpit,
in the army or in Congress, in the meeting of teachers or
in the Board of Trustees, in the mighty campaign or in the
Presidential chair. He seemed "greater than any of his
works, wiser than any of his words."

When he first came to Hiram in 1851 "he came unob-
served, a student poor and plain." In 1880 he came "with
flags and bands of music, with powerful friends and a huz-
zaing multitude, and a troop of corre-
spondents to tell it to all the world." February 4, 1881, he made his last visit to
Hiram, and closed his memorable career
with the College and the place. On that occasion, in part,
he said: "To-day is a sort of burial-day in many ways. I
have often been in Hiram, and have often left it; but, with
the exception of when I went to the war, I have never felt
that I was leaving it in quite so definite a way as I do to-day.
It was so long a workshop, so long a home, that all absences
have been temporary, and involved always a return. I cannot speak of all the ties that bind me to this place. There
are other things buried beneath this snow besides dead people. The trees, the rocks, the fences, and the grass are all
reminders of things connected with my Hiram life. * *
May the time never come when I cannot find some food for
mind and heart on Hiram Hill."

His Last Visit to Hiram.

He was born November 19, 1831, in Cuyahoga Co.,
Ohio. Driver on the Ohio Canal in the summer of 1848.
Entered Geauga Seminary, at Chester, O., March 6, 1849.
Taught his first school in the winter of
1849-50. Baptized by W. A. Lillie March
4, 1850. Entered "Eclectic Institute" at
Hiram August 25, 1851. Was teacher and student at

Summary and Chronology.

Hiram from 1852-54. Entered Williams College July 11, 1854. Graduated with honor from Williams College August 6, 1856. Professor and Principal and Lecturer at Hiram from 1856-1866. Elected to Ohio Senate in October, 1859. Entered the Union Army in 1861. Commissioned Brigadier General January 10, 1862. Elected to Congress in October 1862 and served continuously from December, 1863 until 1880. Commissioned Major General September 18, 1863. Elected United States Senator from Ohio in January, 1880. Nominated for President of the United States June 8, 1880. Elected President of the United States November 2, 1880. Inaugurated March 4, 1881. Shot by the assassin July 2, 1881. Died at Elberon, September 19, 1881.

It would hardly be expected with such a man as Mr. Garfield at the head that the character of the school would remain in all respects as it had been, during the administration of Mr. Hayden. And there were some changes, some of them quite radical. "Its genius was less theological or biblical, and more secular or human. The ecclesiastical way of looking at things somewhat receded with the retirement of Principal Hayden. But morals, religion, and Bible study were by no means forgotten. Noble ideals of life and character, ideals of manliness, courage, reverence, and truth, were constantly kept in view. And such of the students as could receive it were filled with the Principal's own largeness of nature."*

Mr. Garfield was very successful as a school administrator. He understood what was, and what was not, essential to discipline and good order, and he never spent his force on little things. "He always had a code of printed

*Garfield and Education, p. 55.

rules that he expounded each term; he exacted weekly reports of conduct; but his own personality was worth far more than both rules and reports."

Mr. Garfield's administration lifted the Eclectic Institute into new prominence. It took a step in advance; its influence was enlarged; a higher standard of scholarship was demanded; its culture became more mature; its patronage outside the church increased; and educators became familiar with the name of Hiram and the Principal. In 1858 Mr. Garfield made a report to the State Commissioner of Common Schools in which he said: "The aim of the school is to hold the rank of a first-class collegiate seminary; to train teachers for their duty in the public schools, and to prepare students for an advanced standing in college. One of the peculiarities of the Eclectic is a clause in its charter providing for the introduction of the Bible as a text book. It is introduced in no sectarian attitude; but the sacred literature, history and morals of the Bible, are regarded as legitimate theme for academic instruction. The Institute is constantly increasing in influence and number of students, and is now more prosperous than ever."

From some of the letters he wrote to friends from 1857 onward there may be gleaned some of the inner life of the Eclectic during this period. August 30, 1857, he wrote: "There has been a great crisis upon the Eclectic Institute, and I am buffeting such waves as I never before breasted, and doing such work as I never before have done. We have raised over $400 to build a fence around the Eclectic grounds. We have remodeled the government, published rules, published a new catalogue, and have now, the fourth week, 250 students (no primary), as orderly as clock-work, and all hard at work. Our teachers are Dunshee, Everest, Rhodes, and Almeda. I teach seven classes and take the entire charge of the school and its correspondence besides. I have the most advanced classes in the school and deliver the most of the morning lectures."

January 16, 1858, he wrote: "I am doing all the work in the school that I formerly did, and more; I speak somewhere every Lord's day, and have written and delivered several lectures this season."

During this period much attention was given to the teaching and training of teachers for their special work. Classes were formed and conducted with reference to the duties of the teacher. Courses of lectures were prepared and delivered on school government and the best methods of teaching. This arrangement was intended to answer the purpose of a Normal school. Elocution was given special attention. It was held, that "to become a good reader, two things are requisite—first, the power of vocal expression; and second an appreciation of the author's thought. For this reason a part of each recitation will be devoted to vocal gymnastics, and the adaptation of the voice to express the different emotions and passions. Then a close study of the sentiment to be read, will enable the student to read 'with the spirit and the understanding,' instead of merely mouthing the printed words."

Among the teachers who helped to make the Garfield administration successful and strong was J. H. Rhodes. He first came to Hiram from Massillon, Ohio, where his parents lived, in the year 1852-53. He was of a good family and of sturdy German stock. Miss Booth to whom he recited when he first came to Hiram, and with whom he afterwards associated as a teacher, has left on record a little incident of his early Hiram life. In a letter written June 24, 1855, she says: "I was in Hiram Thursday, to their exhibition. It was down

in the corner under the apple trees, just as it used to be
when you were there. You would hardly perceive any
change, only in the performers. Sutton was there with the
same gentle voice and bland smile; yet there are more wrin-
kles in his face, and gray hairs are more abundant. And
Bro. Munnell was there looking as earnest and determined
as ever; and Norman Dunshee, too. Time deals kindly
with him; his lank face has assumed fuller proportions and
ne looks more noble. O. P. Miller was on the discussion,
"Do the signs of the times indicate the downfall of Popery?"
His opponent was J. H. Rhodes, a German boy, from Stark
County. He got up with a little patched coat on looking
very humble; but he is tremendous smart. He rolled off a
perfect torrent of eloquence, and argument, too. Bro. Munnell says he will make James' place good."* Mr. Rhodes
never fell below the estimate Miss Booth placed on him, during his long and honorable connection with Hiram. In 1854
he became one of the teachers of the Eclectic Institute and
remained as such until 1863 with only brief periods of absence. He taught in the English Department, Mathematics,
and Modern Languages. He was one of the best teachers
of elocution ever connected with the Institution. His temperament was so different that his pupils never had that
enthusiastic personal affection for him that they always had
for Miss Booth and Mr. Garfield; and yet, he was generally
well liked. He had a bright, keen intellect; the disposition
of a student; a command of language perhaps unsurpassed
by any student or teacher in Hiram; a character unblemished by scandal or weakness; and he retained his affection
for Hiram from the time he entered a student in 1853 until
his death in 1889, a period of more than a third of a century.
Along these years he was student, teacher and Trustee of
the Institution.

---

*Letter to Corydon E. Fuller.

The following interesting memorandum referring to a meeting in progress is in the handwriting of Mr. J. H. Rhodes, written September 27, 1857: "From this place onward is a short abstract of what the **Memorandum** school (by which is meant the teachers) **by J. H. Rhodes.** is doing for the religious interests of the school and society. Brother Everest up to this time has spoken twice, Brother Garfield twice, and Brother Dunshee several times. There have been some personal interviews with a number of the students. I, myself, have made this to supply, so far as possible, what preaching I might do. On the 13th of this month the following ones were converted: Mary DeWolf, Emma Shattuck, Mary Howe, Minerva Tuttle; on the 20th Mary Calvin; on the 27th H. D. Carlton, M. B. Dawson, Charles Ledwell, J. Pardee, Martha Mathews. Some of these we trust may be useful members of the Kingdom of God. May the Spirit of God brood mightily over this Institution, to the conversion of many souls."

After his death the Board of Trustees placed on record June 2, 1890, the following resolutions prepared by C. B. Lockwood, Andrew Squire, and F. M. Green: "*Resolved,* That this Board, at its first meeting since the death of J. H. Rhodes, desires to express its sense of great loss and sorrow at his separation from us. We cannot forget him as one of the distinguished trio, Garfield, Booth and Rhodes, who so faithfully labored as professors, when it was largely a labor of love in the days of our poverty, and gave to Hiram a permanent place among the colleges of our country; nor his unremitting and unremunerated labor of love as a member of this Board. Qualified by education and experience, and with untiring devotion all these years of his history he has faithfully watched over its interests. *Resolved,* That all who love Hiram, owe him a debt of gratitude for his faithful service for her prosperity; and that this Board wishes to properly emphasize its appreciation of his distinguished aid and assistance; therefore *Resolved,* That these resolutions be made a part of our permanent records."

No Hiram history would be complete without his name written large upon its pages. He was not only a distinguished member in the Hiram Fellowship but he achieved distinction as an orator and counselor at law in Cleveland, Ohio, and as a citizen.

He was born in Summit County, Ohio, July 7, 1836, and died in Cleveland, O., February 14, 1890.

During the administration of Mr. Garfield while the patronage somewhat increased, and the receipts from tuition and other sources were correspondingly larger, the expenses

Financial Matters. likewise increased on account of the increased needs of the school. The debt on the Institution amounted at the close of Mr. Hayden's administration June 17, 1857, to $5,517.95. The receipts for tuition for the year ending June 10, 1858, were $3,218.00, of which $349.20 were used for current expenses, leaving for the teachers $2,868.80. It was found difficult to raise money year by year sufficient to prevent a deficit at the end of each year. For some reason the churches that at the beginning were its largest contributors grew cool in their friendship and declined to furnish the necessary support. In 1855 it was proposed in the Board of Trustees, "to raise ten thousand dollars to liquidate the debt, and for other necessary purposes, by one hundred individuals subscribing one hundred dollars each; no one being bound for his subscription till the number of one hundred of such subscriptions be obtained." The terms were afterwards modified so as to require five thousand dollars to be subscribed before the pledges could be held. A. S. Hayden and Dr. W. A. Belding were put into the field as

agents and solicitors to raise this amount. In 1856 Mr.
Hayden reported "pledges and notes to the amount of four
thousand six hundred and eighty-nine dollars," which
amount lacked three hundred and eleven dollars of enough
to claim the subscriptions "according to the modified resolution of the Board, passed at the last meeting."   April 1,
1856, a Standing Committee of Accounts was appointed by
the Board whose duty, in part, was "to annually report the
state of the funds" and the general financial condition of the
Institution.   The committee was made to consist of Frederick Williams and Cyrus Bosworth, Sr.   June 18, 1856, this
Committee made a carefully prepared report which is interesting even at this day: "The Committee of Accounts, to
whom was assigned the duty of settling with the Building
Committee of the Institute, the Building Committee of the
Boarding Houses, and the Treasurer of the Institute, respectfully submit the following report: That in pursuance
of the duties imposed on them, the books and vouchers of
said Building Committees, as presented by Alvah Udall,
Esq., a member of said Committees, and now President of
the Board, have been carefully examined, and show the following results:

1—That the whole amount expended in land, buildings
and furniture, is sixteen thousand and five hundred dollars
($16,500).

2—That the books of the Treasurer show that the sum
of eleven thousand, one hundred and thirty-four dollars
and twenty-five cents, has been paid out of the Treasury,
partly in liquidation of the foregoing amount, and partly for
incidental expenses, for which no detailed account can be
given ($11,134.25).

3—That the whole amount of outstanding notes against
the Building Committees is seven thousand five hundred
and seventeen dollars ($7,517.00).

4—That to meet this outstanding debt, there are claims, to the amount of one thousand eight hundred and ninety-five dollars in the hands of W. A. Belding, and about one hundred and twenty dollars due on land sold, and a balance on the books of the Building Committees of twenty-five dollars and sixty-six cents, a total of ($2,040.66).

5—That a careful examination of the books and vouchers of said Building Committees, discloses nothing that is not fair and honest, and exhibits on striking a general balance, twenty-five dollars and sixty-six cents in favor of the Institute ($25.66).

6—That the foregoing amounts, in all, $2,040.66, deducted from $7,517.00, leave $5,476.34 as the entire indebtedness of the Institute at the present time."

It may be said that while there was scarcely a year during the lifetime of the Eclectic Institute that there was not a deficit, still no serious debts were ever incurred. If the receipts were not equal to the expectation of those most concerned, they accepted the smaller sum, and forgave the debt. But the school was like a healthy growing boy; it was continually wearing out or outgrowing its garments, and means must be supplied to provide larger and new ones. To this end the Principal and some of his teachers, and members of the Board of Trustees, and special solicitors were sent out among the churches to canvass for funds, But this miscellaneous canvassing was not generally satisfactory.

November 9, 1858, the Board of Trustees on motion of William Hayden resolved "that W. J. Ford be employed to act as solicitor and collector for the Institution; and that the President be authorized to act for the Board in specifying the terms of employment." Mr. Ford had been elected a Trustee in 1856 to succeed his father, J. A. Ford. Mr. Ford is a member of the

W. J. Ford.

present Board of Trustees, and counting from his first election to the present, he has served the Institution for 44 years—a longer period than any other person.   As a solicitor he was successful from the beginning and so far as the records show, no trouble ever arose in the adjustment of his accounts.   His work as solicitor ran over into the College period, and the funds that he secured laid the foundation for the permanent endowment fund of the College, which has steadily grown from its small beginning to its present creditable proportions.   Mr. Ford was so successful in raising funds and creating an interest in the school that June 5, 1861, the Board of Trustees recorded its judgment of his work as follows: *"Resolved,* That the thanks of the Trustees of the Western Reserve Eclectic Institute be tendered to W. J. Ford for the efficient manner in which he has discharged his duties as solicitor for the Institution; and that his services be continued in making collections and in raising funds."   It may also be said that Mr. Ford was a student of the Eclectic in its first and second years.   It is, probably, not an overstatement to say that no other financial agent of the College ever excelled him when the conditions and environments of the period of his service are considered.   He is entitled to this distinct recognition in the history of the College.

Great interest was taken in the Literary Societies of the Institute during Mr. Garfield's administration.   The Delphic, Hesperian and Olive Branch in their respective spheres were enthusiastic and successful.   In the multitude of his duties while Principal at Hiram, Mr. Garfield did not forget or neglect the literary work of the school.   His interest and enthusiasm in the work of the societies did not diminish after he became teacher and Principal; and during his administration the names and numbers of the acting

Literary Societies.

members of each society were published in the annual catalogues.

It has already been said that the character of the school
changed somewhat after Mr. Garfield became Principal.
But these changes were usually in the line of its management, the strengthening of its courses of
study, and method of procedure. Perhaps its genius became "less theological
or biblical, and more secular or human"
than it had been under the previous administration. And yet there appears to have been a strong
desire on the part of many of its friends to change its character from that of a merely literary institution with the
Bible as a book for daily study, to a real Theological Seminary. There had never been entire unity in regard to the
grade of the school. Some were in favor, perhaps the
most, of an institution which finally took form under the
name of "The Western Reserve Eclectic Institute;" others
were in favor of a Theological Seminary; while others were
in favor of a College proper with authority to confer
Degrees.

While Mr. Hayden was Principal his prominent aim
was "to implant deeply in the heart of every student, the
code of morals found in the New Testament, based on the
superlatively glorious and immutable facts of Sacred History;" and "it was deliberately and firmly resolved that this
instruction should ever be held paramount in all its classic
arrangements." To the rule that, "the Bible must be taken
into the school as a book of study; its facts must be studied;
and its own pure and perfect morality must be daily urged
upon the consciences of the students, in view of its fearful
sanctions," Mr. Hayden adhered through his entire administration. June 9, 1858, a large number of the friends of

**Proposed
Changes in the
Character of the
School.**

Convention Resolutions. the Institute met in Hiram to consider the character of the changes they desired, and to form a recommendation to the Board of Trustees then in session. The following Preamble and Resolutions were adopted and sent to the Board of Trustees for their action: *Whereas,* It has been shown, that the great want of our brotherhood is a Theological Seminary, be it therefore

Resolved, That we ask of the Trustees and stockholders of the Eclectic Institute, that the school be so changed as to meet that demand, and that anything of its present character be subordinate.

Resolved, That in case the recommendation of this convention, to make the Eclectic Institute a Theological Seminary, be favorably entertained by the Board of Trustees of said Institute, we recommend to them farther to appoint Symonds Ryder to go before the brethren with this plea, and endeavor to raise the money to cancel the debts of the Institute."

When these resolutions were sent to the Board of Trustees, on motion of Zeb Rudolph they were taken up for consideration. After due consideration, William Hayden moved, "to approve the first resolution and adopt it as a purpose to be carried out as soon as practicable." This resolution was unanimously adopted. The second resolution was, also, unanimously adopted, with the addition of the name of James A. Garfield who with Symonds Ryder was "appointed to carry out the object of the resolution."

As there were certain legal questions involved in the proposed change, Symonds Ryder was appointed to secure "the necessary legal advice" on the following questions:

1—Whether a charter for a Theological Seminary can be obtained without application to the Legislature; and if so, how?

2—How large a proportion of the stockholders of the Institute must consent to the proposed change, before it can be legally made.

3—In what form can their consent be lawfully obtained?"

The President of the Board was authorized to carry out the recommendation of the convention, and take "immediate measures to transfer the real estate of the Institute to the Board of Trustees, and to take from the Trustees a mortgage to secure the Building Committee until the debts of the Institute are paid."

Mr. Garfield was appointed a committee to correspond with the stockholders and others, "with a view to learn the general sentiment regarding the change proposed." The President of the Board was authorized to prepare a balance sheet, for publication, exhibiting the financial condition of the Institute. And, finally, it was

"*Resolved,* That, whenever, in the opinion of the members of the Board living in Hiram, it shall be deemed necessary to call a convention of the friends and stockholders of the Institute, to perfect the proposed change, it shall be their duty to issue such a call."

The proper steps were taken to vest the title of the real estate in the Board of Trustees, and the bond and mortgage ordered were executed. And here the effort to create a Theological Seminary out of the Western Reserve Eclectic Institute ceased to be a question for consideration, and nothing came out of it unless the Course of Lectures given in 1866 and 1867 by Isaac Errett and others, may have been the result of the agitation. The records of the Board do not give the reasons why the matter was so speedily and completely dropped. The probabilities are that the legal difficulties were considerable, but that the main reason was, the intense conservatism of the Disciples, their undying hos-

THE GARFIELD HOME.

tility towards sectarianism, and their fear to lay anything upon an altar from which the slightest puff of sectarian smoke ascended.

Not many months passed before another effort to change the character of the Institute was proposed. This time the proposition was to make it a college. At the call of the President, November 9, 1858, there were present at Hiram of the Board of Trustees, Alvah Udall, William Hayden, Aaron Davis, Frederick Williams, Zeb Rudolph, William Richards, Alvah Humeston and W. J. Ford. After some miscellaneous business was disposed of, Frederick Williams offered the following Preamble and Resolutions:

First Resolutions in Favor of a College.

"*Whereas,* The Board of Trustees of the Western Reserve Eclectic Institute, a Seminary of learning, believing that it is desirable and for the interest of said Institute, to reorganize under the provisions of 'An Act, entitled an Act to authorize Seminaries of Learning to change their names and become Colleges," passed April 8, 1856; therefore, *Resolved,* That the name of said Institute be, and the same is hereby changed to Hiram College.*

Resolved, That under the provisions of said Act, the said Institute, as aforesaid, be and the same is hereby ordered to be organized as a College, with full collegiate powers, and privileges to confer upon the graduates of said College the usual degrees granted by colleges, etc.

Resolved, That said Board of Trustees be instructed to take, at such time as the Board may order, all the necessary steps to carry into effect these resolutions."

---

*The name of the College was apparently not given in this resolution when it was passed, but was inserted afterwards. The resolution was adopted with the space for the name unfilled.

—*F. M. Green.*

The motion to adopt these resolutions was made by Frederick Williams and seconded by William Hayden and received the unanimous vote of the members of the Board present, on November 10, 1858.

Here the matter rested until the meeting of the Board of Trustees, February 20, 1867, when at a meeting, in Hiram, at which were present Alvah Udall, H. Ryder, A. S. Hayden, J. H. Rhodes, Zeb Rudolph, and W. J. Ford, Mr. Ford offered the following resolution which was unanimously adopted: "*Resolved*, That the President of the Board of Trustees of the Western Reserve Eclectic Institute, be instructed and he is hereby authorized to take all the steps necessary to carry out the letter and spirit of a resolution passed by the Board in a meeting held November 10, 1858, making the Eclectic Institute a College; and that the name of the College shall be HIRAM COLLEGE, and so entered upon the Portage County and State Records."

The Civil War dealt Hiram as it did many other similar institutions in the North, a very hard blow. "Many
Hiram and the   students went into the army, and others
Civil War.   fell out of the school owing to the disturbed state of the country, while new ones came in slowly. Garfield left to return no more, and other teachers soon followed, Rhodes in the winter of '63-'64 and Everest the next summer. Partial disorganization reigned until the Institute was merged into the College. Sometimes the Trustees failed to meet at the stated time, and when they did meet they did not always know what to do. They were sometimes obliged to take as teachers those whom they could get, and did not always receive those whom they wanted. At last there was a new Principal every year, and when the doors closed in the spring nobody could tell who would be the head in the fall. Miss Booth held on resolutely until 1866, when the state of her parents' health

compelled her to retire.   Much good teaching was done in all these years, but the school was weak and unstable."*

The sentiment of the people of Hiram as of all the Western Reserve, was that of unmistakable and devoted loyalty to the Government in its efforts to preserve the Union of the States. Comparatively few uttered the growl of the traitor, and refused to sustain the Government at Washington in its hour of peril. But there were a few who tried to uphold the "Stars and Bars" instead of the "Stars and Stripes." Occasionally one of the students "advocated such sentiments" that the loyal girls of the "Olive Branch" drowned the words of the "rebel orator" with the lusty volume of their patriotic songs. The neighborhood squire was roused from his slumbers, and "hurriedly brought upon the scene of action" to administer the oath of allegiance to the "refractory copperhead." May 22, 1863, the Hesperian Society gave an entertainment in their hall and as a part of it, a member of the society delivered an oration on the subject, "Once Happy America," in which "he advocated such sentiments that the Olivites, who were present, or at least a large share of them vacated, and began singing patriotic melodies suitable for the occasion." The tumult in the hall was so great that it was impossible to complete the program, and the society finally adjourned. The person who was the center of the tumult in speaking of the matter afterwards said : "When I started down stairs with two or three friends, the mob gathered at the foot ready to devour, I essayed to ask them a few questions, but Mr. Hinsdale, who had been called in and now stood on the stairs beside me, stopped me, saying it would be of no use for me to speak. Timothy Newcomb was called out of his bed to administer the oath

*"The Eclectic Institute," by B. A. Hinsdale, pp. 15-16.

of allegiance to this refractory copperhead. After some parleying it was changed to an oath to support the Constitution of the United States. While doubting his authority to administer, I did not doubt the propriety under the circumstances of my taking it. I told him I would cheerfully take that oath every day in the week. Discretion was the better part of valor in the matter, for it was just a little uncertain in those days what an enraged crowd would do with a man if they got him into their clutches, especially in the night. I was willing to forego any frog-pond immersion or outside tar application as suggested. I withdrew my name from the Society that evening as did several others. Afterwards, I believe, they went through the form of expelling us, but I don't know that I ever harbored many ill-feelings over the matter. It was a part of the times."* It was, indeed, so much a "part of the times," and caused such a distinct sensation in Hiram, that Gen. Garfield from the Headquarters of the Department of the Cumberland, at Murfreesboro, Tenn., under date of May 26, 1863, wrote to B. A. Hinsdale as follows: "Tell all those copperhead students for me that, were I there in charge of the school, I would not only dishonorably dismiss them from the school, but, if they remained in the place and persisted in their cowardly treason, I would apply to Gen. Burnside to enforce General Order No. 38 in their cases.

If these young traitors are in earnest they should go to the Southern Confederacy, where they can receive full sympathy. Tell them all that I will furnish them passes through our lines, where they can join Vallandigham and their other friends till such time as they can destroy us and come back home as conquerors of their own people, or can learn wisdom and obedience.

---

*Hesperian Reunion Address, by A. Squire, 1876.

I know this is apparently a small matter, but it is only apparently small. We do not know what the developments of a month may bring forth, and, if such things be permitted at Hiram, they may anywhere. The Rebels catch up all such facts as sweet morsels of comfort, and every such influence lengthens the war and adds to the bloodshed."

A complete roster of all who enlisted in the Union army, of Hiram students, has never been made; but the Delphic and Hesperian Societies furnished a large number whose names they have sacredly enrolled. For the three years, 1861, 1862 and 1863 when enlistments were most numerous, the Delphic had an aggregate active membership of 202, and the Hesperian of 198. Of these members, those who were at the time of their enlistment members or had been members in one or more of these years of the Hesperian Society were 79, and of the Delphic 56. It is a list of noble names and worthy of long remembrance. Of course Hiram's leading soldier was Mr. Garfield who in his short service of less than three years won the eagles of a Colonel, and the stars of a Brigadier and Major General; but the service of all from privates to generals was creditable, and often conspicuous. These men were found in nearly every arm of the service, infantry, artillery and cavalry. No invidious comparisons should be made in regard to the relative patriotism displayed by the two societies, then as now, rivals for the best. Each did the best it could, and each is entitled to the honor of supplying from its own loved and bravest, some of the best and mightiest defenders of the Nation. And the names of these young men who helped to fill the ranks of the 42nd, the 23rd, the 41st, the 45th, the 7th, and other regiments of Infantry; the squadrons of Ohio cavalry; and the battalions of Ohio artillery, can never be spoken in Hiram's ears, without feeling the touch of their manly fingers, and hearing the tread of their marching feet. Hiram

"Gave with prayers and tears,
  With mingled hopes and fears,
  Her bravest sons, her treasures rare;
In silent grief she leaves them there,
      Where glory lies."*

(Miss A. A. Booth.)

The annual "Commencement Days" were looked upon as great days during the period covered by Mr. Garfield's administration. The crowds that seemingly came from

Commencements. everywhere on these June days were enormous. They were generally good natured, well-behaved, and interested in the literary and musical features of the occasions. The "marshals" were selected from the student body, and decorated in their bright sashes with brilliant badges, highly magnified their offices and were the cynosure of all eyes. The "Bedford Tent" under which thousands could be seated, was spread to its utmost limits. The character of the programmes varied but little from those that had preceded them. More of the performers, perhaps, had had experience in writing essays and preparing orations, than those who appeared on earlier programmes.

The following programme presented June 7, 1860, represents, probably, more of those known as "old students" than any other in this period:

Forenoon.

	MUSIC,	-	-	-			"Hail! Festal Day"
1	ESSAY,	-	-	-			A Page from the Book of Life

ELIZABETH A. WOODWARD, *Lordstown*

2	ESSAY,	-	-	-	-		South Sea Islands

ADDIE M. ROBBINS, *Solon*

3	ESSAY,	-	-	-	-	-	Pipes

MINERVA E. TUTTLE, *Palmyra*

---

*See Appendix for names, regiments and rank.

4 ESSAY, - - - Between the Tropics
        JULIAETTE COMSTOCK, *Mentor*
    MUSIC, - "Lo! the Rosy Morning Breaking"
5 ESSAY, - - - - Sugar-Coated Pills
        MYRA E. ROBBINS, *Solon*
6 - - - - - - Miscellany
    ELIZA E. CLAPP, *Hiram*; MATTIE RUDOLPH, *Garrettsville*
7 ESSAY, - - - Knights of the Round Table
        LOUISA M. LETCHER, *West Unity*
    MUSIC, - - - "Away! Away!"
8 ESSAY, - - - - - Isabella of Spain
        SABRINA M. CAPRON, *Auburn*
9 ESSAY, - - - - We're All Singers
        HENRIETTA M. JAMES, *Troy*
10 ESSAY, - - - At Home and Abroad
        MARY E. TURNER, *Cleveland*
11 "THE MUSES; OR THE CROWNING OF
                            FLORENCE NIGHTINGALE"

———

DISCUSSION:
*Is the Government of the United States superior to that of
                Great Britain ?*
AFF.—J. W. NELSON, *Auburn*; H. C. NELSON, *Brecksville*
NEG.—M. J. RICHARDS, *Solon*; H. D. CARLTON, *Hiram*
    MUSIC, - - "Star Spangled Banner"

———

Afternoon.

    MUSIC, - - - - "Anthem"
1 GERMAN SALUTATORY, - - Goethe
        B. G. HANK, *Hiram*
2 ORATION, - - - - The Nile
        M. S. CLARK, *Freedom*
3 ORATION, - - The Beautiful an Educator
        F. M. GREEN, *Sharon*
4 ORATION, - - - - Egotism
    AMZI ATWATER, *Mantua*
            MUSIC
5 ORATION, - - Japan and the Japanese
        S. P. NEWCOMB, *Hiram*
6 ORATION, - - The March of Empire
    H. S. GLASIER, *Bedford*
7 ORATION, - - - The Heir of the Ages
        F. H. MASON, *Niles*
8 ORATION, - - - - Duelling
        L. J. BROWN, *Freedom*
    MUSIC, - - " Bright Flag of America "
9 ORATION, - - The Teachings of Revolution
        C. A. DUDLEY, *Freedom*

```
10  -     -     -     -     -     -     -     North and South
       B. A. HINSDALE, Wadsworth; H. S. CHAMBERLIN, Solon
       MUSIC,      -      -       "Hail to Thee, Liberty!"
11  ORATION,   -    -     -     -     -    Sir John Franklin
                 H. C. WHITE, Newburgh
12  VALEDICTORY,      -      -      -      Individual Worth
                 F. A. WILLIAMS, Ravenna
       MUSIC,      -      -      "We Love Our Native Hills"
```

Quite a number of the performers on this eventful day are yet living, but many of them are dead. Elizabeth A. Woodward died the wife of J. H. Rhodes, and Addie M. Robbins survives him as his widow. Eliza E. Clapp bears in her long widowhood the sacred name of H. S. Glasier. Mattie Rudolph is yet living, honored by her children and friends and honoring the name of her lamented husband, H. D. Carlton. Sabrina M. Capron is yet queen in the home of Henry C. White. Mary E. Turner is the faithful wife of B. A. Hinsdale. M. S. Clark is an M. D. of good repute in Youngstown, Ohio. F. M. Green yet lives forty years older than when this programme was presented. Amzi Atwater still honors the name so familiar from Hiram's first days. S. P. Newcomb honors Iowa, his adopted state. F. H. Mason is one of the best Consuls the United States has ever had in France or Germany. B. A. Hinsdale has reached an eminence as a close and subtile thinker and educator, higher than any of his Hiram fellowship. H. S. Chamberlain is one of the "iron kings" of the south. F. A. Williams sleeps in a soldier's grave; and Henry C. White is, and has been, for many years, the upright Judge of the Probate Court in the banner city and county of Ohio. And the rest, their names are precious, whether they be living or dead.

The grounds on which the College buildings now stand, have been justly admired, in recent years. When the old College building was erected, the enclosure, of which it

was the center was mostly a ploughed field.
Several years passed before any attempt
was made to grade its surface, or to
adorn it.   No trees except a few fruit trees were within its
limits.   In the year 1857-'58 Mr. Garfield stirred up considerable enthusiasm among the students, by proposing that
the *campus* be planted with evergreen and forest trees.
Many contributed to buy the evergreens; and the maples
and elms were brought by students from the valley south
of the village.   The planting of these trees was an event
of great interest to the participants.   The most of the trees
lived and grew and are now the stately and venerable trees
on the campus.   Some of the boys whose relations to each
other were intimate joined in the selection and planting of
a tree.   The large elm tree on the circle near the new Y.
M. C. A. Building was brought up from the valley by
Charles P. Bowler and F. M. Green and planted by them.
Some of the trees on the campus are "Class Trees" and were
planted with appropriate ceremonies.

The "Course of Study" during Mr. Garfield's administration was enlarged and strengthened.   Its teachers were
nearly all graduates, or were ready to
graduate; and the course of study was
brought up to correspond with the in-
crease in scholarship and power of the teachers.   In 1863
the curriculum of study demanded:

First Year: Ray's Arithmetic; Grammar, Quackenbos';
and Green's Analysis; Camp's Geography; Mitchell's An-
cient Geography; Murdoch and Russell's Elocution; Loomis'
Algebra, begun; Cutler's Physiology; Arnold's First and
Second Book in Latin; Cornelius Nepos; Crosby's Greek
Grammar; Harkness' First Book in Greek.

Second Year: Loomis' Algebra; Loomis' Geometry;
Willard's Ancient and Modern History; Warren's Physical

Geography; Well's Natural Philosophy; St. John's Geology; Arnold's Prose Composition; Virgil, Schmitz and Zumpt's; Anthon's Sallust; Greenfield's Greek Testament; Crosby's Anabasis; Fasquelle's French Grammar; Wood's Botany; Boise's Greek Composition.

Third Year: Loomis' Trigonometry and Surveying; Cicero's Orations; Odes of Horace; Lincoln's Livy; Owen's Thucydides; Anthon's Memorabilia; Anthon's Homer; Telemaque; Charles XII; Woodbury's German Grammar; Woodbury's German Readers; Youman's Chemistry; Olmstead's Astronomy; Quackenbos' Rhetoric.

Fourth Year: Loomis' Analytical Geometry and Calculus; Horace, Satires and Epistles; Cicero de Officiis; Tyler's Tacitus; Demosthenes' Select Orations; Woodbury's Prometheus; Demosthenes de Corona; Schiller; Kame's Elements of Criticism; Shaw's English Literature; Wayland's Moral Science; Wayland's Intellectual Philosophy; Wayland's Political Economy; Butler's Analogy; and Hopkin's Evidences of Christianity.

This course of study was preserved in the main, until the close of the Eclectic period.

When Mr. Hayden retired in 1857, after seven years of service as Principal, Mr. Garfield was chosen by his associates as Chairman of the Board of Instruction, and afterwards elected by the Board of Trustees

Close of Mr. Garfield's Administration. as Principal. He continued to be the active head of the School until he entered the army in 1861. After that time he held only a nominal relation to the Institute. "From an educational point of view, those were the golden days of the Eclectic Institute. The force of teachers now became more permanent, discipline was keyed up to a higher pitch, and a new enthusiasm was breathed into the scholars. The school advanced its standing in the estimation of the public. The number of students enrolled never quite equalled what it had been under the previous administration, but this was due to the abolition of the Primary Department. Naturally, the students were more mature in character and more permanent as a body than they had been under the previous administration." The coming of Garfield to Hiram as its executive head marked an era in Hiram history. Its educational features were intensified; and while the general Christian tone of the school was well preserved, less attention was given, than formerly, to special doctrines. Some of his brethren, including prominent preachers, were filled with sorrow, when they saw the school pass into Garfield's hands; for they feared that under the enthusiasms he could command, the school would be cut loose from its old moorings, and sail into an unknown sea and touch on alien shores. But their fears were not realized. The school did change, but more by the enlargement of its work and the extension of its horizon of influence, than in any other direction.

Perhaps no better summary of the plans, spirit and work of Hiram during the entire period of the Eclectic Institute can be given than in Mr. Garfield's own words at the "Reunion of 1880." Mr. John M. Atwater had discussed "Our Ideals of Life and Character" with beauty of diction and strength of expression, and Mr. A. S. Hayden had laurelled the memory of some famous members of the Board of Trustees, when Mr. Garfield said: "To my mind the history of Hiram College, and the institution on which the College was built, divides itself into two chapters. The first, both in time, and perhaps in importance, should be headed, what other people did for it; and the second is, what did Hiram do for itself? You have heard one relative to the founders. They were pioneers in this Western Reserve. They were all men of energy, great force of character, and nearly all of them men of small means, but they

Mr. Garfield's Summary of Hiram Life.

planted this Institution. In 1850 it was a cornfield with a solid plain brick building in the center of it; and almost all the rest has been done by the Institution itself. This is the second chapter. Without a dollar of endowment, without a powerful friend anywhere, but with a corps of teachers who were told to go on the ground and see what they could make out of it, and to find their pay out of the tuitions that should be received, who invited students of their own spirit to come here and find out by trial what they could make of it; and the response has been their chapter of work, and the chief part of the response I see in the faces gathered before me to-day. It was a simple question of sinking or swimming. I know we are all inclined to be a little clannish— perhaps we have a right to be,—but I do not know of any place, I do not know of any institution, that has accomplished more with so little means than this school on Hiram Hill. I know of no place where the doctrine of self-help has had a fuller development, by necessity as well as by favor, than here on this hill. The doctrine of the survival of the fittest found its place amongst these men and women gathered here. As I said about them a great many years ago—the theory of Hiram was to throw its young men and women overboard and let them try it for themselves, and all that were fit to get ashore got there, and I think we had few cases of drowning anywhere. Now, when I look over these faces, and mark the several geological ages so well represented by Mr. Atwater in his address, I note one curious fact where the geological analogy does not hold: I find no fossils—no fossils at all. Some are dead and glorified in our memories, but those who are alive, are ALIVE, I think all. The teachers and the students of this school built it up in every sense—they made the cornfield into that handsome campus. These evergreens you see across the road they planted. I well remember the day they turned out and went into the woods to find beautiful maples, and brought them in—when they purchased these evergreens—when each young man for himself, and perhaps a second for some young lady that he loved, planted one or two trees on the campus, and named them after himself. There are many here with moist eyes to-day that can point out the tree that

Bowler planted. Bowler was shot through the heart at Cedar Mountain. Many of you can point out trees, big trees now, called after you many years ago. I believe, outside of the physical features of the place, that there was a stronger pressure of work to the square inch in the boilers that ran this establishment than any other I know of. Young men and women, rough, crude, untutored farmer boys and farmer girls, came here to try themselves and find what manner of people they were. They came here to go on a voyage of discovery to discover themselves. In many cases I hope the discovery was fortunate in all that was worthy of trying, and the friendships that were formed out of that struggle have followed this group of people longer and farther than almost any I have ever known in my life. They are scattered all over the United States, in every field of activity, and if I had the time to name them the sun would go down before I had finished."

Notwithstanding there was considerable opposition to Mr. Garfield at the beginning of his administration, it had mostly ceased when he finally bid its classrooms farewell. Young Hiram was always on his side and clothed itself in the glory of the coming days of his greatness, which they enthusiastically foretold and fondly anticipated. The foundation of the future College was being laid, that necessarily must have a broader view and a wider constituency than the humble academy just chiselled out of the woods.

CHAPTER IV.

The Eclectic Institute—Its Later Life and Close.

1863-1867.

The active work of Mr. Garfield as head of the Eclectic Institute ceased when he entered the army in 1861, and he formally tendered his resignation as Principal to the Board

Formal Resignation of Mr. Garfield.

of Trustees; but, hoping that he might return soon, and resume his work in the Institute, it was not accepted until June 11, 1863. November 18, 1861, Mr. H. W. Everest was "constituted and appointed Principal of the Institute; with full power and authority to act as such, until the next annual meeting of the Board of Trustees, and until a regular election shall be held; and until his successor shall be duly elected and qualified." This commission was given to Mr. Everest by Alvah Udall, the President of the Board of Trustees, because, "it was inconvenient for the Board of Trustees to meet and hold a regular election" at that time. June 11, 1862, the Board, not willing to entirely release Mr. Garfield, elected Mr. Everest to "act as Principal *Pro Tem* in the absence of Mr. Garfield." With him were associated J. H. Rhodes, Almeda A. Booth, and B. A. Hinsdale as teacher in the English Department. All of these except

B. A. Hinsdale a Teacher.

Mr. Hinsdale, had already won a "good degree" as teachers in the Eclectic. In the year ending June, 1861, Mr. Hinsdale had been named in the Catalogue as an "Assistant Teacher." With these years, the formal introduction of Mr. Hinsdale, as one of the most eminent of Hiram's long list of teachers, is found. Mr. Everest continued to act as Principal until the summer of 1864 when he closed his long and honorable relation to the Institute, and went forth to return no more.

Much of the early student and teacher life at Hiram surrounds the name of Harvey W. Everest. He came to Hiram in 1852 a young man twenty-one years of age. He was born at North Hudson, Essex County, New York, May 10, 1831. At the age of sixteen he was a teacher in the common schools of his native town. He was a student with Mr. Garfield in the Geauga Seminary at Chester, Ohio, and came to Hiram about one year later. Here he prepared himself for College and in 1854, he with C. C. Foote, Sterling McBride, A. B. Way, and others entered Bethany College, intending to take his degree from that institution. But the conditions surrounding Bethany at that time were not congenial, and he soon left the place and the College. He entered Oberlin College where he graduated in 1861. In 1855-6 he was elected "Teacher of Natural Sciences" in the Eclectic Institute, which place he held until 1862, when he was made Principal *Pro. Tem.* of the Institute. He held this position until he left Hiram in 1864. May 16, 1864, he notified the Board of Trustees that he had accepted the Presidency of Eureka College, and placed his resignation in their hands. On his resignation the Board passed the following resolution: "We recognize Prof. H. W. Everest as one of the ablest teachers of this Institute; and in him this Board recognize the qualities of a fine scholar, a high-minded gentleman, and a true Christian; and, that in his leaving, this Institution loses one who has long and faithfully discharged all the duties that have been imposed upon him in the various positions in which he has been placed in connection with said Institute; and this Board cheerfully recommend him to the confidence of the Brotherhood and the public in general." He remained in Eureka for nearly eight years, leaving there in 1872 to become the pastor of the Christian Church at Springfield, Illinois. In 1874 he accepted a professorship in Kentucky University at Lexington, and remained there two years. Then after serving the Christian church as pastor, at Normal, Illinois, for one year, he became, in 1877, a second time, President of Eureka College. In the spring of 1881 he accepted the presidency of Butler University at Irvington, Ind., and served there until 1886. He then went to Wichita, Kansas, to undertake as Chancellor, the responsible and laborious work of organizing Garfield University. At its suspension in 1890 in consequence of a failure in the financial management, he became pastor of the Christian Church at Hutchinson, Kansas. In 1891 he was elected to the Southern Illinois State Normal University at Carbondale, where he remained until he was elected Dean of the College of the Bible in Drake University, at Des Moines, Iowa, which place he occupied at the time of his death, May 21, 1900.

He was the author of two books which were largely the product of his study and teaching in the class room. "The Divine Demonstration—A Text Book of Christian Evidence" published in 1884, has been used in a large number of Colleges as a Text Book on the subject of which it treats. His second book "Science and Pedagogy of Ethics" was published in 1899. These books show the clear and critical scholar and thinker, the wise counsellor, and the humble Christian man. He was always most at home where the Christian religious element was predominant. When he came to Drake University he said: "I am thankful every day for my change from the Carbondale (Illinois) State Normal University to Drake University. I am expecting much from the change of climate, but more from the change of

HIRAM COLLEGE: As Remodeled in 1886

work. There I taught one or two classes each day, but was mainly occupied, as President, in adjusting and oiling the machinery. Here I am occupied with classes and have to do with science and practical life. There I was helping to train teachers for public schools, but here I am assisting those who would prepare to preach the gospel of Christ. In a State school one's religious views must be held in abeyance; in this school Christianity is uppermost and all else is subordinate. I rejoice in my freedom, and in my higher work."* He always bore an unblemished character, and filled every post of honor and responsibility to which he was called with distinguished ability, fidelity and success. He was the soul of honor, and believed that: "Honor is a harder master than the law, for it cannot compromise for less than one hundred cents on the dollar, and its debts never outlaw." He administered the complex and perplexing affairs of the various executive offices to which he was called with ability and wisdom. As a preacher and a writer he ranked high, but the schoolroom was his kingdom over which he reigned, everywhere and always, with noble and manly dignity, and with the scepter of an unselfish, consecrated, Christian character.

Hiram college is largely indebted to him for its solid worth and its integrity as a Christian institution of learning.

In 1863 the Board of Trustees adopted a resolution assessing a fee of twenty-five cents per term from each student to create a contingent fund to be applied "to printing catalogues and other incidental expenses." **Matriculation Fee.** The financial condition of the school was stringent, the tuition receipts were the only funds available to pay instructors. As might be supposed, the salaries of teachers were so small as to be almost

*From " Doctrine and Life," by Iowa writers, p. 20.

insignificant, and teaching was a labor of love. This fact goes a good ways towards explaining the frequent changes in the executive and teaching force. At the same time, all of the most prominent teachers remained a number of years, becoming completely identified with the school and doing an amount of excellent teaching in the spirit of self-sacrifice that has never been properly appreciated but by the few.

After the resignation of Mr. Everest the Board of Trustees elected C. W. Heywood to act as Managing Principal.* His administration was a brief one, covering the year 1864-

C. W. Heywood as Principal.
65. Besides the management of the school, Mr. Heywood taught Natural Sciences, Classics and Rhetoric. Miss Booth, who valiantly remained at her post during all these years of uncertainty and frequent changes, was made Preceptress; besides teaching Modern Languages, Classics and Mathematics. It seemed impossible, whatever other changes might be made, to get along under any administration without her. In 1863 the Board of Trustees had declared "that in the person of Miss Almeda A. Booth the Institution has a teacher whose wisdom and experience fit her to hold, under any and all arrangements, a large control in the direction of the affairs and government of the school." Mr. William

William Lowe.
Lowe for a portion of this year was a teacher of Mathematics; Mr. L. G. Felch taught in the English Department; Miss Mary Buckingham, History and Latin; Miss Nellie Rudolph was the teacher of German; Miss Mary E. Moore taught Instrumental Music; Miss Julia A. Wilson was teacher of Landscape Painting and Drawing; and Miss S. M. Newcomb, teacher of Spencerian Penmanship. There is but little data on which to base a judgment of Mr. Heywood as an

*He came from Kingsville Academy to Hiram, a graduate of Rochester University, and a man of versatile talent.

administrator of school affairs. He did the best he could under the circumstances, and he left the Institution after his brief service with the reputation of a good man and a faithful teacher.

Mr. Heywood was succeeded by A. J. Thomson, who acted as Managing Principal during the year 1865-66. Mr. Garfield was still retained as Advising Principal. When

A. J. Thomson as Principal. Mr. Thomson was secured, Mr. Garfield reported to the Board of Trustees that the Committee on securing a Principal and teachers "had engaged Mr. A. J. Thomson as Principal at $1,200 a year; Miss Booth at $700; Mr. H. A. Coffeen at $600; and Mr. L. G. Felch at $400 a year. Miss Booth still held her place as Preceptress. Mr. H. A. Coffeen was the teacher of Natural Science and Elocution; Mr. L. G. Felch, teacher in the English Department, and assistant teacher of Mathematics; Miss Julia B. Treat, teacher of Instrumental Music; Miss Emma L. Johnson, teacher of Landscape Painting and Drawing*; and the Spencer Brothers, teachers of Spencerian Penmanship.

The first name in any catalogue of Hiram in the Department of Penmanship is that of Platt R. Spencer. The Institution was very fortunate to secure the "old man eloquent with the pen" to lead her "foremost files" in this department. Mr. Spencer first came to Hiram in 1854, and the Spencer family was identified with the Eclectic Institute until its close. Mr. Spencer was the originator and author of the "Spencerian style and system" of Penmanship, probably not surpassed by any other in America or the world.

---

*Miss Emma L. Johnson became a student at Hiram in the year 1857-8. As Mrs. B. S. Dean she is yet a teacher in the College. As student and teacher she has had, perhaps, the longest continuous relation to the school of any person.

He was born in East Fishkill, New York, near the Catskill mountains, November 7, 1800. He was the youngest of a family of eleven children. His father was a soldier of the Revolution. He died while Platt was yet a mere child, and the widowed mother, with New England courage and resolution, sought a home in the pioneer lands of northern Ohio; and much of Mr. Spencer's work was accomplished under the difficulties and discouragements incident to the frontier life. The family came in a wagon from the State of New York to Jefferson, Ashtabula county, Ohio. It was a winter's journey of fifty-one days. He was then ten years of age. At the age of fourteen he taught his first writing class. The most unique school of art in the world was his famous log-cabin seminary. This he built on his own farm, two and one-half miles north-east of Geneva, Ohio, in 1848. Here he began teaching his wonderful system of Penmanship. At the age of eight years, and before he had ever seen a sheet of paper, he was seized with a desire to write and draw. "With a penny clutched in his hand, he one day hailed a lumberman going to the nearest town twenty miles away, and asked him to buy him a sheet of paper. Late into the night he waited the return of the man, with the only thought of applying his goose quill to a real sheet of paper. When it came, he went to his room and wrote till morning."* He was elected to several offices in Ashtabula county, among them the office of Treasurer, which office he held till 1850. An incendiary fire, during his last term of office as Treasurer, destroyed the Court House and some of the papers in the Treasurer's office. After his term of office expired, he returned to Geneva, and in the little log-schoolhouse known as "Jericho," began again to teach those who desired a knowledge of his art. Here, away from "the pomp and din

---

*A. L. Arner, M. D., Jefferson, O.

of city life," young men and women came, from all parts of the country. Among these log-seminary students was H. Dwight Stratton, chief of the founders of the great chain of commercial colleges, numbering fifty-two, in the United States and Canada. Mr. Spencer began teaching penmanship in Hiram in 1854. Some of the very best students that Hiram had at that time were in his classes, which were usually large, always full of enthusiasm. He was the poet-penman of the world, and from an original poem which was sung at the closing lesson in March, 1857, the following stanza is given:

"One wish—young friend, ardent, sincere,
    Life be to you a well-writ page.
Each letter perfect, full and clear,
    Linked in bright lines from age to age;
Such records Heaven approves full well,
And such be yours, farewell, farewell."

In the winter of 1864 he delivered his last lecture, and gave his last course of lessons in Packard's Business College, in New York City, and then laid down his "faithful pen," not again to be taken up. He died May 16, 1864, at Geneva, Ohio, and his remains lie buried in the beautiful cemetery at that place.

Referring to Mr. Spencer in an address before the students of the Spencerian Business College, at Washington, D. C., June 29, 1869, Mr. Garfield said: "About forty years ago a young lad who had come from the Catskill mountains, where he had learned the rudiments of penmanship by scribbling on the sole-leather of a good old Quaker shoemaker—for he was too poor to buy paper—till he could write better than his neighbors, commenced to teach in that part of Ohio which has been called 'benighted Ashtabula.' He set up a little writing school in a rude log cabin, and threw into the work the fervor of a poetic soul and a strength of heart and spirit that few men possess. He caught his ideals of beauty from the waves of the lake and the curves they make upon the white sand beach, and from the tracery of the spider's web. Studying the lines of beauty as drawn by the hand of Nature, he wrought out that system of penmanship which is now the pride of our country, and the model of our schools."

Besides his work as Principal of the Institute, Mr. Thomson was teacher of Classics, Rhetoric, and Phonogra-

Mr. Thomson as Teacher. phy. He was a man of fine culture and a devoted teacher, but under the uncertainties, financial condition and other difficulties prevailing at that time, he closed his relations to Hiram at the end of the year.

Adoniram Judson Thomson was born near Burksville, Ky., September 3, 1835. Not long after his parents removed to Louisville, and for a time that city was their home.

Biographical Sketch of A. J. Thomson. Thence they removed to Illinois, which was Mr. Thomson's home until 1883, except one year spent in Hiram in 1865-66. He became a member of the Christian church at the age of seventeen. In 1858 he graduated from Abingdon College, receiving the degree of A. B.; and three years later the degree of A. M. from the same institution. He was ordained to the gospel ministry in 1858, and preached on Sundays almost constantly from that time till 1886. He was teacher in Abingdon College for about twenty-five years, leaving that work to accept the place of Principal of the Western Reserve Eclectic Institute, which he resigned in one year and returned to Abingdon College in 1866.

Alone or associated with another he was pastor of the church in Abingdon about fifteen years. Among other churches in Illinois for which he preached regularly for longer or shorter periods were Blandinsville, Bryant, Denver, Henderson, Monmouth, Plymouth, Peoria, Princeton, and Quincy. In 1883 he was called to the pastorate of the church in Manhattan, Kansas, where he remained three years. During this time he served on the Kansas State Board of Missions as President, and in other relations. In 1891-92 he was employed in the office of the Standard Publishing Company at Cincinnati, O., and a part of that time preached for the church at Carthage, Ohio. In October, 1892, he was elected Principal of the Louisville Christian Bible School, then under the auspices of the American Christian Missionary Society, but lately transferred to the Christian Woman's Board of Missions. In this position he is still at work, most laboriously, conscientiously and effectively. In every relation he has held at Hiram or elsewhere he has maintained a character "void of offense," and a reputation for gifts and acquirements of a high order.

Within the period now being considered, and well towards the close of the Eclectic Institute, and urged on by a number of eminent Disciples, ministers and others, the

Theological
Department.

Board of Trustees proposed to add to the Institution "a Theological Department, distinct from the Literary, in which regular classes would be formed and direct instruction given to those who designed to enter the ministry." It was asserted that the demand for such instruction is imperative; that it is absurd to claim that the teacher of God's Word should be less complete and systematic in preparation for his work than the members of other learned professions; that it was folly and superstitious weakness to neglect that thorough discipline and laborious preparation necessary to fit a man for such high duties, and credulously trust that God will supply both knowledge and culture; and as the success and

permanency of the Eclectic Institute no longer appeared
doubtful, such a department should be established as soon
as possible. The idea of making of the Institute a Theological Seminary had in a large degree, if not entirely,
passed away; and the proposition was now to arrange for a
"Course of Biblical Lectures," which would open the way
for a permanent Theological Department. A committee
consisting of Dr. J. P. Robison, J. A. Garfield and Harmon
Austin was appointed June 20, 1865, to provide for a Course
of Biblical Lectures. This committee, after due consideration, reported that they had received "the advice of a large
number of prominent brethren," and had decided "to profit
by the wisdom of other professions, such as Law and Medicine," and announced that they had secured the services of
able and experienced men who would give in the name of
the Institution, "a Course of Lectures which would be free
to preachers and students of the Bible desiring to perfect
themselves in the ministry of the Word."

A Solicitor had also been appointed to canvass the
churches for the funds necessary to inaugurate the work.
On his report the committee further said: "From the en-
couragements received in the way of cash and pledges we
have agreed with Isaac Errett, that he, together with those
whom he may call to assist him in the course, be paid the
sum of twenty-five hundred dollars, and five hundred dollars for incidentals; this amount to be divided and used as
Mr. Errett might agree with his associates." The Course
of Lectures was to begin Monday, June 4, 1866, and continue for fifteen weeks. Isaac Errett, the chosen head of
the Department, announced that his associates would be
Robert Milligan, of Kentucky University, Lecturer on the
Inspiration and Interpretation of the Scriptures, Historical
and Critical Study of the Old Testament, and Critical and
Exegetical Analysis of the New Testament; Henry T. An-

derson, Lecturer on the Principles of Interpretation as applied to the Greek of the New Testament; David S. Burnet, Lecturer on Sacred Rhetoric, and Preparation and Delivery of Sermons. Other lectures on kindred topics were to be supplied during the term. The Course of Lectures began at the time announced and were so successful that at a meeting of the Board of Trustees held in Hiram, August 14, 1866, the following resolutions offered by Mr. Garfield were adopted: "*Resolved,* That the experiment of a Course of Biblical Lectures, inaugurated by the Board of Trustees, and now in progress, has proved eminently successful, and should be maintained as a permanent means of fitting young men for the Ministry of the Gospel.

"*Resolved,* That the thanks of the Board of Trustees are cordially extended to the brethren who have delivered the Lectures before the Biblical class for the ability and faithfulness of their labors."

While this Course of Lectures was good and wholesome, and a credit to the distinguished men who gave them, they were the last as they were the first of their kind in the history of the Institution.* The voice of its charter, which announced its special purpose to be "the instruction of youth of both sexes in the various branches of literature and science, especially of moral science, as based on the facts and precepts of the Holy Scriptures"; and the early emphatic announcement that "the Bible must be taken into the School as a book of study; its facts must be studied; its own pure and perfect morality must be daily urged upon the consciences of the students, in view of its fearful sanctions," were supreme mandates. Many were in favor of the new departure, but more were against it. Daily Bible instruction has been kept up during the fifty years of the life of the

---

*There were two courses, one in 1866 and one in 1867.

Institution, but nothing like the modern Theological Seminary, or Theological Department, has ever gained a foothold in Hiram. The Biblical languages are daily taught by competent Professors; the Book is studied in the original languages, in the classroom; the history and the doctrine of the Bible are investigated; the power and strength of the church, as well as her weaknesses, are all considered as a part of the purpose for which the Institution was founded.

For sixteen years the Eclectic Institute was without a Commercial Department, where the laws, rules and methods
The Commercial Department. of commercial transactions and business could be studied and illustrated. August 14, 1866, on motion of Mr. Garfield, the Committee on Teachers was authorized to inquire into "the feasibility of establishing a Commercial Department in the Eclectic." This committee appears to have considered the matter "feasible," for in the catalogue of 1867 the name of
Osmer C. Hill. O. C. Hill appears as teacher in "English and Commercial Departments." He was the first instructor in this Department at Hiram, and he remained at the head of the Department until he left the Institution in 1875. He was a student in Hiram when the Civil War broke out. He enlisted as a soldier, served his period of enlistment, and then returned to Hiram to study and to teach. He was an enthusiastic teacher and a useful man. He graduated at Williams College in 1876. For two years he was a teacher in Oberlin College, and for twelve years he taught in the public schools of Oregon, Missouri, and Hiawatha, Kansas. He was the author of a series of school readers. He was a preacher, also, and occupied the pulpit, more or less, on Sundays for thirty years. Wherever he lived he bore an honorable name. He was born in Orange, Cuyahoga county, Ohio, December 31, 1839, and died in Hiawatha, Kansas, June 30, 1899.

John M. Atwater was the last Principal of the Eclectic Institute; and he was one of its first body of students. He

John Milton Atwater as Principal.

also reached over into the College and was one of its first Professors, and afterwards President. It is fitting, therefore, that the glow of the closing days of the "Old Eclectic," and the sheen of the rising College days should fall on him at this point in the History of Hiram College.

After the resignation of A. J. Thomson, the Board of Trustees was under the necessity of finding another Principal, and the lot fell on John M. Atwater. On motion of Mr. Garfield it was *"Resolved,* That the Committee on Teachers be authorized to employ J. M. Atwater, J. S. Ross, and such other teachers as may be necessary, to conduct the Literary Department of the Institute in the future; and that the amount of money received for tuition, *and no more,* be allowed to the payment of such teachers, and for the incidental expenses of the Institution."

Mr. Atwater accepted the place on these conditions; and associated with him were J. S. Ross, teacher of Classics and Natural Sciences; Osmer C. Hill, teacher in English and Commercial Departments; Miss S. A. Bartlett, teacher of Languages, and Botany; Miss Julia E. Pardee, teacher of Mathematics, and Philosophy; Miss Tillie Newcomb, teacher of Instrumental Music; Miss Emma L. Johnson, teacher of Landscape Painting and Drawing; Miss Mary Atwater, teacher of French and German; and W. H. Rogers, Bailey S. Dean, Grove E. Barber, and C. C. Smith, as Assistant Teachers in the English Department.

Of these, J. S. Ross is still living, an honorable and honored man and a Christian preacher of high repute; of Miss Bartlett there are no records at hand; Miss Pardee is the wife of Prof. Asa M. Weston, who was the first Professor of Mathematics and Modern Languages in Hiram

College; Miss Newcomb was for several years teacher of Instrumental Music, and as the wife of J. C. Ellis, yet resides in Hiram; Miss Johnson is the wife of Prof. B. S. Dean, and the present cultured teacher of China Decoration and Pastel in Hiram College; W. H. Rogers is a cultured preacher in Massachusetts; B. S. Dean is Professor of History in Hiram College; G. E. Barber is Professor of Latin in the University of Nebraska; and C. C. Smith is a swift-footed, able, and eloquent messenger of the Church, and assistant Corresponding Secretary of the American Christian Missionary Society. Mary Atwater married G. W. Neely, and died at her home in Bower, North Carolina, April 12, 1900. John M. Atwater, the leader of this band of teachers, died in Cleveland, Ohio, January 17, 1900.

Perhaps the best known family group of students that attended school in Hiram in the early period were the Atwaters, three brothers, Orris, John, and Amzi, and a sister, Mary. "Belonging to a well-known

The Atwater Family.

family of the vicinage, attending for a number of years more regularly, and generally several of them at the same time, and possessing abilities and character, they naturally impressed themselves upon the School, both as a group and as individuals." All have lived honorable and useful lives, and yet it is no invidious judgment that places John at the head of the list. He was born in Mantua, Ohio, June 3, 1837. He became a Christian, upon a profession of his faith and baptism, when he was little more than twelve years of age, and united with the Church in Mantua. His first term in Hiram was in 1851, a year after the School was first opened. He taught school in Solon in the winter of 1854-'55. He preached his first sermon in Hiram in the fall of 1859, and continued to preach one-half time for the church in Hiram until the spring of 1861, dividing the time with Hiram's veteran preacher, Symonds Ryder. During this period he was student and teacher in the Eclectic Institute. In 1861 he entered Oberlin College and graduated under the Presidency of Charles G. Finney in 1863. He was married to Harriet M. Smith at Oberlin, October 1, 1863. He was the pastor of the church in Wellington, Ohio in 1863-'64, and until 1866 pursued the Theological Course at Oberlin, and preached for the churches at Camden, Henrietta and Eaton in Lorain county. In 1866 he was elected Principal of the Western Reserve Eclectic Institute, and in 1867 he was chosen Professor of Latin and Greek, in Hiram College, under the Presidency of Dr. Silas E. Shepard. After the resignation of Dr. Shepard he was elected President of Hiram College, and served from 1868-1870. He thus had "the unique distinction of being both Principal of the Eclectic Institute and President of Hiram College, and strove hard to do his duty in both positions." He served as Professor of Latin and Greek in Alliance College in 1870-'71. After he left Alliance he turned his attention for several years to the ministry and was pastor of the church in Syracuse, N. Y., in 1871-'72; Worcester, Mass., 1872-'76; Wauseon, Ohio, 1876-'78; Springfield, Ill., 1878-'79; Cleveland, Ohio, Franklin Circle Church, 1879-'84; and Ada, Ohio, 1885-'87. While at Ada he published a monthly journal, "The One Principle," which was intended "to emphasize the importance of the union of all Christians upon Christ."

In September, 1887, he was elected Principal of the Normal Department, and Professor of Didactics in Garfield University, Wichita, Kansas, under the Presidency of H. W. Everest. His wife died at Wichita, September 9, 1887. On leaving Wichita he preached for several Kansas churches from 1888 to 1890. He served Eureka College as Professor of Latin in 1891-'92. In June, 1892, he was married to Miss Anna Robison, who became his efficient helper at Oskaloosa, Iowa, whither he went to assume the duties of President of Oskaloosa College in 1892. He remained in Oskaloosa until 1897, when he was elected President of Central Christian College at Albany, Missouri. His health having failed soon after he reached Albany, he was obliged to resign from the Institution, which he did at the close of the College year. This practically terminated the labors of his life. After vainly seeking health in the South, he returned to Cleveland, Ohio, where, in the midst of his friends, he died January 17, 1900, loved and lamented by all. Between his entry into Hiram in 1851 and the close of his life in 1900 is the record of a laborious and busy career. He did much that is not named, and could not be detailed, in a brief sketch. In every position to which he was called he was faultlessly faithful in his effort to meet every obligation. "He was a sound scholar, a good teacher, and excellent companion, and a true man." He excelled as a teacher rather than as a preacher or the executive head of school or college. He was a man of almost infinite detail in his methods of analysis, and administration of affairs. To many this made his addresses and sermons tiresome and his administrative directions bewildering. He was an exceedingly busy man, never sparing himself, if so he might help others. He once wrote to a friend: "I live in one incessant, pelting hailstorm of demands upon my time." He was a pure man in heart, in speech, in life. Robert Moffett, who was one of the speakers at his funeral, said of his goodness of life: "I never saw or heard of, nor did I ever know of anyone else who ever saw or heard, John Atwater say or do anything at any time or place that was not worthy of the upright life." He was tenacious of his opinions almost to the border of stubbornness, as some of his friends thought, and was harder to persuade than the occasion seemed to justify, and yet, his views were maintained most conscientiously and considerately. All in all, he is one of the great men that Hiram, in its first half century, has given to the world.

Mr. W. J. Ford, who was the most successful solicitor or financial agent employed by the Board during the entire Eclectic period, made a strong effort to lay the foundation

Looking towards an Endowment. for a permanent endowment fund for the Institution. November 10, 1866, he reported that he had succeeded in raising reliable subscriptions and notes for the endowment fund, in Hiram and its immediate vicinity, amounting to $16,775; and that he had other subscriptions sufficient to make the total nearly thirty thousand dollars. It is probable that these subscriptions were never all paid, but they laid the foundation for the present creditable endowment of the College. June 12, 1867, on motion of Mr. C. B. Lockwood, a "Finance Committee" was created by the Board of Trustees, "to take charge of all funds for endowment, and invest the same subject to the approval of the Board; and this Board hereby promise the brotherhood that no part of the principal of such funds shall be used, but shall be kept sacred for the purpose for which it was donated." With rare exceptions this rule has always been adhered to by the Board of Trustees; and if at any time, for temporary necessities, any portion of the endowment fund has been used, it has been promptly replaced.

A system of scholarships was also attempted, but so far as the records show, the effort was never of much benefit to the Institution. Some money was, however, raised in this way, though the amount was com-
Scholarships. paratively small. The scholarship method of raising funds for the Institution has never, for some reason, been popular with the constituency of Hiram College.

To the old students of Hiram the sound of the College Bell meant more than it does to-day. Then it announced

The
College Bell.

the hour of rising in the morning and the hour when the students must be in their rooms at night. Now it has little significance save as a warning for the change of classes. For many years the bell was rung at five o'clock in the morning, but this habit ceased about the year 1870. The nine o'clock night bell was discontinued about the year 1884. The rule of the Institution was—

"Early to bed and early to rise,
Makes a man healthy, wealthy, and wise."

But these early habits have long since passed away, either for better or for worse.

Perhaps no one who has made the attempt to describe oldest Hiram and its students, had a more vivid memory of

The Old
Hiram and its
Students.

the persons and events, and has been able to describe them more felicitously and accurately, and sometimes humorously, than John M. Atwater. In 1880 he made an address before the "Hiram College Reunion" on "Our Ideals of Life and Character," which contains so much of interest concerning those early days, that a summary of it is here given:

No one can return, after years of absence, to the school or college where he once studied, at least in the time of its ordinary activity and regular work, without a strong im-

Mr. Atwater's
Memories.

pression, perhaps even a sad one, that he has lost his place; that the waves of the deluge have swept away all his generation, and that a new tribe has taken possession of the earth. But this is Reunion Day; and Reunion Day, it would seem, should be old students' day, when those who at other times might flit silent and lone like uneasy ghosts across these grounds, may congregate in such numbers as to seem for the day to reconquer and repossess the land.

Are you then an old Hiram student? Do you belong to this army? Advance, and give the countersign. But first, pause; there are old *students*, and then there are *old* students. To what era do you belong? In what geologic age did you flourish? You were here, you say, when the corner-stone was laid of the Ladies' Hall! But that was only yesterday. I fear you are a new comer. Do you remember when the seats in the college chapel were first turned to face the west? Do you remember when Prof. Demmon came here to fill the chair now held by Prof. Barber? If you are an *old* student you were here when there was no Hiram College, but rather the old Eclectic Institute. Perhaps you can remember when President Everest, now of Eureka College, was at the head of this institution. It may be you were here when Prof. Rhodes had his great classes in elocution. It is possible that you were here to help plant these trees on the college grounds; if so, we shall admit that you are one of the old students. Do you remember a time when the Delphic, the Hesperian, and the Olive Branch were yet unborn, when little mushroom societies sprang up and died almost every term? (In those days arose the Junto, the Progressionist, the Attic, the Society of Seven, the Washingtonian, the Philomathean, the Eclectic, and many others.) Do you recollect the time when there was a primary department, a school for children, in the south wing of the college? Were you here when Wal. Ford used to call the roll of students in chapel in the morning? Do you remember when N. C. Meeker, the victim of the late Indian massacre, kept a store just west of the church? Were you here when Senator Garfield was employed to ring the college bell? Do you recollect when the last two or three presidents of the college first came here fresh from the farm with the hayseed still in their hair? Can you remember when there was a regular boarding-house in the college basement? Were you a student here when Miss Booth had not yet become a teacher here, but was still teaching district school over in Mantua? Were you in school here when W. B. Hazen, now General in the

U. S. Army, was a school-boy here from Garrettsville?
You were here in those days, were you? Well, then, we
will not require you to go through college, but will confer
upon you at once the degree of O. H. S.—Old Hiram Student—and for this one day your degree ranks higher than
that of those who took the sheepskins yesterday.

When you and I were notified of the approach of this
reunion, and began to make our plans to attend it, we were
naturally led to think of the friends we should meet here;
to call up the once familiar faces, and to speculate as to
which of them would be here, and which would not. And
we thought of some who have drifted so far away from this
place into distant States, that we scarcely expected to meet
them in this reunion; and we thought of some, too, who
have drifted out into that unknown sea whence there is no
returning. And so we have been spending these late weeks
in the companionship, as it were, of old schoolmates, living
over again the half-forgotten days, reciting again the old
lessons, holding anew the old contests, and walking with
old friends over the old familiar paths.

Almost every foot of ground around Hiram Hill, for
miles away, is historic; memories, which link together old
companions, haunt each nook and corner, each field and
hillside.

South of the college, is the old foot-ball ground, scene
of mighty battles. In the northwest corner of the college
campus, base-ball has flourished for many a year. In the
corner northeast of the college, under the old apple trees,
several commencements have been held, and one reunion or
more; and the air down there is thick with mental pictures
of the scenes and the speakers of those occasions. Over
northwest of the village, in the field, then half woods, is the
tree, perhaps only a stump now, under which we sat down
alone to grapple with the "Goose Question," and wrestled
until we gained the victory. I do not know whether Hiram
students, in their march on the road to knowledge still meet
that column of geese marching to oppose their progress, but
I can testify that in my day the approach of those geese
caused great searchings of heart, and it was not every

student by any means who at recitation was found to be "sound on the goose question."

In that same northwest field is the spot where once Amzi Atwater, who had gone out to recite his commencement speech, met a black bear, which had lately parted company with some caravan. The bear was passing through from the southwest, and was just in time to be present at the rehearsal; but as the boy and the bear were not acquainted with each other, he did not interview the beast, and does not know to this day how his speech took with the stranger. The attendance of the bear at his rehearsal must have been very encouraging to the speaker; he had, of course, expected to be something of a lion on commencement day, but not that his first roar would call all the wild beasts together.

Over west of the college, and just south of Tiffany Hall,* is the spot where Abraham Lincoln was first nomi-

---

* While I was a student in Hiram in the winter of 1857-1858, I roomed in what was then known as "Tiffany Hall," a long one-story building, with a hall running the entire length, with rooms partitioned off on either side for student lodging and study rooms. The building is yet standing on the street leading to the residence of Professor Peckham and outwardly is substantially as it was then.

That winter was distinctly marked by the excitement caused by the decision in 1857 of the Dred Scott case by the United States Supreme Court and handed down by Chief Justice Roger Brooke Taney, in which a majority of the Court held that "negroes were so inferior that they had no rights which the white man was bound to respect." There was intense excitement in the Nation over the decision, and especially was this true on the "Western Reserve" in Ohio.

During the winter some of the students in Hiram entered into an arrangement by which the leading features in the evasion and enforcement of the law should be illustrated in a somewhat realistic way. I do not now remember all the details or the names of those who took a leading part in the arrangement. I only know that I was let into the secret, and asked to become a participant, which I declined. Two young men by the name of Mumford roomed in "Tiffany Hall" on the opposite side of the building to my own room, and they were made the victims of the plot. Somewhere near midnight two black-faced students, representing fugitive slaves, on their way to Canada and freedom, attended by two or three men representing farmers of the vicinity, came into the Hall, to Mumford's room, and insisted on having supper, as they had been in hiding all day and

nated for President of the United States. It was twenty years ago! And who would have thought it had been so long! The great Chicago Republican Convention of 1860 was about to hold its three-day session. The leading candidates were Seward and Chase, Lincoln being mentioned only occasionally as a far-off possibility. Some of Mrs. Hart's boarders (among them Harry Glasier, H. D. Carlton, and Amzi Atwater), were fond of pitching quoits as a rest from books. To give zest to the game, the boys enlisted as champions of the several would-be nominees of the Chicago Convention. This was done for several days; and there on the play-ground they declared Lincoln to be nominated, while at Chicago the fight was still raging between Seward and Chase! Moral: Boys are a class of folks that deserve close watching.

In the street, in front of President Hinsdale's (which was then Mr. Garfield's house), is the ground where we played wicket ball; Mr. Garfield was one of our best players. Then there was D. R. Northway, the best batter on

---

were hungry. Willingly and quickly these two good Mumford boys set before the supposed half-starved fugitives the very best they had, and their meal was being disposed of with haste and evident relish, when there appeared suddenly in the midst of the startled company two officers of the Government and their posse, who proceeded to place in arrest in a formal way, the two Mumford boys for the "audacious crime" of harboring and feeding fugitive slaves. The two Mumford boys took the matter seriously and from a farce to begin with it looked for a time as if there might really be a tragedy in the end. Other students who had rooms in "Tiffany Hall" were roused, and word was soon taken to A. S. Hayden, who was living in Hiram at that time, and to James A. Garfield, the Principal of the Eclectic Institute, who soon started for the center of disturbance with the grim determination that "no slave shall ever be returned to slavery from Hiram Hill." But, before they reached the Hall, there had been a general scattering of the principals in the farce and the occupants of the Hall were left to explain matters as best they could. The ring-leaders in the affair were identified, and the next morning the chapel exercises were well-seasoned with "hot stuff," and two of the boys were dismissed from the school. While the affair was only intended for "fun," it had a serious effect on the future politics of some of the students, and especially did it impress Mr. Garfield with the sense of hatred toward slavery and love for liberty as nothing before ever had. This fact I had from Mr. Garfield himself.
—*F. M. Green.*

the ground, and Hi. Chamberlin, and Mose Richards, and that young giant from Virginia, Hoff. He was a good fellow; the boys called him "Old Virginia Never Tire." Has anybody heard from him since the war?*

Down south of Uncle Zeb's, across the street, and across the ravine, is the place where four of us went once to rehearse a discussion prepared for commencement; but, alas, in saying it, I recall that two of the four are long since dead. They died during the war—Will Smith and Gus Williams! They were two of the pleasantest fellows we ever had here in Hiram. How at every turn the faces start up along these paths of those that are with us here no more! * * * * * I was speaking of a place where we once went to rehearse. But where did we not go to rehearse! If the trees about Hiram were phonographs, you could shake orations and debates out of any tree within two miles of this hill. And who knows but Edison or some other son of a Yankee will yet get the hang of making the trees repeat what they have heard! If that time ever comes, then as farmers have some trees that bear greenings, and others pippins, so the folks about Hiram will have some trees for prose and some for poetry; one tree that recites Hiawatha, and another Horatius At The Bridge; one tree that bears salutatories, and another valedictories.

Down in Esq. Udall's sugar camp is the place where we went twenty-four years ago last spring for a Leap Year Sugar Party! It was a merry time. So many fair, bright faces! So much gay and hopeful young life! Where are they all now?

It is pleasant, and yet it is sad too, to wander thus in memory over all these hills and fields where forms invisible to outward eye start up to meet us at every footstep. Perhaps you would pardon me if I should dwell still longer upon these scenes and memories. But as I look back at our student life here in Hiram, at the busy swarming hive of which we were a part twenty years ago to-day, I am led to think of the question what Hiram was in those days; what spirit ruled here, what Hiram taught us, and what it

---

* Mr. Hoff at that time was living at Cadiz, O.

did for us. It was here, beyond question, that many of us took the shaping of our lives. It was here that we consciously and unconsciously received the ideals of life and character which will continue to mould our thoughts and our actions as long as we live.

In answering the question, "What Ideals did Hiram Give Us?" Mr. Atwater in part said:

I shall not attempt to enumerate all the noble conceptions of character which from time to time Hiram held up **The Ideals of Life** before her sons and daughters to win **which Hiram** their admiration. I shall only seize upon **Gave its Students.** a few, and those the ones which most impressed *me,* and which beyond all doubt had a mighty influence for good with many generations of students.

The first which I will mention of those ideals which we learned to admire, is that of *a man standing squarely on his own feet, and not held up or bolstered up by somebody else.*

There are two classes of men whom we meet everywhere and in all situations in life. One of them has some force of his own; the other has to be held up and carried by his father. One of them intends to do something himself; the other can always tell you of great things that his grandfather did. One of them knows how to earn his own money; the other knows how to spend what his father has earned. One of them begins poor and slowly works his way up; the other begins rich and rapidly runs down. One of them sets up a little business and slowly builds it up till he becomes perhaps a merchant prince; the other is set up in business on a large scale by his father and soon runs through with both the business and the capital. One of them begins life in obscurity and rises by his own merits to an honorable prominence; the other is introduced to an admiring public or even to the world, by his renowned father, and is kept by him from sinking into utter obscurity. One of them, in all his plans and undertakings for life, expects to work his own way and carve out his own success; the other never accomplishes anything nor even undertakes anything except as somebody's patronage carries him all the way.

Hiram taught her sons and daughters to admire the one, and to pity and despise the other. She taught us not only to have an honorable pride in winning such laurels as we could, but she taught us to cherish an equally honorable pride in refusing to wear any laurels which we had not ourselves won. I think it is safe to say that Hiram fixed this thought in the hearts of her children.

A second ideal which Hiram taught us to admire was that of *a man who is in reality just what he professes to be; a man who wishes to be known to be just what he is.*

"To be, rather than to seem," this was the motto. This second principle is in very close sympathy with the first. The man who stands upon his own feet, instead of being carried by others, the man who has an honest pride in winning success and reputation for himself, and who feels it to be a species of degradation to wear borrowed honors as being somebody's *son,* such a man is likely also to feel it as a degradation to wear honors which he is supposed to deserve, but which he knows he does not.

Another ideal which was always before us in the days of which I write, and which beyond all doubt made its imprint upon our characters, was that of *a minute man—a man who is always ready, a man who has all his faculties under such discipline and control that they obey his will, and furnish to order the best product of which they are capable.*

When you and I were students here, we were taught to have a genuine pride in being always ready, *"semper paratus,"* as the good old Latin proverb is. And this "always ready" has a wonderful number of applications. It means never tardy, always there on time; it means that you always come prepared, that you have the exercise for which you were appointed, that you have the report which you promised to write for the committee, that you have brought the documents on which the business depends; it means that you always come *well* prepared, that your declamation is committed so you do not blunder and flounder, that in your essay you have done yourself justice, that your committee report is written and in order, not oral and scrappy; it means that you are ready to undertake, to step in, to go forward, to take responsibility; it means that when you are wanted, you can be counted on, if the thing itself is right; it means that you are a ready off-hand speaker, that you can rise without a moment's warning, gather your thoughts together while you talk, speak to the point, strike the nail on the head, drive it home, and clinch it. And this being "always ready" is a habit that can be acquired, an art that can be learned. The reason why one man is always ready and can be counted on, and another always comes too late or unprepared, is that one of them has trained himself or has been trained to be on time and ready, and the other has allowed himself or has been allowed to be sleepy and slow.

Some of the papers told a good story lately to illustrate Russian and Turkish military discipline. Two officers, one of each nation, being stationed near each other during a truce, were boasting of the drill of their respective armies. The Russian declared that so perfect was the discipline in the Russian army that if he sent a soldier on an ordinary duty, he could tell at each instant what progress the soldier had made. To prove this he called an orderly and directed him to make a small purchase at a neighboring shop. The orderly saluted and disappeared. The officer, taking out his watch, marked the time. "Now," said he, "he has turned the first corner; now he has reached the shop; now he has made the purchase; now he is half-way back; now he is at the door." At that instant his step was heard in the passage; he entered, delivered his purchase, saluted and retired. The Turkish officer, with the utmost coolness, declared that that was very well, but his orderly would do just the same. So he summoned Mustapha, and gave him a similar commission. Mustapha disappeared. Looking at his watch, the Turk marked the time, saying: "Now he is half-way there; now he has made the purchase; now he turns the corner; now he is at the door;" and, sure enough, his step was heard in the passage. "Mustapha," said the Turk, "have you fulfilled my orders?" "Most worshipful master," answered Mustapha, "I have not yet found my shoes!" Now the reason why the Russian soldier was ready and on time, was that he had been trained to be ready; and the reason why Mustapha couldn't find his shoes, was that he had been allowed to go in that slip-shod, shambling way.

Hiram students twenty years ago had in a wonderful degree the ideal of the man always ready, *semper paratus.* The whole school was like a well-drilled army, ready at the word "forward!" It is impossible to calculate the worth of that discipline.

The last of all the ideals given us at Hiram which I shall name to-day, was that of *the man who wins by work, not by genius, nor by luck, and therefore always wins.*

There is a class of men in the world of whom Dickens has given us the type in his immortal character of Micawber. They are not destitute of natural ability. They are capable of forming large plans and cherishing great expectations. But they are worshipers of the goddess Luck. They are "waiting for something to turn up." And they are expecting something every day. They are always expecting something; and their hopefulness is unfailing. Disappointment never damps their ardor nor changes their plan. Luck failed them yesterday. Luck has brought them nothing to-day. "But something will turn up by to-morrow." Such men never *do* anything. They are simply waiting for something to *happen.* These worshipers of Luck, these Micawbers, were not all of them born Micawbers. Many of them were made such by some extraordinary misfortune of that kind which people call a stroke of good luck—a windfall. One of them once made fifty thousand in real estate in a few days (and lost it all in a good deal less time); another "struck ile," and was for a few days one of the nabobs; a third made ten thousand in one day in Wall street, (and of course lost it all the next day, and has since lost as much more as he could borrow). And all these men have been completely ruined by the one piece of good luck. They think, and plan and dream of nothing but that stroke of luck and how to make another. They have been so dazzled and bewildered by finding that one nugget of gold, that they just wander round and round the spot in hopes of finding the mate to it. The world is full of Micawbers "waiting for something to turn up."

It would be unsafe to say that there are no Micawbers

among the old students of Hiram; but it is not unsafe to
say that Hiram never furnished one as the natural product
of her soil. Her climate has never been favorable to such
growths. In opposition to all the plans and ways of all the
Micawbers, Hiram has always believed in work—in straight-
forward, unyielding *work,* as the key which opens every
lock, as the "Open, Sesame," for every door.

There is another class of men, very numerous in the
world, which Hiram has never sought to encourage. I mean
now the geniuses, the semi-geniuses, the imitation geniuses,
and the would-be geniuses. The characteristic of this class
is that they do nothing by any set, definite or regular effort;
but they do great things (or at least they intend to, such is
the theory), "when the inspiration comes," when they are
in the mood for it, when they have "a happy thought" or a
"favored hour." I believe most profoundly in these inspira-
tions—these moods, and these favored hours; but the inspiration is to be found by faithful seeking; the mood is to be
secured by patient application; and the favored hour is like
the favored hour of the mother bird, when long brooding
is rewarded by the stir and sound of life. These would-be
geniuses, of course, have no mental drill. To seek anything
like discipline would be to abandon the theory. The immediate practical effect of adopting the genius notion, is to
release all the mental powers from the control of the will.
They become at once like an army with no discipline. Now
Carlyle says: "Every man is as lazy as he dares to be."
But the would-be genius is, by his theory, invited and encouraged to be lazy. And then, it will be found practically,
that the more we wait for moods, the less the moods will
come; and, on the other hand, the more we labor without
the inspiration, the more surely will the inspiration be given.

Hiram has always held before her children the ideal of
the man who wins his success by heroic *work,* and not by
genius nor by *luck.* I am not able, in all cases, to say from
which one of our teachers each lesson came. I do not, in
every case, remember what teacher most emphasized or first
emphasized in our hearing, a given lesson. I know that for
some lessons we are chiefly indebted to him whom we may

well call the father of this institution, its first President, A. S. Hayden.

I know that we are indebted for many lessons of instruction to that teacher of rare power, that woman of rare breadth of mind, Miss Almeda A. Booth. And I know, too, that to many other teachers whom I cannot name, our debt is great.

One lesson, one ideal, the last which I have named, that of the man who wins by work, and therefore always wins, that one lesson (at least), I am able to trace directly to Mr. Garfield. I shall never forget one powerful address which he gave to a large body of young men preparing for the ministry. I preserve for you one grand sentence. "Gentlemen," said he, "I can express my creed of life in one word: *I believe in work!* I BELIEVE IN WORK. In Dickens' Great Expectations, Joe Gargery, the big burly blacksmith, meekly submits to be bulldozed by his small but terrific wife, of whom nevertheless he is very proud. So he tells Pip at one time, as you remember, "She is a fine figure of a woman, Pip, a fine—figure—of—a—woman;" * * * * * but when she—gets—on—the ram—page, Pip, candour compels fur to admit that she—is—a—Buster!!" Dickens says that Joe spoke that last word "as if it began with at least twelve capital B's." If you wish to know the full force of that sentence about the creed of *work*, as Mr. Garfield uttered it, and as his own life habits have enforced it, write it with at least twelve capital W's! To say that we thank him for the lesson, that we thank him for all his lessons, that we love him because we owe to him the best half of all we are, is saying less than the truth, and less than our hearts have always said.

Dear old schoolmates of the days long since passed! I have sought thus to gather up a handful only of the pearls, pearls of greatest price, which were poured out before us here in such glittering abundance in those golden days. The world may have found us rich or poor in mental or moral worth, but be that as it may, it is certain that our teachers, out of full treasure houses, brought forth treasures to enrich us, without measure; yes, without money and without price.

During the seventeen years of the Eclectic Institute 29 persons were chosen on its Board of Trustees: Carnot Mason, Symonds Ryder, Isaac Errett, William Hayden, Zeb Rudolph, Frederick Williams, Aaron Davis, J. H. Jones, J. A. Ford, William Richards, George King, A. L. Soule, Alvah Udall, Dr. M. Jewett, Alva Humiston, Harmon Austin, W. J. Ford, A. S. Hayden, Thomas Carroll, Hartwell Ryder, J. P. Robison, R. M. Bishop, D. W. Canfield, W. W. Richards, A. B. Way, C. B. Lockwood, J. H. Rhodes, A. Teachout, and James A. Garfield. Of these C. B. Lockwood, A. Teachout, and W. J. Ford are members of the Board of 1900.

Number and Names of Trustees.

Outside of the Faculty 17 different persons were chosen to act as Solicitors or Financial Agents for the Institute: William Hayden, Horace Dutchin, Calvin Smith, J. H. Jones, Aaron Davis, Deacon Chapin, S. R. Willard, Symonds Ryder, Charles Brown, J. A. Ford, A. B. Green, Frederick Williams, W. A. Belding, Brown Penniman, W. J. Ford, John Encell, and B. F. Waters. All of these were duly authorized to raise funds for the Institute. All had some success but the largest returns came from the labors of William Hayden, Aaron Davis, Dr. W. A. Belding and Wallace J. Ford.

Solicitors for the Institute.

For 17 years only two persons were elected to preside over the Board of Trustees. These were Carnot Mason and Alvah Udall. Mr. Mason was President for 16 years.

Presidents of the Board.

Dr. L. W. Trask was Secretary of the Board of Trustees for 15 years, and was succeeded by Dr. A. J. Squire, who served the remainder of the Eclectic period, and for many years afterwards for the College Board.

Secretaries of the Board.

Treasurers of the Board.

Symonds Ryder held the office of Treasurer for 11 years, and was succeeded by Zeb Rudolph who held the place until 1868.

Principals of the Eclectic Institute.

Including A. S. Hayden who held the position for seven years the following persons were elected Principal of the Eclectic Institute: A. S. Hayden, James A. Garfield, H. W. Everest, C. W. Heywood, A. J. Thomson, and John M. Atwater.

Teachers of the Eclectic Institute.

Within the 17 years of the Eclectic Institute—58 different persons occupied either principal or subordinate places as teachers in the Institution: A. S. Hayden, Thomas Munnell, Norman Dunshee, Charles D. Wilber, Almeda A. Booth, Phoebe M. Drake, Laura A. Clark, Calista O. Carlton, Sarah Parker, Amaziah Hull, James A. Garfield, Harriet E. Wood, Harriet Warren, S. L. Hillier, J. B. Crane, Mrs. Charlotte R. Crane, Sarah Udall, Julia J. Smith, J. H. Rhodes,* G. C. Reed, Hannah S. Morton, Jen-

---

* The reason Mr. Rhodes gave for going to Hiram is interesting. In his address before the Hiram College Reunion, June 11, 1880, he said:

This Institution, located here in the heart of Yankeedom, thirty years ago and more, was brought to my attention by chance, or mere accident—the simple circumstance that I happened to sleep with a preacher one night. That night as I wished to sleep he wanted to know what I had been doing. I said I had been teaching school that winter. He said, "You had better go to Hiram." I said, "Where's Hiram?" He said, "Here on the Western Reserve." Well, I concluded I would go to Hiram on the recommendation of B. F. Perkey. I came to Ravenna by cars, and through seventeen miles of mud, in March, 1853, landing at the hotel, at that time under the hill.

In the morning I rose up and went to the College grounds, expecting to see, even on that wintry morning, ladies and gentlemen parading round the fountain that I had seen pictured. I went there and saw the gentleman whose silvery hair (alluding to the Rev. Mr. Hayden) was as white then as now.

To his cordial grace and kindness in welcoming me to Hiram I

nie A. Chapin, Platt R. Spencer, J. W. Lusk, H. W. Ever-
est, Mary Atwater, Sarah L. Spencer, H. C. Spencer, H. A.
Spencer, L. P. Spencer, John M. Atwater, W. C. Webster,
Hiram S. Chamberlain, Burke Aaron Hinsdale,* F. A. Wil-
liams, Julia A. Wilson, T. E. Suliot, J. C. Cannon, Nellie
Rudolph, C. W. Heywood, William Lowe, L. G. Felch,
Mary Buckingham, Mary E. Moore, Statira M. Newcomb,
A. J. Thomson, H. A. Coffeen, H. C. Mitchell, Julia B.
Treat, Jasper S. Ross, Osmer C. Hill, Sarah A. Bartlett,
Julia E. Pardee, Tillie Newcomb, W. H. Rogers, Bailey S.
Dean, Grove E. Barber, and Clayton C. Smith.

The students of Hiram have always been an important
factor in its progress and success; indeed, there could not be
a school without students.   Students are the life of a school.

**The Students
of the
Eclectic Institute.**
In general Hiram students have always
been of a high grade.   This is especially
true of the Eclectic period.   Coming as
they did mostly from country homes and
from families in moderate circumstances, with their main

---

think is largely due the fact that I remained as long as I did. I remember him kindly. Most of the places were then filled, and he sent
me to board with a Mr. Packer, in the village here. It has always
been a conundrum to me how Mr. Packer could board me for $1.25
a week, and have my washing and mending done.

I remember a circumstance that had much to do with my remaining at Hiram. I was a little homesick, and one day I went into the
large hall of the College building, and the tall, muscular, tow-headed
man in charge there, who was teaching Algebra, came up to me, and,
seeing a cloud over my face, threw his arms about me in an ardent
way. Immediately the homesickness disappeared. The tow-headed
man (General G.) has not so much hair to-day as he had then. Hard
knocks in public life have uprooted much of his hair. As we are not
permitted to refer to politics, I cannot refer to him any more, as most
of his life has been political.

* As I was writing these names the news came to me that B. A.
Hinsdale died at Atlanta, Ga., Nov. 29, 1900, one week later in the
same month than he entered Hiram as a student 47 years ago.
—*F. M. Green.*

purpose to get as much out of the school as they could, it is not strange that they should manifest a high character and deportment.   Among its thousands of students there were only a few who proved unworthy representatives of their families or the school.   Counting up the footings in the annual catalogues, in the 17 years of the Eclectic Institute there were 6,518 students of which 3,689 were males and 2,829 were females.   This aggregate represents about 4,000 different students.   These students were widely distributed, showing that as an Academy of high grade Hiram was not a provincial school.   They came from Wisconsin, Canada, New York, Illinois, England, Michigan, Pennsylvania, Indiana, Iowa, Virginia, Vermont, Kentucky, Minnesota, Massachusetts, California, Louisiana, Germany, Nebraska, Maine, Missouri, Texas, and, of course, the largest number from Ohio, Northeastern Ohio furnishing the most impressive number.

It has been observed that "every good school has a spirit, and the spirit of one good school is very much like the spirit of another good school."   Every school has some characteristic, distinctive and peculiar if not remarkable.   It may be that its administration is of a superior and brilliant sort as, for instance, in the case of Williams College and Mark Hopkins; it may be that some teacher has shown unusual and prodigious power and skill in the classroom and impressed on all his wonderful personality; it may be that the pupils have illustrated in a large degree, the best features of student life, and have thus given to the School a spirit strongly marked and easily seen.   This "spirit" is not bad unless it becomes extravagant, and it can do a school much good.   During the days of the Eclectic Institute there was a "Hiram spirit" that never went down.   Its sources were from the several springs just mentioned: The administra-

The Hiram Spirit.

tion was attractive and controlling; some of its teachers were of the first rank; and the character of its student body was more than usually homogeneous. In Mr. Hinsdale's address at the "Jubilee of Hiram College" June 22, 1900, and one of the very last addresses he ever delivered, speaking of "the spirit of schools" and of the "Hiram spirit," he said: "It is a kind of poetry that covers the hard, bare, bleak realism of life until the students become sufficiently mature to grapple with those realities. Do not understand me to mean that the Hiram spirit is simply the conceit of youth. Our dear friend Everest, replying to the question, once told me that there was a distinctive Hiram spirit, stating that the directness, clearness of head, and earnestness of purpose which marked the Disciple movement in its early days flowed into the School and gave it character, not merely in religion, but in other things as well. This may well have been so. At all events, I have thought, and still think, that Hiram students as a body have been an earnest, thorough-going, and effective group of men and women. If the old School has never sent out from its halls eminent scholars, great thinkers or distinguished men of letters, it has certainly sent out thousands of young men and women well-equipped in mind and character to do worthily their work in the world. The best thing that Garfield ever did for Hiram students was to teach them to put away cant and other forms of insincerity, to cultivate truth and reality, to be themselves, to be strong, and to quit them like men. It was a great lesson. It still lives in Hiram College."

In the selection of its Board of Trustees, Hiram has always been fortunate. None have accepted a place in that important and honorable body, except those who sincerely

Unity of Action.

desired the success of the Institution; and the meetings of the Board throughout the Eclectic period were characterized by frank and strong discussion and investigation, and, in the

BOWLER HALL: ERECTED IN 1880.

MILLER HALL: ERECTED IN 1889.

end, by unity of action.   This condition of mind and heart
on the part of those who were chosen to guide the interests
of the School had much to do in its progress and prosperity.

But the days of the Eclectic Institute were drawing
towards the close.   Some of its best friends had fondly anticipated the day when the School should reach the stature
of a College.   Not many at the beginning
looked so far ahead as this, but some did;
and the Trustees and friends of the Western Reserve Eclectic Institute finally announced that they had "determined to put
in execution the long cherished purpose of making the
Eclectic Institute a first class educational institution, with
power of conferring degrees.   The subject having been held
under advisement, action was taken at the meeting of the
Board, on the 20th day of February, 1867, to carry into effect this purpose.   The style and title of HIRAM COLLEGE
was adopted.   This movement having been endorsed by a
large convention of the friends of the Institution, held at
Hiram on the 12th of June, the College will go into full operation at the opening of the school year, Tuesday, August
13, 1867."   Nothing remained now except to close the doors
of one school and open the doors of another.

**Closing Days
of the
Eclectic Institute.**

**The Last
Commencement.**

The Commencement programme for
June 13, 1867, has a historic interest for
it marks the line between the Academy
and the College, and it is given here:

Forenoon.

PRAYER

MUSIC   MUSIC

GERMAN SALUTATORY

ALICE SQUIRE, *Bridge Creek.*

ESSAY,   -   -   -   -   -   Under the Juggernaut

CELIA BIDLAKE, *Mantua*

ORATION,   -   -   -   -   -   -   Bismarck

T. A. SNOW, *Auburn*

MUSIC—AWAY, AWAY

ORATION,   -   -   -   -   -   -   How Soon?

J. M. Monroe, *Mogadore*

ORATION,   -   -   -   -   -   Westward Ho!

J. B. Johnson, *Middlefield*

ESSAY,   -   -   -   -   When my Ship Comes in

Helen Kent, *Aurora*

MUSIC—BY THE BAND

DISCUSSION,   Should Polygamy be Suppressed by Force?

Aff.—A. A. Amidon, *Geneva*

Neg.—E. A. Pardee, *Hiram*

MUSIC—BY THE BAND

ESSAYS,   -   -   -   -   Election Day, A. D., 1900

Mattie Moore, *Parkman*

Estella Udall, *Hiram*

THE ECLECTIC MISCELLANY

EDITORS

H. N. Mertz, *Bellair*   Ida M. Slocum, *Pit Hole City, Pa.*

MUSIC—TO-DAY

ORATION,   -   Hearken to me; I, also, will show mine Opinion

D. C. Collins, *Nicholasville, Ky.*

ORATION,   -   -   The Whirligig of Time and its Revenges

S. E. Young, *Hiram*

MUSIC—ALL BY THE SHADY GREENWOOD TREE

Afternoon.

MUSIC—LASHED TO THE MAST

ORATION,   -   -   -   -   -   Mathematics

C. H. Leonard, *Chagrin Falls*

ESSAY,   -   -   -   -   Shall a Woman read Greek?

Blanche Slocum, *Pit Hole City, Pa.*

ESSAY, -   -   -   -   -   John Chinaman

Alice Amidon, *Geneva*

ORATION,   -   -   -   -   -   Obscurity

B. E. Wakefield, *Greensburg*

MUSIC—THE OLD MOUNTAIN TREE

COLLOQUIAL DISCUSSION,   -   -   -   -

Has Secretary Seward Bought an Elephant?

E. S. Hart, *Hiram*   O. C. Hubbell, *Bedford*

MUSIC—BY THE BAND

ESSAY,   -   -   -   -   Exogens or Endogens

Orissa Udall, *Hiram*

VALEDICTORY,   -   -   -   End of Vol. I

B. S. Dean, *Center, Wis.*

MUSIC—THE OLD ECLECTIC BELL

After the Commencement Exercises, the address before the College
Societies will be delivered by

GENERAL J. A. GARFIELD

MUSIC—OLD EASTER ANTHEM

Of the names of those who appear on the programme some are dead, some are in the far West, some in the kitchen or among the "household gods," some are lawyers, some are preachers, and two, E. B. Wakefield and Bailey S. Dean, are able and honorable Professors in the Faculty for 1900. One of these out of the "Obscurity" of the occasion, has risen to a high place as preacher and educator; the other closed for the students Vol I. of the School on Hiram Hill.

It was fitting that Mr. Garfield, the student, the teacher, and the Principal, should make the last address for the "Old Eclectic" and the first for Hiram College.   March 4, 1881, from the East portico of the Capitol at Washington, in his Inaugural address as President of the United States, Mr. Garfield said: "We stand to-day on an eminence which over-looks a hundred years of national life—a century crowded with perils, but crowned with the triumphs of liberty and law.   Before continuing the onward march, let us pause on this height, for a moment, to strengthen our faith and to renew our hope by a glance at the pathway along which our people have travelled."   The great statesman then proceed-ed to reveal the pathway over which the Nation had trav-elled to reach the heights of a century of progress.   When this was done he looked towards the future and forecasted its progress, the expansion of its influence, and the enlarge-ment of its empire.

In much the same way did he make his appeal to the young people of Hiram in his address before the Literary Societies of the Eclectic Institute on this notable Commence-ment Day.   In part he said: "In ordinary times, we could scarcely find two subjects wider apart than the meditations of a school-boy, when he asks what he shall do with him-self, and how he shall do it, and the forecastings of a great nation, when it studies the laws of its own life, and endeav-ors to solve the problem of its destiny.   But now there is more than a resemblance between the nation's work and yours. If the two are not identical, they at least bear the relation of the whole to the part. The nation having passed through the childhood of its history, and being about to enter upon a new life, based on a fuller recognition of the rights of manhood, has discovered that liberty can be safe only when the suffrage is illuminated by education. It has now perceived that the life and light of a nation are inseparable. Hence the Federal government has established a National Department of Education, for the purpose of teaching young men and women how to be good citizens. You, young gentlemen, have passed the limits of childhood, and being about to enter the larger world of manhood, with its manifold struggles and aspirations, are now confronted with the question, 'What must I do to fit myself most completely, not for being a citizen merely, but for being "all that doth become a man," living in the full light of the Christian civilization of America?' Your disenthralled and victorious country asks you to be educated for her sake, and the noblest aspirations of your being still more imperatively ask it for your own sake.

In general it may be said that the purpose of all study is two-fold,—to discipline our faculties, and to acquire knowledge for the duties of life. It is happily provided in the constitution of the human mind, that the labor by which knowledge is acquired is the only means of disciplining the powers. It may be stated as a general rule, that if we compel ourselves to learn what we ought to know, and use it when learned, our discipline will take care of itself.

The student should study himself, his relations to society, to nature, and to art; and above all, and through all these, he should study the relations of himself, society, nature, and art, to God, the Author of them all.

Of course it is not possible, nor is it desirable, to confine the course of development exclusively to this order; for

Truth is so related and correlated, that no department of her realm is wholly isolated. We cannot learn much that pertains to the industry of society, without learning something of the material world and the laws which govern it. We cannot study nature profoundly without bringing ourselves into communion with the spirit of art, which pervades and fills the universe.

While acquiring this kind of knowledge, the student is on a perpetual voyage of discovery,—searching what he is, and what he may become; how he is related to the universe, and how the harmonies of the outer world respond to the voice within him. It is in this range of study that he learns most fully his own tastes and aptitudes—and generally determines what his life shall be."

In the conclusion of his speech Mr. Garfield said: "I beseech you to remember that the genius of success is still the genius of labor. If hard work is not another name for talent, it is the best possible substitute for it. In the long run the chief difference in men will be found in the amount of work they do. Do not trust to what lazy men call the spur of the occasion. If you wish to wear spurs in the tournament of life, you must buckle them to your own heels before you enter the lists. Men look with admiring wonder on a great intellectual effort, like Webster's reply to Hayne, and seem to think that it leaped into life by the inspiration of the moment. But if by some intellectual chemistry we could resolve that masterful speech into its several elements of power, and trace each to its source, we should find that every constituent force had been elaborated twenty years before,—it may be, in some hour of earnest intellectual labor. Occasion may be the bugle-call that summons an army to battle; but the blast of a bugle cannot ever make soldiers, or win victories.

And finally, young gentlemen, learn to cultivate a wise

reliance, based not on what you hope, but on what you perform. It has long been the habit of this Institution, if I may so speak, to throw young men overboard, and let them sink or swim. None have yet drowned who were worth the saving. I hope the practice will be continued, and that you will not rely on outside help for growth or success. Give crutches to cripples; but go you forth with brave true hearts, knowing that fortune dwells in your brain and muscle, and that labor is the only human symbol of Omnipotence."*

The days of the Western Reserve Eclectic Institute were now closed. From a small beginning the Institution had grown in power and influence, until it commanded the respect of all who had touched its horizon, and the admiration and assistance of many. It had broken the bands with which its early nurses had enswathed it; it had outgrown the garments of its childhood; it had come to be known as a stalwart and supple-sinewed representative of its class among educational institutions; and by the very force of the conditions that surrounded it, it became necessary to enlarge its borders, to advance its standard, and to seek to win a place among higher institutions of learning, and an honorable seat in the Parliament of Colleges.

The Close
of the
Eclectic Institute.

---

*President Garfield and Education, pp. 277-313.

CHAPTER V.

Hiram College began its work August 13, 1867; and while the name and rank of the Institution were changed this did not essentially change its aims and spirit. The work formerly done went on all the same. A College had simply been added to an academical and preparatory school. Acting under the statute of April 8, 1856, which empowers seminaries of learning incorporated by general law or special Act to change their name and become colleges, and after such change to confer the usual college degrees the Board of Trustees, February 20, 1867, changed the name of the Eclectic Institute, and clothed it with collegiate powers and responsibilities. June 19, 1872, the Board, in pursuance of the statute for such cases made and provided increased the number of Trustees from twelve, the original number, to twenty-four. With these exceptions the original Act of Incorporation has not been changed. The action of the Trustees by which the Eclectic Institute was made a college was endorsed by a convention of the friends of the Institute held in Hiram, June 12, 1867.

The Beginning of Hiram College.

The humble origin, the feeble beginning, and the uneven steps in the progress of Hiram College are not unlike those of other colleges. In some respects Hiram had a

more promising beginning than many
others. A few facts in regard to other
institutions of learning in Ohio will not
be uninteresting here. When "Ohio University" opened its doors as a college June 1, 1809, "but three students reported for duty, and none of these remained long enough to graduate." The first Faculty of "Miami University," in 1824, consisted of three members. For fifty years Oberlin College "owed its life to the sacrifice and devotion of its founders and instructors" and its benefactors were people of small means who "periodically contributed small sums from scanty earnings." At the outset "the only resources of the Ohio Wesleyan University were the contributions of friends, and for some time these were wholly absorbed by the current expenses and other indebtedness." Kenyon College was located "amid well-nigh untrodden forests, and involved large outlays of labor and heavy sacrifices." Marietta College began as "the Institute of Education;" then it appears as the "Marietta Collegiate Institute," and "Western Teachers' Seminary," and finally "Marietta College." Its first effort to raise funds for an endowment was made in 1833, "when something more than eight thousand dollars was raised of which the seven trustees gave one half." Western Reserve College, now Adelbert College of Western Reserve University, was opened for students in the fall of 1826 and "only twenty-three students were enrolled in the college during the year 1827-'28, sophomores, freshmen, preparatory and special; and the instructional force consisted of one tutor." The financial difficulties of Antioch College which had the distinguished Horace Mann for its first President, began early in the history of the College. Denison University began its work in a Baptist meeting house, in Granville, December 13, 1831, with one teacher; and "for thirty-six years had no productive endowment,

Hiram and Other Colleges.

and its financial crises were many and severe." Mount Union College was first organized as a small seminary in 1846, with only six students. It is well for the friends of Hiram College to know these facts, for though it has had its days of "gloom and thick darkness," other institutions with which it has been an honorable competitor have had like experiences.

"The Association of Ohio Colleges" like all valuable institutions is an evolution or growth. At a meeting of the Ohio Teachers' Association prior to 1867 a committee was appointed to prepare a plan of organiza-

Hiram College a Member of the Association of Ohio Colleges. tion of the colleges of the State; and at a meeting of college officers held at Springfield, Ohio, July 2, 1867, the committee which had been previously appointed made a report on organization—which was discussed and adopted. This report was substantially the present constitution of the Association. Its purpose was stated as follows: "The object of this association shall be an interchange of opinions among those engaged in the higher departments of instruction, and the adoption of such common rules as may seem fitted to promote efficient and harmonious working." In 1875 a committee of five was appointed from Western Reserve, Denison, Ohio Wesleyan, Kenyon and Oberlin colleges "to fix some standard to which a college must conform in order to be received into its membership." This committee reported to the meeting at Cincinnati in 1876, "that it is the judgment of this committee that colleges holding or claiming membership in the Association should be able to fulfill three conditions:

(1)—There should be the four regular college classes in full operation.

(2)—The college course should comprise four years of college work with fifteen recitations per week.

(3)—The minimum of requirements for admission to the freshman class should be, besides the common English branches, from two to three years of Latin study with daily recitations, two years of Greek with daily recitations, and algebra to quadratic equations." This report after full discussion was adopted with slight amendments; and a committee of five was constituted of representatives from Western Reserve, Kenyon, Oberlin, Antioch and Ohio Wesleyan University, "to ascertain what colleges come within the conditions of the resolution adopted in 1877 upon the subject of membership in the Association." This committee reported at the meeting in Oberlin in 1878, and named fifteen institutions in the order of the date of their charters, and whose "right to the title was, in their judgment, not to be questioned." The fifteen institutions were as follows: Ohio University, 1804; Kenyon, 1824; Western Reserve, 1826; Denison University, 1831; Oberlin, 1834; Marietta, 1835; Ohio Wesleyan University, 1842; St. Xavier's, 1842; Otterbein, 1847; Antioch College, 1852; Baldwin University, 1856; Hiram College, 1867; University of Wooster, 1870; University of Cincinnati, 1870; Ohio State University, 1870. This report was adopted, and these institutions were thus made to constitute the Association of Ohio Colleges.

The aim of the College was declared, in the announcement made in 1867, to be, "to furnish a course of training as thorough as any in the country; and while it will bestow

The Aim of Hiram College.

careful attention upon the classical languages, it will aim to give a fuller course than is common, in those branches which are modern and national." In a high degree this last clause describes a distinctive feature of the College. More than ordinary attention is paid to Historical and Political studies, particularly to those that bear upon the duties and rights of the American citizen. Hiram was never intended to be a school of special training, and it has never been a Biblical or Theological Seminary. The Bible is used daily in general service or classroom study, and special instruction in Biblical studies has always been furnished to those desiring it. The agencies employed are text-book instruction, chapel lectures, and special courses of lectures delivered by members of the Faculty or by lecturers called in from abroad. It has sought to prepare young men for the ministry by providing them with general culture supplemented by short courses of lectures and special studies. Of course, these students have been taught the leading tenets and peculiarities of the Disciples of Christ; but all attempts to exercise over the body of the students a peculiar denominational influence have been carefully avoided.

The original charter which has never been changed in this particular, defines the object of the corporation to be, "the instruction of youth of both sexes in the various branches of literature and science, especially of moral science, as based on the facts and precepts of the Holy Scriptures." In Hiram the experiment of co-education has been successful, though, as a rule, ladies have generally chosen one of the shorter courses of study. Like Oberlin, Hiram has found the results and lessons of its experience in the practice of co-education to be:

Co-education of the Sexes.

"First, economy of means and forces, a very evident advantage.

Second, convenience to the patrons of the school, since very many cases are observed where brothers and sisters are attending college together to the advantage of both.

Third, wholesome incitements to study.

Fourth, social culture, which influences powerfully the

manners, feelings and thoughts of both sexes during that period when character is being specially moulded.

Fifth, absence of rowdyism, hazing, and many other disorders.

Sixth, in the relation of the school to the community, a cordial feeling of good will, and the absence of that antagonism between town and college which is often met with."

Without doubt, there are disadvantages connected with the practice but these are clearly outweighed by the advantages.

The first Faculty of Hiram College consisted of Dr. Silas E. Shepard, President, and Professor of Moral Science and Literature, Logic and Rhetoric; John M. Atwater, Professor of Latin and Greek; Asa M. Weston, Professor of Mathematics and Modern Languages; Osmer C. Hill, Professor in the Commercial and Chirographic Department; Miss Lottie M. Sackett, Principal of the Ladies' Department; Miss Julia E. Pardee, Instructor in Mathematics;* Miss Tillie Newcomb, Teacher of Instrumental Music; Miss Emma L. Johnson, Teacher of Landscape Painting and Drawing; Eugene H. Plowe, Teacher of Vocal Music; Edgar A. Pardee, Teacher in Greek; Henry N. Mertz, Teacher in Latin; and Grove E. Barber, Teacher in English Branches. Thus equipped the new College began its work. Of those who formed the first Faculty only Miss Johnson, now Mrs. B. S. Dean, is connected with the College at this time.

The First Faculty of the College.

---

*Julia Eunice Pardee was born at Wadsworth, O., December 11, 1836. She taught school in Wadsworth, O., Corry, Pa., and Hiram. She came to Hiram in 1866 as teacher of Mathematics and Philosophy, and remained in the Faculty until her marriage to Prof. A. M. Weston, July 7, 1868. She was a woman of excellent character and superior intellect, and her class-room work strong and impressive. She is yet living, a grandmother of children, in her pleasant home at New Castle, Ind.

Dr. Silas E. Shepard was the first President of Hiram College. When he entered on his duties he was sixty-six years old. He was a man of strong physical constitution, large brain, remarkably clear intellect, and high moral sentiments, a diligent student, a close thinker, and a speaker of much more than ordinary power. Religiously his first experiences were among the Congregationalists. Afterwards he united with the Baptists, and early in the history of the Restoration of primitive Christianity as contended for by Thomas and Alexander Campbell and others, he became identified with the movement and gave to it the strength of his life. As a preacher he was first known in Pennsylvania where he was very successful, and the influence he established in the early part of his career, remained unbroken to the last.

The First President.

New York was for many years the field of his labors. In that state he published a religious magazine—"The Primitive Christian"—a keen and sprightly advocate of New Testament Christianity. For several years he resided in the city of New York where he preached, and labored in the rooms of the American Bible Union as an assistant in the work of revision, and publishing a magazine of critical character called "The Reviser." He spent a few years in travels in foreign lands. When he came into Ohio he was for several years preacher and teacher in Cincinnati and Cleveland. His studious habits were adhered to through his life, so that his mind was fresh and vigorous to the last.

Socially he was one of the most companionable of men —communicative, genial, witty, yet never disposed to monopolize the conversation or to turn attention upon himself. Never vainly ambitious but always modest in asserting his own claims, he did not grow sour over disappointments, but remained sweet in spirit and cheerful to the close of his life. He was also large-hearted, freely giving of his means for every good work, and performing much labor without regard to compensation. Of him Isaac Errett said: "It was our privilege to know him intimately, and to be often associated with him in public duties. We are able to say that we never shared his society without being a gainer by it, and that from first to last no cloud or shadow ever fell upon our friendship to cast even a moment's gloom. We uniformly found him pure, unselfish, carefully considerate of the rights of others, and supremely devoted to the truth. His superior attainments gave him prominence over many of his co-workers, yet we do not believe that one has ever been found to complain of arbitrariness, assumption, or failure to recognize and honor the merits of his brethren."

D. P. Henderson, another life-long friend, has left the following estimate of him on record: "He was one of the most intelligent and amiable of men. His mind and heart corresponded in their comparative greatness. No envy, no jealousy occupied a place within him. His mind was clear, analytical and full of intellectual power. He was meek and condescending, and childlike simplicity characterized his intercourse with his fellow-men. He was a critical scholar in biblical literature, and one of the most courteous Christian gentlemen in debate. While he was firm and uncompromising in his views, yet he awarded to his opponent the same right to think and express his sentiments as he claimed for himself. He was refined in sentiment and courteous to all men."

Professor B. S. Dean who was a student in Hiram during the Presidency of Dr. Shepard, and conducted the services at his burial ten years later in Troy, Pa., speaking of his standing and influence at his home said: "I think nowhere else was Dr. Shepard so grandly himself as right here in Bradford County, the scene of his earliest advocacy of Primitive Christianity, the arena of his sternest conflicts, grandest triumphs and most continuous service. For a whole year I heard him at Hiram, O., ten years ago, but never did I know the might of the man till I heard him here among the people and the churches to whom he was, indeed, a father. Among the last words that he uttered, he said to his daughter, 'I want you to say *good bye* to my friends for me, and tell them I should like to have seen them all.' His was by no means a perfect character. But his very imperfections were born of those elements which gave him strength and made him so grandly useful. At the age of seventy-six his form was erect, his step elastic; and of him it might almost be said, 'His eye was not dim nor his natural force abated.' Those who got nearest his heart knew it to be young and sweet and tender, and happy are all our homes which have been graced and gladdened by his presence."

Fifty-eight years of his seventy-six he spent in preaching the gospel. He came to Hiram too late in his life and with his habits too firmly fixed to make a successful administrator of college affairs. His mind and body had worked too long on transcendent subjects for study, and themes for speech to be brought down to the consideration of rules for "the intercourse of the sexes," and how to avoid the "clashing of classes." He remained only one year in connection with the College. Notwithstanding it was manifest that he would not be able to guide the College interests to a successful issue his resignation was accepted with great regret by the Board of Trustees, and resolutions to that effect were placed on record at the close of his service. Dr. Silas E. Shepard was born in New Berlin, New York, in the year 1801, and died at Troy, Pa., October 12, 1877, at the age of 76 years.

Asa M. Weston was born of Massachusetts stock September 24, 1836, in Cleveland, O., whither his father came in 1816, and was reared on a farm six miles east via. St.

Prof. Asa M. Weston. Clair Street. He was prepared for College at Shaw Academy in the village of Collamer. Three years of college life was spent at Oberlin, O. In 1857 he finished his college course and was graduated from Antioch College in the classical department, in the first class of that institution, the famous educator, Horace Mann, President, signing his diploma. The course of study was especially thorough in language, mathematics, history, and mental, moral, government science, constitution, the latter under the personal tuition of Mr. Mann.

After graduation he taught in Clinton County, Ohio. For two or three years he was local editor of the "Cincinnati Daily Press," a flourishing daily paper. In 1862 he enlisted as a private (August 11, 1862) in the 50th O. V. I. Regiment and served till the close of the war. During his army service he had almost uninterrupted good health, and was successively promoted from private to Corporal, Sergeant-Major, and 2nd Lieutenant, and mustered out with his Company June 26, 1865. For two years he was Superintendent of Public Schools and Principal of Jennings Academy at Vernon, Ind. In 1867 he came to Hiram and for two years was Professor of Mathematics and Modern Languages, in the Faculties of Presidents Shepard and Atwater. While at Hiram he was married to Miss Julia E. Pardee, Teacher of Mathematics and Philosophy in the closing year of the Eclectic Institute and the opening year of Hiram College. After leaving Hiram he gave private school instruction for two years. He was then called to the chair of Greek and Modern Languages in Eureka College, Eureka, Ill., where he remained for more than six years. As teacher at Eureka he followed H. O. Newcomb, an old student at Hiram, and was associated in the Bible Department with H.

COLLEGE Y. M. C. A. AND Y. W. C. A. BUILDING: Erected in 1895.

W. Everest at one time Principal of the Eclectic Institute. Toward the close of his work at Eureka he was elected President of the College in which position he served only a brief period. On leaving Eureka his work as College Professor closed. For three years he served the Church at Troy, Pa., as preacher and pastor. For the last twenty years he has resided on a farm in Henry County, Ind., preaching as occasion required at various places. He is now living in New Castle, Ind., retired from work of all kinds. After ceasing from College and School work Mr. Weston turned his attention to literature and produced several volumes of more or less merit: "The Maid of Muldraugh's Hill," an army tale of thrilling interest based upon his own army experiences in Kentucky; "The Passing of the Veterans" in verse prepared for a G. A. R. memorial service; "Clipper Jap," a story for boys in six chapters; and "Vanished," a longer story. In 1886 he published "The Evolution of a Shadow" or "The Bible doctrine of rest from the standpoint of a believer in the divine authority and paramount importance of the religious observance of the first day of the week." This was his most pretentious work and reveals the high literary culture of the author, the strength of his thought, the keenness of his perceptions, and the power of his faith. Mr. Weston's instincts are all in the direction of accurate scholarship. As a child and as a young student he was quick to learn and easy to communicate; so that when his college course was ended and he entered the classroom as a teacher he was thoroughly prepared, and popular with his students. As a preacher he was strong as a teacher of the Word of God, and if not eloquent he was impressive in his utterances. He was in Hiram when salaries were ridiculously small, and when the Institution was "farmed out" to the President and the receipts divided among the workmen. His has been an honorable and

Christian life and when he finally rests from his labors his works will follow him.

Miss Lottie M. Sackett, the Principal of the Ladies' Department, brought into her position the fruit of a long **Miss Lottie M. Sackett.** experience as a teacher, the strength of a cultured mind, and the influence of a good reputation and a sterling Christian character. She remained one year. She is yet living at Warren, O., honored and beloved by all.

Osmer C. Hill. Osmer C. Hill remained a member of the College Faculty as Professor in the Commercial and Chirographical Department until 1876, when he closed his relation to the College.

Course of Study. The course of study for the first year of the College was prepared by a committee consisting of John M. Atwater, J. H. Rhodes and Alvah Udall. This course remained for several years substantially as it came from the hands of the committee.

Some changes in the business methods of the Board of Trustees were made, and rules adopted which have been very strictly adhered to ever since. At the first meeting of the Board in the College year a Commit-**Business Methods.** tee on Finance was appointed whose business was to "take charge of all funds for endowment and invest the same subject to the approval of the Board." On the adopting of this rule it was also declared that "this Board hereby promises the brotherhood that no part of the principal of such funds shall be used; but shall be kept sacred for the purpose for which it was donated."

On motion of Mr. Garfield it was Resolved, That the President of this College shall present to the Board of Trustees at each annual meeting a report in writing, setting forth the number of students in attendance during the year; the names of all persons employed as teachers; the work done by each, and any facts showing the general condition of the Institution. The Treasurer shall make as a part of his report a full statement of the receipts and expenditures of all money arising from tuition."

Annual Report of the President and Treasurer of the College.

The first Standing Committee on Finance was constituted of C. B. Lockwood, A. Teachout and Harmon Austin.

First Finance Committee.

Mr. Teachout and Mr. Lockwood are yet living and members of the present Board of Trustees. The Board has never had any abler or more faithful representatives.

A convention of the friends of the Institution met in Hiram June 12, 1867, the closing day of the Eclectic Institute, and recommended to the Board of Trustees, the establishment of a Biblical Department with an appropriate course of study for Hiram College. The Board took immediate action to carry out the recommendation of the convention, and on motion of Mr. B. A. Hinsdale the following resolutions were adopted: "*Resolved,* That we cordially approve of the recommendation of the Convention of June 12th in favor of establishing a Biblical Department, and the Board will appeal to the Christian Brotherhood to contribute fifty thousand dollars to the perpetual endowment of that Department, wherein lectures and other instruction shall be gratuitously furnished to all who are preparing for the Christian ministry; and that we, also, approve the recommendation of said convention that the brethren be asked to

A Biblical Course.

endow one chair in the Literary Department of the College."
It was also declared as the sense of the Board that the President of the College "should also be a Lecturer and Professor in the Biblical Department." The Biblical Department
modified as modifications have been found necessary, is one
of the permanent features of Hiram College.

In changing the school in name and in some respects
in character certain legal questions must necessarily be involved. In 1868 a committee of the
Board of Trustees consisting of Alvah
Udall, J. A. Garfield, and D. W. Canfield,
was appointed to consider all legal ques-
tions arising out of changing the school into a college. The
committee after careful examination reported that "the proceedings had been regular and legal."

The
Legal Status
of the College.

As the College interests began to multiply and its responsibilities, financial and other, increased, the Board of
Trustees decided to have a searching investigation made
into its legal history. Therefore in 1874
a committee consisting of B. A. Hinsdale,
then President of the College, Alvah
Udall, President of the Board of Trustees, and Dr. A. J. Squire, Secretary of
the Board, was appointed to prepare the legal history of the
College, with authority to employ such legal counsel and
assistance as they might need. This committee reported at
the annual meeting of the Board held in Hiram June 17,
1874. Though the report is quite long yet it is of permanent
value, and will be inserted here. To the Board of Trustees
of Hiram College: At a meeting held in Cleveland, January 28, 1874, you adopted the following resolution:

The
Legal History of
Hiram College.

"*Resolved,* That a committee of three, consisting of B.
A. Hinsdale, Alvah Udall, and A. J. Squire be and are here-

by appointed, to examine and look up the records of Hiram College, and ascertain and determine, if possible, whether the whole business as shown by said records was done in a proper and legal manner. The committee shall also ascertain the amount of capital stock of the College, what amount has been subscribed and what amount paid. Said committee is authorized to employ legal counsel, if necessary, if the records are faulty or deficient, the committee shall report such deficiencies, and all other matters pertaining to the subject, to the Board of Trustees at the regular meeting in June, 1874."

Authority of the Committee of Examination.

The committee created by this resolution respectfully reports, that it has sought thoroughly and conscientiously to perform the duties defined, and that the following are the results of its inquiries: The legal history of Hiram College began with an Act of the Legislature incorporating the Western Reserve Eclectic Institute, dated March 1, 1850. By its first section said Act created twelve persons named, together with such others as might be associated with them, a body corporate and politic, and invested them with the power of perpetual succession. It also provided that the capital stock of the corporation should not exceed fifty thousand dollars ($50,000), and that said stock should be divided into shares of twenty-five dollars ($25) each, to be used for no other purposes than in the instruction of youth of both sexes in the various branches of Literature and Science, and in the Holy Scriptures. Section second declared that the corporation should be capable of acquiring and holding property, real and personal, and of disposing of the same, for the benefit of the Institution, in all ways incident to similar corporations. Section third

The Results of the Examination.

provided that the corporate concerns of said Eclectic Institute should be managed by a Board of Trustees, of not less than nine nor more than twelve, of whom five should be a quorum to do business, and one of whom should be elected President. Said section further invested this Board of Trustees with all the powers for the establishment and management of the Institution, specifying all the leading powers in terms. Section fourth of said Act provided that all instruments of writing required to carry into effect any contract made by the Board, should be executed by the President thereof, and be sealed by the corporate seal. Section fifth provided that the corporators named in the first section, or such of them as chose to act, should manage the affairs of the Institution until subscriptions to the stock amounting to seven thousand ($7,000) dollars had been made, at which time a meeting of the stockholders should be called to elect Trustees. It provided that one-third of said Board of Trustees should be elected for one year, one-third for two years, and one-third for three years, and that thereafter there should be annual elections. It further provided that each stockholder should be entitled at each election to one vote, in person or in proxy, for every share of stock owned by him, with the proviso that no stockholder should have more than four votes for one hundred dollars ($100), six votes for two hundred dollars ($200), seven votes for three hundred dollars ($300), and eight votes for four hundred dollars ($400) or more. Section sixth regulated the annual meetings to elect Trustees, and provided for failures to elect. Section seventh empowered the Board to make By-Laws for the management of the Institution, and to prescribe the mode of transferring the stock.

Previous to the passing of this Act, the corporation had been acting as a provisional Board of Trustees, having been chosen for that purpose by a convention of the churches in Northern Ohio. They continued so to act until October 14, 1851, when it appeared that seven thousand dollars ($7,000) of stock had been obtained. At a meeting held on said day the President was instructed to issue a notice to the stockholders to meet in Hiram the 24th of the following November, to elect a Board of Trustees as contemplated by the charter. Said notice was duly issued, and twelve Trustees were elected on the day appointed. From that time there has been an annual election of the requisite number of Trustees, as prescribed by the Charter.

The next step in this legal history is the action of the Board by which the Institution took the name and rank of a College. This action rests upon an Act of the Legislature which took effect April 8, 1856, empowering seminaries of learning incorporated by general law or special Act to change their name and become colleges, and after such a change to confer the usual collegiate degrees. The second section of this Act, which prescribes the manner of the change, is as follows: 'Every seminary availing itself of the power herein given shall, in making such change, enter a resolution with full minutes of their action upon the regular records of the seminary, affixing thereto its common seal; and before the taking effect of such resolution, it shall be accurately transcribed and with the accompanying minutes and the common seal affixed, shall be filed in the office of the Recorder of the proper county and recorded by that officer; and also filed in the office of the Secretary of State to be recorded by said Secretary; and any copy of such file or record duly certified by the County Recorder or Secretary of State, as the case may be, shall be evidence in the courts of the State.' The Board of Trustees acted under this statute on two different occasions. The official record filed in the office of the Secretary of State is as follows : 'The Board of Trustees of the Western Reserve Eclectic Institute, met at Hiram November 9, 1858, at half past two o'clock p. m., pursuant to a call of the President. (Members present), Alvah Udall (in the chair), Wm. Hayden, Aaron Davis, Frederick Williams, Zeb Rudolph, Wm. Richards, Alvah Humiston, and W. J. Ford. In the absence of the Secretary of the Board, W. J. Ford was elected Secretary *pro tem.* Sessions of the Board opened by prayer by Wm. Hayden. Minutes of the last meeting read by the President. After hearing reports of committees, etc., the meeting was adjourned till tomorrow morning, (Nov. 10).

Nov. 10, 1858. Board met pursuant to adjournment, and was called to order by the President. Frederick Williams offered the following resolutions, viz.: 'Whereas, The Board of Trustees of the Western Reserve Eclectic Institute, (a seminary of learning) believing that it is desirable and for the interest of said Institute to reorganize under the provisions of 'an Act to authorize seminaries of learning to change their names and become colleges,' passed April 8, 1856,—

(1)   Therefore *Resolved,* That the name of said Institute be and the same is hereby changed to HIRAM COLLEGE.

(2)   *Resolved,* That under the provisions of said Act, the said Institute by the name aforesaid, as aforesaid, be and the same is hereby ordered to be organized as a college with full collegiate power and privileges, to confer upon the graduates of said college the usual degrees granted by colleges, etc.

(3)   *Resolved,* That said Board of Trustees be instructed to take, at such time as the Board may order all the necessary steps to carry into effect these resolutions.'

On motion of Mr. Williams, seconded by Mr. Hayden,

the foregoing resolutions were adopted by the following vote, viz.: Affirmative, F. Williams, Wm. Hayden, A. Davis, Z. Rudolph, Wm. Richards, A. Humiston, A. Udall, W. J. Ford.—8. Negative—None.

Alvah Udall, President of the Board of Trustees.
W. J. Ford, Secretary, Pro. Tem.

Hiram, February 20, 1867. The Board of Trustees of the Western Reserve Eclectic Institute met pursuant to call of the President. (Present) A. S. Hayden, W. J. Ford, J. H. Rhodes, Z. Rudolph, H. Ryder, and A. Udall, President of the Board. Meeting opened by prayer by A. S. Hayden. On motion of Mr. Ford the following resolution was passed unanimously: That the President of the Board of Trustees of the Western Reserve Eclectic Institute, be instructed, and is hereby authorized to take all the steps necessary to carry into effect the resolutions passed by the Board, in a meeting held November 10, 1858, making the Eclectic Institute a College, and that the name of the college shall be, 'Hiram College,' and so entered on the county and State records.

ALVAH UDALL,
President of the Board of Trustees.

(SEAL.)

A. J. SQUIRE,
Secretary.

5 Cent Internal
Revenue Stamp.

I certify the foregoing to be a true copy transcribed from the regular records of the Western Reserve Eclectic Institute this sixth day of July, A. D., 1867.

A. J. SQUIRE,
Secretary of the Board of Trustees.

Secretary of State's Office.)
United States of America, Ohio)

I, William Henry Smith, Secretary of State of the State of Ohio, do hereby certify that the foregoing is a true copy of the certificate of change of name of the Western Reserve Eclectic Institute, to Hiram College filed in this office July 13th, A. D., 1867.

In testimony whereof, I have hereunto subscribed my name and affixed the great Seal of the State of Ohio, at Columbus, the 13th day of July, A. D., 1867.

(SEAL.)   WM. HENRY SMITH,
                     Secretary of State.
5 Cent Internal Revenue Stamp.

At a meeting of the Board held June 12, 1867, the President of the Board, General Garfield, and D. W. Canfield, were appointed a committee to consider all legal questions arising out of changing the school into a college, and so to arrange the language of transfer as to guard all property rights of the Institution. (See Secretary's Book, page 24.) At the next meeting of the Board held January 1, 1868, this committee submitted the results of its inquiries: "Your committee appointed at the annual meeting held June, 1867, to consider all legal questions arising out of changing the school into a college, etc., beg leave to report, that they have examined and considered all such questions, and find that all the proceedings have been regular and legal, and therefore do not in the least degree prejudice the property rights of the Institution.   ALVAH UDALL,
                     D. W. CANFIELD.

Before dismissing this point, your committee would further represent that the legality of the proceedings by which the Eclectic Institute was changed to Hiram College has been tested by a suit that passed through both the Probate and Common Pleas Courts of Trumbull County, and that no flaw was found.

Your committee next inquired into the proceedings by which the number of Trustees of the College was increased from twelve to twenty-four.   This action rests on a General Statute that passed and took effect April 13, 1865. The first section of said Statute runs as follows: "That the Board of Trustees of any College or University now existing by virtue of any Act of Incorporation, or which may hereafter become incorporated, are hereby authorized to increase the number of Trustees provided for in such Act of Incorporation to any number not greater than twenty-four.   (See Swan and Sayler's Supplement to the Revised Statutes of the State of Ohio, p. 106.)"

On the 19th of June, 1872, the Board adopted the following resolution: "*Resolved,* That in pursuance of law for such cases made and provided, the number of Trustees of Hiram College be increased to twenty-four, and that at the next election of College Trustees, and at each and every such annual election held thereafter, there be elected a number sufficient with those remaining in office, to make twenty-four; electing at the first sixteen, eight for three years, four for two years, four for one year, and thereafter to fill vacancies."   (See Secretary's Book, p. 66.)

In pursuance of this action, on the 20th of June, 1872, the stockholders elected sixteen Trustees, and on the 19th of June, 1873, they elected eight.

On the 11th of January, 1873, the Legislature passed an Act repealing the Act of April 13, 1865, and providing: "That the Board of Trustees of any College or University now existing by virtue of any Act of Incorporation or law, or which may hereafter become incorporated under the Laws of the State of Ohio, are hereby authorized to increase the number of Trustees provided for in such Act of Incorporation or law, to any number not greater than twenty-four. The provisions of this Act shall also apply to all academies, seminaries, and Institutes not originally incorporated as colleges or universities, but which have since become such under the laws of this State." (See General and Local Laws, Vol. LXX, p. 4). There is, perhaps, room for doubt whether the action by which the number of Trustees was increased was strictly legal. This action was taken before the Act of 1873 was passed, and the question is, whether the Act of 1865 applied to a college that had been originally chartered as a Seminary or Institute. More specifically, the question is, whether, in 1872 within the meaning of the Statute, Hiram College was a college "by virtue of an Act of Incorporation." The question is respectfully submitted to the legal talent of the Board.

The inquiries of the committee concerning the capital stock of the College, have led to the following results:—

The
Capital Stock.

"*First.* The charter of 1850 placed the minimum stock at seven thousand dollars ($7,000); the maximum at fifty thousand ($50,000).

Second, It is impossible to ascertain the amount of stock subscriptions. The original subscription books or papers have been lost, and it does not appear that any permanent record of these was made.

Third, The amount of stock that has been paid for, according to the books of the Treasurer, is 673 shares, or sixteen thousand eight hundred and twenty-five dollars ($16,825).

Fourth, The amount for which certificates have been issued is 452 shares, or eleven thousand and three hundred dollars ($11,300); leaving two hundred and twenty-one shares, or five thousand five hundred and twenty-five dollars ($5,525) for which no certificates have been issued. The reason why these certificates have not been issued is, they have not been called for.

Fifth, At the annual meeting in 1872 the Board adopted a resolution authorizing the President to issue new stock in the name of the College in place of the old stock, appointing the President, Hartwell Ryder, and L. Cooley a committee to furnish certificates to the owners of stock who have not received them, and empowering Mr. Cooley to sell one thousand (1,000) shares of the new stock. (See Secretary's book, p. 68.) Your committee has not learned that anything more has been done under this resolution than to issue a few College stock certificates in place of the Eclectic institute certificates. The committee further states that it has prepared a tabular statement of stock showing the names of the original owners, their residences, the number of shares owned, and whether certificates have or have not been issued. (See Secretary's 2nd book, page 107.)

Your committee further represents that it has carefully examined the records of Board meetings from the year 1849 to the present, and that it has found said records, for the most part, kept in a full, clear, and methodical manner. It was discovered that the Secretary's book did not contain the record of one annual meeting, but, fortunately the original minutes were found, and the omission in the record has been supplied. The committee would recommend a little more care in the future in recording reports of committees, and a little more pains in the wording of motions and resolutions, also more care in the kind of ink used by the Secretary. Especial attention is called to this last point, because, owing to the use of poor ink used by the Secretary, some of the records must soon be transcribed. But while the committee calls attention to these minor points, it is happy in being able to state that the records are in such excellent condition that there is no difficulty in tracing the history of the Board from the beginning; and it cannot see that any question affecting the institution can arise out of any imperfections in the work of either the former or the present Secretaries. Your committee has noticed in looking through the minutes that there has been more or less irregularities in organizing the Board and respectfully recommends that some rule be adopted and followed in the future. All of which is respectfully submitted.

                              B. A. HINSDALE,
                              ALVAH UDALL,
                              A. J. SQUIRE,
                                        Committee."

The
Second Faculty of
the College.

On the resignation of President Shepard the Board of Trustees took immediate steps to provide a President and Faculty for the College, but some little time elapsed before it was accomplished. In the meantime Prof. A. M. Weston was authorized to act as correspondent for the college.

The Board met June 11, 1868, and after considerable discussion it was *"Resolved,* That J. M. Atwater be elected President of Hiram College and that a

J. M. Atwater
Elected President
of the College.

committee be appointed who shall in conjunction with him, be authorized to make all arrangements for the organization of a Board of Teachers." The committee ordered was composed of J. H. Rhodes, Alvah Udall, and Hartwell Ryder. A Board of Teachers was finally formed consisting of John M. Atwater, President, and Professor of Mental and Moral Philosophy, and Biblical Literature; Asa M. Weston, Professor of Mathematics, and Modern Languages; Amzi Atwater, Professor of Latin and Greek; Andrew J. Squire, Professor of Chemistry, Anatomy,

Physiology, Hygiene, and Physical Culture; and Miss Cortentia C. Munson, Principal of the Ladies Department.

Amzi Atwater was born in Mantua, O., November 9, 1839. He came to Hiram as a student in the fall of 1853 and his student life continued with some irregularity until 1860. Between these years he taught

Amzi Atwater. school at North Royalton, O., in 1858 and Braceville, O., in 1859. In 1860 he located at Bruceville, Ind., where he taught four terms. In 1862 he entered the North Western Christian University (now Butler), where he remained until 1865, with the exception of a "Hundred Days Service" in the U. S. Army in 1864. In 1865 he entered the State University at Bloomington, and also preached for the Christian Church at that place. In the University he was chosen Principal of the Preparatory Department and Adjunct Professor of Languages, which place he held until June, 1868. In 1866 he graduated from the University, receiving the degree of A. B. In 1868 and 1869 he was Professor of Latin and Greek in Hiram College, and during this time preached for the church at Ravenna, O. In 1869 and 1870 he preached for the church at Mantua, O. In 1869 he received the degree of A. M. from the Indiana State University, and in 1870 was elected Professor of Latin in that institution. August 8, 1870, he was married to Miss Cortentia Munson, an associate of his in the Faculty of Hiram College. From 1870 to 1893 he was Professor of Latin in Indiana State University. His entire service in the University covered a period of 26 years. From 1893 to the present his time has been devoted mostly to preaching; at Franklin, Ind., from 1893 to 1895; Sullivan, Illinois, from 1896 to 1897; and at Bridgeport, Connecticut, while his son Munson D. Atwater studied at Yale University. In 1898 and 1899 he preached at the church at Mantua Station, O. In 1882 he visited Europe and made a partial tour of the continent. He is now living at Bloomington, Ind., and Financial Secretary for the endowment of the Bible Chairs at Butler College, Irvington, Ind.

Cortentia Munson, daughter of Edward Spencer and Sophia Cowee Munson, was born Sept. 29th, 1838, in Mentor, Ohio. After the usual round in the public schools she attended at Hiram two terms—1856-7, under the presidency of A. S. Hayden.

Cortentia Munson.

Afterward she taught several terms in Mentor and vicinity, and in the public schools of Painesville, Ohio, in 1860-61. As her only brother now enlisted in the army she spent the next four years at home with her parents, and was actively engaged with the Mentor Aid Society in preparing and sending supplies to the soldiers in the field and hospitals. Early in 1865 she entered Lake Erie Seminary at Painesville and graduated with the class of 1867. Soon after she went with her brother to Knoxville, Tenn. Returning to Ohio the following year she was chosen Lady Principal of the College at Hiram September, 1868, under the presidency of J. M. Atwater, Amzi Atwater being at the time Professor of Latin and Greek. Miss Munson continued to teach in Hiram till December, 1869, when, on account of the dangerous illness of her mother, her presence was required at home. Cortentia Munson and Amzi Atwater were married Aug. 8th, 1870. Bloomington, Ind., the seat of the State University in which Amzi Atwater was a professor for 26 years, has been the family residence ever since. Two children were born, Munson Darwin and Eva Sophia, the latter dying at two years of age in 1877. Munson graduated at Indiana University in 1894, taught three years in Rayen School, Youngstown,

COLLEGE PRESIDENTS.

E. V. Zollars   G. H. Laughlin   J. M. Atwater
Dr. S. E. Shepard   B. A. Hinsdale

Ohio, studied two summers in Chicago University, and spent two years in post-graduate work in Yale University.

Besides these some changes were made in the assistant teachers and Magnus Buchholz, teacher of German; James M. Hurlbut, teacher in English Branches; Adelia L. Clifford, teacher of Instrumental Music; and Miss Statira Newcomb, teacher of Portrait and Landscape Painting and Drawing, were the new teachers employed. The condition of the affairs of the College during the year was evidently not very satisfactory either to the President and his Faculty, or to the Board of Trustees. It was found that there was an indebtedness near the close of the year for current expenses of $1,691.97. A meeting of the Board of Trustees was called for May 13, 1869. President Atwater made a statement of the condition of the school, after which W. J. Ford moved "That Hiram College be transferred to Dr. Silas E. Shepard for one year on condition that he hire teachers, keep up both the Literary and Theological Departments, and receive the tuition and annual interest of the endowment fund of the College for his compensation." The Board appears to have been divided as to the name to be inserted in the resolution, and Mr. Atwater's name was proposed in place of Dr. Shepard. It was finally agreed that Trustees Ford and Teachout should confer with Dr. Shepard, and Trustees Lockwood and Rhodes with President Atwater, and "ascertain if they would take the College for the tuition and the interest on the endowment fund for one year as per resolution specified." Later on the same day these committees reported the results of their conferences. Each had received an affirmative answer, and either of the gentlemen "would take the College on the terms proposed." The Board then proceeded to fill by ballot the blank in the resolution for President, which was filled by a vote

of 7 for Mr. Atwater and 3 for Dr. Shepard, and the following resolution was adopted:—"*Re-*

Contract with
J. M. Atwater
for Second Year.

solved, That the Board of Trustees hereby authorize J. M. Atwater to take charge
of the College during the next college
year, beginning with the June Commence-
ment of 1869, as its President on the following conditions,
to wit:

(1) Said President shall employ and pay all teachers
and Professors; shall pay incidental expenses; and shall
provide instruction in the Literary, Biblical and Preparatory Departments of the College sufficient to keep up the
present standard of excellence.

(2) That as compensation for said service he shall
receive all receipts for tuition during the said year, to be
collected by him in accordance with the established rates;
one year's interest on all funds, notes, and subscriptions now
in possession of the College; and one year's interest on all
funds which may come into possession of the College by
solicitation or otherwise during the college year, said interest to be collected by said President under the direction of
the Board; Provided, that this resolution shall not deprive
the Board of its full amount of general supervision of the
management and accounts of the College."

Under this arrangement Mr. Atwater served his second
year as President of the College. This arrangement while,
perhaps, the best that could be made at the time, was not
satisfactory to either party. President Atwater was continually oppressed by the financial condition of the institution, making it impossible for him to meet satisfactorily the
obligations he had assumed. Besides, it appeared to the
Board of Trustees and many friends of the College that
Mr. Atwater's administration was not up to the standard

of a College administration. All recognized the difficulties incident to the change of rank of the institution. There were great obstacles in the way of changing academic methods to those which should characterize a college. The man had not yet been found who was able to add to the name of the College the dignity and influence which a college ought to possess. Mr. Atwater in the class room was a teacher of superior ability; before the world he bore an exalted character; and in earnestness of purpose and in the conscientious discharge of every duty, as he saw it, he was without a flaw. But he could not, with his limitations, create of the School anything superior to the Eclectic Institute of which he had been the successful Principal.

The Board of Trustees realized the situation as difficult and even critical. A change of some kind was demanded and must be made. Accordingly, on May 7, 1870, at a specially called meeting of the Board at which were present Alvah Udall, J. H. Rhodes, A. Teachout, James A Garfield, J. F. Whitney, Hartwell Ryder, C. B. Lockwood, and Harmon Austin, the following resolution by Mr. Lockwood was adopted:—"*Resolved,* That we deem it expedient to employ President J. M. Atwater and Professor B. A. Hinsdale to organize and employ a Faculty to take charge of the College the ensuing year in accordance with their proposition to take the same for two thousand ($2,000) dollars and tuition receipts, provided at our next meeting it appears that the funds can be raised."

At the annual meeting of the Board held June 9, 1870, the contract was concluded with J. M. Atwater and B. A. Hinsdale on the following terms:—"That they organize and pay a competent Faculty, and pay all incidental expenses, on the condition that the Board guarantees to them the tuition receipts and fifteen hundred dollars for such service; and also guarantee to them one year's interest on all endowment fund they may raise during the year." Alvah Udall, A. J. Squire, and Hartwell Ryder were made an Advisory Committee of the Board in the organization of the Faculty. It was also *"Resolved,* That in this arrangement J. M. Atwater be President, and B. A. Hinsdale, Vice President, and that *each be endowed with equal and coextensive authority* in the management of the College."

At the same meeting the Board passed the following resolution in favor of Mr. W. J. Ford, who had made a report as Solicitor of the Western Reserve Eclectic Institute and Hiram College. A committee had examined his report of work and results and recommended the resolution. *"Resolved,* That W. J. Ford has served with fidelity and unusual success the Eclectic Institute and Hiram College, and is entitled to the gratitude of the Board of Trustees, the Stockholders, and all friends of the College for the industry, perseverence, and ability with which for a period of twelve years he has performed the duties of Solicitor for the Western Reserve Eclectic Institute and Hiram College."

Thanks to W. J. Ford as Solicitor.

The double-headed arrangement by which J. M. Atwater and B. A. Hinsdale were "endowed with equal and co-extensive authority in the management of the College" was of short life. July 1, 1870, the Board of Trustees met at the call of President Udall, and received the resignation of President Atwater, which was immediately accepted. It was then *"Resolved,* That B. A. Hinsdale be elected permanent President of Hiram College." The vote was taken by ayes and nays, and resulted in a unanimous choice, the following Trustees being present and voting:—James A. Garfield, Harmon Austin, Hartwell Ryder, John F. Whitney, Alvah Udall, and C. B. Lockwood.

Mr. Hinsdale was notified of his election and appeared before the Board and announced his acceptance of the position in an appropriate speech. At the same meeting the committee appointed previously to secure a Financial Agent for the College "was authorized and directed to employ Elder Lathrop Cooley to sell scholarships at one hundred dollars each for a period not to exceed eight years; and that he be authorized to solicit other amounts according to such methods as said committee may direct; provided that not more than twenty per cent shall be paid for the whole cost of any such solicitations and collections." Thus began Mr. Cooley's work for the College which has extended with more or less continuity of service, over many years, even down to the present time. Mr. Cooley made a very efficient and successful Financial Agent for the College. Until 1880 his name was published annually in the catalogue as Financial Agent.

Lathrop Cooley as Financial Agent.

While the administration of President Atwater had not been as successful as many had hoped that it might be, it had developed some facts which have been found essential to the perpetuity, strength, and growth of the College. For three years it had been uncertain whether this one or that one would remain beyond a year at the head of the Institution. Everything was uncertain and temporary. No one had encouragement to do his best or could do his best. But the Board determined that the Financial Agent should have such a tenure of office that he could put into execution plans for raising funds which would require years to mature. It was also determined that the Presidency should not be subject to an annual change; and so they elected Mr. Hinsdale "permanent President of Hiram College."

Close of J. M. Atwater's Administration.

A foundation was laid for an "Endowment Fund" during this period. Mr. Ford had succeeded in getting numerous small sums in various quarters, and one large sum from Mr. Robert Kerr, of Marion, O. July 29, 1867, Mr. Kerr signed a contract to give "fifty thousand dollars to endow a Chair in Hiram College." This amount was somewhat reduced before it was finally paid, by a compromise with the Board of Trustees; but a sufficient sum was realized from it to establish the "Kerr Chair of Natural Science" now and for many years occupied by Professor George H. Colton. Small sums were also realized from bequests that had been made to the College. The endowment of Hiram College has been a matter of slow growth from this small beginning to its present creditable proportions.

An Endowment Fund.

When the institution opened as a College in 1857 some changes in the Literary Societies were made. The Hesperian and Olive Branch Societies joined in a petition to the Faculty for a union society, giving their reasons why such a society would be beneficial. The name of Sutton E. Young heads the Hesperian list, and the name of Alice Robinson the Olive Branch list. After careful consideration the Faculty unanimously decided not to grant the petition.

The Literary Societies.

On March 18, 1868, the Faculty considered a request by A. A. Amidon, and G. E. Barber, representing the College students, for the organization of a distinct College society. The Faculty was a unit in favor of "distinct College and preparatory societies," and gave good reasons why such a society should be established in the College. The name Alpha Delta was finally agreed to and the sentiment

"Let mind rule" adopted as a motto. In 1870, February 17, the society was chartered and M. P. Hayden, T. A. Snow, and E. M. Wilson were chosen trustees. The society was strong and vigorous from the beginning. May 16, 1871, a contract was made between the society and the Board of Trustees "transferring the College library to the society." This society admitted ladies who were College students to membership under certain restrictions. August 21, 1873, the Faculty "after much observation and reflection, reached the conclusion that there should be two, and only two gentlemen's societies in the College," and proposed that the Alpha Delta should "close up its business, dispose of its property, and adjourn *sine die,* leaving the ground to the two old societies." The society considered the advice of the Faculty and August 22, 1873, proceeded to "take steps towards closing up its business," and when the proper adjustment had been made and the property of the society properly distributed, the society was closed. It had had an honorable life but the College conditions would not justify its continuance and it left the field to the old societies.

The life and spirit as well as the method of the "Old Eclectic" could not die at once. It lived on after the form of the Eclectic Institute had passed away, and was plainly discernable in the initial years of Hiram College. The free and unconventional character of the Eclectic did not die instantly with the change of name, and rank. It was desirable to preserve its spirit and at the same time to adjust it to the new forces of education that were beginning to display themselves, and to conform it to the requirements that its new name implied. During its first three years the College kept close to the habits of the old school. Its first Presidents did

The
Life and Spirit
of the
Eclectic Institute
in the College.

all they could under the conditions that prevailed, but a change was needed and a change was made, and a new administration provided.

CHAPTER VI.

HIRAM COLLEGE—B. A. HINSDALE'S ADMINISTRATION.
1870-1882.

July 1, 1870, B. A. Hinsdale, by resolution of the Board of Trustees, was elected "permanent President of Hiram College." Before this time the idea of permanence of administration does not appear to have been before the Trustees in the selection of a President, and an annual election had been an almost established rule. The financial condition of the Institution had made it impossible to secure and retain a President who had already won a place in the world of letters and as an administrator of College interests.

B. A. Hinsdale the Third President.

While literature and science were to have a proper place in its Course of Study, the special purpose of the Eclectic Institute was to be by charter stipulation "instruction in moral science as based on the facts and precepts of the Holy Scriptures;" and this was the distinguishing feature of the Eclectic Institute to its close. But with the change of name from Institute to College, and change of rank from an academy of high degree to an institution with college promises and college ambitions, other changes became necessary. If it was to be a College it must have a college character, a college position, a college curriculum, and a college dignity. To attain to this distinction, it will not seem strange to those who give the matter intelligent thought, that for a time, at least, the distinctly theological or Biblical character of the school should take a secondary place and the secular and classical be exalted to the first; and so, while morals, religion and Bible study were

Mr. Hinsdale's Great Purpose.

by no means forgotten or ignored, the great work of the President during the administration now being considered was to bring the Institution into the fulness of a College, and gain for it a recognition in the educational world.

When Mr. Hinsdale entered upon his work as President of Hiram College he was without experience in the administration of college affairs. He had been a member of the Faculty during the last year of President Atwater's administration, and previously had served a year as Professor in Alliance College under President Errett; he had taught country schools and conducted select schools in country places; but he had never been entrusted before with the heavy responsibilities of a College President.

He brought, however, to his position a knowledge of Hiram second to none. He entered the Eclectic Institute

Some of Mr. Hinsdale's Characteristics.

in 1853 as a student and as a student and teacher he had spent in Hiram a large number of the intervening years. He was well acquainted with the habits, the surroundings, the financial condition, and the influences that had controlled the school from the beginning. He was thirty-three years of age and possessed a strong physical body which was capable of hard work and long endurance. He had a sensitive conscience, and truth and faithfulness were the girdle of his reins. He had been an unwearied searcher after knowledge from his youth and the reasons for things he demanded at every step of his progress. While he was a man of faith yet in large degree, his faith rested on facts which he, by investigation, had been able to discover. His mind was of a logical cast, clear, distinct, and decisive, and his findings were stated with the authority of a judge whose judgments will not allow dispute. All subjects that concerned men were interesting to him, some of more interest than others, and a few of transcendent importance; but in their consideration he took the "pedagogical view" rather than that of the declaimer, the orator or the rhetorician. He was a tireless searcher for the foundations, the sources of things, and he never attempted to build the superstructure until he felt sure that the foundation was solid. In a word, he had the genius and instincts of an educator. There are minds to which environment gives a set from which they never turn:—there are others whose reaction is more powerful than any direct forces that play upon them. The environments of the Eclectic Institute had a strong influence over Mr. Hinsdale but with his cast of mind and temperament they could not absorb him. Hence the changes he inaugurated in the management, the discipline, the curriculum, and the special culture for which he believed the college should stand. For twelve years, "sometimes in gloom and thick darkness," he strove to reach the ideal which was before him when he accepted the President's chair. No one acquainted with the financial condition of the College when Mr. Hinsdale became President, and onward in his administration, will ever accuse him as one controlled by a mercenary spirit. He cared but little for money, but his soul was wedded to an ideal of education which in every possible way he determined to realize both as a personal possession and as a "garment of praise" for the college over which he presided.

*His recent death, in the midst of his mature years and usefulness, will give an added interest to the following biographical sketch of his life and work.

---

*At Atlanta, Ga., Nov. 29, 1900.

Burke Aaron Hinsdale was born in Wadsworth, Ohio, March 31, 1837. His father, Albert Hinsdale, was born in Torrington, Connecticut, July 18, 1809; his mother, Clarinda Elvira Eyles, was born in Ohio July 12, 1815. Both of his parents were of good New England stock.

Biographical Sketch of President Hinsdale

He grew to young manhood on his father's farm in Wadsworth. His home training was all that a Christian father and mother could give him. His school privileges until he came to Hiram were no better than those afforded to other young men of his locality, in the old-fashioned district-school. Physically he inherited a sound body without grace or comeliness, but of good fiber and capable of enduring immense strain. His mother "was possessed of good judgment, very ready to make up her mind, which was not easily turned, and very apt to carry out her purposes." From her he inherited that imperious will that was one of his distinctly marked characteristics.

He was naturally of a studious temperament and usually preferred to read and study than to play in the intervals between the work in the fields and the time for rest and sleep at night. It was a rare thing in his boyhood to see him without a book in his hands during these intervals. His favorite books were history, and those bearing on the philosophy of mind. The strongest faculties of his mind were the perceptive, the reflective, and the logical. It has been said of the scholars of Greece in Alexandrian times that "they were not creative, but rather reflective. They did not produce great masterpieces of poetry or art, nor did they devise new systems of philosophy. They were scholars and critics rather than original makers. They were students and codifiers. They gathered together the wisdom of their forefathers. This they transmitted to posterity." This describes very accurately the character of the product of Mr. Hinsdale's mind. His perceptions were so keen and vivid that he saw clearly what was dimly seen or altogether unseen by others. His powers of reflection enabled him to bring forth lessons of great value from hitherto undiscovered places. And his strong logical faculty enabled him to raise from these discoveries a building not only massive but often beautiful. He came to Hiram on November 21, 1853, and entered as a student on that day. Describing that coming himself, he says:—"I was a big boy, awkward and uncultured enough, with the smell of the furrow upon my garments; but I knew a thing or two, and my mind had opened enough to appreciate what I heard to the full." Until 1861, for the most of the time, he was a student in the Western Reserve Eclectic Institute, leaving Hiram to work on the farm or teach a district school at irregular intervals. In 1861 he was chosen as one of the assistant teachers in the Eclectic Institute; in 1862 his name appears as a full-fledged teacher in the English Department. This position he held until 1864. From this date he does not appear again in Hiram circles until he appears as Professor of History, English Literature, and Political Science, in 1869-1870, the last year of President Atwater's administration. During that year he was elected President of Hiram College, which position he held for twelve successive years. Between the years 1864 and 1869 he devoted himself mainly to preaching. He began to preach in 1862. He united with the Church of Christ, in Hiram, in the winter of 1853-'54 under the preaching of A. S. Hayden, then Principal of the Eclectic Institute. He preached quite regularly for churches during the years 1862-1868, remaining longest with the Disciple churches at Solon, O., and Franklin Avenue Church in Cleveland, and Hiram. He never entirely left the pulpit, though from the time he entered Hiram as President until the close of his life, with the exception of Hiram, he had no regular appointments. Mr. Hinsdale was not a popular preacher. His style of delivery and the minuteness of his analysis of a Biblical theme were not attractive to the most of people. His sermons were always strong and filled with robust thought, and many heard him gladly and with great profit, but it cannot be said of him as was said of his Master, "the common people heard him gladly." His social faculties were not as strongly marked as his intellectual, and yet to many he revealed a strong sympathy and a tender heart. To those whom he accepted as his friends he revealed himself with the cordiality of a great heart and in truest friendship. In his family he was a loving son and brother, husband and father. In June, 1877, in his address to the graduating class at Hiram he related an incident in his life which no one can read without moist eyes and which revealed the tenderness of his love. He said:—

"Not many months ago I hugged a tree. Pardon the egotism that recites how it was.

"It was night, and I was approaching the old home. I was hurrying to one whose bedside I shall never approach again until I lie beside her in the churchyard. Turning into the woods on the left, and eagerly pushing onward by an old path, I found myself in a large open field. A flock of quails rising out of the rank clover flew away into the darkness. Passing by a tree over whose roots I had often tossed the plow in my boyhood, I went up to it, put my arms around it, and hugged it with genuine friendship. I looked down upon the ground; I looked up to the stars; I turned my ear to the silent farm-house to catch, perhaps, the sound of human voice, or even of baying dog or lowing herd; and, as there rushed across my mind the flood of thronging memories, the fountains of feeling were broken up and welled forth in tears."

It is quite possible that there is room for a difference of

judgment among those who were brought into contact with Mr. Hinsdale in their estimate of him as a preacher, of his social qualities, and his religious influence; but there can be no dispute as to his eminence as an educator. This became at last the chosen field for his intellectual enginery and the field whereon he fairly won a place among the very best. To so great a height did he rise in this field that it may rightfully be claimed for him that but few were his equals and none his superiors among American educators. Whatever limitations there were in other departments of his life, in this department there seemed to be no limitations, save those of time and opportunity. His career as an educator began when he became President of Hiram College. The manner in which he handled the educational interests of the College brought him into prominence among the teachers, and friends of higher education in Ohio, and he was called on far and near for addresses to Councils of teachers, Associations of educators, and Associations of preachers before whom he stood in the exalted character of a pedagogue. During this period he was a large contributor to the volume of religious literature. He wrote largely for the Christian Standard of which Isaac Errett was editor, and for the Christian Quarterly conducted by Wm. T. Moore. He never ceased to be a valuable contributor to the religious journals published by the Disciples of Christ, though in his later years he confined his literary contributions to the Christian Evangelist, and these contributions were mostly of a pedagogical character. He was a pamphleteer of unusual fecundity. A large part of his public addresses biographical, historical or literary were issued in this form, and he was prodigal in his distribution of them among his appreciative friends.

His earliest books were on religious subjects. His first

book on "The Genuineness and Authenticity of the Gospels" was published in 1872. This was followed in 1878 by "The Jewish Christian Church," and in 1879 by "Ecclesiastical Tradition." In 1880 he prepared at the request of Mr. Garfield and the Republican National Committee, "The Republican Text Book for the Campaign of 1880." In 1881 he published the Hiram College Memorial, "President Garfield and Education." In 1882 he edited very satisfactorily "The Works of James Abram Garfield." Other books published by him after he left Hiram are "History and Civil Government of Ohio;" "The American Government;" "Schools and Studies;" "Training for Citizenship and Suggestions for the Teaching of Civics;" "The Old Northwest" in 1888; "Jesus as a Teacher;" "How to Study and Teach History;" "Teaching the Language Arts;" "Studies in Education;" "Horace Mann and the Common School Revival in the United States;" and "The Art of Study" in 1900 his latest volume. He was also preparing an elaborate History of the University of Michigan for the great series of college histories called "Universities and Their Sons" which was not completed at the time of his death.

On leaving Hiram College he was elected Superintendent of Public Schools in Cleveland, O., which position he held from 1882 to 1886. In 1888 he was elected to the Chair of the Science and Art of Teaching in the University of Michigan which place he held to the close of his life. He was a member in high repute of educational associations both State and National, and served as President of many of them.

He received numerous literary degrees from colleges and universities though in the regular course he was not the graduate of any. Bethany and Williams Colleges conferred on him the Degree of A. M.,; Ohio State University

COLLEGE FACULTY IN 1900.

the Degree of Ph. D.; Ohio University and Hiram College conferred on him the Degree of LL. D. One of the last acts of the Trustees of Hiram College in recognition of his high standing and worthy life was at its June session in 1900 to confer this degree, only conferred on two or three others in its entire history, as a College; and one of the last addresses of Mr. Hinsdale before his work was done was to recall the memories of the Eclectic Institute which gave him an impulse and helped him to reach the height on which he had long stood a worthy man, a good citizen, and an accomplished scholar and distinguished teacher of his fellowmen. No one who heard his address at Hiram June 22, 1900, will ever forget it. As he spoke of the comrades of the early Hiram fellowship who had recently crossed to the "other side," his voice had a tenderness of tone that revealed his heart, and his words a pathos that lingers like a benediction from a loving father who is about to depart on a journey from whence he will not return. How beautiful are these words descriptive of Hiram scenery: "Seeing is believing; and with all the changes that time has wrought, the landscape is still the same. The woodlands have become fewer and smaller in area, while the fields have expanded; but then, as now, verdure clothed the hills and the valleys in the spring time, while the chestnuts yellowed, the oaks and ashes browned, the sassafras and the pepperidges reddened, and the maples burst into scarlet and gold, as they have done in the autumn for fifty succeeding years. The whippoorwill sang in the woodside at evening then as he sings now." Others have done much to make Hiram what it is today and without their help it could not have been, and it would not be what it is; but take the Institution as it was in 1870, it is not to the disparagement of any others to say that Hiram College owes more to B. A. Hinsdale for its high rank as an Educational Institution than to any other man. To this end he bent his life and he succeeded; and the history of Hiram will never get old or mean, so long as the impulses which he generated in her behalf, and the machinery of which he was a controlling force, remain. His death November 29, 1900, was a shock to all of his friends and co-laborers in church and school, not many of whom had even heard of his sickness.

President Hinsdale's first Faculty. The first Faculty that President Hinsdale gathered about him was a strong one. Isaac N. Demmon was Professor of the Greek and Latin Languages and Literatures. He is now a distinguished Professor in the University of Michigan at Ann Arbor.

Isaac Newton Demmon was born in Northfield, Summit County, O., August 19, 1842. He was the oldest of a **Isaac N. Demmon.** family of nine children. His father, Leonard Demmon, was a native of Massachusetts. In 1884 the family removed to Noble County, Indiana, and settled near the present village of Kendallville.

Isaac acquired the rudiments of education at home, learning to read, write, and cipher before there was any school opened within his reach. When he was seven years old a district school was established near his home which he attended. At the age of eleven he was sent to a "select school" at Kendallville. For several years he attended this village school, and for several more he taught district schools in the vicinity of his home.

At the age of 21 he matriculated at the North-Western Christian University, now Butler College, at Irvington, Indiana. In 1864 he enlisted in the Union Army and went with his company to Stephenson, Alabama. In 1865 he entered the University of Michigan and graduated with the class of 1868. That class consisted of 54 men and was the largest and one of the strongest ever graduated up to that time. In the fall of 1868 he was elected to the professorship of Greek in Alliance College where he served two years with Dr. Isaac Errett, President, and Professor A. R. Benton of Butler College, B. A. Hinsdale and others. In 1870 he accepted the chair of Ancient Languages in Hiram College under President Hinsdale.

In 1872-'73 he was an instructor of Mathematics in the University of Michigan. The three following years he was Principal of the Ann Arbor High School. In 1876 he was again in the University as Assistant Professor of English Language and Literature, and History. On the resignation of Prof. M. C. Tyler in 1881 Prof. Demmon succeeded to the vacant chair, which he has since held with the title of Professor of English and Rhetoric. For this important chair he has a peculiar fitness. His range of study has been broad, and his experience as a teacher varied. "He has the literary sense, justness of perception, catholic appreciation, correctness of taste, and a sympathetic power of interpreting authors of very divergent qualities."

He has received academic degrees: A. B., University of Michigan, 1868 A. M., (ibed) 1871; and LL. D., University of Nashville, 1896. He is a man of high character, a genial companion, a scholar in the first rank, an able professor, and an accomplished teacher. His stay in Hiram was brief but honorable; and the paragraph which he fills in Hiram history is bright with the foregleams of the great success which now crowns and adorns his life.

Wilson S. Atkinson was Professor of Mathematics and Astronomy. He was a strong man in his department but failing health compelled his retirement in 1875. On receiv-

Wilson S.
Atkinson.

ing his resignation the Board of Trustees *"Resolved*, That we accept with sincere regret the resignation of Professor W. S. Atkinson, an act to which he has been reluctantly brought by the protracted prostration of his health; that during his occupancy for the period of four years, of the Chair of Mathematics and Astronomy, to the full satisfaction of the Board, he has proved himself in all respects an instructor and a disciplinarian in his department, of superior skill and ability, and, also, a gentleman, who has secured for himself our sincerest respect; that we deeply sympathize with him in the continued frailty of his health, in the disappointment of the cherished purposes of his life, and also with his family in their present trying situation; that this action of the Board be communicated to Professor Atkinson, and entered on our records."

Edmund B. Wakefield was Professor of Natural Sciences. The entrance of Professor Wakefield into this Faculty was the beginning of his distinguished career as an

Edmund B.
Wakefield.

educator. In 1873 he resigned from the Faculty and for a number of years devoted himself to preaching and pastoral work. In this field he achieved distinction and success. In 1890 he was elected to the chair of Political Science and Biblical Theology and still holds a high place in the Faculty of Hiram College. Of a genial temperament and easily approachable, a virile thinker, a courteous gentleman, with a dignity before students and people that always commands respect, he is a favorite with all.

Osmer C. Hill.

Osmer C. Hill was Principal of the Commercial and Chirographic Departments.

A. J. Squire.

A. J. Squire, M. D., was Lecturer on Chemistry and Physiology.

Miss Ellen Jackson.   Miss Ellen Jackson was the Principal of the Ladies' Department.

Orlo C. Hubbell taught German, Grove E. Barber taught Latin, Sutton E. Young in the English Department, George H. Colton in the Scientific Department, and Mrs. J. C. Ellis was teacher of Instrumental Music.

In 1872 the Faculty was somewhat changed. Teachers Barber, Young and Colton dropped out and Mrs. Marietta Cuscaden succeeded Miss Jackson as Principal of the Ladies' Department. The Board of Trus-

1872.   tees recognized the merit of these young men and placed on record "the thanks of the Board" for "the able and faithful manner in which they had discharged the duties of assistant teachers during the year;" and of Miss Jackson the Board said: "We tender to Miss Jackson our appreciation of the ability and devotion she has evinced in discharging the duties incident to her office, and of her character as a Christian lady."

1873.
Mrs. Mary E. Hinsdale.   In 1873 Orlo C. Hubbell was succeeded by Mrs. Mary E. Hinsdale as teacher of German.

1874.
George H. Colton.   In 1874 Professor Wakefield was succeeded in the Chair of the Natural Sciences by George H. Colton, a chair he has filled with eminent ability to the present time.

Professor Colton was born in Nelson, Portage County, O., October 10, 1848. His parentage was of good New England stock. His boyhood years were spent on the farm, where he was a close observer of the habits and characteristics of plants and animals. Outside of his home his education began in the "old fashioned district school" where the scholars were never graded or grouped, and where the teacher always "boarded around." From the district school he entered Nelson Academy, where he prepared himself to enter college. In the fall of 1867 he entered Hiram College. He graduated in 1871, receiving the Degree of B. S., and in course received the Master's Degree. In 1892 the Board conferred the Degree of Ph. D. on Professor Colton, *Magna Cum Laude*. After his graduation at Hiram he took a special course in civil engineering and science in the University of Michigan. In June, 1872, he was a member of the engineer corps of the Cuyahoga Valley Railroad, and aided in the location and construction of that line. In 1873 he was promoted to the position of Division Engineer, and had charge of a part of the road under construction. In the fall of 1873 he resigned his position to accept the chair of the Natural Sciences in Hiram College, a position he has held continuously ever since. In 1883 he was elected Treasurer of Hiram College, a position he has held with eminent ability to the present time. In 1886 when the main building was enlarged he had charge of the funds and "so satisfactorily did he perform his duties, that the building committee, in token of their appreciation, presented to him a handsome gold watch and chain."

In his department Professor Colton is a superior teacher. He bears an honorable character, and his genial and even temper, and his marked mental ability, and his wide knowledge of men and subjects for study, make him not only a professor of the first rank but also, a desirable companion.

1875.

In 1875 there were no changes in the Faculty.

1876.
Colman Bancroft.
Mrs. Phoebe B.
Clapp.

In the catalogue of 1876 there were several changes. Professor Atkinson was succeeded by Colman Bancroft as Professor of Mathematics and Astronomy, and Mrs. Phoebe B. Clapp took the place of Professor Hill as teacher of penmanship.

Professor Bancroft began his service in Hiram College in the fall of 1875 and with the single interruption of 1879 to 1881 he has served continuously to the present time. He

Professor Bancroft.

was born in Cattaraugus County, State of New York, in 1843, and spent his early years on a farm. When he was twelve years old he attended the Academy at Rushford, New York, and afterward, Pike Seminary in the same state. In 1865 he entered the University of Michigan where he graduated with the class of 1869. In addition to his course at the University he did extra work in French, Italian, Chemistry and Mathematics. In 1870 he was Principal of the High School at La Porte, Indiana. In 1871 he was Professor in Alliance College and remained in that Institution until its doors were closed. In 1875 he came to Hiram where he still remains. He has always held a high rank in the Faculty of Hiram College. He is thoroughly equipped for his work and in his class room everything is thorough and systematic. He is a man of many accomplishments, and not least among them are the adornments of his Christian character, modesty, sincerity, integrity and intelligence.

1877.
Miss Lillie M. Stow.

In 1877 Dr. A. J. Squire retired from the Faculty and Miss Lillie M. Stow took the place of Mrs. J. C. Ellis as teacher of Instrumental Music for a year.

1878.
Arthur C. Pierson.

In 1878 the name of Arthur C. Pierson appears as Teacher of English Studies, dropping out in 1879 and re-appearing in 1880.

Arthur Chester Pierson was born in Keosauqua, Iowa, May 20, 1852, and died in Ravenna, Ohio, June 15, 1900.

At the time of his death he was Professor of English Literature and Psychology in Hiram College, and for the first time in its history his death broke the active teaching force of the college. He had also begun the writing of the History of the College of which his own memorial sketch is now a part. On the day of his burial Prof. E. B. Wakefield, his associate in the Faculty and a life-long friend pronounced the memorial discourse. He so accurately voiced the facts in regard to Prof. Pierson that what he said in large part forms the body of this sketch:

Sketch of Arthur Chester Pierson.

For the first time in its history has the active teaching force of Hiram College been broken in upon by death. And the first stroke has fallen well to the center of the group. What the passing of this life meant to those who have so long shared in its anxious toils and its inspiring hopes, I have no words to tell. Arthur C. Pierson was born in Keosauqua, Ia., May 20, 1852. While he was an infant his parents removed to the Pacific coast. Of his life here, especially of his later years in San Francisco, he had vivid memories, as those who have read his occasional sketches, or listened to his lecture on "The Golden Gate," will well remember.

At the age of thirteen he was left an orphan, homeless, penniless, almost friendless, in a land at that time very far off. But a kind Providence brought him to the home of an uncle in York County, Pa. In later years he expressed gratitude for this passage of his life. He toiled on a farm, he acquired a love for its homely and substantial virtues which he never got over; he felt as many another has, that no other home introduces one so well to the fundamental and unperverted facts that concern our human existence.

In early manhood young Pierson found himself a student and a graduate of the Normal School at Ada, O. He heard the preaching of the gospel under William Dowling (whose memory he always tenderly revered), and the result of that preaching was natural, and, of course, far-reaching. Henceforth his Christian faith was the main fact, and

the great shaping force of his life. Early in 1876 he came
to Hiram, and in 1879 he was graduated. From the first he
loved the college; he found associations such as he was hungry for; he wished them never to be broken off. And now
his wish is gratified. They never will be broken. For three
years after graduation he was a tutor in the college. Then
he was made a full professor in the chair of rhetoric and
English literature; and this place, excepting one year's absence on leave, he filled until he bade farewell to all of
earth.

In reviewing the past twenty years of this life, one is
struck with the prodigious amount of work that he has done.
He has taught incessantly in the classroom; he has preached,
as a rule, every Sunday; he has held meetings, and assisted
in teachers' institutes, and delivered lectures and addresses
of various character, almost without number. Besides all
this, he has written extensively, and in his writing he displayed such aptness and real ability that we mourn today,
and can scarce be comforted, that the limitations of life for-
bade his ever showing his full power to the world.

No man connected with the college has ever done so
much work in the region that immediately environs us. He
has carried the loftiest ideals of life, in their best forms of
expression, into scores and scores of communities. Men
have long said he was an "exceedingly valuable man." But
how valuable he was will be better understood now, when
we try to fill the place where he stood so long. And this
leads me to say that there are some people in the world that
can readily be spared; there are plenty to fill their places.
The man who fills high place in state may fall, and a thous-
and aspirants, with all their partisans, will mourn only in
public. The man who sits environed with wealth may depart, and the world be as well off, and his successors be glad.
But when a man who is inspired and compensated from his
own heart, has carried light where there was darkness, and
comfort where there was sorrow, and made his life a living
sacrifice—when such a man is called away, the world misses
him; and for him remains the sweetest incense earth can
pay—the holy tears of grieving gratitude.

One of the most striking features of Professor Pierson's life was his generosity; perhaps I had better say, his unselfishness. He gave away of his time and money up to his ability, and sometimes beyond. In the college no professor was so ready to take on extra work. Indeed, sometimes it seemed impossible to load him down. If called to outside work, it was always understood that, if possible, he would say "Yes." When sometimes an appointment came due when he was overwhelmed with work, he would declare that he never would make such a promise again. But he would—the very first time that another call came!

And here we have the end of it! Aged forty-eight, in the very prime of a splendid manhood, and he is gone. He literally gave his life away. But, after all, amid all our grief, I don't know as we should have it changed.

In intellectual life one of his weak points was closely allied to a strong one. He had a name for being absent-minded; and while there have been joking exaggerations, there was a good measure of truth in it. But his absent-mindedness never came from vacancy of mind. He had great power of abstraction, and he would lose himself—sometimes inopportunely, of course—in a train of absorbing thought. But when his abstraction met the occasion, it gave him great power. His teaching was not equal, but when he could readily give himself to the subject he taught with surpassing excellence. In his sermons, when he really lost himself in his theme, he would often clothe lofty and symmetrical thought with a beauty of expression that few can attain to. I have often thought that his mind showed itself most truly in his prayers. Bowing in the presence of the Invisible with him compelled abstraction, and often there was a child-like devotion and a beauty of diction that concealed its very excellence by its excellence.

As a preacher, Professor Pierson was not given to doctrinal argument, nor was he famed for exhortation; although he knew sound doctrine, and on occasion could make effective appeals. But he was good at drawing lessons from the Bible and applying them to life. His preaching was, in the nobler sense, rational and practical. He had no art for making compromises, and he could never try to be sensational. But every community loved to hear him preach, and churches usually built up under his ministry, even if he was only a "Sunday pastor."

One secret of his strength in the ministry I am sure is not fully understood. He had a faith in Christ and his gospel that was really as childlike and unquestioning as I have ever known. Doubt seemed utterly foreign to his nature, and the great characters of the Bible were living verities to him. And right here let me say that he was a most guileless man. To conceive of him engaging in any plot to injure another, or to get underhand gain, would be to think the unthinkable. If he had ever anger or ill will toward another, he could not hold it. It would evaporate like dew when the summer sun has risen, and leave no more trace behind. I have heard him mourn over the limitations of his life, and his failure to realize his ideals, but I never heard him speak bitterly of any one, or disclose anything like malice rankling in his heart.

He was a good companion to have wholly to one's self. He was greatly at home in the whole range of English literature; and, when really aroused, it surprised one to find what extensive passages of it he had at his command. When some happy theme was struck, even if wandering in leafy groves far from all books, you might hear "readings from the authors" till it almost seemed that memory was inspired. Of late his mind has greatly centered on the history of the college which he was appointed to write. As he worked upon it, it seemed as though the dreams of earlier days had come back. He would do at length a work with solid literary merit; he hoped, he said, to make it a monument to his memory. Alas! it stands like many another fondly cherished plan—a broken shaft above a grave.

But of all themes that to which his mind would most surely turn concerned the Christian faith. The burden of churches was always upon him, and he thought unceasingly upon their welfare. He studied with sincere concern the great struggle that goes on to establish or destroy the kingdom of God on earth. To him, he once said, the struggle to make the faith in Christ triumphant, was like the struggle of the patriot to save his country—his home and altar and heart and hope, were all dependent on it. His convictions were deep, and they held with remarkable firmness. There might be waves on the surface, but his soul had depths where changeful storms had small effect and wrathful billows never rolled.

There are some lives that face so many adversities, and move on against such cruel headwinds, that the whole voyage grows heroic and pathetic. No gilded caraval, no flowery beds of ease, bore this life. Alone, through years of utter poverty, the boy fought his own way to cultured manhood. His married life was broken by death, and long sickness and death again. Through years of heart-breaking burden he still went with high purpose on. And he has fallen still in the front of life's battle, with his face full front to duty. His life honors all who walked beside him. To his stricken wife and his orphaned children he has left the best heritage a man ever leaves—a name unsullied by dishonor, and a memory dearly loved.

His last hours were a fitting and natural close to the life he had lived. Through bitter pain he was called suddenly to face the ending of every earthly hope, and every fond and familiar association. And he was not dismayed, he was not unmanned, he was all himself. He calmly arranged his earthly affairs. He said he had the dread of dissolution and separation from friends natural to man, and yet he did not fear to die. And then

"Beyond our voice and sight
He drifted out."

O my brother! It dazes my brain and rends my heart to speak these words over your cold form. And yet it comforts me. We have sometimes talked of what the passage from this life to the other meant. In higher or in lower sense we found no vision of the great transition. But we did trust, in the "vague beyond," to find One who once walked lovingly with men; and on that hope we rested. Now you behold with open vision, and we, too, shall soon behold what you beheld.

In our chapel, not long ago, in speaking of the death of one of our former teachers, he quoted a passage from the poet, wherein the death of a good man is likened to the going down of the sun. As, when the sun has gone, the golden sunset lingers, so the departing life leaves golden memories gleaming in the westward sky. But the clouds are golden because the sun still shines. Indeed, it seems to me utterly true that moral goodness and love do not belong to things that die. Our friend has gone from our sight, but love grown more tender, and memories hallowed, linger; and that they linger is assurance that in immortal scenes, beneath a fairer sky, he still lives on.

We lay down such a life as this as soldiers do their dead upon the hard-fought battlefield—with a proud sorrow and exultant grief. We miss our comrade, but he fought well. He was wounded in the conflict, but he stood fast to the end, and did not falter. The march was long and rough, and his feet grew weary, but he finished it. Clouds rolled until the way was dark sometimes, but he kept his faith. Now the march and the battle are all over, and the crowning time has come. It is death that sets the seal to victory in life. If truth and honor and pure fidelity be kept until this hour, they are kept forever.

And so today, like Evangeline—only with far more reason, after all the faithful years, in view of all we have had and all that we hold—we can clasp our dead to our hearts, and say, "Father, we thank thee."

1879.
C. D. Hubbell.
Alpha A. Boynton.
Louis C. Force.

In 1879 C. D. Hubbell and Miss Alpha A. Boynton were teachers of English Studies, and Louis C. Force a special teacher of Elocution.

1880.
Miss Mary B. Jewett.
Fred A. Niles.
H. M. Stone.

In 1880 Miss Mary B. Jewett became Principal of the Ladies Department, and Professor of Modern Languages; Fred A. Niles was teacher of Penmanship and Bookkeeping; and H. M. Stone was teacher of English Studies.

1881.
George A. Peckham.
Charles F. Schovanek.

In 1881 Charles F. Schovanek taught Penmanship and Bookkeeping, and George A. Peckham began his long service in the College as Professor of Mathematics and Astronomy.

George A. Peckham was born in Akron, O., July 17, 1851, and is the oldest of four children in his father's family. His father is a Connecticut Yankee, and his mother of the best of Pennsylvania stock, her ancestry embracing some of the best families of Holland. His first school experiences were in the public schools of his native city. He was naturally studious and his progress was rapid. He came to Hiram as a student in 1869, and began the study of Latin. The year 1870 he spent in Bethany College. At the opening of Buchtel College in 1872 he entered in its classical course and graduated in the class of 1875, in the meantime doing a year of extra work in both Latin and Greek. He remained after his graduation, for two years as a teacher in Buchtel.

November 1, 1877, he was ordained to the ministry and located with the Disciple Church in Granger, Medina County, O., where he remained for one year. In 1878 he accepted a call to the chair of Ancient Languages in Buchtel College, which place he held with rapidly growing distinction until he entered Hiram in 1880. Since his ordination in 1877 he has preached with more or less regularity to the present time. His sermons are scholarly and sound, but his throne is not the pulpit but the professor's chair. Here he is perfectly at ease and his will is imperious. He is a linguist of high rank having few equals and fewer superiors. He is a diligent student and a discriminating thinker. He makes no parade of his learning, but the sons of many countries could speak with him in their mother tongue, with ease and pleasure.

As a Christian man his character is unstained by fault or foible; as a friend he is honorable and faithful; and as a companion always cheerful and agreeable. At its June meeting in 1900 the Board of Trustees of Hiram College conferred on him the Degree of Doctor of Philosophy *Magna cum laude.*

1882.
Mahlon H. Wilson.
Anna M. Wing.

In 1882 Mahlon H. Wilson became teacher of Penmanship and Bookkeeping, and Anna M. Wing teacher of Instrumental Music.

Thus twenty-two different persons served in the Faculty of President Hinsdale during his administration of twelve years; but it will be observed that the changes were mainly in the subordinate departments of the College. The idea of permanency was being emphasized by the continuous service of those who were elected to professor's chairs. A College Faculty was being created that could not be changed except for extraordinary reasons. In his effort to secure this condition the President of the College had the cordial support of the Board of Trustees. At a meeting of the Board in May, 1871, the following resolution was adopted: "That the arrangement made by the Board with the present Faculty in July, 1870, be continued hereafter as a permanent arrangement for management and instruction in the College."

President Hinsdale on entering upon the presidency of Hiram College chose for his inaugural address "The Secularization of Learning," in which he stated with considerable emphasis what he considered necessary in a course of college study. This address can be found in full in the volume "Schools and Studies" which he issued in 1884. Only his analysis and summary are given here. After an extensive argument as to the relative value of the classics and the sciences for the purposes of liberal study he said: "Separate and apart from all arguments, we have here the best of reasons for includ-

President
Hinsdale's
Inaugural Address.

ing the classics in a liberal curriculum—they are the best breaking-in studies. At the same time they cover only a small part of the whole educational field. The mathematics, the sciences of nature and man, the modern languages, have each a place, and a place that the classics cannot fill. No wise educator will attempt to fit the modern mind to any single curriculum. My claim is that these languages and literatures are invaluable in their own place. They should, moreover, be studied according to modern methods and in the modern spirit, and should be combined with a judicious selection of other studies. At this point educational conservatism has already been compelled to yield ground, and to find room for studies that the mere classicist cannot bring himself rightly to value. Some of these studies may be set down in this place.

1—Such books of history and geography as will give a knowledge of the world of today.

2—More work should be done in political or governmental science. In Europe, where the citizen has but small share in the conducting of State affairs, it is not surprising that little or no attention should be paid to political science, save in its higher speculative phases; but in the United States, where the people govern, where at stated periods all political power returns to their hands, it is astonishing that the schools deal so little with the duties of citizenship. The result of this neglect is that a majority of our citizens are ignorant, not only of political science in general, but, what is worse, of the nature and working of our own political institutions. I am not now referring to such political education as can be gained from partisan newspapers or party platforms. I mean a well-grounded knowledge of the nature and history of our constitutions and laws. Above all, every American boy should be so familiar with American

EDWIN L. HALL, A.M.
LATIN.

GEORGE H. COLTON, A.M., Ph.D.
NATURAL SCIENCE.

EDMUND S. WAKEFIELD, A.M.
LAW.

GEORGE A. PEGRAM, A.M.
MODERN LANGUAGES.

COLMAN BANCROFT, M.S.
MATHEMATICS.

MARCIA HENRY, A.B.
ASS'T PROF. IN LATIN.

COLLEGE FACULTY IN 1900.

history as to be thoroughly alive with the American spirit.

3—Something more should be done for those studies which relate to the physical and spiritual nature of man,—those studies which together make up a science of humanity. Here we meet the sciences of anatomy and physiology upon the one hand, and those of mental and moral science upon the other. The last have indeed long been prominent; the others are now compelling a recognition.

4—Larger room should be found for our own incomparable English language and literature. I have spoken of various educational facilities and instruments to which the old scholars and teachers had no access. Here is one of them. Here is enough material to make a very thorough course of literary study,—poetry and oratory, history and philosophy, science and theology, wit and wisdom.

The extension of education has led to another demand which must be briefly considered, namely,—the demand for what is called 'practical education.' Now I approve of an education that is really practical, and I approve of no other. The merits of the question hinge on the meaning of the term. In popular estimation it means an education that is cheap, an education that is speedily obtained, an education that soon begins to put money in the pocket,—in a word, it means the 'bread and butter sciences,' and these taught in a hasty, superficial manner. That such a demand as this should exist is natural; it is the inevitable result of the attempt to educate the people. Education for the million means cheap education, for the million cannot afford any other; and, in the best sense, cheap education means poor, or at least, meagre, education. This is all very well understood. But the trouble comes in the attempt to make the popular standard the measure of higher education. French cannot be taught in twelve lessons, or Latin in two years;

nor can a decent collegiate education be furnished when the pupil is graduated in four years from the time that he leaves the common school or the academy. Whenever a college proposes to teach ten books of Homer in four or five months, it is safe to conclude that something is wrong; and when an institution of any sort proposes to give what is called a 'practical education,' and contemns the accepted methods of mental discipline, it is safe to conclude that its managers are more interested in getting the money of their pupils than in promoting their mental growth. The two great elements that enter into thorough mental training are time and application; and without these such training is impossible. An old Greek said: 'The gods sell everything for toil.' Bacon's test in philosophy is the only one to apply to education,—it is the test of utility, or of fruit. The popular talk about 'practical education,' save in the case of the million, is a piece of cant. All studies that develop mental power and put the student in possession of valuable knowledge, are practical, but the men who publish programmes and courses of instruction that fit boys and girls for the work of life over night are sciolists that ought not to be countenanced.

Finally, it may fairly be said that the secularizing of learning has brought up the question of woman's education. For this reason, as well as for the reason that this Institution is dedicated to co-education, I shall say a word or two about this question. Hitherto girls have been educated with too exclusive attention to 'their sphere.' There is no reason why girls should not have as broad, strong, and thorough a general training as boys; nor do I see any reason why, to a great extent, it should not be the same training. I do not indeed advise that as many girls as boys should take a classical course of study; but a girl has as

good a claim as a boy to high mental cultivation. At the
same time, her education should have a shaping towards the
place in nature and in society that God has assigned her.
There are some things that men may profitably know which
it is almost criminal for a woman not to know.   Many
topics lying in the field to which we are now brought are
tabooed in public discussion; but I may close with a quota-
tion from Mr. Herbert Spencer that suggests more than it
says: 'When a mother is mourning over a first-born that
has sunk under the sequelæ of scarlet fever; when, perhaps,
a candid medical man has confirmed her suspicion that her
child would have recovered had not its system been en-
feebled by over-study; when she is prostrate under the
pangs of combined grief and remorse,—it is but a small con-
solation that she can read Dante in the original.' "

The financial condition of the College during President
Hinsdale's administration was exceedingly stringent.   There
was but little income from endowment for there was but
little endowment, and the principal in-
The Financial   come was from the receipts from students
Condition.   for tuition.   The Board would not allow
any debts to accumulate and the receipts
from tuition were compelled to bear the burden of expenses.
The financial struggle in the College was not altogether peculiar for the country during this period passed through one
of the most terrific financial crises in its history.   The entire receipts of the College for the twelve years of President
Hinsdale's administration did not average over seven thous-
and dollars a year; and out of this every expense must be
paid.   As the President was obligated out of the annual ap-
propriation made by the Board, to pay the teachers and other
expenses, it often left a very small amount for his own compensation.   In his report for 1872 as President of the Col-

lege he said: "It is well understood by
The President's the Board that the President has no regu-
Salary. lar salary. The Board has for two years
appropriated five thousand five hundred
($5,500) dollars per year to defray current expenses, and
the President has received what is left after all other items
of expenditure are paid. Last year his compensation was
$1,135.46; this year $1,056.46. It must be remarked, however, that no account is made of postage, stationery and ordinary traveling expenses, which together amount to a considerable sum. If these items were aggregated and sub-
tracted from the nominal salary the real one would be something less than it appears to be. As I have consented to all
the arrangements of the Board thus far, I have no com-
plaint to offer touching the past. But I would respectfully
submit to the Board that $1,056.46 is an inadequate compen-
sation for the duties performed. I would further represent
that the Board should fix a definite salary for this office, or
officer, and not subject him to the humiliating consciousness
that his compensation *is the leavings.*"

At the beginning of the College in 1867 Mr. W. J. Ford
had, as Financial Agent, received a promise of fifty thous-
and dollars from Mr. Robert Kerr of Marion, O., for endowment purposes. This was the first large
Lathrop Cooley. sum ever promised to the permanent endowment of the College. In 1870 La-
throp Cooley was employed as Financial Agent, a position
which he held for several years. Mr. Cooley was quite successful in his work. Among the larger sums he received was
seven thousand dollars from Mr. Thomas N. Easton of
Hinckley, O. The proceeds of this sum were not immediately available to the college. Smaller sums were received

from various sources which aggregated a considerable sum. The contract with Mr. Robert Kerr was modified so that the College came into possession of thirty thousand dollars of available funds from that source during this period. An effort was also made to sell scholarships and to increase the stock of the College which resulted in considerable success. Mr. Cooley's wide acquaintance with the Disciple churches of Northern Ohio, and high standing as a preacher among them, enabled him to press the claims of Hiram as no one else could. In becoming a preacher he did not lose his business sagacity and this gave him great influence with business men. While the financial condition of the College did not improve rapidly the business methods pursued by the Board and all concerned were clear and clean. From year to year a balance sheet of the College was presented showing its resources and liabilities to date. One of them is here given—that of June 8, 1881—which represented the College resources at the end of Mr. Hinsdale's administration: Real estate, $4,600; buildings, $17,500; tabernacle, $1,500; boarding hall, $10,000; building improvements, $2,312.16; furniture, $1,021; museum, $500; library, $1,000; endowment, $50,000; and cash in hands of the Finance Committee, $61.96, making a total of $88,495.12.

In June, 1879, Alanson Wilcox was employed as Financial Agent of the College, a position he held for several years with marked ability and success. The reports which **Alanson Wilcox.** he made to the Board and on record show that he was vigilant and active in the interests of the College. The "Ladies' Hall" and "Tabernacle" were built and for these he had much to do.

The annual reports of President Hinsdale to the Board of Trustees reveal the condition of the College, his own anx-

The
Annual Reports
of President
Hinsdale.

ieties and desires, and the great difficulties in the pathway of its progress. In his address at Hiram June 22, 1900, he spoke of the "gloom and thick darkness" in which he strove to keep its "lamp trimmed and burning." To cheer the students and in a measure lift himself above the "gloom" he would recite stanzas of Ferguson's poem, the "Forging of the Anchor," of which the following is one of the most appropriate:

"Leap out, leap out, my masters! leap out, and lay on load!
Let's forge a goodly anchor—a bower thick and broad;
For a heart of oak is hanging on every blow, I bode;
And I see the good ship riding, all in a perilous road—
The low reef roaring on her lea; the roll of ocean poured
From stem to stern, sea after sea; the main-mast by the
        board;
The bulwarks down; the rudder gone; the boats stove at
        the chains;
But courage still, brave mariners—the bower yet remains!
And not an inch to flinch he deigns—save when ye pitch sky
        high;
Then moves his head, as though he said, 'Fear nothing—
        here am I!'"

In his report in 1872 President Hinsdale said: "I think I am not mistaken in saying that the College is growing in public confidence and favor. At the same time, however, I do not look for any striking or rapid growth. There are probably few members of the Board who appreciate the difficulty of building up a college in Hiram. Our State is thickly strewn with colleges and the number is constantly increasing. Graded schools are springing up in every village; and young men well qualified to teach them go out from our own halls to receive better salaries than we pay our professors. The place is small, inconvenient of access, not a cheap place to live in,

1872.

destitute of social attractions and many conveniences. We are rowing against wind and tide. Under the circumstances nothing can keep up the reputation of the Institution but good instruction and wise management. The Faculty are doing their utmost to meet the demands upon them, which none understand better than themselves."

Mr. Hinsdale's report in 1874 showed "a large falling off in the patronage of the Institution as compared with the previous year, and the diminished attendance was followed by a correspondingly diminished income from tuitions." The total outstanding obligations for that year for current expenses were $3,234, to meet which the total resources were $2,285. This condition of things gave the President great anxiety, notwithstanding he could say: "The interior history of the College for the year has been highly satisfactory to the Faculty, and I believe to the great body of students. In respect to devotion to work, discipline, moral tone, etc., the behavior of our students has been all we have any right to expect. In no previous year since my administration began have the results, all things considered, been so satisfactory. By examining the catalogue the Board will see that the falling off of students has been almost wholly confined to the lower grades of study."

His report for 1875 was one of the most carefully prepared of President Hinsdale's annual reports. In detail it touched every point which to him seemed important. His comprehensive grasp of College conditions in Hiram and elsewhere was clear and convincing. Among other conclusions to which he arrived he said: "We cannot materially increase the number of our students except in two ways: First, by enlarging our college classes. This is greatly to be desired, but will be found to be very difficult. It can only be done by elevating the character of the College, at least in the popular estimation. Second, that any considerable enlargement of our work must be in the field of common English, and High School studies. Here, too, we are met by a difficulty, the cost of our education. If this could be reduced a few dollars per term, I am satisfied we could exhibit an increase of students. Until that is done, I am satisfied we cannot expect any material growth in that direction. If the business of the country improves, all schools may expect to feel its results, and we with the rest; but no improvement in general business can carry us to our former level."

Concerning himself he said: "During the last year I have received unmistakable warnings that I cannot press my powers with safety any farther, nay, that I am now an overworked man. I ought to be free to respond to occasional calls from the churches, to go as I am able, here and there. My estimate of my influence upon men, with whom I am not immediately connected, is humble; but I am sanguine enough to think that, in this way, I could be of some service to the College. What is more, I have some cherished plans of literary labor that I am anxious to prosecute to completion, which I can never do so long as I am overweighted as at present."

The year 1876 revealed no improvement and in the particular of patronage and tuition income was a depressing one. The number of students had de-

1876.

creased from 235 in 1875 to 179 in 1876, and the receipts from $3,409, in 1875 to $2,208 in 1876. These facts gave a gloomy tinge to the report of that year.

The report for 1877 was not more encouraging than those that had immediately preceded it. The interior work of the College had been good and the student life almost unexceptionable. But the student body

1877.

had been reduced from 179 in 1876, to 137 in 1877, while the College receipts had decreased in the same time from $2,208 to $2,058. The teachers had "had only a mouthful of pay each during the year," and some of them had been compelled to contract debts which were already becoming embarrassing. Of this condition of the College President Hinsdale said: "In my opinion the College is in a critical financial condition. What shall be done, if anything, the Board must determine. The closest economy has been practiced, and the expenditures for the year have been kept considerably below the amount contemplated by the Board. There can be no material reduction, unless the whole scale of the Institution is cut down; that would involve the securing of a cheaper, and, therefore, a new Faculty. Whether that, even, would be financial wisdom in the long run, is a question to determine. * * * * I have only one thing more to present, and that is this: It seems to me that there is a great want of public interest in Hiram. The general public may be assumed to be as indifferent to Hiram as to any other school; but there is a body of people who ought to feel more interest and responsibility than they do. Of course, I mean the people who planted the Institution—The Disciples of Ohio. Whether anything can be done to awaken more interest and a greater feeling of responsibility, perhaps the Board will do well to consider."

In 1878 there was a gleam of light through the clouds. The patronage of the College had increased by a gain of 31 per cent. in different students, and the gain of cash tuition receipts about 26 per cent. There was an unusual warmth in the report for that year and all concerned felt its influence. The position that Hiram College held among similar institutions was considered creditable not so much on account of the large place it filled as in the quality of the work it had done. Of this President Hinsdale said: "Educational work is very gener-

1878.

ally undervalued, especially when done on a small scale.
Large numbers and great sums are thought by the majority
of men to measure the value of educational work. I protest
against this standard as delusive and mischievous, and
affirm that the quality of what is done even more than the
quantity is to be considered. But even on the score of statistics our showing is not a mean one. The Institution at
Hiram became a College with the year 1867-8. Since then
there have been enrolled on her catalogues 121 preparatory
students, 124 freshmen, 104 sophomores, 57 juniors, and 47
seniors. The grand enrollment counting by years has been
2,719, or an average of 247 per year. How many different
students there have been in the eleven years cannot be told
without more labor than I can give to the subject."

In 1879 the outlook was not so hopeful for the College,
and President Hinsdale was greatly discouraged and about
ready to give up. The attendance was growing less and the

1879.   deficits for current expenses were grow-
                   ing larger. The Board found it neces-
sary to still further reduce the teaching force and to cut the
salaries of the already overworked President and Professors
down to a sum which was a humiliation for them to accept.
The President's report for 1879 was as sharp as a surgeon's
scalpel. He reviewed the condition of the Institution from
its beginning in 1850 to the present and showed that the attendance of students had gradually declined from 1853
when the attendance reached 529, to 1879 when there were
only 169. The Institution had been in existence for 28 years
counting to 1878. Dividing the 28 years into four equal
periods the average yearly attendance was as follows: 1850
to 1857, 450 4-7; 1857 to 1864, 411 1-7; 1864 to 1871,
291 1-7; 1871 to 1878, 227. Concerning these figures President Hinsdale said: "When a school reaches its climax in

three years, when its average attendance the second seven years is 39 less than the first seven, the third seven 120 less than the second, and the fourth seven 64 less than the third, it is idle to seek to explain the facts by referring them to accidental circumstances; there is at work some persistent and powerful tendency from first to last." He then proceeded to give what, in his judgment, were the elements that had produced this tendency:

1. "The unfortunate geographical location of the College as things have turned out.

2. Unfortunate economic and social conditions at Hiram.

3. The decay of interest on the part of the public, especially the Disciple churches.

4. The enormous development of the common schools.

5. The decline of the rural population in the northeastern counties of Ohio.

6. The ever-increasing competition of academical and collegiate schools.

7. The relative failure of the school to keep up with the times in mechanical equipment. The machinery for illustrative study at Hiram is no better than 25 years ago. Within that time, however, immense progress has been made all around us. These forces have acted so powerfully and so constantly that, had it not been for the devotion and sacrifice of a small number of persons, ere this Hiram would have been a thing of the past. The forces that have acted since 1853, persistent as gravitation, will draw Hiram nearer and nearer the earth unless something is done to counteract them. Something must be done for Hiram or Hiram must die; at most it can do no more than live on in a starved and dwindling condition. To me after as profound attention as I am capable of giving to any subject this is an incontro-

vertible fact. If the name College could be dropped it would be well; but probably it will be necessary to retain that to hold the funds. A humble school with a cheap corps of teachers could probably be kept up at Hiram for many years; but to think of supporting a College on $3,000 or $4,000 a year is simply farcical. For nine years I have worked with might and with main, making reasonable allowances for human infirmity. I have done my best to make good scholars at Hiram; to make good men and women of our pupils; and to give the College standing abroad. I can do no more. I confess I am discouraged. The consciousness that the work is becoming less on my hands, and that I am often blamed as the cause of the decline, weighs on my spirits. I could work on with heart and with hope, if I could see a prospect of future enlargement. But unless I can see some larger hope in Hiram than I have seen in the last few years, then I must begin to lay my plans with reference to some other work."

In 1880 President Hinsdale's report was more hopeful. Some improvements had been made in buildings begun, and provisions made for the better accommodation of students.

1880. The attendance had been increased by the addition of 40 students. "Putting all things together, the outlook is to me more hopeful than for many years. For obvious reasons Hiram can never become a foremost name in educational works, but I am sure that a general co-operation of its friends would add considerably to its facilities, and add to its patronage."

The report for 1881 is hopeful. The attendance had not sensibly diminished from the year before and the College receipts had been somewhat larger. By the election of Mr.

1881. Garfield as President of the United States in 1880 the name of the College had unexpectedly "become a foremost name in educational works" and among educational institutions. A new boarding hall had been completed and furnished and a commodious tabernacle had been built for the larger gatherings on the Hill.

In 1882 President Hinsdale made his last report as President of the College. He said: "The College year now closing has been a year of ordinary prosperity in all departments of our work. Upon the whole the impetus that was gained in 1880 has been maintained, but no new one has been received. In respect to instruction and discipline nothing in particular needs to be said. The usual efforts have been made by students and by instructors, and with the usual results."

1882.

On the question of "Accommodation for students," he said: "There has been much talk about increasing the attendance at Hiram. I would call the attention of the Board to the fact that there is no room in Hiram for more students than we have had for the last two or three years. With 150 students Hiram is full to her utmost capacity. I would suggest that the Board consider the question whether they can do anything themselves, or by stimulating private enterprise to improve the accommodations for students."

These paragraphs from the annual reports of President Hinsdale reveal many facts concerning the inner life of Hiram College during this period. Whether he probed to the bottom of the case or not, he made an honest effort to find the real difficulties and manfully and fearlessly to meet them. Though he did not reach the measure of success he desired in bringing the Institution out of the swaddling bands of the old Academy and clothing it with the real garments of a College, yet he succeeded in laying foundations, the strength of which is felt to this day.

What These Reports Reveal.

At its meeting June 12, 1879, the Board of Trustees

unanimously adopted the following reso-
A New Boarding Hall. lutions presented by a Committee on a Boarding Hall consisting of C. E. Henry, Harmon Austin, and Dr. W. S. Streator.

1 "We would recommend the erection of a moderate-sized building, the cost thereof not to exceed five thousand dollars, suitable for enlargement.

2. That three thousand dollars of available funds in the hands of the Finance Committee may be used for the erection of said building, the sum to be refunded to the Finance Committee from special subscriptions to this purpose after the building is paid for.

3. That the money received from rental of rooms in said building shall be first applied to the payment of interest on the three thousand dollars.

4. That all notes or subscriptions now in the hands of the College Treasurer be collected and applied as far as practicable toward the building as a part of the three thousand dollars.

5. That vigorous efforts be made to raise at once by subscription the requisite amount to pay the remaining two thousand, and that there be no relaxation of effort until the whole amount of the cost of the building is raised, and the money advanced by the Finance Committee be returned to them for investment."

The ladies of Hiram to the number of 45, through Mrs. Hinsdale, Mrs. Hank, Mrs. Stanhope and Mrs. Ellis had presented an earnest petition to the Board for the construction of a building "so built and furnished as to accommodate a large Boarding Club, and also, have a certain number of furnished rooms to rent to students."

They also promised that if the Board would "build or cause to be built such a house, we will undertake to furnish it from top to bottom with all appliances needed for its successful management; and we will appoint from our number an Advisory Board to act with the College authorities in its management after it is opened."

This was the beginning of what is now known in Hiram as "Bowler Hall."

The new hall was located on "the Smith property," which consisted of a frame house and five acres of land, and which formerly belonged to John Smith, the father of C. C.

The Smith Property. Smith, now Assistant Corresponding Secretary of the American Christian Missionary Society. The Hall was put up according to plans and specifications drawn by "Heard and Smith," architects of Cleveland, Ohio. The work was pushed forward with vigor so that that in June, 1880, the Building Committee presented the finished product to the Board of Trustees at a total cost of $8,935.78. The committee having charge of the building and other improvements connected with it, consisted of John J. Ryder, Alvah Udall, and R. Stanhope. In the conclusion of their very clear, comprehensive and intelligent report they say: "It will be seen that this gross amount considerably exceeds the expenditures originally contemplated. The explanation is not that the original work cost more than was expected, but that much more work has been done. In the first place the purchase of the Smith place, furnaces, water in the house, side-walks, etc., were not included in the estimates. Your committee beg leave to say, that they have never gone beyond the letter of their instructions save in cases where it seemed necessary to do so. The Smith lot and house will be sources of income. Two terms experience with the Hall shows that if properly managed, it will return a fair interest on the money the Board has put into it, and that it will be a valuable auxiliary to the college."

The building of the Boarding Hall with its furnishings at a cost of about $10,000, and of the Tabernacle at a cost of $1,500, added greatly to the accommodations of the college. It forecasted also what could be easily done of a like character when the determination to do it had been fixed.

The Financial Agent, Alanson Wilcox, had been untiring in his efforts to increase the interest in Hiram and to raise money for the new buildings, and **Financial Agent.** for other purposes. Through his efforts the attendance of students had been sensibly increased. A large territory was traversed into which the "enthusiasm for Hiram" was carried by the agent. In his canvass he found some of the elements which had worked against the progress and success of the College. He found the Disciples, the natural patrons of the college, were not wealthy and the times were hard; that these same Disciples "seemed to lack a spirit of liberality in educational matters;" and that the ministry among the Disciples were not specially interested in the college work. Much good in many ways resulted from Mr. Wilcox's labors. The Board of Trustees appreciating what had been done, and the small cost of the year's canvass, gave "a vote of thanks to the agent, Alanson Wilcox, for his untiring zeal and successful labor in the interests of the college, and especially for the unlooked for meagre traveling expenses to the college during his year's service."

With the completion of the Boarding Hall and Tabernacle, Alvah Udall, Esq., practically closed **Alvah Udall, Esq.** his long and faithful service in behalf of Hiram College, though he remained a member of the Board of Trustees until his death in

COLLEGE FACULTY IN 1900.

1887. He was elected a member of the Board in 1854 and served continuously for a third of a century, and from 1856 to 1880 he was President of that body. On account of failing health and lengthening years he resigned as President in 1880. His resignation was accepted with sincere regret in the following appreciative terms:—*"Resolved,* That this Board of Trustees of Hiram College have a high appreciation of the faithful and valuable services of the retiring President of the Board, Alvah Udall, Esq., who has with untiring fidelity served in that capacity for twenty-four years, giving to it the best energies of his business experience and counsels, and that we hereby tender our thanks to him for the same."

Mr. Udall was an interesting character and a man of marked personality. Never a member of the church he was a lover of good men and a willing helper of Christian people. He was honorable in all his business relations, calm and judicial in his estimate of men and things, dignified in his intercourse with society, a lover of his own family, and in every way merited and received the esteem of all classes of people. He was born September 14, 1807, the eighth child in a family of thirteen children. His father, Samuel Udall, came to Hiram in the winter of 1818 from Hartford, Vermont. He came with his family all the way on sleds. It may be only a legend, but it is said: "That Col. Daniel Tilden, who crossed the Delaware with Washington, came to Hiram a little earlier, and with others of its proprietors who were 'Free Masons' named the township Hiram, after Hiram Abif, King of Tyre."

At the age of 22 Alvah Udall was elected Clerk of Hiram township. He was afterward elected Justice of the Peace and served for fifteen years. He was also Assistant

Revenue Collector for the Government for eight years. In 1831 he was married to Phoebe Ann Udall, the marriage ceremony being performed by Joshua R. Giddings, Esq. Mrs. Udall was a noble woman—a Christian in name and in fact. The Udall home was like Paradise to many of the earlier students at Hiram. In the maple-sugar season the old "sugar-camp" north of the house was the place for an annual rendezvous of teachers and students, where Mr. and Mrs. Udall delighted in their entertainment. Mr. Udall was one of the earliest friends of the Institution at Hiram and his influence had great weight in the location of the school. The brick for the old building were made on his farm east of the center and he delivered them at the building place for $2.25 per thousand. He was deeply interested in every movement toward higher education. When Mr. W. J. Ford was chosen Financial Agent he wanted to be sure that he was the right man for the place, and with his wife drove from Hiram to Bazetta to hear for himself. He had fine qualifications as a presiding officer of the Board elements much needed in the earlier days of Hiram. He was always ready in his rulings and considerate of the feelings of his associates. During the Civil War he was a rock on which many of the interests of the Institution leaned, and in whose shadow many of its friends were refreshed. When Mr. Ford returned from "the front," General Garfield said to him: "Report to Squire Udall for instructions," and Mr. Udall said, "Keep the field of the school at home open, until the boys come again." Hiram owes much to him both for the "Eclectic Institute" and for Hiram College, and his name will be found written large on its walls and in the first fifty years of its history. He died May 2, 1887, at the age of fourscore. The Board of Trustees took suitable action on his death and placed on record an appreciative tribute to his memory.

Trustees of this Period.

1870-1.

The Board of Trustees during President Hinsdale's administration was composed at the beginning of the following persons:—Judge D. W. Canfield,* W. J. Ford, Charles B. Lockwood, Thomas W. Phillips, J. H. Rhodes, Alvah Udall, B. F. Waters, John F. Whitney, Harmon Austin, James A. Garfield, Hartwell Ryder, and Abram Teachout. These were somewhat changed year by year, though the larger number served to the close. In 1873 the Board of Trustees was enlarged to twenty-four members. The following names will mark the changes during this time:

1871-2.   Freeman E. Udall, and Dr. Worthy S. Streator.

1872-3.   F. W. Andrews, H. L. Morgan, Thomas N. Easton, J. M. Parmly, R. M. Hank, A. S. Hayden, J. J. Ryder, A. J. Squire, Albert Allen, George A. Baker, Lathrop Cooley, A. J. Marvin.

1873-4.   William Bowler, John T. Phillips.

1874-5.   No change.

1875-6.   Dr. J. P. Robison, W. P. Hudson.

1876-7.   Charles E. Henry, Charles W. Hemry.

1877-8.   Cyrus Ryder.

1878-9.   Judge H. C. White.

1879-80.   O. G. Kent, R. Stanhope.

1880-1.   B. A. Hinsdale, Andrew Squire.

1881-2.   No change.

The steadiness with which the Trustees held their places had much to do in keeping the affairs of the college in a favorable condition though its growth for numerous reasons was necessarily slow.

---

*Judge Canfield died suddenly at his home in Chardon, O., December 29, 1900, at the age of 72 years.

During the period of his administration Mr. Hinsdale's endurance seemed to be inexhaustible. In addition to his administrative duties he taught classes in history, philosophy, rhetoric, and literature, gave frequent public lectures, preached on Sundays, and made numerous contributions to the press. His first books were of an entirely religious character. His first book published while at Hiram ,appeared in 1872, on "The Genuineness and Authenticity of the Gospels;" his second a monogram on "The Jewish Christian Church," in 1878; a third in 1879 on "Ecclesiastical Tradition." Much interested in 1880 in the success of General Garfield for President of the United States, at the request of the National Republican Committee he wrote a "Campaign Text Book" besides making numerous speeches in favor of Mr. Garfield. On the death of the President he wrote in 1882 "President Garfield and Education," a memorial volume, and in 1883, before he finally left Hiram, he collated General Garfield's speeches and addresses in two large octavo volumes. All of these works show wide reading, deep and comprehensive study and thought, and that honesty of purpose and expression which always characterized his literary endeavors.

President Hinsdale's Literary Work.

But the time had come, in his judgment, and it is only fair to say, in the judgment of many of his best friends for his work at Hiram to close. He had done all that he could for Hiram, and Hiram had done all that it could for him. He had worked heroically towards an end— a distinct purpose for the college, and his work had not been without success. He had not accomplished all that he desired to accomplish, but all, under the conditions that pre-

Close of President Hinsdale's Administration.

vailed, that could reasonably be expected.* His pulses were set toward a larger field wherein he would not be disturbed by fitful finances, or burdened with the almost countless details of college administration.

From Hiram he went to Cleveland, where for four years he gave himself, as Superintendent of the Public Schools of that city, to the study of great educational problems, from the standpoint of the Public School System. His annual reports won attention from educators of the highest character and accomplishments throughout the State and Nation. His contributions to educational journals, and his public addresses on educational topics brought him into the front rank, where he remained easily to the close of his life.

In 1888 he was elected to the Chair of "The Science and The Art of Teaching" in the University of Michigan and entered upon his labors at the University in February of that year. Here he remained, rising higher every year in the estimation of his associates, in an almost unbroken

---

*President Hinsdale's formal resignation of the Presidency of Hiram College was received by the Board of Trustees, May 3, 1883: "Gentlemen: I deem it fitting, if not necessary, to resign formally the office to which you elected me July 1, 1870, the Presidency of Hiram College, said resignation to take effect at the close of the commencement exercises at Hiram, June 14 next. The reasons that impelled me to sever my practical connection with the College last year, as I now sever my formal connection, which are many, need not here be recited; but I am happy in being able to say, want of good understanding with you was not one of them. So far from it, in now laying down this office, the duties of which I strove to fulfill for twelve years, I cannot forbear placing upon record my generous appreciation of and thankfulness for the confidence and support that you have always given me. No man in such a position could rely upon a Board more fully than I always have relied upon you for co-operation and strength in whatever could be made to appear at once reasonable and right. In so doing I hope you have found some reward in the results that have followed our joint efforts to make the College strong and useful. Hoping that all your future efforts in the same direction may be abundantly blessed, I am,
Very truly,
B. A. HINSDALE, President of Hiram College."

service, until the "silver cord was loosed, the golden bowl broken, and the pitcher broken at the fountain" November 29, 1900.

The college had now reached a crisis and its most steadfast and far-seeing friends were unable to forecast its future. It had won the name and rank of college but whether it would be able to carry it with honor was a question. Its oldest, ablest, and most consecrated sons and daughters had until now filled its highest places and led its "foremost files." From now onward its fortunes must be trusted mainly to those who called other Institutions *Alma Mater,* and to whom the early struggles and traditions of Hiram were unknown as personal experiences.

A Crisis in
College Affairs.

CHAPTER VII.

HIRAM COLLEGE.—A CRISIS AND HOW IT WAS MET.
1883-1888.

"Where McGregor sits is the head of the table," and if he has sat there long it is difficult for another to take his place. The resignation of President Hinsdale, who had

The Old Traditions to the Front.

occupied the place so long, and had impressed some marks indelibly on the college, laid a great burden on the Board of Trustees in the selection of his successor. He had advanced its standard much beyond the traditions of the "Old Eclectic." And whether there should be a retreat from the point gained, or an advance was the question. At the battle of Cedar Mountain, where Charles P. Bowler, a Hiram student, gave up his life, a part of the brigade commanded by Rutherford B. Hayes, had gotten quite in advance of their comrades in a seemingly perilous position, and the Division Commander, seeing the situation, commanded that the colors should be brought back. General Hayes, the Brigade Commander, with better knowledge of the real condition of affairs, and unwilling to beat a retreat, called out in tones that thrilled the hearts of the men, "Bring the men up to the colors!" In reaching the rank now held by the college some elements which an institution depending for its support on the patronage of the Disciples of Christ must not ignore, had been, in a measure, left behind, and the time had now come to bring them up to where the college colors had been carried.

Some of the friends of the college clearly recognized the necessities of the hour, and June 7, 1882, the Board of Trustees placed on record the following Preamble and Resolutions: *"Whereas,* Religious instruction is a most desirable part of education, and in accordance with the ideas of the founders of this Institution; and,

Special
Biblical
Instruction.

Whereas, It is necessary that our Financial Agent should be aided in his endeavors to present the interests of this Institution to the Disciple churches of Ohio, therefore

Resolved, That there should be maintained a high degree of religious interest in the college; That a suitable amount of Bible study should be made a part of the college course; That classes should be provided for those desiring special instruction; That the Financial Agent be requested to give especial attention to the matter of raising funds for endowing a special chair of religious literature, and that the Board pledge the churches of Ohio to establish a chair for this purpose as soon as funds can be raised or secured so to do."

At a special meeting of the Board held in Cleveland March 15, 1883, on motion of C. B. Lockwood, Bailey S. Dean was elected Professor and Vice President of the college at a salary of five hundred dollars a year. The Faculty as finally arranged and provided for consisted of Bailey S. Dean, Vice President and Professor of Mental and Moral Science; George H. Colton, Professor of Natural Sciences; George A. Peckham, Professor of Greek and Latin Languages and Literatures; Colman Bancroft, Professor of Mathematics and Astronomy; Arthur C. Pierson, Professor of Rhetoric and English Literature; Mary B. Jewett, Principal of Ladies' Department and Professor of Modern Lan-

Election of
B. S. Dean,
Vice-President.

guages; M. J. Grable, Teacher of Mathematics and English Studies; M. H. Wilson, Teacher of Penmanship and Book-keeping; Lizzie A. Clapp, Teacher of Instrumental Music; and Emma Johnson Dean, Teacher of Drawing, Oil Painting and China Decoration.* The teaching force of this Faculty was strong, perhaps stronger than ever before in some of its points.

Bailey S. Dean, Vice President and acting President, was well qualified in character and education to act as Inter-rex until a President could be found. He

Biographical
Sketch of
B. S. Dean.

was born at Canfield, O., in 1845. He was of Connecticut stock on his father's side. His father was Orsemus Dean, a man of sturdy character and one of the pioneer farmers of Mahoning county. His mother was Rhoda Hayden, and sister of William and A. S. Hayden, the first and foremost in the projection and execution of the educational idea which finally became the Western Reserve Eclectic Institute. Mr. Dean was nursed and trained in the country home of his parents; and his early years were spent as a farmer's boy. His school privileges were as many, perhaps no more, than others had in that day. He entered Hiram as a student in 1861 and continued with somewhat irregular intervals, as student until 1868, about four years in all. In 1868 he entered Bethany College and graduated with the Class of 1869. For eight years afterward he was pastor of the Disciple Church at East Smithfield, Pa., which proved to him a pleasant and fruitful field. In 1878 he became pastor of the Disciple Church at Bellaire, O., where he remained until he was called to the Hiram Church in 1882 for which he preached for about six years, resigning to accept the Chair of History

---

*Willard W. Slabaugh and Duane H. Tilden were employed as tutors in the Preparatory Department, and Allie B. Merriam as assistant in Penmanship and Bookkeeping.

in Hiram College, a place he yet occupies. As a student at Hiram he is one of the links between the old and the new. He belonged to the last classes of the Old Eclectic and to the first classes of Hiram College. As the valedictorian in June, 1867, he closed Vol. I. of the school's history and threw some of the light of the past on the yet untrodden walk of the future. Considering what has come to pass since 1882 it seems like a provision of Providence that he was at hand and qualified when the Board of Trustees called him to administer the duties of the College President.

It was not an easy task to find the man who would satisfy all concerned for President; but the Board looking

Finding a President. at all the interests involved determined to find the best one who could be persuaded to accept the position. Their motto now became, *"Non Progredi—Regredi Est."* The Board called to its assistance the members of the "Ministerial Association

Help from the Ministerial Association. of the Disciples of Christ in Eastern Ohio" and asked them to nominate three persons from which the Board might select. The ministerial committee appointed by the Association to select names consisted of J. M. Atwater, C. C. Smith, and Martin L. Streator. This committee secured answers from 58 preachers; and in their report to the Board said:—"We believe that in view of the origin and original objects of Hiram College, it is, in the highest degree important, indeed absolutely essential that its President should be not only a believer in the Christian faith, but also an acknowledged Christian and distinctively identified with the Disciples. In this remark we believe we express the unanimous feeling and conviction of the Association that appointed us, as well as the entire body of the Disciples. We also believe that the Disciples of Northern

Ohio and their preachers are ready, as indicated by their recent action in convention, to co-operate with the Board in giving to the college increased means of usefulness."

The committee of the Board appointed to nominate a President consisted of Lathrop Cooley, J. J. Ryder, and

Committee of Trustees.

C. W. Hemry. They reported that they had canvassed the field with care, and nominated Joseph King, of Alleghany City, Pa., a preacher of excellent scholarship and distinguished ability. With one exception the members of the Board voted in favor of Mr. King and a committee was appointed to notify him of his election. His salary was fixed at $1,500.

At the same meeting, held May 3, 1883, the Board announced that "we contemplate the organization of a Biblical Department in Hiram College early in the coming year."

For what appeared to him good and sufficient reasons, Mr. King declined the offer of the Presidency, closing his letter of May 11, 1883, with these words:—"I have regretted

Mr. King Declines the Presidency.

the wide publicity given to the matter and if I have caused delay or embarrassment to the Board by encouraging the hope that I would accept if elected and by finally deciding not to, I shall regret it still more. I sincerely trust that the Board will be wisely guided in the selection of another, and that one abler and better qualified in every way to fill the position than I am will be obtained."

Notwithstanding the embarrassments incident to the changing of the college administration Mr. Dean's report

Vice-President Dean's Report.

to the Board of Trustees was hopeful. There had been a net increase of 21 students, and a considerable increase in the financial receipts for college purposes. In some departments the classes were overcrowded and the demand for the enlargement of the college buildings was becoming imperative. On this matter Mr. Dean said: "I

The Need of New Buildings. most earnestly hope that the Board will not suffer the question of a new building to drop out of mind. It is an urgent need; the libraries are crowded; the Societies have no suitable halls; the museum is ill accommodated; there is no laboratory; and no suitable room for music or art. The old building will serve for recitations for a century to come perhaps; but for the purposes specified it is not suitable. A new and modern building would without doubt tend to increase the attendance, as it would be a mark of progress. I believe that the friends of progress would respond to a move in that direction. In conclusion I would most gratefully testify to the hearty co-operation of my co-workers in all the cares and responsibilities of the year. No one could ask for more perfect harmony than has prevailed. Thanking you for the confidence reposed in me, and deeply sensible how imperfectly I have discharged the duties of my position, I lay down the trust which I reluctantly assumed."

At the annual meeting of the Board of Trustees held June 13, 1883, the financial condition of the college was

Financial Condition. reported in a carefully detailed report from the Finance Committee, showing a total of producing capital of $42,840. Concerning the securities of these funds the Committee said:—"Your committee have endeavored to secure the best rates consistent with unquestioned security, and so far the Trustees can rejoice with us that there has been no loss to interfere with the productive resources of the college, or to admit of any doubt as to the judicious management of our Endowment Fund."

June 13, 1883, the Board of Trustees took action on the

recommendation of the Committee on President and unani-

Election of G. H. Laughlin President. mously elected George H. Laughlin President of Hiram College and fixed his salary at $1,500. Mr. Laughlin accepted the position and entered on his duties immediately. The Faculty at the beginning of his administration was substantially the same as that which served with Vice President Dean. Jessie F. Horton became special Teacher of Elocution, and Walter C. Spaulding, and Frank W. Norton were tutors in the Preparatory Department; and Minnie E. Robinson took the place of Mary B. Jewett as Principal of the Ladies' Department.

George Hamilton Laughlin was born December 28, 1838, at Quincy, Illinois. He was third in a family of eight

Biographical Sketch of President Laughlin. sons. On his father's side he was of English ancestry and on his mother's, Scotch, and in the line of his father he was related to President James Madison. His early training was received on an Illinois farm, and his first educational opportunities were furnished by the "district school" of his neighborhood. Physically he was not a large man either in height or weight. He was five feet eight inches in height, and he never weighed over one hundred and fifty pounds. In October, 1857, he entered Berean College, at Jacksonville, Illinois, where he remained less than one year. He then entered Abingdon College at Abingdon, Illinois, where he remained for four years as a student. He graduated from Abingdon College in 1862 with the highest honors of his class, delivering the Greek Salutatory. He united with the Christian Church in 1859. He was married August 21, 1862, to Miss Deborah J. Ross, who yet survives him. About the time of his marriage he began teaching and preaching, which he steadily continued until his death, November 16, 1895. For three years immediately following his marriage he taught in the public schools of Illinois. For eight years following he was Principal of Ralls County Academy at New London, Missouri; and for five years of this time he was County Superintendent of Public Schools.

In 1874 he was called to fill the chair of Ancient Languages in Oskaloosa College, Oskaloosa, Iowa. He held this position for seven years. In 1881 he was elected President of the college, resigning to accept the Presidency of Hiram College in 1883, which position he held for four years. After he left Hiram for three years he was Professor of Ancient Languages in Garfield University, Wichita, Kansas. He was also pastor for one year of the Christian Church at Wichita. After he left Wichita he was pastor of the Christian Church at Kirksville, Missouri, and for three years filled the Chair of English Literature, in the State Normal School at Kirksville. He received several academic Degrees besides those granted by his *Alma Mater;* LL. D.; Ph. D., and was a member of a Society of Science in London, England, and a Councilor of the American Institute of Civics. He was a very busy and useful man, but his best work was done in the Professor's Chair and in the pulpit, places for which he was better equipped than for the distracting details of college administration. He bore a blameless character in his private and public life. Coming to Hiram as he did in a critical period in her history; a stranger to the larger part of his supporters; and unacquainted with the methods and traditions which had prevailed for a third of a century; it was impossible for him to do what another, trained and learned in these things might have done; and yet it may fairly be questioned whether any other could, under the circumstances, have done better than he did. The time had not yet come for the distinct, and strong forward movement.

When President Laughlin began his work in Hiram he had understood that the college would be provided with a

The Need of Larger Buildings. better building for its work. The need for such enlargement of college facilities was manifest to all. But the Board of Trustees was conservative and would not move except on safe ground. President Hinsdale had frequently insisted on the great need of enlarged accommodations. Vice President Dean had done the same. Several of the Professors had emphasized these numerous requests. Finally a tentative movement was started February 11, 1884, by Trustees A. J. Marvin and William Bowler. Mr. Marvin moved "that a subscription paper be drafted for the purpose of raising funds to build a new building at Hiram and for making repairs on the old." Mr. Bowler moved "that the amount which it should be attempted to raise be $15,000, all subscriptions to be paid when $10,000 of good and valid pledges shall have been taken." Both of these motions prevailed but with the proviso:—"That nothing which has been done at this meeting be construed as committing this Board to the proposition to build at Hiram and that the committee on subscriptions be instructed to take no steps whatever that shall in any way commit the Board in any financial sense, until the Board shall have taken further action in the premises." But this was a beginning—a beginning which silenced, at last, all clamor for the removal of the college from Hiram to any other place, and resulted in the enlargement of the material facilities of the college more than one hundred per cent.

President Laughlin's reports from year to year are interesting. His first report was made June 11, 1884, in **President Laughlin's Annual Reports.** which he said in part:—"In many particulars the scholastic year now closing has been a prosperous one. There had been an increase of the number of students in **1884.** college classes, a slight decrease from the previous year in the Preparatory classes; while the aggregate financial receipts were about the same as for the two years preceding. Hiram's standard of scholarship is high; it shall not be lowered during my administration. The scholarly attainments and teaching capacity of my fellow-teachers will go far towards maintaining the present high standard of scholarship in the Institution and increasing the number of students in the regular college classes. But success in college work depends upon a great variety of helps. The pressing need of Hiram is a new college building. Although your attention has been frequently called to the fact, yet it is my firm conviction that unless Hiram shall keep pace with the other colleges of Northern Ohio in supplying educational facilities, that her days of usefulness will be numbered in the near future. Hiram does not ask for a costly building and artistic display, but for a plain building —simply for more room. * * * I am also heartily in sympathy with the desire that Hiram should be distinctively a Disciple School, and it seems to be the general judgment of the Disciples in Northern Ohio that a Biblical Department should be sustained in Hiram College. It is sincerely hoped that you may adopt wise measures as to ways and means of sustaining this Department as an essential feature of the general curriculum of studies at Hiram."

President Laughlin's report for 1885 presented a generally favorable condition of affairs at the college. The Bible Department had been quite prosperous. The financial condition had not materially changed except in the diminished revenue from the Boarding Hall. In regard to the new building President Laughlin said:—"One year ago the Faculty were authorized by the Board to assist the Building Committee in soliciting subscriptions. All that I am now able to report is that through my own solicitations subscriptions to the amount of nearly $4,000 have been made since February, 1884. Possibly other subscriptions have been secured by the Building Committee. The members of the Faculty heartily join me in recommending you to place in the field, at an early date, an agent whose special business shall be to solicit students for the college."

President Laughlin's report for 1886 was not as hopeful in some of its features as the two preceding. One reason that he gave was "the uncertainty whether or not the college would remain at its present location." The financial condition of the college was about at its lowest ebb, and a reduction of the teaching force had become necessary. Persistent rumors were in the air that the college was to be removed to Warren or to some other location. But there were hopeful signs and favorable features. He said:—"One of the written conditions upon which I accepted the Presidency of Hiram College was that the facilities of the Institution should be increased by the erection of an additional college building as soon as possible. The assistance given to this enterprise by members of your own body in generous subscriptions made two years ago supplemented by numerous smaller subscriptions made within the past year, chiefly in Portage county, has greatly encouraged both my co-laborers and myself. From the first, I have had confidence in the ultimate success of the enterprise, believing that the increased facilities of the Institution would in the 'logic of events,' be brought about in a few years, if not at Hiram, certainly at some point in Northern Ohio. What we have seen by the eye of faith for several years is now beginning to materialize. The present Commencement is, in a certain sense, an auspicious occasion in that the corner stone of the new building is now to be laid. And now that your Institution is, in quite a definite way fixed permanently at Hiram, I doubt not that the loyalty of its old friends and that of its new friends will be its source of strength. And although we are fully at the turning point of a new chapter in Hiram's history, yet I presume that it is a wise statement to make, and that the members of the Board, the Alumni, the Faculty of the College, and all the genuine friends of the Institution realize that it will require 'a long pull, a strong pull, and a pull altogether' to consummate fully the work now inaugurated."

President Laughlin's last report was made June 15, 1887. The report was brief but indicated a good condition of college affairs. Quite an increase had been made to the college classes, and the financial condition was somewhat better than in the previous year. The Literary Societies had been stimulated to better work by the hope of soon having better halls for their sessions. Joseph King, who had declined the offered Presidency of the college, had donated his large private library to the college, which largely increased and enriched that department. The one sad event of the year and of the administration now drawing to its close, was the death of James Edgar Norton, of whom the President said:—"In the midst of the spring term (May 5) we were called upon to mourn the death of J. E. Norton. His death, which was caused (April 29) by a very peculiar accident, cast a deep gloom over the college community. He was a member of the Junior Class. In faithfulness and thoroughness of work, in integrity of Christian character, and in friendship for all he had no superior among our students."

President Laughlin's connection with the college closed with Commencement day, June, 1887. In accepting his resignation the Board of Trustees placed on record the following appreciative resolution:—"That this Board take pleasure in recognizing the faithfulness with which President Laughlin has discharged his duties as President of Hiram College for the past four

years, and desire to express their appreciation of his honest
and zealous labor to forward the interests of the college
during his entire connection with it."

The event of greatest importance to Hiram College
during the period from 1883 to 1888 was the enlargement

**Completion
of the
New Buildings.**

and renewing of the college building
which for a long time had been inadequate for the needs of the Institution. As
in all such enterprises a few men are at
the front and plainly in sight, so it was here. President
Hinsdale had begun the agitation of the question of a new
building in his report to the Board of Trustees for the year
1881-2. Vice President Dean had given emphasis to the
necessities of the case. President Laughlin had brought
the matter forward in each of his annual reports until the
Board had actually and seriously considered the question
and set in motion the forces that finally resulted in the successful completion of large and well-arranged buildings.

It will not be invidious to name with the foregoing
B. S. Dean, D. H. Beaman, G. H. Colton, O. C. Atwater,
William Bowler and Abram Teachout. Others did good
work and are entitled to credit; but these were the swift-
footed runners, the hands that never hung down, the knees
that were never feeble, and the minds that were quick to
discern and liberal to devise.

At a meeting of the Board of Trustees held in Garrettsville March 31, 1886, Mr. Abram Teachout offered the
following resolutions, which were unanimously adopted:—

**Mr. Teachout's
Resolution
in 1886.**

"Whereas, At a meeting of the Board
held in Cleveland February 11, 1884, initial steps, looking to the erection of a
new college building at Hiram, were
taken; and

"Whereas, Subscriptions amounting to about ten thou-

sand ($10,000) dollars have been secured for erecting said building,

   Therefore be it Resolved, That a Building Committee be elected on nomination, and be clothed with power to build the said building on the following terms and conditions:—*First,* Said committee is authorized to procure plans, to make contracts, and to supervise the work of erection. *Second,* Said committee is authorized to collect the subscriptions already made with which to pay for said building, and also to secure and collect additional subscriptions for the same purpose, provided that the total amount raised, including the ten thousand dollars, shall not exceed seventeen thousand five hundred dollars ($17,500) ; and the committee are hereby authorized to expend any balance that may remain after building and paying for the new building, in repairs upon the old building. *Third,* All contracts made by said committee shall be made in their own names and in the names of such other persons as they may associate with themselves for their purposes; it being expressly provided that the committee shall not in any way involve the college in such contracts, and that the college shall not, in any particular, be responsible for the transactions of said committee. *Fourth,* On the completion of said building, and on the final payment being made therefor, it shall be turned over to the Board of Trustees and shall be accepted by the same as a part of the college property."

   On the adoption of these resolutions it was resolved that the Building Committee to be elected should consist of ten persons, five of whom should be **The Building Committee.** members of the Board. The committee selected from the Board consisted of William Bowler, Abram Teachout, J. J. Ryder, B. F. Waters, and Charles E. Henry; the others were F. E. Derthick,

George H. Colton, D. H. Beaman, J. E. Norton, and Arthur Crane.

At this meeting the Board authorized the Building Committee to employ Orris C. Atwater to act as Financial
Agent for the present. Mr. Atwater had
O. C. Atwater.   already been active in proclaiming the
necessity of new buildings at Hiram and pushing their claims among the people. A meeting of the citizens of Hiram and vicinity had been held in the College chapel July 17, 1885, and a committee of fifteen citizens appointed to take the necessary steps for a thorough canvass, especially of Portage county. This committee met July 30, and chose Mr. Atwater to represent them in the canvass. In writing of this particular time to Prof. B. S. Dean, Mr. Atwater says: "You know the work of 1885, 1886, 1887, and how many dark days there were, how many questions and plans, how many doubts and fears. You remember well the committee of fifteen that met in the Delphic room; and that they put the whole matter in my charge as to a sub-committee of one: and when I dared not go on alone, for I had never been tried in any similar work, they increased the sub-committee to three and insisted on my naming the other members of that local working committee. There would have been no new building, and no Y. M. C. A. Building, and no glad triumph and jubilee, if somebody had not been found to carry the burden that committee of fifteen had laid on me. You never knew how grateful I was for the cheer I got by going up to consult with you in your study, nor how many prayers went up for help from on High. There ought, too,
to be mention made of D. H. Beaman's
D. H. Beaman.   courage and generosity in the dark days
of 1885. When he urged me to undertake the canvass he offered to pay all the salary and all the expenses. He laid no restrictions upon me and he paid every dollar, and paid

it promptly and cheerfully—that, too, while it was still doubtful whether any good would come out of it, or whether other subscribers would have to pay a cent."*

The tribute paid by Mr. Atwater to Mr. Beaman is not too great. The local committee would have been greatly weakened if he had not been a member of it, and the local work of Hiram will always bear witness to his public enterprise and liberality.

Mr. Atwater was unremitting and conscientious in his canvass. He could speak from the heart for Hiram, for he was one of her first students in time and in ability. He knew her needs for his own growth had been at her side. He could not do great things for the day of great things had not yet come. Of this he says:—"Nobody realizes more than I do that that day was the day of small things and nobody rejoices more heartily over the great advances being made. But in the condition Hiram then was after so many years of weakness, and with all the discouragements, and with the 'Warren movement' hanging over us, there had to be a day of small things before there could be a day of great things."

During this struggle Prof. B. S. Dean was not in the rear rank of efficient helpers. He canvassed Hiram and suc-

B. S. Dean.   ceeded in raising about four thousand dollars, nearly all of which was paid. He also assisted in the canvass of Mahoning and Trumbull counties. In his Hiram canvass Mr. Dean was a volunteer.

Mr. W. H. C. Newington was chosen by the committee

W. H. C. Newington.   of fifteen to solicit funds from the College Alumni. The records do not reveal the result of his labors but with his energy put into the canvass something came out of it.

---

*Letter of O. C. Atwater, Bethany, Neb., June 15, 1900.

The Committee of Ten elected by the Board of Trustees met in Hiram April 16, 1886, and organized by selecting Abram Teachout, Chairman, and George H. Colton, Secretary and Treasurer. The Committee had the authority from the Board of Trustees to build a new and separate building or remodel the old one. They chose the latter after an examination of carefully drawn plans from various architects. The plan adopted was prepared by S. W. Foulk, of New Castle, Pa. The contract for building was awarded to C. W. and J. L. Weaver, of Sharon, Pa., and work was begun on the 8th of June and pushed so rapidly that the corner stone of the structure was laid on Commencement Day, June 17, 1886, with appropriate ceremonies, and the traditional box containing papers, coins, etc., was deposited under the stone. On this occasion speeches of the proper sort were made by Dr. I. A. Thayer, Prof. B. J. Radford, of Eureka, Ill., William Bowler, and Abram Teachout, who concluded the exercises in an appropriate manner. The contract called for the completion of so much of the building by September 28, 1886, as to accommodate the regular classes, and the whole was to be completed by December 1, 1886; but a failure on the part of the brickmaker to furnish the brick in time delayed the work so that the carpenters did not get through until February 19, 1887. During the fall term of 1886, and the first part of the winter term the Town Hall, and the "Baker House" on the west side of the campus were used for college purposes. The new building was dedicated on January 11, and its recitation rooms opened on January 12, 1887. On the day of dedication the weather was extremely cold, but nevertheless a large audience assembled in the new chapel at 1 :45 p. m., the time appointed for the exercises. President Laughlin presided on the occasion and after the opening

Organization of the Committee.

Dedication of the New Building.

prayer by Prof. B. S. Dean the students of the college sang "Ho! Reapers of Life's Harvest." Prof. George H. Colton presented the financial statement of the Building Committee. All this prepared the way for the address of Mr. Abram Teachout, the able chairman of the Building Committee. As his address touches every essential phase from the inception to the completion of the new building the

Mr. Teachout's Address and Report. larger part of it is given here. Addressing the Trustees and friends of Hiram College, Mr. Teachout said:—"This college has for many years been far behind her sister colleges of the State in accommodations for its teachers and students. The want has been referred to in the annual report of its president for several years. It has been seriously considered by the friends of the school. Many valuable students have been lost because of this want. The lack of means to make the necessary improvements has been the chief trouble. It is well known that Hiram College is the outgrowth of the great religious reformation of the nineteenth century which culminated in the organization of what is known as the Christian or Disciple Church. 'Colleges and churches,' said the great Alexander Campbell, 'go hand in hand in the progress of Christian civilization.' 'The number of colleges and churches in any community,' said he, 'is the index and exponent of its Christian civilization and advancement. Colleges and schools of every rank are or ought to be founded upon some great principle in nature and in human society.' As chairman of the Building Committee I think I can safely say that our belief in the above sentiment has stimulated us to accept the heavy responsibility and undertake the work. We have got it where it is, and have invited you here to see what we have done. In behalf of the committee, I thank you for coming, so many of you, and hope you will not have occasion to regret having spent

the day at Hiram.   Your Building Committee was appointed
at a meeting of the Board of Trustees at Garrettsville, held
to consider the matter of expending $10,000 that had been
subscribed for building purposes. Its members were selected
from the store, the farms, the machine shop, and the lumber
yard; also one from the College Faculty, who was quickly
made secretary and treasurer of the committee.   We were
given power to collect the $10,000 subscribed, to employ a
solicitor to continue the subscription, and to go ahead with
the work provided that we would assume all responsibility,
and not encroach upon the endowment fund, or incur any
obligations the college would be required to pay. When that
resolution was passed the members of the committee looked
into each other's faces rather hesitatingly. But, never having
had such honors conferred upon them before, after a few
brief consultations, they concluded to accept, and try their
luck.   There were eight of us, and we were permitted to add
to our number as our judgment should dictate.   At our
second meeting we appointed Rev. E. B. Wakefield, of Warren, O., and Dr. I. A. Thayer, of New Castle, Pa., to act
with us on the committee.   They have been a help to us, for
if they could not furnish much money, they could pray for
us and our success, which we felt at times we very much
needed.   We at once invited plans and estimates for a new
building, not to cost over $15,000.   Three competent archi-
tects furnished plans, which were investigated thoroughly
on the 27th of April, 1886.   The plans were all good and the
estimates reasonable, but they did not give the room needed.
The old building was carefully looked over from basement
to garret, with the idea of building the new in connection
with the old so as to have all in one building, as more room
and a better looking structure could be obtained for the
money.   It could be warmed with less expense, and would
in every respect be more convenient.   We, therefore, asked

the competing architects to submit plans and estimates of
that kind, which they did. We finally adopted the plans
proposed by Mr. S. W. Foulk, of New Castle, Pa. Permit
me to say that there were great misgivings about altering
or changing the old building so that its identity would in
any way be lost. There was a unanimous feeling that, if
practicable, it should stand upon Hiram Hill a monument of
its thirty-six years' work and of the noble men who had
occupied its presidential chair and are now numbered among
the dead. The honorable and godly A. S. Hayden, the scholarly Dr. Silas E. Shepard, the young, active, energetic
teacher, brave soldier, distinguished statesman, and martyred
President, James A. Garfield. I take time only to mention
those that have finished their work and have gone to their
reward. May not some inquiring mind of generations yet
to come, in looking over the records of this Institution and
reading the life of the lamented Garfield and his connection
with the history of our country from 1860 to the time of
his death, September 19, 1881, look up to heaven and say:—

> 'In those dark and stormy days of old
> Arose among the risings of his age,
> A man of massive and gigantic mold,
> Whom we must measure as the Cretan sage
> Measured the pyramids of ages past
> By the far-reaching shadows which he cast.'

Yes, my friends, the shadow of that wonderful man will
reach far down into the ages. But I am digressing and must
return to my work. Your committee held three meetings at
Garrettsville, on May 15, 23, and 28, to open bids and consider and adopt a system of heating and ventilation. In the
meantime Mr. Bowler and myself visited Oberlin and Toledo
to get all the information we could in regard to the most
improved system of heating. On the 29th day of May contract was made with C. W. Weaver, of Sharon, Pa., to erect

the building, and with Isaac D. Smead & Co., of Toledo, O., for heating and ventilating. It became necessary to bargain for extras with Mr. Weaver from time to time, principally to make the old part of the building entirely new in all of its rooms. The work of excavating and quarrying the stone for the foundation was commenced on or about the 8th day of June, and the work was pushed as fast as possible. The corner stone was laid June 17, 1886, the day of the Commencement exercises. There has been general harmony in the committee. Some of them were thought to be a little slack about attending the called meetings, but when called to account for it gave us about the same satisfaction as the preacher received when he took his deacon to task for going to sleep every Sunday as soon as he had commenced his sermon. The deacon's answer was, 'My dear brother, I have perfect confidence in you, and when you get fairly started in your sermon I know everything will be going right anyhow.' I shall not be detracting one syllable from the efficiency of any member of the committee when I say to you that Brother William Bowler has been untiring in his efforts; has spent more time here than any other member of the committee; has watched with a critical eye the work in every department; and, has, I think, made a lasting impression and acquaintance with nearly every workman on the job. He has our sincere thanks. You have heard the report of the Secretary and Treasurer. Every dollar of the money has passed through his hands, and when we consider his duties as teacher in the college, it is almost a marvel that we find his book and statement in so accurate a condition as they are. Our soliciting agents, O. C. Atwater and B. S. Dean, have been industrious and have succeeded as well as could be expected. We have, as the treasurer's report shows, incurred a debt for which we are personally responsible; but we believe you have got value received, and will, according to your abilty, help us to liquidate it. The money we have borrowed is for a reasonable length of time, and at a low rate of interest, all of it drawing only six per cent. We have been kindly tendered more money at that rate of interest than we needed, so that we are flattered that our credit has not suffered, and if you help us out we believe you will be doing a good work. We should labor for the good of our race. This would be a dark and cheerless world if we lived for ourselves alone. We should live for one another."

Mr. Teachout was followed by Rev. Jabez Hall, then of Cleveland, O., in an able and scholarly address in which he urged that the original thought and purpose of the founders of Hiram College should be adhered to, viz.:—"To erect an Institution sacred to Christian learning in which the Living Oracles—the Word of God—should faithfully and fully be taught to all who should resort to this place for the purpose of being educated."

Address of Rev. Jabez Hall.

In impressing this thought Mr. Hall in part said:—

1—"Inasmuch as it was the principal thought of the founders of this college to make it a 'School of the Bible,' there rests upon us an obligation to foster this design. For we have received this Institution thus planned and organized with this special character stamped upon it and wrought into its character. The moneys contributed to the founding and perpetuating the Institution were given for this purpose and with this end in view. The appeal urged constantly on the brotherhood of the 'Disciples' has no other ground to stand on than this: that this Institution is a school of the Bible, a Christian college. From the standpoint of obligation, then, we ought earnestly to strengthen and enlarge the department of Bible instruction in this Institution.

2—"We ought to do this because it is a thing eminently fit and wise to do. Whatever views we may hold of the origin of the sacred books of the Christian religion, we cannot place them in a position inferior to other literatures. The Bible, as a classic, is at least entitled to a prominent place among the best the world possesses. If the future shall not reverse the history of the past, the race will continue to draw from these fountains its richest nourishment for the life that now is. The knowledge it imparts can be gained from no other source, or from no other source so well. Nor is any other knowledge so important to man as that given in the Bible. It has the promise of the life that now is, and of that which is to come. The great books, the enduring books, the vital books, have owed their best inspiration to its influence. Its vitality is only to be accounted for by its intrinsic excellence. As literature has no peer to this matchless 'book of books,' so it can have no substitute for it.

3—"We ought to strengthen and enlarge the department of Bible instruction in this Institution because we believe in it. The body of people known as 'Disciples' have from the first placed special emphasis on Bible study. The college founded at Bethany, West Va., by Alexander Campbell, made this its corner stone. In an address delivered at Bethany, May 31, 1858, on the laying of the corner stone of Bethany College, Mr. Campbell said:—'From the origin of Bethany College on the first Monday of November, 1841, till this day, a period of sixteen years, there has been a Bible study and a Bible lecture for every college day in the college year. The Bible is read, as it was written, in chronological order, and a lecture on every reading is delivered, exegetical of its facts and documents, historical, chronological, geographical; whether they be natural, moral, or religious, in reference to the past, the present, and the future of man. Theories, speculations sometimes called doctrines, faith, orthodoxy, heterodoxy, come not within the legitimate era of collegiate, literary, moral, or Christian education. * * * * In this corner-stone we deposit a copy of the Holy Bible, not to bury it in the earth, but as a monumental symbol of the fact that this Book, this everlasting document ought to be the true and proper foundation of every Literary, Scientific, Moral and Religious institution— essential to the perfect and complete development of man in his whole constitution—as a citizen of the commonwealth, a citizen of the Kingdom of Heaven, and heir of the universe through all the cycles of an eternal future.'

"As a people we have an abiding faith in these principles and in this book. We believe that any education which is not molded by the teachings of the Bible, is so far defective. We believe that the Bible as a text book should be studied every day in everyone of our colleges, and that a student graduating from one of these institutions should know the Bible better than he knows any other book. Ought we not to conform our practice to our faith?

4—"We ought to give more, and *more* thorough attention to Bible instruction in this Institution, because it is a crying need of the times. We want this Institution to be abreast of the needs of the hour. On account, therefore, of the pressing need, we ought to meet this demand.

5—"And finally, numbers of young men come to this Institution for the purpose of fitting themselves for the ministry of the Word of God, and this number could be easily increased if the Institution were fairly well equipped to give the requisite training. It surely needs no argument to prove that if this Institution invites and encourages such persons to come here, it is under weighty obligations to furnish suitable instruction; that the whole man may be educated, body and soul, and so fully equipped for every good work in the world."

Mr. William Bowler followed Mr. Hall in a brief ad-

dress full of thankfulness for what had been done and full
of hope for the future. Among all the
**Address of
Wm. Bowler.** Trustees from the beginning none is
worthier of the title "Trustee of Hope"
than Mr. Bowler; and his hope was always based on his
invincible faith—a faith always supplemented by his unselfish works.

Brief addresses were made by Judge H. C. White, and
W. J. Ford, students of the old Eclectic, and by E. B. Wakefield, one of the first graduates of the col-
**Other
Addresses.** lege. Mr. Teachout then presented the
new building to the Trustees, which was
accepted on their part by Mr. J. H. Rhodes, with appropriate remarks; who in turn committed it to the care of the
Faculty through President G. H. Laughlin.

It was a great day for the college when the new building was completed and ready for use. It settled the question
of location permanently. It established
A Great Day. the fact that the Institution had friends
that would not let it starve or perish. It
also settled the question whether the "Disciples of Christ"
would sustain an Institution whose management was loyal
to the terms of its charter and true to the faith which inspired and moved its founders. The many friends of Hiram
were agreeably surprised when they came to look through
the completed edifice so elaborate and withal so roomy, on
that bleak winter day. The original building at Hiram was
small compared with the new one of which it was now a
part. The front of the new building is the same in width
as the old. Its depth is 103 feet. It is three stories high
exclusive of the basement, and its tower has an elevation of
113 feet. In the basement are found the furnaces by which
the building is heated. As it was when it came from the
hands of the Building Committee in 1887, on the first floor

was a large hall, at the end of which were the commercial room and the laboratory. On one side was the apparatus room and two large recitation rooms. At the end of the hall in the second story was the chapel, large, airy, and beautifully frescoed. On this story also were found the library and reading rooms and four large recitation rooms. In the third story were the museum, the Y. M. C. A. rooms, and the three society rooms. By the erection of other buildings in Hiram the purpose of some of the parts of the building described has changed, but outwardly it is as it appeared in 1887. The entire cost of the work up to the day of dedication as shown by the carefully prepared report of the Treasurer was $22,999.47, of which $9,286.80 remained unpaid but with $2,875 of unpaid subscriptions to be collected, leaving a debt over all pledges of $6,411.80.

During the fifty years of its history Hiram College has employed a large number of persons as Solicitors or Financial Agents. Some of these have served for only a brief period, others for a longer time. Some have had but little success, others have done much. During the lifetime of the Eclectic Institute not less than twenty-five persons were elected solicitors. William Hayden is the first one named. Of all these Dr. W. A. Belding was by far the most successful in his efforts to raise money. The records do not show in any detail the aggregate amount of work that he did or its result; but they do show that from October 14, 1851, when he was first "employed by the Board to act as general solicitor and collector" to the end of his service which covered several years, that he was active and successful. Dr. Belding was present at the meeting at A. L. Soule's in Russell, O., when the first formal steps were taken to establish the Western Reserve Eclectic Institute. So far as known

A Financial Agent's Experiences.

Dr. W. A. Belding.

TEACHOUT LIBRARY ANL OBSERVATORY: ERECTED IN 1900.
(UNFINISHED.)

he is the only one living of all those who made up that important body June 12, 1849. Referring to that meeting and to his work for Hiram Dr. Belding says:—"I was present at that meeting, and when the plan was agreed upon and the determination was made to go ahead with the work, I was selected as its financial and general agent. The raising of the sum needed for such an enterprise seemed like a great undertaking for a people so weak financially and so few in numbers. But I succeeded in raising the first twenty-five thousand dollars to lay the foundation of the Western Reserve Eclectic Institute, which has since grown into the well-known and reputable educational institution called Hiram College. I naturally feel proud of the work there inaugurated and so prosperously carried on. God's blessing has attended it from the first, and many noble men and women have gone forth from its halls, who have honored the Institution, and aided to fill the world with the knowledge and spirit there impressed upon them."* Warren Asa Belding was born at Randolph, O., September 5, 1816, and is yet living in Troy, New York, in his 85th year serene and tranquil in the "full assurance of faith" that he will soon enter that city whose "builder and maker is God." During his long ministry he has baptized over 12,000 persons; has raised large sums of money for church buildings, and for other purposes; has established many churches and is entitled to the quiet he now so much enjoys.

W. J. Ford was first "employed to act as Solicitor and Collector" for Hiram November 9, 1858. In years of continuous service he held the place longer than any other person in the history of the Institution. He was elected a member of the Board of Trustees in 1856 to succeed his father, J. A. Ford. He was

W. J. Ford.

*Biography of Dr. W. A. Belding, p. 72.

a faithful and successful agent and well merited the thanks of the Board, frequently and freely tendered to him. He had many interesting experiences during his long period of service. He is still a member of the Board of Trustees, and retains much of the ardor of his first love for the Institution for which he has done so much. He was born in Burton, O., Nov. 23, 1832, and is living on a farm north of Hiram at the present time. The following resolution was passed by the Board at the conclusion of Mr. Ford's long term of service:—"That W. J. Ford has served with fidelity and unusual success the Eclectic Institute and Hiram College, and is entitled to the gratitude of the Board of Trustees, the stockholders, and all friends of the college for the industry, perseverence, and ability which for a period of twelve years he performed the duties of Solicitor for the Western Reserve Eclectic Institute and Hiram College."

Lathrop Cooley was elected Financial Agent of Hiram College May 16, 1871, at the beginning of the administra-**Lathrop** tion of President B. A. Hinsdale, and **Cooley.** served through a very critical period in the financial history of the college. When he began his work Mr. Cooley had been for many years a noted preacher among the Disciples in Northern Ohio. He had a wide acquaintance with the membership of the church, and a business sagacity which had its influence among business men. His experiences during his numerous canvasses would make an interesting story if given in detail. Mr. Cooley's history is full of interesting facts. He was born in Genesee county, New York, October 25, 1821. In 1829 he came to Mantua, Ohio. From the age of nine until eighteen he worked on a farm and in a shop summers, and attended District school in the winter. In this way he learned to be a farmer and a wagon-maker. At the age of twenty, with the ministry of the Word of God in view, he entered Brooklyn Academy, near Cleveland, paying his expenses while there by working morning and evening at his trade. At the age of twenty-two he began to preach; the first two years of his ministry were spent mostly in Lorain county, traveling on horseback and preaching in school-houses and in shops. At that time there were no settled preachers between the Cuyahoga and Vermillion rivers. Some of the time he traveled in company with William Hayden, who was preaching and holding meetings in that territory. At the age of twenty-four he was called to the pastorate of the Franklin Circle Church in Cleveland, then Ohio City, which had been organized by John Henry February 20, 1842. Mr. Cooley was a charter member of this church, which at that time met in a little hall on Detroit street hill. His first salary was $100 and board with the brethren. On April 12, 1846, he organized a Sunday-school or "Bible School." This was probably the first Sunday-school organized by the Disciples in the State of Ohio. In 1851 he was sent into northern Illinois as a preacher and missionary. For a time he located there preaching in Chicago and outlying districts. In 1853 he returned to Ohio and for a year was employed as an organizing evangelist by the Ohio Christian Missionary Society. During the same year he took charge of the church at North Royalton, O., where he remained for eight years, supplying the pulpit at different times outside of Royalton, at Cleveland, Bedford and Stow. In the spring of 1862 he was called to the Church at Painesville, Ohio, where he remained until 1866. From Painesville he went to Akron as preacher and pastor of the High Street Church, where he remained until 1872. After leaving Akron he preached for the churches on Miles avenue and Franklin avenue in Cleveland for about two years. At the beginning of President Hinsdale's administration at Hiram, he was elected Financial Agent of the college but was not able to devote himself wholly to that

work until 1874. In the fall of 1874 he made a journey to
Egypt and Palestine. On his return in the spring of 1875
he was called to the church in North Eaton, where he remained until 1877. He then returned to Cleveland, where,
unaided and with little encouragement from anyone, he purchased from the German Reformed Body, a church building
on Erie street and organized what is now known as the
Cedar Avenue Disciple Church. This church, with its convenient building, growing from a little handful of members
to its present large and influential membership, will, so long
as it endures, testify to Mr. Cooley's courage, devotion,
liberality and faith in the triumph of the simple story of the
primitive and Apostolic doctrine. In 1880 he took charge
of the Cleveland Bethel, and for several years was its Superintendent and Chaplain. From 1889 to 1892 he was pastor
of the church in Medina. Though he does not now take
upon himself the burden of regular local work, yet the Sundays are few that he does not preach somewhere. For 57
years his voice has been a familiar one to the people and
churches of northern Ohio. He is in good health and vigorous for a man of four-score years and anticipates completing
his 60 years in preaching the simple Gospel of Christ.

June 11, 1879, the Board of Trustees adopted the following resolution: "That Alanson Wilcox be employed as
Alanson   Financial Agent of Hiram College for the
Wilcox.   coming year—his whole time to be given
to the interests of the college, providing that it can be done
without interfering with the present obligations of the
Board." At the time of his election Mr. Wilcox was not a
novice in the kind of work which was required of him. He
had had considerable experience in raising money and in
interesting the churches and people in special enterprises.
He was vigorous in body, quick in action, with tact that
enabled him to find the right side of approach generally

without giving offense, a good evangel of the interests of Hiram. He was especially valuable in interesting young people in the school, and in searching for those who by their wills would make the Institution a beneficiary. His annual reports, extending over a period of five years, are models in that they present in detail what he did, where he went, and the results so far as they could be tabulated. At the time of his service he found that the Disciples within the territory traversed were not a wealthy people; that having made what property they had "by economy and not by commerce," they lacked a spirit of liberality in educational matters; that the ministry of the Disciple churches were not specially interested in the college and its work; and that the old students of Hiram lacked an enthusiasm in her behalf that he had hoped to find. He also found the foot-tracks of the agents of other colleges ahead of his. He made a vigorous effort to change these conditions and he had a fair measure of success. On his election as Corresponding Secretary of the Ohio Christian Missionary Society in 1884, he closed his work as Financial Agent of the college, though his interest in behalf of Hiram and work in her behalf have continued to the present time. In 1889 he was elected to the Board of Trustees, a position he yet holds. He has held the office of Secretary of the Board since 1898. Mr. Wilcox was born in Hinckley, Medina county, Ohio, February 23, 1832. His father, Dr. Orlando Wilcox, was an eminent physician of Connecticut birth and a strenuous advocate of temperance. It is said of him that he organized the first temperance society ever organized in Ohio. He traces his ancestors back 260 years to the north of England. He received his earliest education in the common school at Hinckley, and in the academies at Hinckley and Richfield, and Baldwin Institute at Berea. He entered Hiram as a student in the fall of 1855 and received instruction from Thomas

Munnell, Norman Dunshee, Almeda Booth, H. W. Everest, J. H. Rhodes and James A. Garfield. He was a student in Hiram for three years and received a certificate of scholarship from his teachers when he left. The college conferred on him the degree of A. M. in 1892, and assigned him to the Class of 1871. He began to teach school at the age of sixteen. He began to preach before leaving Hiram and occupied pulpits at Garrettsville, Burton, Mantua, and Crestline, in Ohio. He spent several years in Michigan at Vandalia, and Paw Paw, where his work was successful. He then evangelized in Pennsylvania and West Virginia. After this he spent three years with the church at Muir, Michigan, and in 1866 did evangelistic work in that state. From Michigan he went to Worcester, Mass., where he remained three years, in the meantime planting two churches in New Hampshire and one in Rhode Island. From 1871 to 1873 he was pastor of the Hazlewood Church, Pittsburg, Pa. From 1874 to 1878 he was pastor of the Franklin Avenue Church in Cleveland, O. From 1879 to 1884 he was Financial Agent of Hiram College. From 1884 to 1895 he was Corresponding Secretary of the Ohio Christian Missionary Society. From that time he has been an all-around helper in Sunday-school, college, and church work. At present he is pastor of the Third Christian Church in Youngstown, Ohio. He has been a faithful and tireless worker during all these years and is worthy of the high regard in which he is held. He united with the Church of Christ at Stow, O., in 1851, and counts himself as starting from that place, which he denominates "The mother of preachers," for out from that church have gone J. Carroll Stark, Leonard Southmayd, Alanson Wilcox, F. M. Green, George Musson, and others.

O. C. Atwater, as Financial Agent of the college, began his work April 1, 1886, and continued until the new building

Orris C. Atwater.

was completed in 1887. He had a difficult field to work and the obstacles in his way were many, but with unfaltering faith he proceeded on his mission until he reached a good measure of success. His reports were not so plethoric of money, as of certain other facts which impressed themselves on him as he went on with his work. These facts represent the experiences of all financial agents in a greater or less degree.

First, he was requested not to canvass certain places, thus closing the door for some possible returns; second, he was received by most people kindly, though occasionally the reception was hostile; third, he found that there was an undeveloped interest in the work, and for the most part this interest centered in its religious work; fourth, that it was needful to push on the religious work of the college in order to draw both pupils and funds from wide fields; fifth, that no help is so cheap or so effective as that of preachers when they are once interested in the work. They are *free agents* in the churches they represent; sixth, there is need of continual advertising by the Financial Agent, in the papers, by circulars, by the President, by the Faculty, by the preachers, and by the students; and finally, "Our churches have not been enthusiastic about Hiram, because Hiram has not been enthusiastic about them. Once show them that Hiram will do the work that they desire and help will be found for us." Mr. Atwater's work was well done. His subscriptions were carefully taken and there was but little shrinkage on collection.

A brief chronology of his honorable and faithful life follows:—ORRIS CLAPP ATWATER, the oldest son of Darwin and Harriet Clapp Atwater, was born at Mantua, Portage county, Ohio, September 6, 1833. He was educated first of all, at home by godly parents. His school life began in the

district school of his vicinity. He entered Hiram in 1850 on
the first day of the Western Reserve Eclectic Institute. He
attended the school at Hiram about one term a year until
1858, when he went to Oberlin. He remained at Oberlin
through the college years 1859 and 1860. In 1861 he entered
Williams College and graduated with the class of that year,
receiving the academic Degree of A. B. In 1861-2 he taught
school at Edwardsport, Ind. September 3, 1862, he married
Miss Huldah A. Jackson, a student at Hiram for three years
and a graduate of Oberlin. In 1862 and 1863 he and his
wife taught at Eaton Rapids, Mich. From 1863 to 1865 he
and Mrs. Atwater taught in the High School of Circleville,
Ohio. In 1866 he was a teacher in the schools of Rushville,
Ind. During the same year he returned to Hiram to attend
the first course of lectures to preachers. From 1867 to 1872
he had charged of his father's farm in Mantua, preaching
on Sundays at Mantua, Shalersville, Newton Falls, and occasionally elsewhere. July 8, 1873, he was formally set apart
to the ministry of the Word of God. In 1874 he preached
for a mission church at East Brimfield, Mass. From 1874
to 1879 he preached for the churches at Carthage and South
Butler, New York. From 1879 to 1884 he was pastor of
the church at Randolph, Ohio. From 1884 to 1887 he
preached at Mantua, and April 1, 1886, he was elected Financial Agent of Hiram College and served for a little more
than one year. In 1887 he located at Greencastle, Ind., where
he remained until 1889. From 1890 to 1893 he preached in
Iowa and Nebraska, principally at Falls City and Kearney.
Since then his home has been at Bethany, Nebraska. From
here he goes out to preach but without removing his family.
His two children, Charles Jackson Atwater, and Ellen Bessie
Atwater, were both much loved students of Hiram College.
Ellen was at Hiram from 1884 to 1888, received the Degree
of A. B. from Cotner University in 1891, and at present is

Professor of History and English in that Institution. Charles graduated at Hiram in 1888. He was also a graduate student in De Pauw University, and the University of Chicago. After serving as Professor of Ancient Languages, in Fairfield College, Nebraska, from 1892-1894, and Professor of Greek in Oskaloosa College, Iowa, from 1895 to 1896, he died greatly mourned at Oskaloosa March 4, 1897. He was greatly beloved for many admirable qualities of mind and heart.

In these sketches of Financial Agents from the founding of the Eclectic Institute to the close of the period under consideration no special mention is made of a large number of persons who did much in raising money and creating interest in the Institution; but only those are sketched who were formally elected by the Board as Financial Agents, and in time and results made an impression on its affairs. Principals and Presidents of the Institute and the College, members of the Faculty, trustees, preachers, and distinguished citizens, at one time or another, have done much in the same field for the financial and other interests of Hiram, and deserve to be remembered for what they have done.

Immediately on the resignation of President Laughlin the Board began a search for a successor. After considerable correspondence Professor W. H. Woolery, of Bethany, West Va., was unanimously chosen, at a salary of $1,500. June 7, 1887, Mr. Woolery accepted the position. In his letter of acceptance to O. C. Atwater, Secretary *pro. tem.* of the Board, he said:—"Yours of June 4, informing me that I am elected President of Hiram College, came to hand yesterday. I accept the position, and express through you to the Board of Trustees my appreciation of the high place with which they have honored me. I promise with the co-operation of the friends of Hiram to work for

Looking for a New President.

the continued usefulness of the school and for a large constituency to which we may appeal. With many thanks for the Board's confidence, Yours Fraternally, W. H. Woolery."

Mr. Woolery was a man of fine physical presence, a well-cultured mind, a genial heart, and good executive ability, and his selection was looked upon with great favor by the friends of Hiram who knew him. But in less than a month from the date of his letter of acceptance he wrote another recalling his acceptance and declining the election. This letter was accompanied by one from President W. K. Pendleton, of Bethany. It is not necessary to enter into details concerning the matter. It is sufficient to say that the reasons given for his change of attitude by Mr. Woolery were accepted by the Board of Trustees of Hiram and a new committee began its search for a President. That committee consisted of B. A. Hinsdale, William Bowler, and Lathrop Cooley.

During the year ending June, 1888, the college was without a President and the modest Professor of Mathematics and Astronomy, Colman Bancroft, was chosen "Chairman of the Faculty" and acted as President for the year. In his report June 14, 1888, to the Board of Trustees Mr. Bancroft said:—"You are familiar with the circumstances that led to my very reluctant acceptance for the year now closing, of the title "Chairman of the Faculty." This modest place brought upon me in addition to the work of an instructor, a considerable part of the duties usually devolving upon the College President. Though unaccustomed to such duties, and having at my disposal little time to do all that clearly ought to be done for a school by its presiding officer, the ready co-operation of the Faculty has secured a fairly prosperous year. The teachers have without exception been competent and thorough in their instruction, and, for the most part, the students

Prof. C. Bancroft, Chairman of the Faculty.

have taken satisfactory rank in their classes." An epidemic of measles among the students seriously interfered with the work of the winter term, and resulted fatally in the case of two or three students. There had been, however, no serious diminution of interest in any of the college departments and the year came to its close with numerous signs of promise.

In the meantime the committee to select a President had not been idle, and at a special meeting of the Board of Trustees January 18, 1888, they made the following report: — "The undersigned committee respectfully recommend the election of E. V. Zollars as President of Hiram College at a salary of $1,600 per year, his term of office to begin at the close of the current college year." The report of the committee was unanimously adopted by the Board and Mr. Zollars was declared elected. He was notified of the action of the Board and on March 5, 1888, his letter of acceptance was received and placed on file.

Election of E. V. Zollars.

At the close of Professor Bancroft's service as "Chairman of the Faculty," the Board expressed its appreciation of his work in the following resolution: "That the thanks of the Board of Trustees of Hiram College be hereby expressed to Professor Bancroft for the invaluable service he has rendered the college during the past year by acting as its President, and that we place on record our grateful recognition of his faithful and efficient services."

Thanks to Prof. Bancroft.

The Institution had now passed thirty-eight years of its history. It had had its days of doubt and its days of hope. Sometimes its garments had been too small to cover its nakedness and again they were full size. Through all of its difficulties and over all the obstacles in its way, it had made a steady though slow progress until it was recognized as a College of no mean rank.

Getting Ready for the New Administration.

It had enlarged its material equipment until it was able to accommodate a hoped-for increase of students. Its society halls were new and handsomely furnished. Its Board of Trustees was composed of men, many of whom had never flinched in the face of its greatest difficulties.

Its Faculty had been tried under the most adverse conditions and had been found true. In temper they were congenial and they worked in harmony for the interests of the College. Their pay was small but their hope was large. In ability and experience they were able to command consideration for the departments they respectively controlled.

The question of change of location had been hushed by the logic of events; and the evidence of a return to their "first love" was manifest on every hand among the old constituency of Hiram. One had been called to the presidency who was not a novice in the management of schools; and although a stranger to the personal traditions of Hiram, had fairly compassed the situation and was ready to act.

During the great contest at Gettysburg, when the life of the Republic was the prize of battle, a color-bearer was struck down, and then another and another, and courage was put to the highest test. The colonel of the regiment called one of his trusted men to him and said: "Sergeant, take this flag, bear it aloft, do not surrender it in dishonor, return with it or report the reason why." The sergeant received the colors and marched against the pitiless hail of war. He did not surrender and he did not return but when the battle ceased his commander knew the reason why. The Board of Trustees said to the President-elect, "Take the banner of Hiram College and bear it unsullied and without dishonor or report the reason why." He accepted the trust and what he did, and how he did it, will be the interesting subject of the next chapter of Hiram's history.

CHAPTER VIII.

HIRAM COLLEGE—ADMINISTRATION OF E. V. ZOLLARS.
1888—1900.

There are certain qualities of mind and character essential in a College President to fit him for the successful administration of college affairs. It is impossible to manufacture College Presidents to order; like poets they must be born, not made. He should have judgment, tact, and be well-informed; with grace of speech and "persistent though cautious in method;" joined to a natural fondness for administrative detail and for problems of classification and of organization. And above all he must have confidence in himself and faith in his undertaking.

Essential Elements in a College President.

In the selection of E. V. Zollars the Board of Trustees were fortunate. He had the essential qualities of mind and character. Years of experience had demonstrated his ability as an administrator of the details of a successful school. He had a fixed and clear ideal of what a Christian College should be, with confidence that it could be reached if the proper assistance was rendered. In his acceptance of the Presidency he was not hasty but took time to consider the question from the various standpoints of personal interest, local and general church interests, and the interests of Hiram College. February 10, 1888 he accepted the trust in a letter of considerable length addressed to the Board of

E. V. Zollars a Good Selection.

Trustees of which the following are a few sentences: "Allow
me, first of all, to express to you my sin-
cere thanks for this mark of your confidence, manifested in calling me to a position not only honorable in itself, by reason of the wonderful possibilities it affords for doing a great and important work, but rendered
doubly so by reason of the able and distinguished men that
have filled it with such credit to themselves, to the Institution and to the cause of Christian education. Realizing the
weight of responsibility imposed by these considerations, I
would shrink from assuming such a burden were it not for
the fact that your call comes to me supplemented by the solicitations of disinterested men for whose judgment I have
a profound respect, and in opposition to which, I feel loath
to move. Another important circumstance in enabling me
to reach a decision is the fact that your call invites me to a
kind of work to which I have given ten years of valuable
time, and for which I have a passionate fondness. Moved,
therefore, by the advice of men of discriminating judgment,
who know me and understand the work to which you call
me; attracted both by the greatness of the work and my personal love for it; looking upon the successful past history
of Hiram College as the guarantee of an honorable
future, I am constrained to accept your most flattering call, believing that in doing so I am moving not simply
in a path marked out for me by the judgment of wise yet
fallible men, but in a line of duty to which I am called by the
Divine Father, to whom I may, therefore confidently look
for wisdom and support in discharge of the grave responsibilities imposed upon me. To maintain the present high literary standard of the Institution, and at the same time supplement the various courses with such a liberal measure of
Bible study as the exigencies of the case and the demands

*Mr. Zollars
Accepts
the Position.*

of the times require, is, in my judgment, the problem of the immediate future. Furthermore the question of ministerial education is one of increasing interest and transcendent importance. Never before was the call for educated preachers so great as it is at the present time. To the solution of these questions I shall, therefore, give my best thought and greatest energies, being strengthened by the consciousness that I shall have your most hearty sympathy and co-operation, as well as the cordial support of Hiram's many friends."

When Mr. Zollars entered upon his work as President of Hiram College he was 41 years of age. Physically he was strong and his body was built for hard service. His mind had been well disciplined by his college course and by many years of service as teacher. He was a good judge of men and strong in his power to persuade them. He had an idea that a teacher who could teach was one who could "push forward the limits of human knowledge in some direction, or who could add to the interpretations of the knowledge which we already possess; and that he must be devoted to a particular line of study; and must have the power to pursue researches, the will to continue and interpret them, and the magnetic attraction which will draw students to them and fire them with his teacher zeal and ambition." This ability enabled him to usually select the right persons for his assistants in school and College work. His parents were Christians and they did not neglect the heart culture of their son. From his mother's knee he was trained in a life of virtue and of Christian service. He became a member of the Christian Church June 7, 1863, and along the pathway he then entered he has not faltered for a day. He entered Bethany College in 1871 and graduated from that institution in 1875, sharing the first honors of the classical Course with E. T. Williams, now a missionary in China, delivering the

A Character Sketch of E. V. Zollars.

Greek salutatory. Shortly before his graduation he began preaching, a business for which he showed a decided talent. Mr. Zollars is a strong preacher, and on great occasions his efforts are of the best. His Baccalaureate sermons have been superior in thought and expression. He is especially strong in enforcing the moral phases of his theme, and in his power of persuasion. For a year after his graduation he taught Ancient Languages in Bethany College. He then spent a year as Financial Agent of the College with good success, making a thorough canvass wherever he went. It was of little use for another to follow him after he had gone over the field. He became President of Kentucky Classical and Business College at North Middletown, Ky., in 1877, and remained there until 1884, when he was elected President of Garrard Female College at Lancaster, Ky., where he remained one year, resigning to accept a call to the pastorate of the Christian Church at Springfield, Illinois, from whence he came to Hiram in 1888.

The blood of the sturdy Hollander and the dauntless Puritan mingles in his veins. His great-grandmother was the daughter of a soldier of the Revolutionary War. Socially he is warm-hearted and sympathetic, quick to perceive and prompt to act, and his friendships are strong and abiding. Of academic degrees he received that of A. B. and A. M. from Bethany and LL. D. from Hiram. He is of restless temperament and his energy is incarnate in every vital force of his distinctly marked personality. Much was expected of him when he came to Hiram and much has been accomplished. A brief chronology of his life follows:

E. V. Zollars' Chronology.

E. V. Zollars was born Sept. 19th, 1847, on a farm near lower Salem, Washington County, Ohio. He attended a select school in Marietta, Ohio, taught by Miss Mary Cone for about two years in 1860 and 1861. Attended preparatory department of Marietta College for about two years from 1862 to 1863, completing the work required for entrance to the freshman class of this institution. Clerked in a grocery store in Marietta in 1864 and married October 26th, 1865 to Miss Hulda Louise McAtee of Washington County, Ohio. Engaged in mercantile business for a short time in 1865. Engaged in farming in Washington County from the spring of 1866 to the summer of 1871. Entered Bethany College 1871, graduated from Bethany College in 1875. Taught in Bethany the session of 1875 and '76, filling the adjunct chair of Ancient Languages. Acted as Financial Secretary Bethany College 1876 and 1877, still retaining the position of adjunct Professor of Ancient Languages. Resigned work in Bethany College in June, 1877 and accepted the presidency of Kentucky Classical and Business College, filling this position for seven years. Became President of Garrard Female College in the fall of 1884. Became pastor of the church at Springfield, Ill., 1885. Served in this capacity three years. Became President Hiram College, 1888. The following is a list of books and pamphlets written by E. V. Zollars: 1893 and 1894, Holy Book and Sacred Day, a work on Biblical introduction printed in Garrettsville and issued by Standard Publishing Co. 1894 and 1895, Bible Geography, published by Standard Publishing Co. 1895, Great Salvation, being a discussion of the first principles of the gospel. Published by Standard Publishing Co. Hebrew Prophecy. This book is in process of preparation at the present time and is nearly completed; besides numerous pamphlets.

The first Faculty of Hiram College led by President Zollars consisted of Colman Bancroft, Professor of Mathematics and Astronomy; George H. Colton, Kerr Professor of Natural Science; George A. Peckham, Professor of Ancient Languages and Literature; Arthur C. Pierson, Professor of English Literature and Modern Languages; Bailey S. Dean, Professor of History; Edwin L. Hall, Adjunct Professor of Ancient Languages; Mary B. Hamilton, Principal of the Ladies' Department; Addie L. Zollars, Teacher of Music; Lilian E. Morgan, Teacher of Painting; Benjamin F. Pritchard, Principal of Commercial Department; A. B. Russell, Teacher of Elocution; W. H. Mooney, and G. A. Ragan, Tutors in English and Preparatory Departments. Several of these were teachers of long experience and held a high place as scholars in their respective departments. In 1890 Edmund B. Wakefield was elected Professor of Political Science and Biblical Theology; William A. Knight, Assistant in English Department; E. A. Ott, Teacher of Elocution; John Shackson, J. B. Works, Mrs. A. A. McCorkle, Angie B. Proctor and H. D. Messick, Tutors in English and Preparatory Departments. In 1891 a few new names appear: Cora M. Clark was elected Professor of Modern Languages; Helen B. Pettibone, Principal of Ladies' Department; C. B. Ellinwood, Assistant Teacher of Music; Helen E. King and Jennie A. Robison, Teachers of Painting; Carl B. Harris, Principal of Commercial Department; and John G. Scorer, Teacher of Elocution.

In 1892 the names of H. H. Howard, Teacher of Painting, and Calvin C. Ryder, Instructor in Natural Science, appear. In 1893 Alonzo Skidmore appears as Professor of English and Instructor in Ancient Languages; Lola E. Scott, Instructor in the English Department and in Mathematics; Mrs. Emma J. Dean, Teacher of China Decoration and Pastel; Homer W. Campbell, Principal of the Business Department; Mrs. Hattie L. Barclay, Principal of Ladies' Department; John T. Bridwell and Myrta G. Parsons, Tutors.

In 1894 Harlan M. Page was elected Professor of Biology and Medical Science; Marcia Henry, Instructor in Ancient Languages and English; Arthur G. Harshman, Teacher of Music; A. M. Newins, Teacher of Elocution; Miss Mary Graybiel, Principal of Ladies' Department; and E. J. Smith, Tutor in Mathematics.

In 1895 Marcia Henry became Principal of the Ladies' Department, a position she holds to the present time; Silas Warren Pearcy, Assistant in Ancient Languages; Lula Freeman Pearcy, Teacher of Music; Alice Cornelia Brooks, Teacher of Landscape Painting; William Edward Adams, Principal Department of Oratory; Lora Elma Wire, Instructor in Physical Culture and Elocution; Grace Greenwood Finch, Instructor in Physical Culture; and Belle Griffith, Della P. Hart, Mary B. Logue, Charles A. Niman, Vernon Stauffer, Mary Wilson, Tutors in Preparatory Department. In 1896 Hugh McDiarmid was elected Professor of New Testament Introduction and Christian Doctrine; Mrs. Dasa Boden, Teacher of Landscape Painting; Robert P. Shepherd, Instructor in Law and Political Science; Elmer E. Snoddy, Instructor in Greek; Risher W. Thornberry, and Olive D. Pearcy, Instructors in Gymnasium Work; and Charles G. Phillips, Helen Stoolfire, Lulu Phinney, Ella R. Dodd, Eugene B. Dyson, Walter S. Hertzog, William D. Van Voorhis, Marc O. Pinney, Laura F. Craft, Tutors in Preparatory Department.

In 1897 Mayme C. Fuller became Assistant Instructor in Oratory; Eugene Feuchtinger, Director of Music Conservatory and Teacher of Voice Culture, Piano, Composition, Theory and History; Allie M. Dean, Teacher of Flower and Figure Painting; James Earnest Dean, Teacher of Free Hand and Mechanical Drawing; and Errett W. McDiarmid, Tutor in Latin.

In 1898 Kate S. Parmly was elected Assistant in Ladies'

Department and Teacher of Elocution; Clara L. Whissen, Teacher of Piano and Violin; Elisha Blackburn, F. B. Messing, Elizabeth Carlton, Instructors in Gymnasium Work; and J. A. Miller, R. O. Newcomb, Karl Hertzog, Elizabeth Scott, Tutors in Latin, Algebra, German, and English.

In 1899 Ellsworth F. Burch was chosen Teacher of Commercial Arithmetic and Correspondence; and C. M. Young, S. H. Calender, F. C. Landsittel, Tutors of French and English.

In 1900 Frank Home Kirkpatrick was elected Professor of Oratory; William McKenzie, Principal of the Business Department; Josephine E. Line, Instructor in Physical Training; and J. W. Wiseman, W. W. Frost, W. W. Wager, Tutors.

The annual reports of President Zollars are clear, comprehensive, and in detail cover all departments in the life and progress of the College. No better view can be had of the internal affairs of the College, and no better general view of the condition of the various interests involved, than is furnished by these annual reports.

The Annual Reports of President Zollars.

President Zollars made his first report to the Board of Trustees in 1889. It was the twenty-second annual report of the Institution since it was incorporated as a College. The total increase by terms in the enrollment was 102. The excess of enrollment over the preceding year was 30. The per cent of gain 22. The total enrollment by terms was 545, which represented 251 different students. Of the year's progress Mr. Zollars said: "Hiram College has passed through the most prosperous year in its history. Never before has the future seemed so full of promise. The problem as to how the new lines of work could be carried on without in any way curtailing or weakening the former work

1889.

has been solved. The friends of the College have shown a disposition to lend such financial support as may be necessary to accomplish the much desired object. Such interest and enthusiasm seem to have sprung up for Hiram and its work, that today we are enabled to look into the future with highest anticipations and fondest hopes." The permanent producing endowment of the college was represented as $51,240, and a temporary five-year endowment had been secured during the year of $30,000. The income from tuition was $4,300, and the total income $8,731. A new piano was purchased, improvements had been made in the Laboratory, and some repairs on the College buildings which created a deficit of less than two hundred dollars. The College had been well advertised during the year through the College paper, the weekly papers published by the Disciples, by willing friends, by the Faculty and by the President.

The report for 1890 was full of hope and enthusiasm. The permanent endowment fund was reported at $53,652.26. The temporary endowment had reached $61,500, and the entire income from all sources was $14,-193.18. Permanent improvements had been made at a cost of $2,060.72, on which there was a deficit of $1,140.39. The increase in the number of students had been sufficient to increase the tuition receipts to $6,029.33. The total number of different students enrolled had reached 324, and the total by terms 746. Of this number 27 were pursuing the Classical Course; 72 the Philosophical; 20 the Ministerial; 106 the Scientific; and 9 the Special Ministerial Course.

Of the year's work and results President Zollars said: "In visiting churches during the past year in Hiram's interest I have discovered that the Institution has a firm hold upon the affections of a large number of people. I have yet the first appeal to make for Hiram without meeting with a generous response. The feeling is not only one of interest but of real enthusiasm. True, we have many hard problems yet to solve, many difficulties still to overcome, but the success of the past and the honor and love in which Hiram is held give me large hope for the future. Great possibilities are certainly within our reach."

The report for 1891 opens with the declaration that, "In a history covering twenty-four years of college work, the chapter that the session of 1890-'91 has added, deserves an

1891.
important, if not indeed the first place." The number of different students enrolled was 325, and the total by terms 759. Of the different students there were 205 gentlemen, and 120 ladies. Mr. B. F. Pritchard, who had charge of the Commercial Department of the College, died. He was a faithful worker and much beloved by all who knew him. The permanent endowment fund was reported as $61,199.23, and the temporary endowment as $63,077. The receipts from tuition were $6,324.51, and from all sources $16,576.79. In closing his report President Zollars said: "Everything looks hopeful and encouraging. Everywhere throughout the State the interest in Hiram is rapidly growing, as well as in many other States. The churches approve our work and are more willing to assist us than ever before. My appeals for help have met with uniform success. We hear of many new students who expect to come and a smaller per cent. of our old students will drop out at the end of the year than heretofore. There is a general feeling of hopefulness and confidence among Faculty and students that is truly inspiring. To the College authorities the future never looked so bright as it does to-day."

In beginning his report for 1892 President Zollars said: "We are brought to the satisfactory close of the most suc-

1892. cessful year that Hiram College has ever witnessed. The Hiram tide, which has been gradually rising for the past four years, reached proportions during the past session exceeding the expectations of its most ardent friends. We need no longer look into the past to see what may be accomplished in the way of numbers, but we may confidently look to the future for still greater things. The question of numbers will be largely determined by the facilities which Hiram shall provide for taking care of those who may desire to come. The indications are that our numbers will increase faster than our facilities will grow."

During the year 372 different students were enrolled, and a total by terms of 860. These were distributed in the Classical Course, 37; Long Ministerial Course, 31; Philosophical Course, 61; Scientific Course, 50; Four Years' Literary Course, 45; and Four Years' Ministerial Course, 33.

The permanent endowment fund had reached $69,198.15, and the temporary endowment yielded returns from $60,000. The total receipts for the year were $17,614.87, and the total expenses were $15,960.97. In the conclusion of the report President Zollars said: "The work that Hiram College is doing is meeting with general favor, as is shown by the continually increasing attendance. We confidently expect a still larger increase of patronage during the coming year."

The report for 1893 was full of the elements representing substantial growth. The results were very gratifying **1893.** to the Faculty, the Board of Trustees, and the rapidly growing constituency of the College. The glory of each year had been swallowed up by the greater glory of the year that followed, and so filled the President with the hope that like the path of the just, the future course of the Institution might be as "the shining light that shineth more and more unto the perfect day."

Thirty States and countries were represented in its student body, the larger portion, of course, being from Ohio. The intellectual standard of the school was high, and the moral tone exalted. The religious life was vigorous, and the physical man was not neglected. True manhood and womanhood at Hiram counted for more than anything else. The false and superficial standards of wealth or position are swept away by the higher considerations of real merit. An honest, earnest young person, possessed of noble purpose and high ideals, becomes at once a member of Hiram's aristocracy, "no matter how poor and humble he may be."

The total number of different students enrolled during the year was 405; and the total by terms 931, a large increase over the preceding year. The invested funds of the permanent endowment and permanent endowment notes had reached an aggregate of $115,000. The cost of the school for the year had reached $18,300, of which about $600 were for permanent improvements. A detailed list of donors to the silver jubilee endowment fund was given, their gifts amounting to $75,333.92. More money had been contributed to the College than in any other single year of its history.

The report for 1894 did not reveal an increase in patronage, but notwithstanding the great business depression that existed throughout the country, causing a

1894.

serious loss of patronage to many schools, the average term enrollment was up to that of any former year. The work accomplished during the year was of excellent quality, and the results were very gratifying.

The President said: "Hiram can in no sense be considered a local school. True, it draws very largely from Northeastern Ohio, but every section of the State is represented, and we also have students from at least twenty-five other States and countries. Not only has Hiram won a national reputation, but she is rapidly securing a national patronage."

The number of different students enrolled was 395, of whom 253 were young men and 142 were young women. The total enrollment by terms was 925.

The total income from all sources for the year was $20,350, and the amount expended for permanent improvements $3,396.62. During the College year Harmon Austin, who had been a life-long friend of the College, died, which led the President to say: "In his departure Hiram College sustains a loss that will be deeply felt. Hiram cannot boast of massive buildings, large endowments or extensive equipments, but she is rich in the memory of many great and noble souls, who have labored unselfishly in her advancement."

In opening his report for 1895 President Zollars said: "We are permitted under Divine Providence to chronicle the
1895. history of another most prosperous session; perhaps, all things considered, we may say, the most prosperous year that our College has ever passed through. The winter and spring terms have shown a decided increase over the corresponding terms of any previous year, which, considering the general business depression, must be regarded as phenomenal. It is the universal verdict that the work of the school was never more satisfactory, and the quality of the students is a cause for profoundest satisfaction. It has never been my privilege to come in contact with a body of students of higher moral and intellectual quality."

The number of different students had reached 395, and the total by terms 939. The receipts for current expenses for the year were $17,169.20. The President, under the direction of the Board of Trustees, devoted a large portion of his time to the financial interests of the College, and the results were, for the time actually engaged, $500 a week. Meanwhile the Financial Secretary, Mr. O. G. Hertzog, had received, in pledges, money and various gifts, $10,095.70. The hamlet of Hiram had grown in a substantial way, thus adding to the accommodations for the school.

The report for 1896 showed the largest average term attendance in the history of the school. The work of the school had been highly satisfactory and marked by great earnestness on the part of the student body. This was accounted for in part "by the very high intellectual and moral character of the Hiram students, in part by the fact that a large majority of the students were self-supporting, and consequently were working with a definite purpose in view, and in part by the location of the College relieving them from distracting influences, and enabling the students to concentrate their thought and energy upon the immediate work in hand." Looking backward seven or eight years and comparing with the present, Hiram had doubled itself in several particulars, viz: In the capacity of the town to accommodate students; in the actual number of students in attendance; in the number of courses offered; in the number of studies provided; in the number of professors and teachers; in its endowment; in its income; in its buildings; and in the number of its alumni.

During the year there were 422 different students, and a total by terms of 1,018. The receipts from all sources for College purposes were $19,605.46. The total of invested funds was $84,417.41. As the College had grown in the increase of public interest, and the enlargement of its student body, its expenditures and necessities had correspondingly increased, and the President's recommendations for more endowment, more teachers, more apparatus, more library and more of many other things were persistent and emphatic.

The report of 1897 showed a less number of students than were enrolled in the preceding year; though the number of different students enrolled reached 400, and the total by

1897. terms was 934. This falling off was generally attributed to the financial stringency of the country at that time. The year, however, had been very satisfactory in the work done in the College, in the improvements in buildings, and especially in the completion of the new Y. M. C. A. building. Of the new building the President said: "We scarcely knew how badly we needed this building until we got it. We felt the pressure of more room very greatly and knew that our work was suffering for lack of room, but since we have gotten into the new building we do not see how we got along without it so long. We now have sufficient room for our present teaching force." The receipts for the year from all sources, for current work, were $21,487.52, of which $7,733.84 were from tuition. The friends of the College had abundant reason for rejoicing in the success of the year.

The report for 1898 was very encouraging and hopeful. The falling off the year before had been more than made good. The enrollment had reached **1898.** 421 different students and a total by terms of 1,015. The receipts for the year amounted to $25,142.86 and the disbursements to $24,864.15. The total invested funds of the college amounted to $85,-486.21; and the aggregate value of the college property, including endowment, was represented as $204,333.18. The imperative need of a large endowment was emphasized by the President. It now costs the College in round numbers $20,000 to carry on its work; and in his judgment it was "practically impossible for Hiram College to do less work than it is now doing. There is not a single department of work that we can cut off without seriously crippling the school." On the question of more endowment he said: "It will be seen that more endowment is imperatively demanded if the school is to be placed on an enduring basis. At present the legitimate income of the school from tuition and endowment falls, at least, four thousand dollars short of meeting the necessary current expenses. This would soon bankrupt the school if it were not provided for in some way. An additional endowment of one hundred thousand dollars would solve the Hiram problem for an indefinite time to come. No measures should be left untried that promise to secure this much-needed endowment. This is the one overshadowing problem that the Board of Trustees of Hiram College are compelled to confront."

President Zollars, in his report for 1899, says: "It affords me great pleasure to say that the year just closing has been most satisfactory in all respects.

1899.

We have made the largest enrollment the Institution has ever had. Each term shows an increase in attendance over the corresponding term of any previous year. While this increase has not been large, yet it is sufficient to show that the vitality of the school has not been lost or impaired. The fact is being demonstrated every year that the growth of the last few years is not spasmodic or uncertain and liable to be followed by reaction, but, on the contrary, that it is solid and substantial, and has a basis in the growing confidence of the people in the work and stability of the Institution."

The necessity for a larger income to meet the expenses of the college was made apparent by the increasing patronage, and the increase in the number of teachers to supply the demand. A committee had been appointed by the Board of Trustees to formulate a plan for the raising of the much-needed endowment. This committee decided to inaugurate a movement to add two hundred and fifty thousand dollars to the endowment of Hiram College by the close of its jubilee year—the fiftieth since the Institution was opened for students. This plan contemplated a "popular movement" in which a large number would be interested in its success.

The enrollment by terms reached the large number of 1,075, represented by 443 different students. Of these 93 had decided to enter the ministry; 7 to be missionaries; 81 teachers; 23 studied music; 28 medicine; 41 law; the remainder undecided.

The number of students from other States and countries had become so large that several clubs or associations had been formed to cultivate fraternal relationships, for social pleasure, and to keep the interests of Hiram before their respective localities. These organizations were known as "The Empire State Club," "Canadian Society," "Pennsylvania Club," "Indiana Club," and "Dixie Club."

The receipts of the college for the year were $27,043.93, of which $8,686 were from tuition. In closing his report the President said: "The great work of the past simply makes a much larger future work a possibility. A great weight of responsibility is laid upon those to whom the destiny of the Institution has been committed. We cannot be satisfied to do even as well as our predecessors have done. We must do much better or we will do much worse. The history, the prestige, the glory of the past lay upon us a burden of responsibility which we dare not, which we must not cast aside."

The report for 1900 showed the college receipts from all sources to be $24,642.77, of which $10,356.50 were from **1900.** tuition. This was the largest amount ever received in any one year from tuition, in the history of the Institution.

The enrollment of students included the names of 436 different students, of whom 200 were ladies, and 236 gentlemen, and the total enrollment by terms reached 1,080. The personnel of the student body had never been better. The moral tone of the school had been of the best quality, and the religious life intense. There had not been a case calling for discipline during the year; and with an average term attendance of 360 this fact was remarkable. The reports from the various departments of the College were indicative of strength and progress. Each Professor and Teacher made a report from his particular field. The Conservatory of Music, under the direction of Prof. Eugene Feuchtinger, with only three years behind it, began the year with a large attendance, which was kept up during the year.

The literary societies—the Delphic, Hesperian, Olive Branch, Alethean, and Garfield—all had had marked success during the year. There were students enough from New England to form a "New England Club," which its members hoped would be sufficiently strong to become a connecting link to "closely join our far-away New England to our dear old Hiram Hill."

In closing his comprehensive and carefully detailed report, President Zollars said: "Fifty years of history are completed. From small beginnings the Institution has steadily grown, strengthening itself with each year. Wonderful has been the work accomplished. Its name and history are cherished by thousands of those who have enjoyed the benefits of the instruction it has given, and by tens of thousands who know it only because of the reputation it has made and because of the work that it has done. Hundreds of earnest young men and women have gone forth from the Institution during these fifty years who have left a deep impress upon the day and generation in which they lived. Their influence has been felt to the very ends of the earth. In the pulpit, in medicine, in law, in business, in all the varied fields of human activity Hiram men have honored themselves and the Institution by the efficient service that they have rendered. This current of young life that has been flowing out from Hiram these fifty years with an ever-increasing volume, has been a stream of blessing to the whole wide world. The work has been done in a modest, unpretentious way. There has been no flourish of trumpets, no pompous display, but quietly, modestly, yet with wonderful efficiency, the work has moved forward with ever-increasing momentum like the current of a mighty river. To-day we stand looking both to the past and to the future. We feel that a great weight of responsibility rests upon us. We must do a great deal better than Hiram has ever done or we will do a great deal worse. There are traditions to be cherished, there are ideals to be upheld, there are lofty purposes to be fostered, there is noble service to be emulated. The great sacrifices of the past, which are indeed the glory of Hiram, demand greater sacrifice of us to-day because of the larger possibilities within our reach. The noble workers who have been connected with Hiram in the past point out to us the line of duty that lies before us, and indicate the high grade of service that is demanded at our hands. It is not sufficient that we hold Hiram up to the early standards. The Hiram of the early day was a mighty advance upon the standards of its time, but we must recognize the exalted position that the Hiram of the past occupied and see that the Hiram of the present is lifted up to the highest standards of to-day, and that it shall maintain that lofty position that the ever-advancing standards of the future shall demand. Truly we may be thankful to our Heavenly Father for what, under Him, we have been able to achieve. We may certainly take an honest pride in a worthy work well done; but let us turn our faces to the future, and with an unwavering trust invoke the help of Him who has never forsaken us, and go forward to our duties with strong faith and large expectations. Let us make the past glorious as it has been, but the beginning of the great things along the line of higher education that shall be wrought out by the Hiram of the future, so that our children, when the centennial shall have come, will rejoice in the Hiram of that day as we now rejoice in the Hiram of the present."

There are some elements in these annual reports that are particularly noticeable, and which reveal the character of
Character of Annual Reports. President Zollars. Among them is the broad and comprehensive view which he takes of the College requirements, present and prospective, and his distinct perception of what is needed to meet these requirements. His annual reports show a patience of detail that is remarkable. Nothing is overlooked, and every worker and every department receives its due recognition. And though he sees the difficulties of the situation and with vigor insists on having what ought to be had, and must be had, in order to meet these difficulties, he does not become despondent if the response is not as immediate as he could wish; but with an optimism that always carries encouragement, he sheds the light of his faith and hope upon the problem, and with invincible courage throws the whole power of his personality upon it until it is solved. He has thrown no doubt on the educational function of the presidential office; but he has exalted the administrative side of the office so that the twelve years of his administration have shown, with no disparagement to any other, that a master has been at the head of the school.

Beginning with a total of 221 different students, and a total by terms of 443 in 1888, the successive years have shown a change in these respective numbers as follows: 1889, 251 and 545; 1890, 324 and 746; 1891, 325 and 759; 1892, 372 and 860; 1893, 405 and 931; 1894, 395 and 925; 1895, 395 and 939; 1896, 422 and 1,018; 1897, 400 and 934; 1898, 421 and 1,015; 1899, 443 and 1,075; 1900, 436 and 1,080; or, counting by years, 4,589 different students, or counting by terms, 10,827; or an average per year of 382 different students, and by terms 301.

By years and by terms the figures that follow represent the number of the student body from the opening of the col-

CAMPUS IN WINTER. From College Tower, Looking East.

Similar Statistics from 1867-1888. lege proper to the administration of President Zollars: 1867, 308 and 526; 1868, 277 and 403; 1869, 278 and 438; 1870, 267 and 401; 1871, 302 and 483; 1872, 270 and 390; 1873, 235 and 373; 1874, 233 and 368; 1875, 179 and 288; 1876, 153 and 262; 1877, 201 and 320; 1878, 169 and 283; 1879, 209 and 391; 1880, 214 and 387; 1881, 205 and 384; 1882, 224 and 411; 1883, 202 and 375; 1884, 205 and 406; 1885, 190 and 373; 1886, 186 and 378; 1887, 221 and 443, or a total for twenty-one years of 4,728 students, and by terms of 8,083, an average per year of 225, and by terms of 128.

All of the Presidents of Hiram College have been men physically and mentally capable of hard work, and their **Hiram Presidents Hard Workers.** power of endurance has been tested to the extreme limit. Like the rest, President Zollars has been a very busy man. Besides his administrative duties he has canvassed a large number of the Disciple churches of Ohio and many in other States in the interest of the college; visited and preached at great meetings and conventions; written books for the class-room and the people; conducted an immense correspondence; taught his classes in the college; kept in touch and informed in the work of other institutions of learning; prepared elaborate lectures on a variety of subjects for the college; and as a solicitor for the finances of the College he has gone far beyond the best results of any of his predecessors, in the entire history of the Institution. They, indeed, laid the foundation on which he has builded so rapidly and so successfully, and all are entitled to rejoice with him in the success that has followed their works.

In 1888, besides the annual catalogue, a general catalogue of the Institution from the beginning was issued, with

General Catalogue
in 1888.

a brief history of the first years. From that document the attendance of students during the period of the Western Reserve Eclectic Institute is found to be, by years, as follows: 1850-1, 312; 1852, 254; 1853, 529; 1854, 523; 1855, 445; 1856, 494; 1857, 440; 1858, 487; 1859, 502; 1860, 462; 1861, 427; 1862, 315; 1863, 296; 1864, 389; 1865, 402; 1866, 352; 1867, 250, making a total of 6,879 and an average for seventeen years of 404.

A college paper, issued at regular intervals, appears to be a necessity of college life; if not a necessity, it is often-

College Papers.

times found to be of great interest and value. About the time the College was opened, a monthly paper was issued called "The Hiram Student," and edited by Prof. A. M. Weston. This paper

Hiram Student.

had a brief existence. Fugitive papers, mainly for the purpose of advertising the College, have been issued from time to time under the control generally of the Faculty or some member of it; but in 1887 a real effort was made to establish a permanent college paper in which the interests of Hiram College received proper at-

Hiram College
Star.

tention. This paper was called HIRAM COLLEGE STAR, and was under the sole management of the Hesperian Literary Society. Its chief editor was Frank W. Norton, with John Shackson, Nathan Johnson and G. W. Moore, associates. Its first editorial declared its purpose to be to furnish "a spright-ly college paper to advance the interests of the school and community; and, while the paper would be under the man-agement of one society, it will be a college paper and will be fair and liberal on every question." It announced its politics to be Re-Dem-Procratic and its guiding motto "*Candor dat viribus alas.*"

Under the management of the Hesperian Society the

paper proved a success and was issued for three college years semi-monthly. Its last number appeared in August, 1890. At this time an arrangement was made by which the "Hiram College Star" ceased to be, and a new paper appeared in October, 1890, called the HIRAM COLLEGE ADVANCE, under the joint management of the Hesperian, Delphic, Olive Branch, and Logomathian Literary Societies. The new staff consisted of G. A. Ragan, editor-in-chief, and E. W. Allen, F. A. Bright, Adelaide G. Frost, Marcia Henry, H. D. Messick, Loa E. Scott, A. J. Sever, and A. V. Taylor, associates, with George H. Rymers, business manager. This paper has been continued without interruption to the present time; a credit to the young people who have successively and successfully managed it, and to the college. The Hesperian Society is entitled to high praise for the origin and successful management of the college paper for its first three years. The Advance holds a creditable rank among papers of its class.

In 1890 THE SPIDER WEB, a serio-comic annual of Hiram College was first published by the Junior Class. Since then these volumes have appeared annu-

The Spider Web. ally. In general appearance and in the contents these volumes have steadily improved until the annual issue is anticipated with great eagerness by the friends of Hiram who desire to know its serious and humorous current college life, and is especially interesting to the Junior Class responsible for its issue.

August 31, 1888, the Ministerial Students of Hiram College organized themselves into a society, which was named "Logomathean," for the purpose of

The Logomathean Society. promoting their efficiency in ministerial work. It began its work with 19 members. Their regular programs consisted of sermons, essays, exegeses, declamations, impromptu speeches, Scripture recitations, and discussion of religious questions. The Society prospered for several years, but was finally abandoned for what appeared to be good reasons, and only exists as "a reminiscence of the piety" of its founders.

April 9, 1894, the Garfield Literary Society was organized with ten members chosen from the Delphic and Hesperian Societies respectively. Its charter members gave the following as the reason for the new organization: "We, the Preparatory Students of Hiram College, regarding the benefits of a Literary Society in connection with our school work of the highest importance in disciplining and liberalizing the mind, do mutually agree to form ourselves into a Literary Society, and, for the government of the same, do hereby ordain and establish the following constitution and by-laws, etc." Its first year was a very successful one and its progress from year to year has been highly creditable to the class of students admitted to its membership. During its first year the Society had an average membership of fifty. It has proved to be a liberal feeder to the college societies from which it sprang.

The Garfield Society.

The Alethean Society was organized June 18, 1895. Its charter members and first signers of its constitution were Clara B. Russell, Carrie Goodrich, Margaret Frost, Edith Robinson, Helen Stoolfire, Myra Pow, Florence Oliver, Annie Gould, Florence Campbell, and Josephine Line. The ladies' society of the college, "The Olive Branch," was unable to properly provide for the literary society culture of all the young ladies attending the College. A preamble and resolution were adopted as follows: "Whereas, the Olive Branch Society has proved itself inadequate to meet the demands for literary work by the young women of Hiram College, therefore be it *Resolved,* that the following young women be hon-

The Alethean Society.

orably discharged for the purpose of forming themselves
into a society: Elizabeth Carlton, Blanche Beck, Bessie
Crosse, Inez Prickett, and Lucile Woodward, besides those
whose names appear as charter members—15 in all. The
Alethean Society has prospered from the beginning. During
its first year it added 26 new names to its charter members,
making a membership of 36.

The Young Men's Christian Association of Hiram College was organized in 1870, and has kept in touch
with all the other departments of
Y. M. C. A. college work since its organization. It has
been a great help to the College in many
ways. It has performed the usual functions characteristic
of the organization, besides organizing special Bible classes
for the study of such subjects as "The Life of Christ,"
"Christ as a Personal Worker," "The Life of Paul," "The
Book of Acts," etc.; contributing to the social life of the
college; assisting to adjust new students to their home in
Hiram; providing a lecture course which brought to Hiram
some of the best talent on the American platform; and ren-
dering great assistance in the erection of the new Y. M. C. A.
building.

The Young Women's Christian Association of Hiram
was organized and has contributed in many helpful ways to
the life and prosperity of the college. Each
Y. W. C. A. young woman entering the school for the
first time is warmly welcomed, and,
through the efforts of the Association, is made to feel that
there are many friends ready to love and help her. Substantially the same kind of work is done by this Association
for the young women that is done for the young men by the
Y. M. C. Association. The religious work carried forward
by the two Associations has been of very great value. The
daily and weekly prayer meetings maintained throughout the

year, have added much to the vigor and strength of the religious life of the College.

The Student Volunteer Band was organized in 1889 and
is an association of Hiram students whose purpose is to go
to foreign lands as opportunity offers for
missionary work. Several of its members
are in China and India and elsewhere, engaged in the work of their choice. There
were thirteen charter members, of whom William Forrest
and Edward Allen were the first president and secretary.
Miss Carmie Hostetter and Miss Lucia Scott were the first
members of the Band to take up active work on the mission
field. The following is a list of the Hiram students on the
mission fields of China, Japan, and India. The following
are in the employ of the F. C. M. S.:

The Student
Volunteer Band.

INDIA

Miss Mildred Franklin	Hurda C. Prov's
G. W. Brown	Hurda C. Prov's
Mrs. G. W. Brown	Hurda C. Prov's

CHINA

Miss Mary Kelly	Nankin
E. I. Osgood, M. D.	Chu Cheo
Mrs. Fanny H. Osgood	Chu Cheo
C. B. Titus	Lu Cheo Fu
Mrs. C. B. Titus	Lu Cheo Fu

JAPAN

Miss Carrie Hostetter	Sendai

The following are under the C. W. B. M. in India:

Miss Susie Rawson	Mahoba, N. W. Provinces
Miss Rose Lee Oxer	Mahoba, N. W. Provinces
W. M. Forrest, Y. M. C. A.	Calcutta, Bengal
Mrs. W. M. Forrest, Y. M. C. A.	Calcutta, Bengal
Miss Adelaide Gail Frost	Mahoba, N. W. Provinces
(Home on Furlough)	
Miss Mary Graybiel	Mahoba, N. W. Provinces
(Home on Furlough)	

Mr. B. J. Grainger, of Deerfield, expects to go to India
this Fall.

The missionary spirit of the college has been greatly stirred by the devotion of the members of the Band, and by the joint meetings with the other college associations. In these meetings the needs of the various mission fields have been studied, the history of missionary movements learned in detail; and through addresses by different members of the Band the neighboring churches have been brought into closer and more intelligent relationship with them. Hiram has always been interested in the local interests of the churches and in the world-wide movements of the Church of Christ.

In May, 1889, steps were taken which resulted in the organization of an Ohio Hiram College Association. The

The Ohio Hiram College Association. purpose of the Association is to cultivate the Hiram fellowship and push forward the interests of the college throughout Ohio and other States. All former students and friends of the college are eligible to membership, and its influence has been positive in behalf of the Institution.

This Association was organized in 1885, and consists of

Hiram Association of Cleveland. the many residents of Cleveland who have been Hiram students. The Board of Trustees are made ex-officio members of the Association. It now numbers about 300 members.

This Association was organized in 1889 and a constitution adopted. Its object is: To renew and cultivate the

Ohio Hiram College Association. fellowship begun at Hiram; to organize the friends of Hiram College into an efficient working force; to increase the interest in Hiram's welfare among all its friends; to devise ways and means for enlarging the patronage and advancing the general interests of Hiram College. Its annual meetings are held in connection with the annual convention of the Ohio Christian Missionary Society.

The interests of the physical man have not been over-

looked. The gymnasium has been well patronized since it
was furnished and opened in the new Y.

Athletics.   M. C. A. building. The Athletic Association of Hiram College is a member of the Northern Ohio
Inter-collegiate Athletic Association and has maintained a
good standing. The permanent grounds of the Hiram Association are convenient and kept in good order. Provision is
also made for tennis courts and other physical exercises.

In 1888 a joint stock company was formed, known as
the Hiram College Building Company, for the purpose of
erecting such buildings as were needed

Miller Hall.   for the accommodation of students. This
company erected what is now known as
"Miller Hall." This building is now joined with "Gerould
Cottage," the gift of Dr. Henry Gerould, and is one of the
most commodious buildings in Hiram for the use of young
ladies.

In 1889 a committee was appointed to consider the
"possibility and advisability" of establishing a summer

Hiram   school at Hiram, modeled somewhat after
Summer School.   the Chautauqua plan. This committee reported in favor of the Assembly, and the first program was
prepared and arrangements made for the sessions to begin
August 11 and continue to August 29, 1890. The course of
study was quite elaborate, and included a School of English
Bible, Sunday-school Normal, Teachers' Normal, Miscellaneous Lectures, School of Music, School of Art, School of
Oratory, and a department of college work. The purpose of
the Assembly was three-fold: First, for the benefit of
preachers who may wish to spend their summer vacation in
lines of helpful study; second, for Sunday-school teachers
who may desire to enlarge their store of Bible knowledge;
third, for all persons who may wish to obtain a better knowledge of the Bible while they are seeking rest and recreation.

A large corps of instructors was secured, nearly all of whom were present for the part assigned them: English Bible Work, B. S. Dean, E. B. Wakefield, G. A. Peckham, E. V. Zollars, J. H. Garrison, H. McDiarmid, Robert Moffett, W. F. Richardson, B. B. Tyler, and Alanson Wilcox; Sunday-school Normal Work, F. M. Green, C. C. Smith, and J. S. Ross; Common School Normal Work, A. C. Pierson, G. H. Colton, and Miss Maggie Umstead; Miscellaneous Lectures, Judge George M. Tuttle, Dr. I. A. Thayer, H. A. Garfield, Hon. E. B. Taylor, A. McLean, Jessie H. Brown, Virgil P. Kline, and John G. Scover; Music, Dr. J. B. Herbert and Miss Addie Zollars; Art, Mrs. Alanson Wilcox, and Mrs. Emma J. Dean; Oratory, John G. Scover; and College Work, by the Professors of Hiram College. Some of the instructors were assigned duties in more than one department. The result of the experiment was very satisfactory and the Summer School was continued for several years at Hiram. It was a good advertisement for the college, besides being a good school for those who attended it.

As early as 1888, President Zollars and the Y. M. C. Association began to agitate the question of a new college building. The increasing interest in Hiram College over a widening territory, and the consequent increase of students, made it manifest that larger accommodations must be provided. More room was needed for chapel services, recitation rooms, laboratory, gymnasium facilities, for the Art department, for Christian Association work, and other purposes. Every available part of the old building had been called into service from basement to dome. Realizing the need of more room in which to successfully prosecute their work, the Young Men's Christian Association of Hiram took the initiative looking in the direction of a new building. On invitation Mr. John R. Mott, the National Secretary of

The New
Y. M. C. A.
Building.

the Y. M. C. Association, came to Hiram and addressed the students. His presence and address aroused such an enthusiasm that $7,000 was subscribed by the students for the new building. The college was invited to unite in the enterprise, and thus secure a building that would meet the wants of the various Hiram interests. This was the beginning, but just at that time the financial depression burdened the country, and the work was delayed, but not abandoned. In 1894 the enterprise was revived, and a "rally day" was appointed in the building interest, which resulted in pledges from students, Faculty, and citizens to the amount of $12,000. Other friends came to the rescue, an architect was employed, and general plans were agreed upon, and work actively begun about June 1, 1895. The plans agreed upon were prepared by Mr. C. C. Thayer, of New Castle, Pa. The anticipated building was to consist of two full stories in front, besides the attic story and the basement and sub-basement. The first floor was to be used for library, reading room, and a small Association chapel. The Association parlors and Bible class rooms were to occupy the second story. The attic story was to be used for art purposes and for other needs. In the basement were to be found the kitchen, dining room, art room, and barber shop, while the sub-basement would be given up to the furnace and coal rooms. In the upper part of the rear portion of the building was the general chapel, with a seating capacity on floor and in gallery of about 750. Under the chapel was the gymnasium and bath rooms for ladies and gentlemen. These arrangements have been somewhat changed in the final adjustment, but the building stands, finished, convenient, and complete, a monument to the enterprise and liberality of the students, the Faculty and many other friends of Hiram College. The entire cost of the building was $30,000. The value of the new building to the College was instantly felt, and the wonder grew how for so long a time the school had prospered without it. Following the completion of the Association building, changes were made in the old building which added much to the material equipment of the Institution.

The musical department of Hiram College has always been an important department. The best that could be done

Hiram College
Conservatory
of Music.

under existing circumstances has been done by those who successively have been honored with its administration. The conditions have varied greatly and the measure of success has varied in consequence. Among those who have honored the department and whose names should be written large in the annals of Hiram are Mrs. Tillie Newcomb Ellis, Mrs. Lizzie Clapp Robbins, Mrs. Addie Zollars Page, and Mrs. Lulu Freeman Pearcy. Others have taught music, vocal and instrumental, for brief periods, but these were at the head for a series of years. In 1897 the Board of

Eugene
Feuchtinger.

Trustees secured Professor Eugene Feuchtinger to take charge of the Department of Music. He had already proved himself to be a teacher of rare ability and an accomplished musical scholar. He had already won a high place among the foremost concert pianists, composers, and teachers of music. He was highly recommended by such composers and teachers of music as Constantin Von Sternberg, of Philadelphia, Pa.; Wilson G. Smith, of Cleveland, O.; and John Howard, of New York. Mr. Howard said of him: "I certainly consider him to be a very rare prize. It is very seldom that the combination of talents and the executive ability that he possesses can be found." On coming to Hiram he immediately enlarged the Department of Music to proportions hitherto unattempted. His success has been greater than the most sanguine anticipated, and the Hiram College Conservatory of Music has an acknowledged place in the front rank. The enrollment of the first year reached 74, with an average enrollment of 60 students each term. His assistants, especially Miss Clara L. Whissen, deserve the praise which the Director has generously given them. The following chronology of Professor Feuchtinger's life is interesting:

"Among the younger circles of German-American musicians Professor Eugene Feuchtinger has made himself especially prominent. As a son of the celebrated teacher, chorus director, organist, Franz Joseph Feuchtinger, in Wuerttenberg, he had the privilege from earliest youth of gaining a deep insight into the mysteries of music. The fullest comprehension and greatest success in art is mostly gained by those who from earliest childhood have been surrounded by a pure art atmosphere. That which Richard Wagner so much deplored—the decay of musical worship in the home—did not find its application in their home. The works of the old masters were with love and devotion played and studied. Piano, organ, string quartettes, songs, especially, too, the old classic church music, all of these furnished an art atmosphere of rare purity and beauty, and the love for this beauty destined our subject for the profession of music, where he has since achieved eminent success. He began music study under the eyes of his father at the age of six years. His studies were chiefly piano, voice and organ. At the age of ten he was selected as a boy alto for the Cathedral of his city. Two years later he accompanied a then very celebrated tenor in concerts on the piano. During his years at the Gymnasium (German equivalent for our college) he was director of local singing societies. Later he continued music study, especially piano, voice and theory, under the direct pupils of Kullack and Liszt. After having taught and played for several years in Germany, he followed an urgent invitation by his uncle to America, where he has since become favorably known through his teaching, concerts and lectures in many cities of the eastern and western States. In 1892 he accepted a call to Bethany College, and in 1897 to Hiram College, where he established the Conservatory of Music which, with the assistance of able teachers, is rapidly gaining a large influence in the musical life of America."*

There have been many and radical changes in the Institution at Hiram since its first building towered above the growing corn on its campus in 1850; but in nothing is the change more noticeable than in the condition of the place itself. Then it was only the township center with the usual cross-roads marking the four points of the compass. Its buildings were few and mostly plain farm houses, with their attendant out-buildings. A small school house, a shop or two, a country store with its miscellaneous assortment of shoes and boots, sugar and salt, herring and powder, dry-goods and eggs, and a plain church building exhausted its public buildings. The surrounding country was not yet denuded of its forests of oak and maple, beech and elm, whose green pinnacles had for centuries caught the evening dew, and tossed the morning sunshine in golden flakes on the few cleared fields below. But now what a change! The forests are mostly gone, the fields are under the cultivation of the intelligent and well-read farmer, the sugar-orchards are about the only evidence that forests were ever there; and on every hand the country house, beautiful in design and convenient for its purpose, is seen from Hiram Hill. Instead of a country cross-roads, a hamlet with several hundred people covers the hill, in the center of which are the old and the new college buildings; around the campus are the many new and well-furnished residences with their inviting verandas and well-

Hiram in 1850 and 1900.

---

*From the "Centralblatt fuer Instrumental Music, Solo und Chorgesang," published at Stuttgart and Leipzig, Germany, September 14, 1900.

kept lawns; a system of water works which supplies the
hamlet from never-failing springs; an electric lighting plant
which provides abundant light for all the inhabitants; good
roads leading to the railway stations; and a college whose
past is more than a reminiscence and whose future is full of
hope.

During the period under consideration much had been
done to increase the influence and efficiency of the College.

**What
had been done for
the College.**
Its endowment had been more than doubled; its facilities for taking care of young
ladies had been greatly increased by the
building of a new hall and the improve-
ment of the old one; a music building had been provided to
the great advantage of the Music Department; the beautiful
and commodious Young Men's Christian Association building had been built; the teaching force had been greatly increased and strengthened; accommodations had been secured
for the special departments of Art and Oratory; through the
generosity of Dr. Henry Gerould a Missionary Home for
young ladies of limited means and Christian ambitions had
been provided; and the hamlet had been well provided with
light and water and improved sidewalks.

But all these improvements had cost money which, with
the most rigid economy, the Board of Trustees found themselves unable to meet from the resources of the Institution.
Besides, other needs were continually arising, which in some
way must be met. Manifestly the income of the college was
too small and must be largely increased or its advance must
be checked. There are opportune times in the history of
men and institutions when certain things in their interest
may be done easiest and best. To take advantage of these
occasions is prudent and wise. Such a time was rapidly
approaching in the history of Hiram College. Its fiftieth
year would close with the century, and why not make a jubi-

lee year out of it, and ask, not the rich nor the poor, but the people without distinction, to help to send it into the new century with a generous purse and untrammeled by financial embarrassment.

In his report for 1898 President Zollars spoke with much earnestness and in favor of immediate action by the Board of Trustees to provide means to increase the permanent endowment fund one hundred thousand dollars by the time of the Jubilee Commencement in 1900.

Committee on Permanent Endowment.

The Board resolved to place the whole question of "methods for increasing the endowment in the hands of a committee of seven persons, three of whom shall be members of the Finance Committee, the remaining members to be .appointed by the chair." The committee appointed consisted of W. G. Dietz, O. G. Kent, B. L. Pennington, H. E. McMillin, Alanson Wilcox, C. E. Henry and A. Teachout.

This committee had numerous meetings during the year and on April 4, 1899, decided "that all endowment pledges taken for Hiram College be taken on approval pledge blanks and deposited with W. G. Dietz, chairman of the Endowment Committee; that the territory canvassed should include a complete canvass of Ohio, Pennsylvania, New York, Michigan, and New England, and that agents appointed should confine themselves to the respective fields given them to canvass; and that the assignment of territory and instruction to agents and other details be left to President Zollars, his action to be approved by the Endowment Committee, and that he should be the agent of the committee to solicit funds from the alumni."

The method by which the canvass should be made, after much thought, consideration and consultation, finally embraced the following particulars: The effort should be made to increase the endowment fund of Hiram College, a quar-

The Plan Adopted.

ter of a million of dollars by the close of its Jubilee year; an effort should be made for a great popular movement whereby thousands of the friends of higher education, and of Hiram College in particular, would unite in one supreme effort to place the college on a permanent financial basis; the weekly newspapers among the Disciples were asked to lend their assistance to the movement, and without exception generously and gladly consented to do so; the Christian Standard was especially liberal; and large space was given in all the papers, and the movement was extensively advertised in the United States and in every other country where the Disciples of Christ are found; special agents were placed in the field to visit churches, give addresses on higher education, and present Hiram College and its work by stereopticon lectures; all were asked to pledge something, from one dollar upwards, and pledge cards were furnished for this purpose; individuals were to be solicited for larger sums; and the alumni were asked to raise not less than twenty-five thousand dollars.

There were many details that cannot be inserted here and some changes made necessary as the canvass went on. The work was well started early in the year 1899 and prosecuted vigorously by President Zollars, to whom had been assigned the general management; the Financial Secretary, members of the Board of Trustees, special friends of Hiram, members of the Faculty, and agents selected to canvass special fields. The result equaled the most sanguine expectations. Perhaps no religious people were ever more widely interested in an educational question than were the Disciples of Christ in this effort to endow liberally Hiram College. It was the first really great thing that had ever been attempted in the history of the Institution. Comparatively it was a prodigious undertaking; but from the time the movement

BIG HOLLOW.

THE SUGAR CAMP.

was fully begun to its close no one who put his hand to the plow looked back.

A complete report of the work done and the results achieved could not be made in June, 1900—the Jubilee Commencement week. It is not likely that it ever will be made. Springs of resource were opened that had only begun to flow when the canvass closed on Jubilee Day. But of that which could be seen and tabulated the following was the result: Money, pledges, annuity funds and otherwise, $242,488. The cost for all the agencies employed was about $7,000. Besides President Zollars and Financial Secretary Hertzog, J. L. Darsie, J. L. Garvin, Alanson Wilcox, C. R. Scoville, B. H. Hayden, J. T. Bridwell and others canvassed in special fields. The sums contributed were from one dollar up to twenty-five thousand dollars. The contributors numbered many thousands.* When all promised is gathered together the college will enter upon its second fifty years with a clear endowment of not less than three hundred thousand dollars.

It would be impossible to give to any one of the more prominent persons engaged in this movement to largely increase the permanent endowment of Hiram College the lion's share of credit for the results, without doing a wrong to the others. Of necessity there was a leader and he was the President of the college, but with him were many others, whom without he could have done but little. Among those who did much in the accomplishing of the glad results was the Financial Secretary or Agent of the college, Oliver Gans Hertzog. Mr. Hertzog began his work as Financial Secretary September 1, 1891, and has been in the service of the college for

The Final Report.

Oliver Gans Hertzog.

---

*No names of contributors are given because of the desire of some of the largest donors not to be known, and the impracticability of getting all the rest.

nearly ten consecutive years. With one or two exceptions he has served longer in this office than any of his predecessors. Only five, from the beginning of the Western Reserve Eclectic Institute, to the present, have been in continuous service over two years. These are: Dr. W. A. Belding, W. J. Ford, Lathrop Cooley, Alanson Wilcox, and O. G. Hertzog. The value of a long service in this department of College work is seen in the annual results of Mr. Hertzog's labors. He is able to do much more now than he could do at the first. The seed of the financier must have time to ripen before he can gather his crop. Against many obstacles and under many embarrassments he has been able every year to add something to the material resources of Hiram College. When he began his service he was 47 years of age. His body was sound, his presence cheerful, his mind well disciplined, his acquaintance extensive, his standing among the Disciples favorable, his extended business training was in his favor, his genius for hard work was soon apparent, and his interest in young people—all these qualifications have made him one of the best all-around helpers Hiram has ever had. The chronology of his busy and honorable life is full of interesting facts: He was born in Fayette county, Pennsylvania, April 9, 1899, the sixth child in a family of eleven children, and of good old German stock. His mother's name was Susan Gans, from whom he takes his middle name. He was reared on a Pennsylvania farm. In his young manhood he learned the carpenter's trade. His public education began in the schools of the neighborhood, and at the age of twenty he taught school. Afterwards he took the full course in the Southwestern Normal College at California, Pa., and entered Bethany College, where he remained two years. He joined the Baptist Church at the age of sixteen, and united with the Disciples of Christ under the ministry of Alanson Wilcox at the age of twenty-one. At twenty-five he was ordained to the ministry of the Word of God by John F. Rowe and Samuel B. Teagarden, and began his life-work as a preacher with the old Pigeon Creek Church in Washington county, Pennsylvania.   October 28, 1869, he was married to Ella M. Reader, of Coal Center, Pa., a former classmate of his at school.   As a pastor and envangelist he was successful, as well as in the business management of churches.   He was elected Corresponding Secretary of the Pennsylvania Christian Missionary Society, and about the same time he was elected to a similar position by the Disciples of New York. He chose the New York work and began his labors at Suspension Bridge, October 1, 1870, where he remained for three years.   During this time he planted a church at Pekin and held a successful meeting in Buffalo.   In 1874 he located in Buffalo, where he remained two years and then took up evangelistic work for the "Wellington Co-operation" in Canada, where he labored successfully for three years.   He then returned to Suspension Bridge, where he remained for a year.   He then returned to Canada, holding meetings and planting churches.   During his entire service in Canada he baptized several hundred people and organized eight churches.   June 1, 1881, he received the appointment of special agent of the United States Treasury for the Niagara District, which position he filled for four and one-half years, resigning to accept the work of Evangelist under the direction of the New York Christian Missionary Society.   This place he held for nearly seven years, preaching almost constantly.   During this period churches were established at Freedonia, Wellsville, and Rochester; and more than four years of this time was spent with the church in Rochester. It is not possible to sum up the results of these busy years. It can be said, however, that they were not small and they were highly appreciated by the beneficiaries.   September 1, 1891, he began his work for Hiram College.   He has been a faithful servant to the Institution and a most valuable adjunct to all its other agencies in increasing the number of students, enlarging its finances, and advertising its interests far and wide. He has never been a beggar for position, but his services have always been in demand; and it was providential that he was so well equipped morally, intellectually, physically, and in business capacity for the time and place he has filled in the history of Hiram.

Early in the administration of President Zollars it was suggested that "a fund that could be used to aid students in limited circumstances would contribute largely to Hiram's power for good." Acting on this sugges-

The Phillips Ministerial Loan Fund.

tion, Hon. T. W. Phillips, of New Castle, Pa., a Christian man of financial ability, excellent judgment, and generous impulses, in 1891 placed $5,000 under certain limitations at the disposal of the College. This sum was accepted as the "Phillips' Ministerial Loan Fund," and has been of great benefit to a large number of young men, as the annual reports of the President show. This fund is managed by special trustees who are at this time Alanson Wilcox, E. V. Zollars, and E. B. Wakefield. By an agreement with Mr. Phillips in 1897, the trustees were permited to use a portion of this fund in the erection of a building named "Independence Hall," which will accommodate twenty young men. Rooms are furnished at twenty-five cents a week for each student and board costs one dollar. Mr. Phillips has always been a warm friend of the College and his gifts, though liberal, have never been heralded by noise.

Biography of T. W. Phillips.

Thomas W. Phillips was born February 23, 1835, in Lawrence county, Pennsylvania, the youngest of eight children. His father died when he was ten years of age. His early school life was limited, and of college opportunities he had none; but he was of studious habit and inquiring mind and through books, observation and experience, he compassed the range and purpose of college work, and became well informed in history, biography, science and literature. While yet a young man, he became a member of the firm of Phillips Brothers, which ranked among the greatest oil producers of the world. In his business he has been remarkably successful though like thousands of others he has seen densely dark days, but in every hour of gloom or sunshine the eleventh chapter of Hebrews has been his "Confession of Faith." He has been entrusted with numerous honorable and responsible positions by business associates and fellow citizens and in all of them he has proved himself to be a man of judgment, honor, and business sagacity. From 1892 to 1896 he represented his Congressional District in the Congress of the United States. Here as elsewhere he held an influential position among the best Representatives of the country. His home life is happy; his service to the church unostentatious and generous; and as a friend of Hiram and Bethany, a Trustee of both Institutions, his presence is always grateful and his friendship greatly prized.

In the progress of the work at Hiram a cottage for young women of limited means became as much of a necessity and as desirable as a Hall for young men in similar circumstances. It was suggested that a building be provided in which room rent could be provided at a nominal sum, and the young women could have the privilege of doing their own work, and avail themselves of the benefit of co-operative boarding at the lowest possible cost. In 1897 Dr. Henry Gerould, of Cleveland, O., proposed to solve this problem by the erection of an addition to Miller Hall to be known as "Gerould Missionary Cottage," into which young ladies preparing for the home or foreign missionary fields, and the children

A Cottage for Young Women.

of missionaries should be received free of charge. This cottage, comfortable and convenient, was built and equipped by Dr. Gerould, and is a monument at Hiram of the great-hearted, humble, and generous Christian man. Many loved him while he lived and labored, but more will speak his name with pleasure and appreciation as the years go on.

Henry Gerould was born in Smithfield, Pa., March 6, 1829. He was five generations removed from a Huguenot ancestry. The fact that the blood of that brave, intelligent and liberty-loving people flowed in his veins accounts for many of the traits of character that distinguished him and adorned his life. In 1847 he united with the Church of Christ under the preaching of Dr. Silas E. Shepard and devoted himself from that time to a life of service and self-sacrifice.

Biography of Dr. Henry Gerould

In 1864 he graduated in medicine, having studied for several years in a medical college at Geneva, New York, and later at Hudson, O.

He practiced medicine for several years at Bedford, Ohio. From Bedford he went to Boston, Mass., where he spent some time in the hospitals of that city. From Boston he came to Massillon, O., where he remained until 1874, when he removed to Cleveland, O., which was his home until his death November 10, 1900.

In 1870 he married Julia J. Clapp, a daughter of Thomas Clapp, of Mentor, O. It was a happy and strong union of heart and soul; and in all his planning, and giving and doing he had her encouragement and approval. To them three children were born, but in 1883 all of them passed out of their home to the "home appointed for all the living." From that time Dr. Gerould and his wife determined to make their own home, though deserted by children, beautiful by filling other hearts and homes with joy and sunshine, and thus brighten and bless the world.

He was an active worker in Sunday-school and church; and for educational and missionary interests he had an intelligent zeal and a philanthropic impulse. He was a man of clear-cut convictions; and those who knew him, knew where he stood on all questions of temperance, morality, religion, education, and all needed reforms. His personality was forceful and he could not efface himself. Dr. Gerould was a man of admirable qualities. He was prompt and exact in keeping his engagements. He was honest and honorable in all his dealings with men. He was courteous, considerate and faithful in every relation of life. He knew how to be abased and how to abound. "He stood the test of poverty and adversity; and the severer test of prosperity. He endeared himself to many thousands as a physician, as a friend, and as a worker in the cause of God and humanity. When the ear heard him, it blessed him; when the eye saw him, it gave witness to him. The blessing of him that was ready to perish came upon him; caused the widow's heart to sing for joy. He was a father to the poor and his name shall be held in everlasting remembrance and honor;" and Hiram will not be among the least of those who honor his name and bless his memory.

Among the institutions related to Hiram and not in Hiram is the "Hiram House" located in Cleveland, O. At the opening of the college year in September, 1895, the Home Mission class was organized among others.

The "Hiram House" in Cleveland, O. It took up at once the study of sociological questions, as outlined in the Y. M. C. A. Hand Book by Prof. Graham Taylor, the leader in the "Common's work" in Chicago. The class grew in numbers and in enthusiasm until at the suggestion of Mr. F. G. Strickland a Sociological Club was formed which finally resulted in establishing the Hiram House—a social settlement in one of the poorest and most needy wards in the city of Cleveland. The original "Social Settlement Board" consisted of E. V. Zollars, A. C. Pierson, B. S. Dean, E. B. Wakefield, H. M. Page, A. P. Frost, May Strickland, Helen Stoolfire, Carrie Goodrich, G. A. Bellamy, H. C. Kenyon and F. G. Strickland. At the beginning of the work in Cleveland Mr. F. G. Strickland became manager. He was succeeded by Mr. G. A. Bellamy who still holds the position.

"The 'Settlement' is simply a houseful of open-hearted and intelligent men or women who approach the poor, not as visitants from another world, but as dwellers in the same block or ward, as finding a pleasure (and

What the Settlement is.

it is a real pleasure, not a fictitious one) in the acquaintance of their fellow-inhabitants, and as claiming a share in the life of that quarter of the town, and a right to contribute whatever they may have in the way of books, or music, or pictures, or general information, or meeting rooms or acquaintances to the well being of the community to which they belong. This establishes the relation of the 'Settlement' to its environment as natural instead of artificial, it leaves no room for patronage on the one side or servility on the other."

Hiram House is founded on the principle of brotherhood. Its method of work will be neighborliness. Its efforts will be undenominational, and its work will be religious only as human brotherhood is religious. Its

The Aim and Principle of the Hiram House.

hope is to become a part of the life of its own ward, becoming so by personal helpfulness. In helping the masses, its wish is to help to remove the cause of distress. Further than this we do not commit ourselves to any social program regarding the vexed industrial and economic problems of the day. Our aim is to give not alms but life, not charity but love.

From the beginning the "Hiram House" has been a success; and it is now recognized as a valuable agency by the city authorities and many citizens, in the solution of the problem of the social condition and life in the submerged districts of large cities.

Brief Sketches of Members of Hiram Faculty for 1900.

There are some members of the Faculty of Hiram College for 1900 whose names have already been mentioned but concerning whom no sketch of their lives has been given. The following brief sketches are in their honor:

Edwin Lester Hall, Professor of Latin Language and Literature, and Principal of the Preparatory Department was born in Richfield, Summit County, Ohio. He was a farmer's boy and obtained his earlier education in the District School, and later at the High School of that place. He entered Hiram College in 1882 and graduated in 1886. After his graduation he spent one year in Hiram as Assistant Professor of Latin. He then went to New Castle, Pa., and taught one year in the High School of that city. In 1888 he returned to Hiram, where he has remained ever since. He fills his place in the College Faculty with dignity, and with a growing influence and scholarly grace. He is faithful in the discharge of his duties, kind and obliging, and worthy of the love and esteem in which he is held.

Edwin Lester Hall.

Harlan Myron Page was born in Kalamazoo County, Michigan, May 30, 1867. He graduated from the Bedford High School in 1867. After spending one year in the University of Michigan he entered Hiram College and was graduated with the class of 1890. In 1891 he attended two full courses of lectures in the medical schools of the Western Reserve, and Wooster Universities. In 1892 he received the de-

Harlan Myron Page.

gree of M. D. from Jefferson Medical College in Philadelphia, Pa. For one year he practiced medicine at Warren, O. In 1893 he was elected to the Chair of Biology and Science in HiramCollege, which position he still holds. With a cultured mind, a true heart, a careful medical student and a successful practitioner; quick to discern and apt to teach, he is well fitted for the responsible position which he holds in the College Faculty.

Hugh McDiarmid was born near Morpeth, County of Kent, Ontario, Canada, June 10, 1837, where he received his early education. For five years he was a teacher in the common schools of his vicinity. In 1863 he

Hugh McDiarmid. entered Bethany College, West Va., where he graduated with honor in 1867. After leaving Bethany he preached for the church at Barnesville, O., from which place he was called to the head of a collegiate Institute at Winchester, Ky. In 1875 he removed to Toronto, Canada, where he did evangelistic work for the Wellington Co-operation and edited "The Christian Sentinel," a religious magazine, at the same time. In 1883 he became associate editor of "The Christian Standard" at Cincinnati, O., then under the superb management of Isaac Errett, a prince among editors. After the death of Mr. Errett December 19, 1888, he became editor of the Standard and held the place until his election to the Presidency of Bethany College in 1892.

In 1896 he came to Hiram as Professor of Church History and Homiletics, a position he yet occupies. In 1896 Bethany College conferred on him the degree of LL. D. an honor most worthily bestowed.

As a citizen his loyalty is unquestioned; as a man his character is stainless; as a scholar he holds no mean rank; as a thinker and logician he is worthy of the steel of any foeman; and as a Christian his faith in the Word of God is uncorrupted and incorruptible.

Elmer Ellsworth Snoddy, Professor of Classical Greek
was born May 13, 1863, in Stilesville, Ind. His first years
were spent in Delphi and Indianapolis.   When he was five
years old his parents moved to a farm near
Elmer E. Snoddy. Remington where he received his early education, partly from the district school and
partly from his father, who was an able and experienced
teacher. At the age of sixteen he began to teach, teaching
during the winter months and spending the summers on his
father's farm. In 1882 his parents moved to St. Lawrence,
South Dakota, and were among the first settlers of Hand
County in that new state. He still continued teaching during
the winter months in Indiana. In 1887 he became a Christian and in 1888 he began to preach. He preached for one
year in Indiana, and for two years in South Dakota before
coming to Hiram. He was State Evangelist of South Dakota when he entered Hiram College in the fall of 1891. He
was graduated with the class of 1896, and during his Senior
year he taught in the Greek Department of the College. Immediately after his graduation he was chosen as Instructor of
Greek in Hiram College; but he soon reached the rank of
Professor of Classical Greek, a position for which he is eminently qualified. As a Greek scholar he is brilliant as well as
accurate; and for his age it would be difficult to find his superior. He is a born teacher and the Professor's chair is his
throne rather than the pulpit. Courteous, intelligent and
genial, he is a favorite with students and citizens alike.

Charles T. Paul was born in Bowmanville, Ontario,
Canada, in 1869. Educated first in the Public and High
Schools of that town. Afterwards for ten years pursued the
study of Modern Languages principally
Charles Thomas Paul. under French, German and Italian Spe-
cialists.   Also took special university
courses in Philosophy and Oriental Languages.

In 1888 founded the Meisterschaft School of Linguistry in Toronto, Ont., an institution which still exists in a flourishing condition under a well known European master.

In 1890 became principal of the Toronto School of Languages, in which seventeen languages, including orientals, classics and moderns were offered. On the faculty were associated with Mr. Paul lecturers and honor graduates of Toronto University, and one graduate of a Japanese University. The majority of the students of this school were teachers or professors who came to avail themselves of the special advantages in Modern Languages. The work differed from the ordinary university courses in that the students were given *an actual speaking knowledge* of French, German, Spanish, and Italian.

While in Toronto Mr. Paul was in frequent demand to interpret public lectures for foreign speakers.

In 1891 he was married to Miss Jessie Williams, of Oakville.

In 1894 he was appointed Professor of English Rhetoric in the Delsarte College of Oratory, also in the same year became editor of "The Tibetan," a journal devoted to the religious, philological, and ethnological questions of Central Asia. The journal attracted considerable attention in America and Asia, and from its scientific value was recognized by the Smithsonian Institution at Washington. He also delivered lectures in many cities and towns of Ontario on Central Asiatic questions.

In 1895 Mr. Paul united with the Disciples of Christ, and began the publication of "The Christian Messenger," which is still the organ of the Disciples in Ontario. Shortly afterwards he was called to the pastorate of the Cecil Street Church, Toronto, where he succeeded W. J. Lhamon, and carried on a successful work until January, 1900, when he came to the chair of Modern Languages in Hiram College.

Miss Marcia Henry, Assistant Professor of Latin and Greek, and Principal of the Ladies' Department, is of direct descent in the student line of the Hiram fellowship. Her father, Captain Charles E. Henry was a student in the days of the Eclectic Institute, his name appearing on the roll of the Institution for the year 1858. Her mother, Sophia Williams Henry, made her first entry into Hiram as a student in the year 1859. Her grandfather, Frederick Williams, was a member of the first Board of Trustees, and one of the incorporators of the Institution; and he offered the first resolution in a meeting of the Board of Trustees providing for the change from Western Reserve Eclectic Institute to Hiram College. Miss Henry was born October 13, 1869, at Geauga Lake near Solon, O. Her student life at Hiram was always faithful and efficient. She graduated from Hiram College in 1891, and after her graduation accepted a position in the public schools of Mentor, Ohio. In the fall of 1893 she returned to Hiram as Assistant Professor of Latin and Greek and Principal of the Ladies' Department, a position she has held with credit to herself and to the college ever since.

Frank Home Kirkpatrick, Professor of Oratory, has conducted his department with credit to himself and to the College.

Miss Kate S. Parmly, Assistant in the Ladies' Department of Hiram College, was born in Perry, Lake county, Ohio, September 20, 1855. She was a student at Vassar in 1872. In 1892 she took the Degree of Bachelor of Elocution from the Cleveland School of Oratory, and later the Degree of Master of Elocution from the same school. In the fall of 1897 she came to Hiram. Her work at Hiram has revealed the cultured Christian woman and the accomplished and faithful teacher.

Miss Clara Louise Whissen, Teacher of Piano, Violin,

etc., in the Department of Music, is worthy of high praise. In natural gifts, culture in the theory and practice of music, in enthusiastic devotion to her work she excels. She studied under the celebrated Henry Schradrich in the Cincinnati Conservatory of Music, and later was a pupil of Jacobsohn. She has taught in Westminster College, Pa.; Shepardson Seminary and Mt. Vernon College. In the fall of 1897 she accepted her present position in Hiram College, as teacher of violin and stringed instruments and assistant instructor of piano. She is a pianist and violinist of rare ability, and as a teacher she has been eminently successful.

Clara Louise Whissen.

William A. MacKenzie, who has charge of the Business Department of the College is steadily growing in favor; and as his ability as a teacher becomes manifest his patronage correspondingly increases.

William A. MacKenzie.

Mrs. Emma Johnson Dean's connection with Hiram College as student and teacher is earlier than that of any other of the present Faculty. From 1866-'68 she had charge of the Art Class. In 1882 after an absence of thirteen years, she returned to Hiram and again took up her work in the Art Department. She has thoroughly prepared herself for the position she holds under the best teachers accessible. Within recent years she has added the art of China decoration to her other accomplishments, and at present is teacher of China decoration and pastel. Her character and generous gifts of mind and heart have received a just tribute from all who have come under her influence, and her life has been an adornment to Hiram and Hiram College.

Emma Johnson Dean.

Miss Allie Mabel Dean, Teacher of Still Life and Drawing, daughter of Professor B. S. and Emma Johnson Dean,

Allie Mabel Dean, graduated from Hiram College in 1895, receiving the Degree of Ph. B. In 1896 she went to Oberlin to study art, and later studied at Cleveland in the Art Club. In the fall of 1896 she began to teach in the Art Department of Hiram College, a position she still holds. Her work is highly commended and her personal character commands the respect of all.

Miss Emma O. Ryder received the Degree of A. B. from Hiram College in 1890 and the Master's Degree in 1894. For several years after her graduation she was **Emma O. Ryder.** engaged in public school work, in which she was very successful. In the fall of 1896 she was chosen Librarian, and Secretary of the Faculty of Hiram College. For this work she is well prepared and the College interests are the gainer by her service.

The standard and literary curricula of Hiram College are very complete, and rank in strength with the courses of the best American Colleges. They are designed for such persons **Courses of Study.** as have the time and means and desire to pursue an extended course of study. If there were nothing else the discipline of such a course is of the highest value.

The Ministerial, Legal and Medical courses meet the wants of some students who wish to shape their college course with special reference to their chosen field of work. Each of the professional courses, however, represents as much work, and yields as much mental discipline, as the regular Classical, Scientific or Literary Course. The Teachers' Course is arranged with special reference to the wants of common school teachers. The English Ministerial Course is intended to meet the wants of persons who, through force of circumstances, have been denied large educational advantages until it is too late to undertake a long course of study, or who may have been prevented for other reasons from undertaking extended lines of work. The Business Course provides two years of solid work, and is designed to furnish ample preparation for mercantile and general business pursuits. The Post-Graduate Courses are arranged for the accommodation of students who have graduated in some regular course and desire to win the Master's Degree. The annual catalogs of the College furnish information in detail concerning these courses.

Commencement week, June 16 to June 22, 1900, marked a distinct period in the history of Hiram College. A half century had passed since its founders had stood in joyful anticipation by its new-laid foundations.

Commencement Week, 1900. The most of them had gone within "the low green tent whose curtains never outward swing." The enthusiastic motor which had moved the Institution in its earliest years had been replaced by the sober, steady push of later years, made necessary by competition, financial stress, and a faith made strong by works. Nearly all who had honored the classrooms of the Institution at the beginning and made them famous were only memories to those who constituted the student body of 1900. The ten thousand students who had entered its halls in the days long since past, if living, were among the old and gray-headed men and women of the present and their children were the stars that shone in the sky of their evening. The evening and the morning had appeared in regular alternation for more than eighteen thousand times since Principal A. S. Hayden, then in the prime of his young manhood, led the "foremost files" of young men and women who became at the last the queens of the home, the masters of the farm and the counter, the wizards that play with elemental forces, the great lights of the school and the college, the expounders of law, the able and skillful practitioners of medicine, the eloquent preachers of the "faithful word," and the ruling hands of the great Republic.

STREET VIEW.

This great week had been looked forward to for many months as the crowning period of an honorable history begotten of good; and like a carefully trained and nurtured life had reached a summit from whose height could be seen to its hungry horizon the unmistakeable signs of success.

In the vigor of its administration, in the number and deportment of the students, in the strength of its work, in the scope and strength of its teaching and teaching force, in the cost of its work, in its religious fervor and results, in attention to the physical needs of the students, in the sharp competition of its literary societies, in the large increase of its permanent endowment, and in the general interest awakened in favor of the Institution, the jubilee year had surpassed all others.

The program for the week was elaborately prepared and covered a wide field. For the sake of those who may in the future read this portion of Hiram's history the program for the jubilee week will have a decided interest. The week was opened by the Commencement of the Preparatory Department on June 16, 1900. On Sunday, June 17, 1900, and on the one hundred and twenty-fifth anniversary of the famous battle of Bunker Hill, President Zollars delivered the Baccalaureate Sermon, taking for his subject "Saving others the true work of life." Mark 15: 31. "Likewise also the chief priests mocking said among themselves with the scribes, He saved others; Himself He cannot save."

The Program.

On the evening of the same day the Christian Associations of the College held their anniversary exercises. On Monday, June 18, the various Literary Societies held their annual open sessions and presented thoroughly prepared programs. The rest of the week was divided according to the following arrangement:

Under=Graduate Day
TUESDAY, JUNE 19TH
CHAIRMAN—E. V. ZOLLARS

FORENOON, NINE O'CLOCK

MUSIC - - - - - - - Cornet Band. Vocal
INVOCATION - - - - - W. W. Sniff, *Cleveland, O.*
ADDRESS - - - - - H. B. Hazzard, *Deerfield, O.*
ADDRESS - - - Miss Florence Hathaway, *Cleveland, O.*
MUSIC - - - - - - - - - -
BENEDICTION - - - R. A. Nichols, *Worcester, Mass.*

AFTERNOON, TWO O'CLOCK

MUSIC - - - - - - - Cornet Band. Vocal
INVOCATION - - - - John E. Pounds, *Cleveland, O.*
ADDRESS - - - - - Clyde W. Wells, *Grindstone, Pa.*
ADDRESS - - - - - Miss Adda Jobes, *Erie, Pa.*
ADDRESS - - - - - E. B. Kemm, *Hiram, O.*
MUSIC - - - - - - - - - Vocal
ADDRESS - - - - A. B. Philputt, *Indianapolis, Ind.*
BENEDICTION - - - - - J. W. Kerns, *Steubenville, O.*

EVENING, 7:30 O'CLOCK

MUSIC - - - - - - - Cornet Band. Vocal
INVOCATION - - - - G. L. Wharton, *Hiram, O.*
MUSIC - - - - - - - - - -
ADDRESS - - - President C. L. Loos, *Lexington, Ky.*
MUSIC - - - - - - - - - -
BENEDICTION - - - - S. H. Bartlett, *Cleveland, O.*

Alumni Day
WEDNESDAY, JUNE 20TH
CHAIRMAN—PROF. W. H. C. NEWINGTON, *Niles, O.*

FORENOON, NINE O'CLOCK

MUSIC - - - - - - - Cornet Band. Vocal
INVOCATION - - - - - M. L. Bates, *Newark, O.*
ADDRESS - - - Judge Henry C. White, *Cleveland, O.*
MUSIC - - - - - - - - - Vocal
ADDRESS - - - - F. W. Norton, *Niagara Falls, N. Y.*
POEM - - - - - Miss Adelaide Frost, *Hiram, O.*
ADDRESS - - - - - - F. A. Henry, *Cleveland, O.*
BENEDICTION - - - - J. H. Goldner, *Cleveland, O.*

AFTERNOON, TWO O'CLOCK
CHAIRMAN—H. R. COOLEY, *Cleveland, O.*

MUSIC - - - - - - - Cornet Band. Vocal
INVOCATION - - - - - - I. J. Cahill, *Dayton, O.*
ADDRESS - - - - W. M. Forest, *Ann Arbor, Mich.*
MUSIC - - - - - - - - - Vocal
ADDRESS - - - - - Miss Cora Allen, *Cincinnati, O.*
ADDRESS - - - - - J. K. Baxter, *Mt. Vernon, O.*
BENEDICTION - - - - F. A. Bright, *Painesville, O.*

EVENING, 7:30 O'CLOCK
Entertainment of Hesperian Literary Society

Jubilee Day
Thursday, June 21st
Chairman—E. V. ZOLLARS

FORENOON, NINE O'CLOCK

Music - - - - - - - - Cornet Band. Vocal
Invocation - - - - Lathrop Cooley, *Cleveland, O.*
Address - - - - - - J. A. Lord, *Cincinnati, O.*
Music - - - - - - - - - - -
Address - - - - Hon. T. W. Phillips, *Newcastle, Pa.*
Address - - - - - Gov. F. M. Drake, *Des Moines, Ia.*
Music - - - - - - - - - - Vocal
Benediction - - - - - J. M. Van Horn, *Warren, O.*

AFTERNOON, TWO O'CLOCK

Music - - - - - - - Cornet Band. Vocal
Invocation - - - - - - F. M. Green, *Kent, O.*
Jubilee Endowment - - - - Announcement of Results
Address - - - - - J. H. Garrison, *St. Louis, Mo.*
Music - - - - - - - - - Vocal
Addresses of Class Professors - - - - - - -
Presentation of Diplomas - - - - - - -
Music - - - - - - - - - - -
Jubilee Poem - - Mrs. Jessie Brown Pounds, *Cleveland, O.*
Closing Prayer - - - - - R. Moffett, *Cleveland, O.*

EVENING, 7:30 O'CLOCK
Entertainment of Alethean Literary Society

Eclectic Day
Friday, June 22nd
Chairman—B. A. HINSDALE, *Ann Arbor, Mich.*

Music - - - - - - - - - - Vocal
Invocation - - - - - - - B. S. Dean, *Hiram, O.*
Historical Address - - B. A. Hinsdale, *Ann Arbor, Mich.*
Music - - - - - - - - - - -
Address - - - - - - R. H. Gano, *Dallas, Tex.*
Five Minute Speeches:
  J. H. Jones, *Mt. Union, O.*; R. Moffett, *Cleveland, O.*;
  F. Treudley, *Youngstown, O.*; Wallace J. Ford, *Hiram, O.*;
  Lathrop Cooley, *Cleveland, O.*; W. A. Belding, *Troy,
  N. Y.*; S. L. Hillier, *New York City*; J. S. Ross, *Oneida
  Mills, O.*; Amzi Atwater, *Bloomington, Ind.*; W. L.
  Hayden, *Edensburg, Pa.*; H. S. Chamberlain, *Chatta-
  nooga, Tenn.*; E. A. Ford, *Pittsburg, Pa.*

Others of the early students and pioneers will be present,
and will make short speeches.

Closing Prayer - - - Prof. E. B. Wakefield, *Hiram, O.*

Nearly all whose names appear on the program were present and filled the place assigned to them. Some were absent in person but present in their letters of regret. Of eminent men who made addresses it will not be uninteresting to specially name a few.

Charles Louis Loos of Kentucky University, Lexington, a French-German by birth and a Yankee by adoption, in his 77th year, with characteristic force of language and gesture declared his convictions of the value of the Bible as the supreme authority in all education from lowest to highest. His sturdy words of intelligent conviction were heartily endorsed by all who heard him.

C. L. Loos.

Judge Henry C. White, of Cleveland, O., the "plumed knight" of the old and the new Hiram fellowship, represented most worthily the Alumni of the Institution.

Henry C. White.

J. A. Lord, the accomplished editor of the Christian Standard, Cincinnati, Ohio, commended the College for making the Bible the crown of its curricula of study. His address was delivered with power and earnestness and was heartily enjoyed by the great audience present.

J. A. Lord.

A. B. Philputt of Indianapolis, Ind., in his address to the under-graduates spoke to their hearts as only he can speak who has traveled the same road and had the same experiences.

A. B. Philputt.

J. H. Garrison, the veteran editor of the Christian Evangelist, felicitously and strongly presented the subject of "Christian Education, Its Nature and Value." In the enlargement of his thought he declared: "It is not extravagant to say that education is the supreme need of the world, and that to impart this education is the supreme work of life. This broad use of the

J. H. Garrison.

term education, however, includes in it Jesus Christ as the world's great Teacher, and His divine command, 'Go teach' is the charter for the highest education, for the truest culture. Any idea of education that leaves out Christ is vitally defective. It leaves undeveloped the highest ranges of human nature. Christian education is only another name for true education, or for a full and complete education. This is the one reason that justifies the establishment and maintenance of institutions of learning that are distinctively Christian in their aim, methods and results."

T. W. Phillips.   Thomas W. Phillips of New Castle, Pa., briefly and fervently emphasized the creditable work the Institution had done in the past, and the obligations that were laid upon it for future good and influence.

The closing day was given to the pioneers, i. e., those who had to deal with the Institution in the days of the "Old Eclectic." On this day Prof. B. A. Hinsdale presided and made the principal address. It was of a

B. A. Hinsdale. historical character and had in it an element of pathos uncommon in Mr. Hinsdale's addresses. It proved to be one of the last of his public addresses, and the last for Hiram. A few months later his heart ceased to send the life-current to his busy brain, his voice was silent, and his earthly pilgrimage completed. As the substance of this address is found in other parts of this volume, and sometimes in the exact language used, it is not necessary to insert it here.

The Jubilee Poem, "The Old to the New," by Mrs. Jessie Brown Pounds of Cleveland, O., was by one of Hiram's true daughters by birth and education. In

Jessie Brown Pounds. exquisite phrase she sung the story of Hiram's fifty years. In verse that carried its thought felicitously Mrs. Pounds said:

"The trumpets sound at last the Fiftieth Year;
    From far away to near,
    From near to far away,
    The welcome notes are swelled,
    And joyously they say
To those in Toil's insistent bondage held,—
    The captives of the mart,
    The cup-bearers of Art,
The bowed field-laborers from the world of thought
Who in the mid-day's burning sun have wrought,—
    "Come hither! ye are free
    To keep the Jubilee!"

We come to claim our own;
The lands the miser Time has wrenched away
    Are ours again today;
    Our castles, overgrown
With moss and ivy through neglectful years,
And dimly seen through mists of envious tears,
In spite of Life's pursuing "might-have-been,"
    We stand again within;
For in the dreamed-of Year of Jubilee
    All forfeit lands are free.

We come in joyous answer to the call;
    We come, but ah! not all.
Some whom we miss, and seek with wistful eyes,
    Walk not in mortal guise.
The night shall come to all, we say.   Alas!
The shadows fall at noon; the strongest pass
Before the night has come.   We prate of "Why?"
    When shadows linger nigh,

And stretch our short philosophy to reach
 Beyond the blue.   In vain.
 In vain our tricks of speech;
 We can not make it plain.
Only our hearts this world-old lesson teach:
 That these in youth abide
 Forever at our side,
 Forever strong and free,
 And fresh for victory!

  * * * * * * *

When the half century again shall call,
How many will respond among us all?
 But here and yonder one
 Remaining there will be
Who faces now the East, and fronts the sun,—
Whose present wealth is hope, not memory.
The rest?   It shall not matter.   God is God.
 A tiny ridge of sod
Is all He needs.   The world He made goes on;
 We crowd it, and are gone.
Though human love and memory grow dim,
 He cares, and He is just;
A handful more or less of scattered dust,
Though naught to man, is still enough for Him.

The hour grows chill and late;
 Our Argosies of gold
 Return not, though we wait,
 And waiting, we grow old.
But they are safe.   Beyond some harbor bar,
 In some glad land afar
 Our treasures all are stored;
 Not ours to have and hoard
 Is all the truth we sought,

The high achievements that we would have wrought;
But safe beyond all selfish power and pride,
  Beyond all stress of tide,
  On some fair, friendly shore,
Our ships of Hope are anchored evermore;
And soon or late, we know not how or when,
  Each claims his own again!"

The exercises of jubilee week, while of a joyful and encouraging character, were tempered with seriousness by the sudden death of Prof. A. C. Pierson, who for twenty-five years had been connected with the College.

Conclusion.

Nearly every year of its history was represented among the multitude of guests who came from every direction and from distant places to the jubilee. J. G. Coleman, who was President, at the conclusion of the meeting in Aurora November 7, 1849, when the decision was reached to locate the school at Hiram was present and like Jacob, "leaning on the top of his staff;" Mrs. A. S. Hayden, the faithful wife, the blessed mother, who with her distinguished husband formed the center of the charmed circle of the early fellowship of Hiram. Her presence was as a benediction of the past upon the hopeful future. J. H. Jones, a member of the first Board of Trustees, erect as a mountain pine but with shattered voice and failing memory, barely a gleam from the full-orbed sun of his glorious life; Hartwell Ryder, one of the delegates to the Aurora meeting, for many years a Trustee, and always a friend; son of Symonds Ryder, the sturdy oak, out of which the Eclectic Institute made its Treasurer from 1849 to 1860; W. J. Ford, who laid the foundation for the permanent endowment of the College, and who was elected to its Board of Trustees in 1856; Charles Brown Lockwood, a member in continuous service on the Board of Trustees from 1866 to 1900; Henry Clay White, who represented the first year of its student body; Mrs. F. M. Green who as Ellen E. Stow was a student of the second year; Mrs. Robert Moffett, who as Lucy A. Green was a student of the third year; and Warren L. Hayden, Francis M. Green, Alanson Wilcox, Mary A. D. Williams, Mrs. Emma Johnson Dean, Charles E. Henry, Sophia Williams Henry, Jasper G. Ross, Howard A. Treudley, Andrew Squire, F. A. Derthick, E. B. Wakefield, Grove E. Barber, Charles Fillius, J. M. Van Horn, William H. C. Newington, William G. Dietz, Frederick A. Henry, Harlan M. Page, Fred A. Bright, Warren S. Hayden, Samuel H. Bartlett, A. G. Webb, Adelaide G. Frost, R. A. Nichols, B. C. Caywood, R. P. Shepherd, William G. Frost, Leon C. Vincent, Walter S. Hertzog, W. J. Crum, Guy Hoover, Frank C. Rulon, Fred Kline, Justin N. Green, D. R. Moss, and Charles E. Benlehr—these represented nearly every successive year from the time the decision was made to locate the Western Reserve Eclectic Institute at Hiram in 1849 to the crowning of Hiram College in 1900. Hiram College is the growth from a living seed planted fifty years ago, wisely and with prayer. It does not owe its origin to any one man whose name can be spoken with positiveness. Its progress has been due not to one but to many. Men planted it ; men watered it ; men cherished and nourished it ; and men threw the safeguards of common sense, the common and statute law around it. But all the while it has grown because of the living and energizing idea which informed it. For the same reason it has yielded its seed after its kind and become the cherishing mother to many thousands of sons and daughters. Hiram College is a monument to the devotion of an intelligent and God-loving, conscientious people interested in the welfare, present and future, of humanity. Its birth was with pain and sacrifice. It has been nursed by the tears, the prayers, and the anxious watchings of many ; and its semi-centennial has been crowned with the praise of its sons and daughters and with the love and blessings of God. This chapter cannot better close than with the song in almost faultless rhyme and rhythm, by Hiram's laureate, Mrs. Jessie Brown Pounds:

> "Secluded village of the hills,
>   I own thy witching spell;
> The charm that all thy lovers thrills
>   Is over me as well.
>
> The Mystic Fount of Youth is thine;
>   There is no 'now' or 'then,'
> But underneath thy spell divine
>   We all are young again.
>
> Slight, shadowy forms from far lands come
>   At Love's insistent call,
> And voices cry, 'Oh, sweet, sweet home,
>   We love thee best of all!'
>
> Dear hands long still again I claim,
>   From out the Used-to-Be;
> Each breeze that passes speaks a name
>   And stirs a memory.
>
> O, Hiram, thou are surely blest!
>   The world thy story hears;
> Sweet thoughts of thee like flowers are pressed
>   Within the Book of Years."

APPENDIX.

HIRAM COLLEGE ALUMNI.

1869

Andrew A. Amidon......................................Deceased
James E. Hurlburt, Attorney........................Cleveland
Mrs. Elma Dunn Truesdall........................Garrettsville, O.
*L. L. Campbell, Teacher........................Youngstown, O.
*Henry Clay White, Probate Judge..................Cleveland, O.
*Hiram S. Chamberlain, Business.............Chattanooga, Tenn.
*William H. Clapp, U. S. Soldier................Pine Ridge, S. D.
*Frank H. Mason, U. S. Consul..................Berlin, Germany

1870

Alexander C. Parker....................................Deceased
Edmund B. Wakefield, Professor of Law and Economics,
   Hiram College ....Hiram, O.
*Frank M. Green, Preacher............................Kent, O.
*Clayton C. Smith, Preacher.......................Cincinnati, O.
*I. A. Thayer, Preacher.........................New Castle, Pa.
*William H. Rogers, Preacher.....................Milton, Mass.
*Charles E. Henry, Business.....................Geauga Lake, O.

1871

Grove E. Barber, Professor of Latin in State University....
   .... Lincoln, Neb.
George H. Colton, Professor of Natural Science Hiram
   College .... Hiram, O.
Edgar A. Pardee, Minister....................Williamsville, N. Y.
Mrs. Inez Slocum Black........................Boston, Mass.
Mrs. Julia Smith Leavitt.......................Eden Valley, Minn.
Taylor, A. Snow, Real Estate Agent....................Austin, Ill.
Mrs. Orissa Udall Arner.................................Jefferson
Sutton E. Young, Mining Business................Rapid City, S. D.
*Alanson Wilcox, Preacher..........................Cleveland, O.
*Jessie Brown Pounds, Literary....................Cleveland, O.
*P. H. Dudley, Business.........................New York City.

1872

William P. Cope, Superintendent of Schools............Hamilton
Morgan P. Hayden, Minister....Portage la Prairie, Manitoba, Can.
Charles W. Hemry, Minister........................Fairfield, Neb.
Orlo C. Hubbell, Superintendent of Schools..........Fairfield, Neb.
Mrs. Seleucia Newcomb Hayden.............................
   ....Portage la Prairie, Manitoba, Can.
Joseph W. Robbins..................................... Deceased

Mrs. Alice Squire Hemry.........................Fairfield, Neb.
Andrew Squire, Attorney..............................Cleveland
*Frank A. Derthick, Farmer........................Mantua, O.
*Lucy B. Dudley...................................New York City.
*James M. Van Horn, Preacher......................Warren, O.

*Names marked with a (*) were students of the Eclectic Institute on whom the Board of Trustees conferred Degrees and assigned them to the classes where their names appear.

1873

William A. Babcock, Attorney.........................Cleveland
Frank A. Beecher, Attorney...........................Cleveland
James H. Griffith.......................................Deceased
William I. Hudson, Attorney.........................Chicago, Ill.
Enoch Leavitt, Minister.......................Edon Valley, Minn.
Worthy T. Newcomb, Business......................Dewesse, Neb.
Andrew R. Odell, Attorney...........................Cleveland
Alpheus W. Russell, Editor.......................Mantua Station
Frank L. Summey, Merchant.................Washington, D. C.
Alvin C. White, Attorney...............................Jefferson

1874

William R. Harris ....Deceased
George A. Robertson, Editor...........................Cleveland
Mrs. Rose Tilden Cope.................................Hamilton

1875

Florence Bidlake, Teacher...............................Mantua
Charles Fillius, Attorney.................................Warren
Byron E. Helman, Book Seller.........................Cleveland
Wilbert B. Hinsdale, Dean of the Homeopathic Faculty, Michigan University ....Ann Arbor, Mich.
John F. Rodefer, Manufacturer.......................Elwood, Ind.
Charles H. Ryder.......................................Deceased
Burnett T. Stafford, Minister......................Cleveland, N. Y.

1877

Harris R. Cooley, Minister.............................Cleveland
Charles L. Hall...Deceased
Lee Helsley, Attorney ....Omaha, Neb.
Fayette J. Morton, Physician..........................Cleveland
Galen Wood, Minister.......................Cripple Creek, Colo.
Orlando M. Woodward.................................Deceased

1879

Edwin S. Bower...................................Lincoln, Neb.
Clifton D. Hubbell, Professor of English in Cleveland Public Schools .... Bedford

William H. C. Newington, Principal of High School..........Niles
Arthur C. Pierson....................................Deceased
Adelaide Rudolph, Teacher in Lake Erie College......Painesville
Mrs. Clara Stanhope Hall............................Lincoln, Neb.

1880

Lyman W. Gilbert....................................Deceased
Louis H. Hoffman, Business..........................Cleveland
Edward J. Robison, Banker.....................Indianapolis, Ind.
Colwell P. Wilson, Banker..........................Youngstown

1881

Mrs. Lizzie Clapp Robbins...........................Cleveland
William G. Dietz, Banker............................Cleveland
William F. Fairbanks, Teacher.......................Montville, O.
Vanton O. Foulk, Business...........................Cleveland
Marion J. Grabel, Pastor of Dunham Avenue Christian Church.
.... Cleveland
Carroll H. Parmelee..........................Buffalo, Wyoming
Mrs. Minnie Robison Robinette.......................Macedonia
Henry M. Stone, Merchant Broker.................Denver, Colo.

1882

Charles N. Works, Business.....................North Bloomfield
Edna I. Allyn, Teacher.............................Ottumwa, Ia.
Mrs. Lizzie Gans Kriechbaum........................Canton
Mrs. Jessie Pettibone Dietz........................Cleveland
Mrs. Helen Pettibone Robison...................Indianapolis, Ind.
Mrs. Anna Robison Atwater..........................Macedonia
George C. Russell, Teacher....................Santa Maria, Cal.

1883

Charles Taylor, Attorney...........................Cleveland
Mrs. Minnie Allen Stone............................Deceased
Franklin P. Allyn, Teacher.........................Forrest
Howard H. Baker, Minister..................San Bernardino, Cal.
Floyd N. Barber, Attorney......................Washington, D. C.
George A .McFarland, Principal of State Normal School........
....Valley City, N. D.
Mrs. Lucy Noble Harmon.............................Akron
Lyman A. Reed, Business............................Cleveland
Willard W. Slabaugh, Judge.....................Omaha, Neb.
James G. Warren, Banker.....................Los Angeles, Cal.
Clark M. Young, Professor in State University....Vermillion, S. D.

1884

William B. Clark, Farmer...........................Bedford
Warren Craig, Insurance Agent..................Buffalo, N. Y.

Hattie E. Robison, Teacher.....................Indianapolis, Ind.
Mrs. Ida Sherman Merriman.............................Burton
Walter C. Spaulding, Banker...........................Cleveland
Duane H. Tilden, Attorney............................Cleveland
Almon P. Turner, Manager of the Canadian Copper Co.,......
....................................Sudbury, Ontario, Canada
Mrs. Lilian Works Robertson....................Camp Point, Ill.
Mrs. Cora Amphlett Downs...............Wellesley Hills, Mass.
Mrs. Mabel Bowe Ackerman...........................Cleveland
Mrs. Laura Gerould Craig, Author...............New York, N. Y.
Robert Hoffman, Civil Engineer.......................Cleveland
Ida A. Preston, Teacher.............................Larnard, Kan.

1886

Mrs. Catherine Beattie Hall.............................Deceased
Edwin L. Hall, Professor of Latin in Hiram College......Hiram
Nimrod D. Laughlin, Business.........................Alma, Ill.
Clarence E. Wier, Attorney.....................Indianapolis, Ind.

1887

Mrs. Cora Clark Cooley..............................Cleveland
John W. Damel, Teacher.......................Jefferson City, Mo.
Mrs. Nettie Hopkins McCorkle, Teacher................Cleveland
Mrs. Flora James Collyer............................Beloit, Wis.
Mrs. Laura Laughlin McGinnis..................New Kirk, Okla.
Frank W. Norton, Minister.......................Irvington, Ind.

1888

Charles J. Atwater......................................Deceased
Frederick A. Henry, Attorney..........................Cleveland

1889

Isaac J. Cahill, Minister...................................Dayton
William A. Knight, Minister....................Fall River, Mass.
William H. Mooney....................................Deceased
Arthur B. Russell.......................................Deceased
John Shackson, Editor.................................Glenville
M. Ellen Stevens, Teacher............................Akron, O.

1890

Mrs. Louise Adams Henry.............................Cleveland
John K. Baxter, Superintendent of Schools............Mt. Vernon
Nellie A. Craft..Deceased
William J. Dodge, Principal of High School..............Raven.1a
Edgar R. Fuller, Minister.........................Bakersville, Cal.
Adda M. Hathaway.....................................Bedford
Harlan M. Page, Physician, Professor of Medical Science Hi-
ram College ....Hiram

ABRAM TEACHOUT.

Lucius W. Prichard, Physician.........................Ravenna
Mrs. Angie Proctor Ragan...........................Batavia, Ill.
Emma O. Ryder, Librarian of Hiram College..............Hiram
Benjamin J. Sawyer, Attorney...........................Cleveland
John B. Works, Banker...............................Cincinnati

1891

Mary E. Clark, Modiste...............................Cleveland
Marcia Henry, Professor in Hiram College, Lady Principal..Hiram
Robert M. Marshall, Minister....................Belle Vernon, Pa.
Archie A. McCorkle...................................Deceased.
Homer D. Messick, Attorney..........................Cleveland
Myrta G. Parsons, Teacher..........................Athens, Ga.
Mrs. Carrie Patch Norton............................Cleveland
George A. Ragan, Minister........................Batavia, Ill.
Calvin C. Ryder, Business..........................Cleveland
George H. Rymers, Banker...........................Fremont
Edwin O. Trescott, Superintendent of Schools........Columbiana
Julius V. Wilson, ...Deceased

1892

Edgar W. Allen, Minister.........................Ft. Wayne, Ind.
Cora A. Allen, Teacher...............................Lockland
Fred A. Bright, Minister.............................Painesville
Warren D. Calvin, Physician.....................Ft. Wayne, Ind.
Mrs. Josephine Clark Works..........................Cincinnati
J. Ernest Dean, Illustrator...........................Cleveland
Jacob D. Forrest, Professor in Butler College......Irvington, Ind.
Charles A. Freer, Minister...........................Columbus
Albert H. Hurd, Minister.........................Lone Pine, Pa.
Warren S. Hayden, Banker...........................Cleveland
J. Herman Norton, Printer and Publisher...............Cleveland
Perry J. Rice, Minister.........................South Bend, Ind.
Loa E. Scott, Physician...........................Kirksville, Mo.
Hiram Van Kirk, Professor of Bible Chair of California Uni-
    versity ....Berkeley, Cal.
George W. York, Banker..............................Cleveland

1893

Samuel H. Bartlett, Corresponding Secretary of Ohio State
    Missionary Society ....Cleveland
William A. Brundige, Minister...........................Lima
Mrs. Albertina Allen Forrest.....................Irvington, Ind.
Mrs. Jessie Hall Wood...............................Painesville
Mrs. Mary Henry Webb............................Mineral Ridge
Mary A. Lyons, Ohio State Secretary for C. W. B. M.......Hiram
Roger H. Miller, Business..................New York City, N. Y.
Clayton P. Rockwood, Attorney.........................Cleveland

Claude E. Sheldon, Attorney.............................Windham
Mrs. Blanche Squire Hayden.........................Cleveland
Lewis J. Wood, Attorney............................Painesville
Abner G. Webb, Banker...........................Mineral Ridge
John H. York, Business..............................Cleveland

1894

Clarence R. Bissell, Attorney..........................Cleveland
David D. Burt, Minister.............................Marion, O.
Della P. Craft, Teacher..................................Warren
Forrest D. Ferrall, Minister.....................Pleasantville, Ia.
Adelaide G. Frost, Missionary to India....................Hiram
Mamie Gould, Teacher................................Cleveland
Bert E. Hathaway, Attorney..........................Cleveland
Raymond E. Hull, Business......................Petosky, Mich.
Austin Hunter, Student in Chicago University......Chicago, Ill.
Herbert L. Jones, Teacher............................Hubbard
Alfred M. Kenyon, Instructor in Mathematics in Purdue University ....La Fayette, Ind.
Alfred Vernon Kontner................................Nelsonville
Henry F. Lutz, City Missionary of Pittsburg..........Pittsburg, Pa.
Mattie M. Marsh, Teacher..............................Bryan
Roland A. Nichols, Minister.........................Chicago, Ill.
E. B. Watson, Minister...........................Ballinger, Texas
Allyn A. Young, Fellow in Wisconsin University..Madison, Wis.
William M. Forrest, Missionary....................Calcutta, India

1895

Howard L. Atkinson, Minister........................Chicago, Ill.
Miner L. Bates, Minister...............................Newark
Martin L. Buckley, Minister.........................Rushsylvania
Ben C. Caywood, Minister.................................Akron
Mabel G. Crosse, Teacher of Music................Hazel Green, Ky.
Edwin C. Davis, Minister.............................Bedford, O.
Lincoln Davis, Insurance Agent.........................Cleveland
Allie M. Dean, Teacher in Art Department of Hiram Colloge.. .... Hiram
George B. Dilley, Attorney.............................Cleveland
Frances Hertzog Osgood, Missionary.............Chu Cheo, China
Harry H. Hudson, Attorney............................Cleveland
Harry W. Jewell, Attorney.............................Delaware
Jay E. Lynn, Minister...............................Springfield, Ill.
P. W. McReynolds, Minister.....................Marshall, Mich.
Charles A. Niman, Attorney.......................Cleveland, O.
Dallas J. Osborne, Banker................................Tiffin
Elliott I. Osgood, Medical Missionary............Chu Cheo, China
Maria Parker Bellamy..................................Cleveland
Frank M. Ryder, Business..............................New York
Robert P. Shepherd, Student in Columbia University....New York

Frank H. Simpson, Minister.............................Massillon
Emerson J. Smith, County Auditor.......................Ravenna
H. Maude Thompson, Teacher.........................Malvern
Charles V. Trott, Teacher............................Martinsburg
Edwin T. Wakefield, Physician....................Youngstown, O.
Royal M. Wheeler, Business.........................Mantua Sta.

1896

J. P. Allison, Minister...............................Uhrichsville
William T. Barnes, Minister...........................Wellsville
Claude C. Blair, Business....................................Girard
George A. Bellamy, Warden of the Hiram House......Cleveland
Floyd H. Bogrand, Teacher............................Sharon, Pa.
Elizabeth Carlton, Kindergartner.....................Chicago, Ill.
Bertha A. Clark, Teacher in Cleveland Schools..........Bedford
Laura A. Craft, Teacher.................................Warren
Ira H. Durfee, Minister...........................New Castle, Pa.
Eugene B. Dyson, Physician............................Rootstown
James H. Erskine, Physician..........................Albany, Or.
William W. Frost, Student in Chicago University......Chicago, Ill.
J. H. Goldner, Pastor of Euclid Avenue Christian Church....
....Cleveland, O.
Mrs. Bessie Grabel Frost.............................Chicago, Ill.
John W. Kerns, Minister.......................Steubenville, O.
Raphael H. Miller, Minister.....................Wellsville, N. Y.
Lulu P. Phinney...............................Mulberry Corners
Edith P. Robinson......................................Deceased
Mrs. Clara Russell Anders...........................Youngstown
Elmer E. Snoddy, Professor of Greek in Hiram College....Hiram
Frederick G. Strickland, Minister.........................Chicago
Carrie S. Tibbits, In Public Library.....................Cleveland
Amos Tovell, Minister......................Guelph, Ontario, Can.
William D. Van Voorhis, Minister.......................Akron, O.
Leon C. Vincent, Dentist...............................Ravenna
W. R. Walker, Minister..............................Martinsburg
Daniel G. Wagner, Minister...........................Lordstown

1897

George W. Brown, Missionary.......................Hurda, India
Margaret J. Calvin, Teacher.........................Transfer, Pa.
Samuel G. Carson, Attorney..............................Warren
Mamie B. Colton Vincent..............................Ravenna
Lovina R. Cook..Weston
Van C. Cook, Attorney................................Mansfield
W. S. Cook, Minister...............................Fayette, O.
Henry J. Derthick, Minister.........................Berea, Ky.
Emmitt C. Dix, Editor..................................Wooster
Jay A. Egbert, Minister............................Buffalo, N. Y.
Mrs. Grace Finch Kenyon.........................La Fayette, Ind.

Mrs. Lulu Gault Lynn..............................Springfield, Ill.
William Harris, Minister................................Paulding
Walter S. Hertzog, Principal of High School......Beaver Falls, Pa.
John A. Longmore, Physician....................New York, N. Y.
John P. Myers, Minister...........................Muncie, Ind.
Charles R. Scoville, Evangelist....................South Bend, Ind.
Albert F. Stahl, Minister...........................West Mansfield
C. B. Titus, Missionary.......................Lu Chu Fu, China
Lloyd D. Trowbridge, Physician ....Piqua, O.
Frank A. Turner, Teacher.........................Everett, Wash.
W. G. Voliva, Minister.............................Cincinnati, O.
Pearl H. Welshimer, Minister.......................Millersburg
A. E. Wrentmore, Minister..........................Decatur, Mich.

1898

Howard A. Blake, Minister....................Washington, N. C.
William H. Boden, Minister....................Battle Creek, Mich.
Mrs. Mary Canfield Ewers..............................Fayette
William J. Crum, Minister...........................Hubbard, O.
William R. Davis, Teacher..........................Hillsville, Pa.
Alonzo W. Fortune, Minister.......................Chagrin Falls
Annie L. Gould, Teacher.................................Bedford
Delbert E. Graver, Principal of High School..............Claridon
John S. Kenyon, Professor in Christian College........Canton, Mo.
Ernest D. Long, Professor at Angola, Ind., Normal....Angola, Ind.
Mrs. Ella Poppy McConnell, Minister................Mineral Ridge
Willard R. Moffett, Minister.......................Belle Center, O.
H. Wallace Murry, Medical Student................Camden, N. J.
Earl B. Newton, Business.............................Cleveland
Mrs. Myra Pow Kenyon............................Canton, Mo.
Elizabeth Roberts, Teacher.......................Owosso, Mich.
William A. Scott, Minister.......................West Point, Miss.
Mrs. Lorena Way Newcomb.........................Shalersville
Bert W. Wilson, Medical Student......................Cleveland
Percy H. Wilson, Minister...........................Austintown
Clinton M. Young, Professor at Add Ran University..Waco, Texas

1899

Albertus H. Alden, Medical Student....................Cleveland
J. Everest Allyn, Farmer..................................Hiram
Will A. Bellamy, Minister..........................Evansville, Ind.
Myrta M. Bennett, Teacher at Chagrin Falls........Chagrin Falls
John T. Bridwell, Minister.........................McArthur, O.
Albert W. Cinniger, Attorney............................Medina
Edwin B. Collister, Law Student................Wellsville, N. Y.
Clara C. Darsie, Secretary of Y. M. C. A.............Pittsburg, Pa.
Benjamin M. Derthick, Minister...........................Solon
J. Ray Ewers, Minister............................Bowling Green
Lester B. Gary, Student at Case School................Cleveland

Ross D. Gates, Teacher..................................Chardon
Arthur Holmes, Minister...........................Philadelphia
Guy Hoover, Minister.....................................Minerva
Harry C. Hurd, Medical Student.......................Cincinnati
Mervin L. Jenney, Minister...........................Cleveland
J. Norman Johnston, Minister...........................Augusta
Yetaro Kinosita, Student at Columbia University....New York City
Fred Kline, Minister.....................................Ravenna
Josephine A. Line, Medical Student...................Ann Arbor
Frederick S. Linsell, Minister.....................Paw Paw, Mich.
Frank M. Longanecker, Professor at Fayette Normal School..
.... Fayette
William A. McCartney, Minister.........................Granger
Bruce McCully, Student at Chicago University........Chicago, Ill.
Arthur S. Mottinger, Law Student.......................Akron
Florence E. Oliver, Teacher.......................Princeton, Mo.
William L. Parsons, Business...........................Cleveland
Bernice M. Phinney, Teacher...........................Cleveland
J. Caldwell Price, Medical Student....................Cleveland
Frank C. Rulon, Assistant Professor of Mathematics Hiram
College .... Hiram
J. Hubert Turney, Attorney...........................Madison, O.
Cora M. Turney...Deceased
Katharine M. Weeks, Teacher.................St. Lawrence, S. D.
Clifton C. Wise, Business...........................Millersburg, O.

1900

Webb Parks Chamberlain.............................Twinsburg
Virginia Dillinger ....Findlay
James Hermon Dodd.......................................Hiram
Frank Milton Field.............................Sandy Lake, Pa.
Thomas Alfred Fleming...................Kilsythe, Ontario, Can.
George Berle Fox ....Welshfield
Joseph Laurel Garvin ....Hiram
Oswald Joseph Grainger..........................De Soto, Mo.
Edward Atwood Henry......................Canandaigua, N. Y.
James Garfield Henry...............................Geauga Lake
Henry Daniels Herrick...............................Twinsburg
Walter Chesterfield Gibbs............................Ludlow, Ky.
James Byron Kahle..Tedrow
John T. Le Fevre.....................Hamilton, Ontario, Can.
Erwin Henry McConoughey...............................Solon
Firman C. McCormick.....................................Hiram
Ada May McCormick.............................Ft. Wayne, Ind.
Olney Lee Mercer.......................................Rudolph
Frederick Bernard Messing..............North Tonawanda, N. Y.
Ralph Otis Newcomb.................................Garrettsville
Fred Andrew Nichols.....................................Hiram
John Charles Rhodes.................................Portland, Ore.
Alice Townsend Robinson...........................Angola, Ind.

William Frederick Rothenburger.........................Holgate
Walter Sleeper Rounds.........................Kalamazoo, Mich.
Ward Cleland Sager...Bryan
Charles Sumner Smith.............................Newton Falls
Warren William Wager..Bryan
Arthur Paul Wakefield.......................................Hiram
Walter D. Ward..Winfield
John Warren Wiseman..........................North Royalton

ALUMNI, LITERARY COURSE.

1893

Howard H. Bean, Physician.......................Barberton, O.
L. A. Chapman, Minister..............................Lorain, O.
J. H. Mohorter, Minister............................Boston, Mass.
Charles E. Rose, Farmer...............................Lordstown
Joseph T. Shreve, Minister................................Shreve

1894

Mrs. Francis Barbe Webb....................................Deceased
T. A. Cooper, Minister............................Atlanta, Ind.
Z. O. Doward, Minister......................Grand Island, Neb.
U. G. Gordon, Teacher...........................Taylorsville, Ill.
Mary F. Kelly, Missionary.........................Nankin, China
Octavius Singleton, Teacher........................Louisville, Ky.
John H. Stove, Minister............................Hamilton, Ind.
G. B. Townsend, Minister............................Troy, N. Y.
Norman C. Yarian, Physician...........................Cleveland

1895

Jacob W. Baker, Insurance Agent.......................Cleveland
Mrs. Ada Linton Patterson..............................Hudson

1896

Edward Bower, Insurance Agent.......................Cleveland
Florence M. Campbell.................New Cumberland, W. Va.
Ella A. Caine......................................New Castle, Pa.
Mrs. Ella Dodd McGill.....................................Paulding
Mrs. Carrie Goodrich Kelly, Missionary............Nankin, China
Mrs. Jeanette Howe Wilson.........................Richmond, Ind.
Otto A. Meredith, Medical Student.................Cleveland, O.
Webster G. Moore, Minister............................Akron, O.
James A. Wharton, Minister.................Niagara Falls, N. Y.
Will B. White, Business.................................Cleveland

1897

Dennison R. Moss, Minister.................................Niles
Charles F. Schovanek, Minister......................North Lindale

1898

Tom L. Baxter, Medical Student...............Ann Arbor, Mich.
Blanche M. Beck..Deceased
Ethel C. Caskey, Teacher..............................Bedford, O.
Harvey F. Fetzer, Student in Case School............Cleveland, O.
Justin N. Green, Assistant Secretary of Foreign Missionary
    Society ....Cincinnati, O.
Z. A. Harris, Minister..............................Ft. Wayne, Ind.
James Johnston, Minister..............Adelaide, South Australia
O. T. Manly, Physician...........................Garrettsville, O.
L. J. McConnell, Minister.......................Mineral Ridge, O.
Mrs. Clara Worst Miller............................Ashland, O.
L. O. Packer, Teacher........................Deckers Point, Pa.
Esther B. Patterson, Secretary of Hiram College Faculty..Hiram, O.
Susie L. Rawson, Missionary......................Mahoba, India
Carl D. Thayer, Business............................Cleveland, O.
Samuel Traum, Minister........................Wilmington, O.
Leonard J. Wilson, Student in Case School........Cleveland, O.

1899

M. H. Axline, Medical Student.......................Cincinnati
Jennie E. Britton, Teacher.........................Edwards, Miss.
Charles T. Fredenburg, Minister......Bingham Roads, Ontario, Can.
Daniel B. Grubb ....Mt. Vernon
Homer H. Heath, Medical Student..................Cleveland, O.
Laurence E. Heiges, Teacher...........................Churchill
Carl S. Hertzog, Professor of Mathematics......Los Angeles, Cal.
Lois Hurd ....Dexter City
John T. LeFevre, Minister.................London, Ontario, Can.
Harry W. McMahon, Business..........................Cleveland
Harrison F. Miller, Minister............................Lowell, O.

1900

Ora Carlton Arndt.....................................Sullivan
Roy Bayard Bacon.....................................Cortland
Silas Haydn Calender....................................Milton
Florence Hathaway ....Cleveland
Howard B. Hazzard...................................Lordstown
Kromer C. Ice......................................Salem, W. Va.
Adelaide A. E. Jobes....................................Erie, Pa.
Manley Spaulding Lawrence.....................East Canton, Pa.
Louis John Leet...Freedom
Randolph Yates McCray..............................Mansfield
Asa McDaniel ....Waco
Grace Elizabeth McKibben..........................Newton Falls
Charles Grier Robinson...............................Rockaway
Charles Scott Rowley............................North Fairfield
Nella Luella Shriver.................................Dexter City
Celestia May Turnbull.................................Edinburg
Ralph Tiffany Williams............................Chagrin Falls

At the opening of the Western Reserve Eclectic Institute in 1850—a Primary Department was a prominent feature, and children not yet in their teens were gathered into classes and special teachers provided for them. This arrangement continued until 1857, when it was discontinued. This department was in charge of a woman who not only taught the primary scholars, but also looked after the interests and conduct of the young women of the school.

Principals of the Primary Department of the Western Reserve Eclectic Institute.

During the period from 1850 to 1857 five ladies had charge of this Department:

Phoebe M. Drake ....1850—1851
Laura A. Clark ....1851—1852
Calista O. Carlton ....1852—1853
Harriet E. Wood ....1853—1854
Sarah Udall ....1854—1857

After the discontinuance of the Primary Department Miss Almeda A. Booth had general charge of the Ladies' Department of the school until the establishment of the College in 1867. Since that time 15 different ladies have been elected to the position:

Lottie M. Sackett ....1867—1868
Cortentia C. Munson ....1868—1869
Juliette Comstock ....1869—1870
Ellen Jackson ....1870—1871
Mrs. Marietta Cuscaden ....1871—1877
Mrs. Phoebe B. Clapp ....1877—1880
Mary B. Jewett ....1880—1884
Minnie E. Robison ....1884—1886
Phoebe T. Sutliff ....1886—1887
Kate I. Beattie ....1887—1889
Mary B. Hamilton ....1889—1891
Hellen B. Pettibone ....1891—1893
Mrs. Hattie L. Barclay....................1893—1894
Mary Graybiel ....1894—1895
Marcia Henry ....1895—1901

The character and ability of each and all of these ladies,

were of such a grade that the Institution was honored by them and their assistance in its administration highly appreciated.

The
Board of Trustees.

The Board of Trustees of Hiram College has always been composed of men, honorable, faithful and capable—some of them of exceptional ability as business men.

Presidents
of the Board.

Of the entire number of Trustees for fifty years six only have been elected President and two Vice President. Those who have filled the office of President are:

Carnot Mason .... 1849 to 1856
Alvah Udall .... 1856 to 1880
John J. Ryder .... 1880 to 1890
A. Teachout .... 1890 to 1892
Charles E. Henry .... 1892 to 1899
Charles B. Lockwood .... 1899 to 1901

Those who have been elected Vice President are:

Sutton E. Young .... 1894 to 1896
F. M. Green .... 1896 to 1901

For fifty years six persons have filled the office of Secretary of the Board of Trustees. In many respects this is the most important and difficult of the offices created by the

Secretaries
of the Board.

Board. The value of the records depends very largely on the ability of the Secretary to get accurately, to record legibly and intelligently, and to register systematically the action of the Board at its regular and special meetings. Those who have occupied this office and their terms of service are as follows:

Dr. Lyman W. Trask .... 1849—1864
Dr. Andrew J. Squire .... 1864—1875
Grove E. Barber .... 1875—1882
Arthur C. Pierson .... 1882—1889
Bailey S. Dean .... 1889—1899
Alanson Wilcox .... 1899—1901

It is only justice to say that the records of Dr. Trask are models, and characterize all the elements of a first-class

Recording Secretary. The printed page is not more easily searched than are his written lines.

Treasurers of the Board. Five persons have held the office of Treasurer since 1849:

Symonds Ryder ....1849—1860
Zeb Rudolph ....1860—1868
Richard Hank ....1868—1876
Burke A. Hinsdale ....1876—1883
George H. Colton ....1883—1901

In personal honesty, in financial capacity, in all the sterling qualities of men their record is unchallenged and unstained.

Members of the Board of Trustees. The *personnel* of the Board of Trustees is represented by the following names, the year of election, and in most cases the year when their service ended:

Carnot Mason ....Hiram ....1850—'55
Samuel Church ....Pittsburgh, Pa. ....1850—'51
George Pow ....New Albany ......1850—'51
Kimball Porter ....Wooster ....1850—'51
J. H. Jones ....Wooster ....1850—'53
Frederick Williams ....Ravenna ....1850—'63
Isaac Errett ....Warren ....1850—'58
J. A. Ford ....Burton ....1850—'58
Symonds Ryder ....Hiram ....1850—'60
Aaron Davis ....Bazetta ....1850—'69
Wm. Hayden ....Chagrin Falls .....1850—'63
A. L. Soule ....Russell ....1851—'55
George King ....Chardon ....1851—'59
Wm. Richards ....Hiram ....1851—'61
Alvah Udall ....Hiram ....1853—'87
Alvah Humeston ....Hiram ....1855—'61
Dr. M. Jewett ....Mogadore ....1855—'59
Harmon Austin ....Warren ....1858—'94
W. J. Ford ....Hiram ....1856—'01
Thomas Carroll ....Munson ....1859—'62
A. S. Hayden ....Euclid ....1859—'68
Hartwell Ryder ....Hiram ....1860—'79
J. P. Robison ....Bedford ....1861—'86

R. M. Bishop .... Cincinnati .... 1863—'65
D. W. Canfield .... Chardon .... 1863—'71
A. B. Way .... Alliance .... 1863—'66
J. A. Garfield .... Hiram .... 1864—'82
C. B. Lockwood .... Cleveland .... 1865—'01
J. H. Rhodes .... Cleveland .... 1866—'90
A. Teachout .... Cleveland .... 1869—'01
Thomas W. Phillips .... New Castle, Pa.... 1868—'01
B. F. Waters .... Hiram .... 1869—'90
John F. Whitney .... Freedom .... 1869—'75
W. S. Streator .... East Cleveland ... 1871—'86
Freeman Udall .... St. Louis, Mo..... 1771—'77
F. M. Andrews .... Titusville, Pa. ..... 1872—'76
H. L. Morgan .... Newburgh .... 1872—'97
Thomas N. Easton .... Hinckley .... 1872—'73
J. L. Parmly .... Painesville .... 1872—'01
R. M. Hank .... Hiram .... 1872—'80
J. J. Ryder .... Hiram .... 1872—'92
A. J. Squire .... Hiram .... 1872—'80
Albert Williams .... Akron .... 1872—'75
Geo. A. Baker .... Cleveland .... 1872—'84
Lathrop Cooley .... Cleveland .... 1872—'01
A. J. Marvin .... Cleveland .... 1872—'99
Wm. Bowler .... Cleveland .... 1873—'94
W. P. Hudson .... Cleveland .... 1875—'90
C. E. Henry .... Cleveland .... 1876—'01
C. W. Hemry .... Solon .... 1876—'85
Cyrus Ryder .... Hiram .... 1877—'84
H. C. White .... Cleveland .... 1878—'85
O. G. Kent .... Cleveland .... 1879—'01
R. Stanhope .... Hiram .... 1879—'82
Andrew Squire .... Cleveland .... 1880—'01
B. A. Hinsdale .... Hiram .... 1880—'92
A. A. House .... North Bristol ..... 1882—'00
Lucretia R. Garfield .... Mentor .... 1882—'97
C. H. Ryder .... Hiram .... 1883—'85
W. U. Masters .... Cleveland .... 1883—'86
O. C. Atwater .... Hiram .... 1884—'89
E. B. Wakefield .... Warren .... 1884—'92
Charles Fillius .... Warren .... 1885—'01

John F. Rodifer	Bellaire	1886—'89
I. A. Thayer	New Castle, Pa.	1886—'89
D. H. Beaman	Hiram	1887—'90
Albert Allen	Akron	1873—'89
F. M. Green	Kent	1889—'01
Alanson Wilcox	Cleveland	1890—'01
Frank A. Derthick	Mantua	1892—'01
F. Treudley	Youngstown	1892—'01
O. G. Kent	Cleveland	1892—'01
B. L. Pennington	Cleveland	1892—'99
V. A. Taylor	Bedford	1892—'93
Sutton E. Young	Rapid City, S. D.	1893—'98
William G. Dietz	Cleveland	1893—'01
H. R. Cooley	Cleveland	1894—'01
Robert Miller	Tiffin	1894—'01
W. B. Hinsdale	Ann Arbor	1895—'01
H. E. McMillin	Cleveland	1895—'01
Henry C. Christy	Cleveland	1896—'01
Charles Babcock	Cleveland	1897—'98
W. J. White	Cleveland	1898—'99
Frederick A. Henry	Cleveland	1899—'01
Frank C. Robbins	Niles	1889—'01
Warren S. Hayden	Cleveland	1900—'01

The total number of different persons elected to the Board of Trustees is 86. The first date in the table represents the year in which the member was elected, the second date represents the period to which the member has served.

W. J. Ford.

Of those who are members of the present Board Mr. W. J. Ford was first elected in 1856, succeeding his father, John Augustus Ford, who was a charter member of the Institution. Mr. Ford's service, however, has not been continuous, though he has served from the time of his first election to the present 35 years.

Mr. C. B. Lockwood was elected in 1865 and has served continuously to the present time. He has been longer in service than any other of the 86 Trustees. For more than thirty years as Chairman of the Finance Committee of the Board, he has had the oversight of all the funds of the College; and very largely to his business foresight and devotion to the interests of the

C. B. Lockwood.

College "without money and without price," is the College indebted for its present substantial financial basis. No member has ever served more faithfully or intelligently and no member is worthier of the sincere regard of the friends of Hiram College than is Charles Brown Lockwood.

He was born in Mexico, Oswego County, New York, in 1829. In 1832 he came to Ohio, his father settling at Solon. Here and at Bedford Academy he was educated. In 1850

Chronology.   he went to California. Returning in 1854 he entered a law school at Poughkeepsie, New York, where he graduated and was admitted to the New York bar in 1856. In 1857 he engaged in business at Solon. In 1864 and again in 1866 he was elected from Cuyahoga County to the House of Representatives in the General Assembly of the State of Ohio. In 1877 he commenced business in Cleveland; and since the organization of the Lockwood-Taylor Hardware Company he has been its President. For five years he was a member of the Board of Trustees of the State Asylum for the Insane at Newburgh; and for twelve years he has been Chairman of the Tax Commission of the city of Cleveland. In 1899 he was elected President of the Board of Trustees of Hiram College, a position he now holds.

Thomas W. Phillips first became a member of the Board of Trustees in 1868 and is a member of the Board of 1900. Besides giving freely of his time to the interests of the Col-

T. W. Phillips.   lege he established what is known as the "Phillips Loan Fund" in 1891 which has grown through his aid and the contributions of others from $5,000 to $12,504.45 in 1900.

J. L. Parmly has served the College from 1872 to 1901. He not only has contributed of his time and ability to the

J. L. Parmly.   influence of the Board but he is also a large contributor to the permanent endowment of the College.

Abram Teachout has served on the Board since 1809 and his interest in the College is still unabated. The Teach-

A. Teachout.   out Observatory and Library Building erected in honor of the Semi-Centennial Jubilee of the College will stand, so long as it endures as the material monument of his faith in the future possibilities of the College for which he has given generously of time and money for almost a third of a century.

Lathrop Cooley began his service as Trustee in 1872 and with a slight intermission has served ever since. Be-

Lathrop Cooley.   sides other contributions from time to time his gift of a telescope to crown the Teach-out Observatory will reflect his name from every star that shines over Hiram Hill.

Among the honorary members of the Board of 1900 the name of William Bowler is written large. He was elected a Trustee in 1873, and from that time onward until his ac-

Wm. Bowler.   tive work ceased on account of failing health no form was more frequently seen in Hiram and no face more gladly welcomed than his. His devotion to the College had no limitations save those of opportunity and ability.

He was born March 25, 1822, in Carlisle, New York. When only a boy he came to Ohio, where on the Western Reserve his early education was received. Since 1851 he has resided in Cleveland, where he has lived an active public life. In one of the crises through which the College has passed he came to the front and with almost limitless patience and faith he continued until success was assured.

Other members of the Board of 1900 deserve mention for what they have done in bringing the College up to the present high standard financially and otherwise: Wm. G.

Other Members of the Board of 1900.   Dietz, the present Chairman of the Finance Committee, a most worthy successor to C. B. Lockwood; O. G. Kent, in an emergency always ready with person and money to help; Robert Miller, quiet but faithful; Charles E. Henry, whose wide acquaintance with countries and people has been of great value to the College; H. E. McMillin, whose business sagacity, and generosity have never failed to be found in the right place; and Fred Treudley who more than any other member represents the schools of the State.

Of those who have died and remembered Hiram in the distribution of their estates Albert Allen stands among the

first. He was elected to the Board in 1873, the year the
Albert Allen. number of the Trustees was doubled, and
remained a member until his death in 1888.
Fearless in the discharge of every duty as he saw it, and
faithful in every business obligation, he was a model for the
business world.

He was born in Coventry, near Akron, O., March 12,
1827. His parents, Levi Allen and Phoebe Spicer Allen,
were of the sturdy pioneer stock of Ohio. He was raised on
a farm and attended such schools as were accessible in that
day. He was a very capable business man and ranked high
among business men. He became a Christian early in life
and was always a generous and liberal giver to church and
educational enterprises. For many years he was one of the
strong members of the High Street Church in Akron and its
most liberal supporter. He gave ten thousand dollars to the
endowment fund of Hiram College and for years the trio
who had contributed ten thousand dollars or more to Hiram
included the names of Albert Allen, Flora C. Randall, and
Robert Kerr—their gifts aggregating $52,000. He died
September 25, 1888.

Thomas N. Easton, who was elected a member of the
Board in 1872. He was a friend to higher education and
became a special friend of Hiram College
Thomas N. Easton. and added $8,000 to its endowment.

By occupations the Board of Trustees for 1900 consists
of 13 business men, 4 preachers, 3 lawyers, 1 farmer, 2 phy-
sicians, and 1 teacher. Of these 11 be-
Occupations. long to the Alumni of the College and
hold its degrees.

Its honorary members in 1900 were Wm. Bowler, B. A.
Hinsdale, W. S. Streator, B. L. Pennington and A. J. Marvin.

June 10, 1868, W. J. Ford, Financial Agent for the
Eclectic Institute and Hiram College was asked by the Board
of Trustees to submit a summarized statement of his collections, disbursements and services for the
A Statement of period between 1859 and 1868 inclusive.
Account As this is the only report of like character
by W. J. Ford. on record the conclusions are here given
as a matter of interest: Cash collected,

$16,228.15; pledges for stock and Endowment Fund, $77,-180; out of this was paid $4,978.64 on Boarding House debt, and to teachers; for two courses of lectures to preachers, $4,421.47, leaving on hand September 22, 1868, stock $1,000; in the hands of Finance Committee, $2,000; for the Biblical Department, $5,155; for a Professorship in Biblical Department, $17,125; for endowment to College on the scholarship plan, $1,400; to be used for repairs, $1,500; in bonds and contracts for Endowment Fund, $51,000; $452.86 on salary of Principal and for catalogues; and for the services of the Agent, $4,375.18, making a total of $93,408.15.

The cost of soliciting the entire amount was less than six per cent., and the per cent. for cash actually received nearly twenty-one. In his canvass during the time from 1859 to April 23, 1868, Mr. Ford worked 944½ days, and the total amount of railroad fare, carriage hire and hotel expenses was $1,290.82.

Mr. Ford began his work as Financial Agent with the Church of Christ at Huntsburgh in Trumbull County, and closed with the church in Stow, Summit County. In writing of his first plea for Hiram Mr. Ford says: "When the subscribing was done a little girl came down the aisle with tears shining on her cheeks, and took the paper to the back part of the house, and doubled the amount. This act I took as the Lord's promise to me that we should go forward and not fail."

Of those who greatly assisted Mr. Ford at the beginning of his canvass was Benjamin F. Waters who is yet living in a serene old age near Hiram. Mr.

B. F. Waters.   Waters always was a warm friend to Hiram and as Trustee, liberal giver and canvasser for funds, and in continued friendship he is worthy of long remembrance.

May 7, 1850, at the first meeting of the Board of Trustees after the granting of the Charter, Isaac Errett and A. S. Hayden were directed to prepare a circular for publication "to give general information relative to the objects and plan of the school and the state of progress."

First Circular Advertisement of W. R. E. Institute.

WILLIAM BOWLER.

As this is the first literature issued by the authority of the Board of Trustees it is of interest:

WESTERN RESERVE ECLECTIC INSTITUTE.

Dear Brethren:—We affectionately solicit your attention to a statement of facts, touching an enterprise very dear to our hearts—the contemplated school at Hiram—THE WESTERN RESERVE ECLECTIC INSTITUTE.

It is generally known, that at a meeting of Delegates from thirty-one Churches on the Western Reserve, held in Aurora, Nov. 1849, it was agreed to establish an Institution of learning, such as might meet, in the character and scope of its instructions, and especially, its moral and religious instructions, the wants of the brotherhood; and that such Institution should be located at Hiram, Portage County, Ohio. At another meeting of Delegates in Hiram, Dec. 1849, the preparatory steps were taken towards the establishment of such an Institution. A Board of Trustees was appointed, composed of the following brethren: George Pow, Samuel Church, Aaron Davis, Isaac Errett, Carnot Mason, Zeb Rudolph, Symonds Rider, J. A. Ford, Kimball Porter, Wm. Hayden, Frederick Williams and A. S. Hayden; a Charter drafted and approved, and forwarded to the Legislature—a Charter making special provision for instruction in the Holy Scripture, as an essential part of the course of Education in the Institution. Subsequently, the Charter passed the Legislature; stock in shares of $25 each, having been taken to the amount of $5,000, the Board of Trustees energetically pushed forward the enterprise through its incipient stages. A Farm of fifty-six acres has been purchased at the centre of Hiram, embracing one of the most beautiful sites for buildings anywhere to be found, and containing ample grounds for lots to be occupied by those wishing to enjoy the benefits of the Institution, which the Trustees can sell at reasonable rates. A Building Committee appointed by the Trustees, have let out contracts for the stone, brick and woodwork of the School Edifice—an Edifice intended to be substantial, tasteful, and sufficiently large to accommodate one hundred and fifty students. *The foundations of the building are actually laid,* the work is rapidly progressing, and the building will be ready for use by next Fall. A Committee has also been appointed to secure the services of Teachers, that the first Term may commence by the first of October next.

Thus you will see, dear brethren, that the Board of Trustees are disposed to act with energy in the work committed to their trust. But to carry forward their work to completion, will require greatly increased liberality on the part of the brethren. Below is an estimate of the cost of farm, buildings, etc.

Farm $1,800.00
Building 7,500.00
Furnishing 1,000.00
_____
Total $10,300.00
To meet this, we have subscriptions to the amount
of $5,000.00
Leaving a deficit of 5,300.00

We have been cheered by assurances that the Churches generally, were favorable to the enterprise, and would certainly sustain it. The time has come, when this must be done, or the consequences must be disastrous to the enterprise.

We make an affectionate and earnest appeal to our brethren in behalf of this Institution, just struggling into life. We need such a school. The highest religious considerations demand that we go on with it. We cannot fail in it without dishonor. We cannot succeed in it without the most desirable results flowing to our children and children's children. "Why should the work cease?" Will you be ready dear brethren, when a solicitor calls, to aid as largely as possible? Or will you, without a solicitor, forward your donations or subscriptions, and by timely aid in a most righteous and benevolent work, do honor to your Christian profession, and "lay up in store a good foundation against the time to come." By order of the Board of Trustees.

CARNOT MASON, President of the Board.
L. W. TRASK. Secretary.

May 13, 1850, the Board of Trustees resolved "That

Aaron Davis be empowered to solicit funds, and to spend as much time as shall be in his power, in Trumbull county,
Ohio. The following autograph declara-
Aaron Davis a Solicitor. tion of his authority is in the handwriting of Dr. Lyman W. Trask, Secretary, and Carnot Mason, President:

The Trustees of the Western Reserve Eclectic Institute, hereby authorize Aaron Davis to act as a solicitor to obtain funds and subscriptions for the establishment of said Institute. By order of the Board of Trustees,

> CARNOT MASON, President.
> LYMAN W. TRASK, Secretary.

Hiram, May 13, 1850.

The first subscription paper circulated for funds for the school was prepared shortly after the meeting in Aurora in November, 1849. The heading reads as follows: "We, the
The First Subscription Paper. undersigned, do hereby subscribe the several sums annexed to our names, to the capital stock of the Western Reserve Eclectic Institute to be established in the township of Hiram, Portage County, Ohio, upon the following conditions: Twenty-five dollars to constitute one share and the right to one vote; one hundred dollars the right to four votes; two hundred dollars six votes; three hundred dollars seven votes; four hundred dollars or more eight votes. Said sums payable to the Treasurer of said Institute in quarterly payments. First payment due on the first of September, 1850."

The first signatures are from the Church in Bazetta: Aaron Davis, $100; Daniel Faunce, $50; Moses Bacon, $25;
Bazetta. J. Y. McKinney, $25; Otis R. Coburn, $25; Robert S. Faunce, $25; Eldad Barton, $10; and Edwin Wakefield, $25—a total of $285.

The Lordstown Church was represented by Moses Haskel, Abraham Leach, Peleg Lewis, Peter Wilson, Irvin P.
Lordstown. Gordon, Peter Snyder, I. Tait, B. Tait, Robert Tait, and Orman Dean to the amount of $36.50.

Howland.

The Church at Howland was represented by Simeon Drake, Aaron Drake, Jacob Grove, Joseph Williams, Rhoda Logan and John Buckingham, Sarah Drake, Phoebe Drake, to the amount of $86.50.

Hartford.

The Hartford Church was represented by Rufus Chapman and Milo Dugan to the amount of $50.

Champion.

The Champion Church was represented by Thomas Packard and Samuel McCollum to the amount of $6.

Newton Falls.

The Church at Newton Falls was represented by David Robbins, Jacob Hawn, William Cook, Edward T. Caldwell, Joseph M. Brockett, George Earl, Cyrus Taylor, Sarah C. Cole, Mary M. Caldwell, and Almon Cook, to the amount of $64.

Southington.

Sharon, Pa.

Milton Rice of Southington contributed $10.50; Thomas Hazeltine for the Church at Sharon, Pa., $50; Isaac Arkwright, Niles, $25; and Isaac Errett, Bloomfield, $25. The old document is badly worn, but these interesting facts are gleaned from it. This paper is the one carried by Aaron Davis.

Abraham Teachout.

Abraham Teachout is one of the best friends Hiram College ever had. He has been a trustee nearly ever since the Institution became a College in 1867, commencing his service in 1869. He was born in Ontario County, New York August 17, 1817. The family is of Dutch ancestry. Its earliest representatives came to America in the 16th century and settled in the Mohawk Valley, and from them all the people in the country bearing the name have descended. In religion the family were Baptists. In politics his father was a Whig.

In 1837 his father's family moved to Ohio and settled at North Royalton. Soon after he was of age Abraham went into Cleveland to seek employment, and finally accepted the position of bowsman on a canal boat, rising soon to the position of steersman, then captain, and at last became the owner of a boat. He also secured a situation in the first elevator erected in Cleveland. Later he became a partner with Robert Brayton and built a steam sawmill at Royalton, whch was put in operation November 10, 1845.

He then embarked in mercantile trade at Madison in Lake County. In 1857 he purchased the mill privilege at Painesville. In 1862 he turned his attention to agricultural pursuits which he followed for several years.

In 1869 he engaged in the lumber trade and the sale of doors, sash and blinds at Chattanooga, Tennessee. This laid the foundation of his present business in Cleveland, which he began in 1873. In company with his son, Albert R. Teachout, he has continued to the present with great success.

He was married February 22, 1842, to Julia Ann Tousley. His second marriage was to Mrs. Laura E. Hathaway, in 1881. His third marriage was to Mrs. Mary B. Hamilton in 1896.

A. B. Green, one of his favorite preachers, performed the ceremony at both the first and second marriage. W. N. Arnold at the third.

He was converted to Christianity by the preaching of Alexander Campbell, Walter Scott, A. B. Green, William Hayden, and A. S. Hayden. He was baptized in Royalton in June, 1851, by Wiliam Hayden, and united with the Church of Christ in that place. In 1873 he removed his membership to the Franklin Circle Church in Cleveland, and soon was elected to its eldership, a position he still retains.

He has always taken an active interest in educational affairs. He was a member of the Board of Education in Madison for four years, and in Painesville for nine years.

He has been a member of the Board of Trustees of Hiram College since 1859, and President of the Board for six years. He was chairman of the Building Committee in the erection of the new college buildings, and superintended the construction of Miller Hall. More recently he has erected the Library and Observatory building at his own expense. This building so long as it endures will stand as a monument to his love for Hiram, and his generosity to the College in every hour of its necessity. Lathrop Cooley, his life-long friend, will furnish the Observatory with a first-class telescope, and the two names will be indissolubly linked together as long as the stars shine over Hiram Hill.

Mr. Teachout is a man of great business capacity, sterling integrity, an abiding friend, a Christian without stain, and held in the highest esteem by all who know him; and his name will not perish as long as Hiram and its ever increasing influence continue on the earth.

But few of the details of College administration are ever known to the public, and yet every well-organized faculty has its secretary and keeps a record term by term and day by day of its transactions. Incidents, transactions, and **Faculty Meetings.** results can be found in the records of every faculty to fill a volume with romantic interest from cover to cover. For instance the following is the record for January 14, 1857; and signed by J. A. Garfield, secretary: Teachers met, President Hayden in the chair. On motion of J. A. Garfield it was unanimously *Resolved,* That Messrs. ———— and ———— be required to perform some rhetorical exercise before the school prior to next Monday morning on pain of expulsion. Also it was unanimously *Resolved,* That Miss ———— and Mr. ———— be requested to take their places in Miss Booth's grammar class, on pain of expulsion.

At another meeting in the same month "some irregularities were reported; that Messrs. ———— and ———— had been found in the room of the Misses ———— at 2 o'clock at night. It was known that they had been very irregular in their school duties during the whole term, and after a full investigation of the case it was unanimously *Resolved,* That Messrs. ———— and ———— be dismissed from the school for the remainder of the term.

At still another meeting in the same month "the propriety of having budgets read before public lyceums was discussed, and finally it was unanimously *Resolved,* That no budget should be read unless it had been seen and approved by some one or more of the teachers."

May 20, 1857, the teachers received word from the

Board of Trustees that Mr. A. S. Hayden had resigned as Principal, and asking them to take charge of the school which they agreed to do, "if satisfactory arrangements can be made." A week later the following articles of agreement were settled upon: The Board of Education agree upon their part to conduct the school, furnish the wood and chalk, provide for cleaning the seminary, ringing the bell, making the fires, and pay for printing rules and term reports. The Board of Trustees agree on their part to pay to the Board of Education the entire receipts of the tuition, to publish the annual catalogue, to furnish chemicals, and make all necessary repairs of the buildings, and pay for advertising.

May 30, 1857, Mr. Garfield was chosen chairman of the Board of Education and J. H. Rhodes, secretary. At this meeting the relative wages of teachers was fixed: Mr. Garfield and Mr. Dunshee were to receive $600 each; Mr. Everest and Mr. Rhodes $480 each; and Miss Booth $400. At other meetings following, Mr. Garfield and Miss Booth were "endowed with excusing powers and in their absence any teacher may exercise this power;" it was agreed to have "a religious meeting every Thursday night for one hour to consist of a short discourse and social exercises;" that "the cost of the winter's wood should be paid for from the winter's receipts;" and "the game of chess discouraged among the students."

One of the most noticeable features of the annual reports of President Zollars to the Board of Trustees is the emphasis which he places on the enlargement and strengthening of the Courses of Study. When he came to Hiram in 1888 there were three distinctly marked Courses leading to degrees, viz.: Classical, Philosophical, and Scientific. Provisions, however, had been partially made for a Biblical or Ministerial Course but this movement was not strong. During the first year the great effort was to strengthen this course. During the second year besides these four courses, all of them strong, other courses were maintained: A Normal Course, a Commercial Course, a two-years' English Ministerial Course, and a

Courses of Study in Hiram College.

four-years' Ministerial Course. In 1891 two four-years' Courses, one purely literary and one ministerial in character were arranged with a view to meet the wants of many students who came to Hiram well advanced in years but with little more education than that afforded by private study or the common country schools. In amount of work these courses are about two years shorter than the long course. These courses have been quite popular and yet have not had the tendency feared by some of weakening the longer courses. It was found by experience that only in rare cases did a student change from the long course to the short one, but cases were quite frequent where students changed from the short course to the long one. In recent years the changes in the curricula of studies leading to graduation and college degrees have been many. The policy of granting elective studies has grown in favor, both with college authorities and with students. This is true of the oldest institutions in the Nation as well as of those of later origin. President Zollars and his Faculty have been in entire harmony in regard to these various changes. The result has been that the Preparatory Department has been increased in length one year, making three years of preparatory work instead of two as before. The added studies in the Preparatory Department and to the College courses require seventy one term studies for graduation in the long courses as against fifty-four one term studies before 1888.

At present there are twelve clearly defined courses, leading to degrees, viz.: Four Classical, four Scientific, and four Literary of equal length. Besides these the special courses, Oratory, Music, Commercial, Teachers, English Ministerial and three post graduate courses of a year resident work for which no degrees are granted. Nearly twice as many studies are now taught in the College as were taught at the beginning of this administration, and the Faculty has been doubled in numbers and increased in efficiency. In the variety and strength of the work offered Hiram College holds a high rank among the colleges of the State and Nation.

Historically the Master's degree is the first of the degrees in the liberal arts. In the earlier days of Oxford University in the twelfth century and Cambridge in the thir-

College Degrees. teenth century "a degree was a license to teach. It carried with it the *jus docendi*. Master, Doctor and Professor were at first interchangeable words designating one who had received a license. The Bachelor was a student and apprentice. He could teach under the direction of a Master but not independently. Still he had taken a step (*gradum*) towards the mastership or doctorate and so may be said to have obtained a degree, or been graduated." In Universities like Oxford and Cambridge in England, and in Italy and France, the teachers who constituted the faculty of each of these universities were granted by the pope or the monarch the privilege of teaching, and this developed into the right to grant licenses to teach, or confer degrees.

The first meeting of the stockholders of the Western Reserve Eclectic Institute was quite largely attended and its essential action most carefully recorded. The following is the record: At a meeting of the stockholders of the Western Reserve Eclectic Institute, held in Hiram, November 24, 1851, pursuant to previous notice, Alvah Udall was appointed President and Lyman W. Trask, Secretary. It appearing that the sum of seven thousand dollars has been raised, therefore *Resolved,* That we proceed to the election of a new Board of Trustees, according to the provisions of the charter. Whereupon Isaac Errett and Symonds Ryder were appointed tellers, and the stockholders present proceeded to vote by ballot for the new Board of Trustees. After the ballot the tellers reported "that the following is the result of the election for Trustees of the Western Reserve Eclectic Institute, held on this day November 24, 1851, viz.: For three years, Carnot Mason,* Symonds Ryder, Isaac Errett, William Hayden, 59 votes. For *two* years Zeb Rudolph, Frederick Williams, Aaron Davis, J. H. Jones, 59 votes, except J. H. Jones, who received 57 votes. For *one* year, J. A. Ford, William Richards, George King, A. L.

The First Meeting of the Stockholders.

---

*Carnot Mason received only 58 votes, manifestly not voting for himself.

Soule, 59 votes. Whole number of votes, 59. Signed Isaac Errett and Symonds Ryder, Tellers. *Resolved*, That the tellers' report be adopted, and that Carnot Mason, Symonds Ryder, Isaac Errett, William Hayden, Zeb Rudolph, Frederick Williams, Aaron Davis, J. H. Jones, J. A. Ford, William Richards, George King, and A. L. Soule are elected Trustees of the Western Reserve Eclectic Institute for the term mentioned in that report. Whereupon the meeting adjourned. Lyman W. Trask, Secretary.

At the laying of the corner stone of the extension to the old college building June 17, 1886, the following articles were placed in it: Swiss and American coins of recent date; Proceedings of the Reunion of 1880 and the Centennial History of the College by B. A. Hinsdale;

Articles Placed in the Corner-stone. Histories of the Literary Societies; Programs of recent Commencements and Catalogues of the College for 1883-4-5-6; Report of Ohio Meteorological Bureau; one copy each of the "Saturday Item," Garrettsville Journal, Beaman's Bugle, Democratic Press, Cleveland Leader, Cleveland Plain Dealer, Hiram College Student, Cleveland Herald containing President Hinsdale's Baccalaureate of 1880, New York Tribune, Christian Standard, Chagrin Falls Exponent, the Detroit Plain dealer, Republican-Democrat, the Epitome; Harper's Weekly; a glass plate having a brief history of the building etched upon it; an M. T. badge; a copy of "The Disciple;" a picture of the new building; a piece of Colonial money; Penny Press; a Greek newspaper; a photograph of James A. Garfield; and a copy of the Holy Bible.

Eminent Representatives of the Eclectic Period. Of the student body of the Eclectic Institute from 1850 to 1867 who have risen to eminence since in law, business, the gospel ministry, statesmanship, military life, and above all in noble manhood and womanhood, the following names are among the most noticeable and representative:

1850. Lucretia Rudolph Garfield, one of the "first ladies of the land," and a woman of exalted character; William B. Hazen,

1851. scholar and brave soldier; Henry Clay White, upright judge and distinguished citizen; Orris C. Atwater, and John M. Atwater, preachers and educators of wide distinction; John Encell, preacher and legislator; James A. Garfield, *facile princeps* as man, citizen, statesman, President; Corydon E. Fuller, author, editor, and business man;

1852. the Haydens, W. L. and many others, preachers and authors; Henry O. Newcomb, preacher, professor and lawyer; A. E. Rood, business man; J. Carroll Stark, preacher; Simon Perkins Wolcott,

1853. lawyer and legislator; Chauncey F. Black, lawyer and Governor of Pennsylvania; William Dowling, preacher; Henry M. James, educator; Joseph King, preacher of wide experience; Leonard Southmayd, preacher; Jennie Gardner Encell Mary Turner Hins-

1854. dale; Hiram S. Chamberlain, business; William H. Clapp, military; L. L. Campbell, teacher; C. P. Evans, preacher; Chas. C. Foote, preacher; Robert Moffett, distinguished preacher and missionary secretary; A. H. Pettibone, member of Congress; Joseph Rudolph, farmer and business; Freeman E. Udall, business; Wealthy A. L. Hayden; Perlea Moore Derthick;

1855. Charles P. Bowler, soldier; Harrison S. Glazier, preacher; John B. McCleery, chaplain in regular army; Herman L. Morgan, business; Edwin H. Rogers, preacher; L. D. Woodworth, lawyer and member of Congress; Rufus E. Belding, phy-

1856. sician; H. D. Carlton, preacher; E. A. Ford, railroad; Roldon Hinsdale, farmer and legislator; Frank H. Mason, U. S. Consul; Wallace Coburn, soldier;

1857. Richard S. Groves, preacher; Hiram H. Mack, teacher and legislator; Rufus H. Moss, preacher; Marion F. Pratt, business; Hiram Woods,

1858. preacher; Mary L. Root, teacher; Amzi Atwater, preacher and teacher; Clark

Braden, preacher and controversialist; W. O. Beebe, busi-
1859.   ness; W. H. H. Flick, lawyer and judge;
                   O. C. Hill, teacher and author; C. C.
Smith, preacher and missionary secretary; F. A. Williams,
1860.   soldier; Henry N. Allen, preacher; Myron
                   S. Clark, physician; P. H. Dudley, busi-
ness; Jasper S. Ross, preacher; Grove E. Barber, educator;
1861.   C. W. Clark, lawyer and judge; J. L. Dar-
                   sie, preacher; O. A. Richards, preacher;
A. A. Amidon, lawyer; E. S. Hart, preacher; E. L. Lemert,
1862.   business; J. M. Monroe, preacher; An-
                   drew Squire, lawyer; E. S. Woodworth,
farmer and legislator; Sutton E. Young, lawyer and legislator; E. A. Bosworth, preacher; W. H. Rogers, preacher;
1863.   J. C. Cannon, preacher; Howard A.
                   Treudley, business; Morgan P. Hayden,
preacher; B. H. Hayden, preacher; Wilbert B. Hinsdale,
1864.   physician; O. C. Hubbell, teacher; Virgil
                   P. Kline, lawyer; Webster O. Moore,
preacher and writer; D. L. Rockwell, lawyer; E. B. Wakefield, preacher and educator; B. S. Dean, preacher and edu-
1865.   cator; W. H. Crafts, business man and
                   legislator; J. P. Teeple, business; A. J.
1866.   Laughlin, preacher; O. Q. Oviatt, preach-
                   er; S. M. Cook, physician; Fred Treud-
1867.   ley, educator; J. M. Van Horn, preacher;
                   and Frank L. Gilson, lawyer and judge.

F. M. Green was born in Norton, Summit County, Ohio,
September 28, 1836.

His father, Philander Green, for 57 years in the min-
istry, died April 18,1900. His uncle, Almon B. Green, one
F. M. Green.   of the founders of Hiram College, a
Chronology of   preacher for 55 years, died March 31,
His Life.   1886. From childhood to manhood his
                    main field of labor was the farm. Until
1853 his school life was in the district schools, and Granger
Academy, in Summit and Medina Counties.

November, 1853, he entered the Western Reserve Eclectic Institute at Hiram, O., as a student and remained with
some irregularity until 1860.

From 1855 to 1863 he taught in the district schools of Summit and Medina counties and in the Academies at Granger, O., and Lordstown, O.

March 11, 1862, he was married to Ellen E. Stow, who was a student in Hiram in 1851.

In 1863 he entered the Gospel ministry among the Disciples of Christ and in which service he still continues.

September 9, 1852, he was baptized by Dr. Warren A. Belding, one of the founders of Hiram College.

During his long ministry he has been pastor and preacher for churches in Cleveland, Toledo, Akron, Wilmington, and Kent, in Ohio, and Duluth in Minnesota.

From 1867 to 1870 he was County School Examiner for Mahoning County, Ohio.

From 1870 to 1878, State and National Sunday-School Secretary for the Disciples of Christ.

From 1878 to 1882, Corresponding Secretary of the American Christian Missionary Society.

From 1863 to 1865, Chaplain of the Northern Ohio Hospital for the Insane.

From 1867 to 1874, Associate Editor and regular correspondent of the "American Christian Review," edited by Benjamin Franklin.

From 1876 to 1887, Associate Editor of the "Teacher's Mentor," and "Bible School," published by the Standard Publishing Company.

From 1866 to 1888, regular correspondent for the "Christian Standard," Isaac Errett, editor, and in 1882 Associate Editor.

From 1863 to 1901, for 25 years of that time Corresponding Secretary of the Ministerial Association of the Disciples of Christ in Eastern Ohio.

As author, he issued "The Standard Manual," for Sunday-school workers, in 1878; "A Royal Life," a story of Garfield, in 1882; "Christian Ministers' Manual," in 1883; "Christian Missions and Historical Sketches," in 1884; "Life and Times of John F. Rowe," in 1898; "History of Hiram College," 1901.

Since he entered the ministry in 1863 he has delivered of sermons and other addresses 7,203.

Of academic degrees he has received from Hiram College, A. M.; Bethany College, M. L.; Drake University, LL. D.

From 1889 to 1901, Trustee of Hiram College.

In 1886 and 1887, member of the General Assembly of the State of Ohio.

In 1896, first vice-president of Ohio State Conference of Charities and Correction.

In 1901, preacher for church in Stow, O.

Mr. J. M. Atwater in a unique way has given the relative position of those places which are most prominently connected with Garfield's life in Ohio. He borrowed the method from Victor Hugo, who in his famous account of the battle of Waterloo, describes the field

The Capital A and Garfield's Ohio Life.

of the battle with its roads as shaped like the capital letter A. His description of that battlefield is perhaps the clearest and best ever given. Mr. Atwater says: On the map of Ohio, from Cleveland east and southeast, let the reader imagine a gigantic capital A—the top of the letter at Hiram, the right foot at Cleveland, and the left at Mentor. The base of the letter is thus on the south shore of Lake Erie, and the letter itself points to the southeast. The cross-bar starts a little north of Solon station on the Erie railroad and runs northeast to Chester and a little beyond. The right bar of the A is a little more, and the left bar a little less than thirty miles long. From foot to foot of the letter is a little more than twenty miles, and the length of the cross-bar about twelve. On this letter A can be arranged and kept clear in the mind all of Garfield's home life, except that which was spent in Washington. Along the line of the *cross-bar* are all the scenes of his childhood, and most of those of his youth and early manhood. A little north of the point where the cross-bar joins the right side of the letter is the spot where he was born, the home of his boyhood, in Orange, 3½ miles north of Solon. From this point down the right side of the A to the foot at Cleveland, he went at sixteen to be a sailor on the lake, or, as it turned out to be, a driver on the canal. Along the cross-bar ten miles to the northeast he went to Chester, his first schooling away from home. Two miles south of his home, at the junction of the cross-bar with the right side of the letter, is the Ledge, where at eighteen he taught his first school. Close by is Bentleyville, where he attended meeting, and the little stream in which, March 4, 1850, he was baptized. Hiram, at the top of the A, is the school where he prepared for college, and took half his college course, and where he afterwards did his grand work of teaching. Mentor, at the left foot, was his later home, the Mecca for the throngs of pilgrims in his Presidential campaign, and is the permanent home of his family. Cleveland, at the right foot, was the place of his funeral, and is the place of his tomb and of the Garfield monument. All along the right bar of the letter are the churches to which he preached most frequently, and in several cases regularly, Hiram, Mantua, Aurora, Solon, Bedford, Newburgh, and Cleveland.

Mr. James G. Coleman, of Chagrin Falls, who represented the church at Munson at the meeting in Aurora November 7, 1849, which gave the final decision where the school should be located, and who presided over that meeting when the decisive vote was taken, A Reminiscence says: "There were 31 churches repreby J. G. Coleman. sented by 31 delegates; that the weather was pleasant and he went to the meeting on horseback; that Dr. J. P. Robison presided until the vote rejecting Bedford was taken, when he withdrew and J. G. Coleman presided; that the feeling ran very high, and foolish things were said, but we worked on and succeeded by 4 o'clock p. m. and then adjourned to meet in Hiram; that the meeting was held in the Disciple church at Aurora; and that if Hiram was ready at any time to give up the fight for the location, he did not know it." Mr. Coleman also says: "My wife and I lived in Hiram and attended the Bible lectures in 1866 and 1867; and now, in my 81st year, much weaker in mind and body than I was then, I love to think of the good and faithful ones with whom I lived and labored for Hiram."

HIRAM—FIRST TERM.

Reaching Hiram about dark the evening before school was to open, I found a boarding place at Charles Raymond's, a mile south of the Center. Four of us were to occupy one room. Two of the boys, New Yorkers, were already on hand. A fourth came later.

Reminiscence by O. C. Atwater.

With a table, stove, four chairs, two beds and four boys, the room might be called full. To any one who ever sat at the Raymond table it need not be said that we fared well. For room, board, fuel and lights we paid "ten shillings" ("York shillings")—(all such prices were reckoned in shillings in those days)—a dollar and twenty-five cents a week. Those who had washing done—no laundries in small places then—paid "sixpence," six and a fourth cents more.

The next morning I went up early to see the building. Found "Uncle Zeb" hurrying to finish putting down chairs and desks. As he had an extra screw driver, I was soon hard at work. The last ones were in place before the hour of assembling—perhaps 10 o'clock.

The opening exercises were held in "the meeting house" (*church* was not commonly used by our people on the Reserve then),—this was not the brick church burned a few years since, but a frame building which occupied the same site and was burned some forty years ago. The stand, a high, small stand at the north end of the house between the front doors, was occupied by four persons—A. S. Hayden, the Principal, (commonly called Sutton Hayden); Symonds Ryder, the patriarch of Hiram; Amzi Atwater (better known to all old Portage County residents as "Judge Atwater"), and a fourth person, perhaps William Hayden, possibly Isaac Errett. Do not recall the exercises.

The grounds were an old cornfield, partly surrounded by a rail fence and with the hills left from the last crop not even smoothed down, and without a tree, save a few old apple trees in the northeast corner. It may be that the outer row of trees along the center road that was and the other streets that were to be, had been planted, but if so, they were quite insignificant. There was not a single dwelling around the campus on any side. The only building nearer than "the meeting house" was the Methodist church, on the site now occupied by the Y. M. C. A. building. "The district school" was kept in "the stone jug," a low, square, stone building just east of "the meeting house." There were four or five houses to the west of the corner and near at hand; and one house to the east, the Edwards house, so well known to generations of Hiram students as the Reno place, one to the south, two to the north, and four or five to the west within half a mile. These last are in addition to the few already mentioned as near the Center corners.

A few students found quarters in the basement of the building. Bro. Hayden (he was only occasionally called *Principal*, very rarely indeed *President* Hayden), with his family, and possibly a boarder or two, occupied the south wing of the basement, some three rooms. The remainder of the students, besides those in the basement and in the few houses near "the Center," had to be stowed away as best they could be in farmhouses for a mile or more round about. Favorite boarding places were the Packer place to the north; George and "Squire" Udall's, to the east, and Charles Raymond's, a mile south. Zeb Rudolph, "Uncle Zeb," as he was affectionately called by everybody, lived in the first house west of "the meeting house sheds," the house so long occupied afterwards by Deacon Young. His house and Pelatiah Allen's ("Pati Allen's") were crowded to overflowing.

The only store in the place was kept by N. C. Meeker, afterwards Horticultural Editor of *The New York Tribune*, and later murdered by the Indians while serving the U. S. Government as Indian Agent. His store was kept in the little black (or brown) house west of ———— Young's, since the home of Mrs. Deihl. There the ambitious youth could invest in slates and slate pencils, sticks of candy, foolscap, matches, stearine candles, japanned candlesticks, and the indispensable snuffers. The days of camphene had not yet come. And as for coal oil and electric lights, they were still further away in the unknown future.

The post office was kept by ———— Young in the

kitchen of his old farmhouse. This house occupied the corner where Clinton Young's house now stands. The mail came after dark on those winter nights and was often late. Waiting in the long, dimly-lighted kitchen (one candle does not make a very brilliant illumination) was trying to the students and to Mrs. Young as well.

Ravenna, fourteen miles away, was the nearest railroad point. But to most of the students this was a very small matter, as indeed such inconveniences were to most people west of the Alleghenies. The only railroads in that part of Ohio were the original Cleveland & Pittsburg Railroad and the Lake Shore Railroad. Men were toiling across the plains and over the Rockies to California, the land of gold, on foot and with ox teams. Years were yet to pass before the famous "Pony Express," harbinger of our great western railroad lines, should win its amazing triumphs.

The school opened in November with three teachers— A. S. Hayden, principal; Thomas Munnell, assistant, and Mrs. Phoebe M. Drake, teacher of the primary department. The primary occupied the south wing below. Nearly all the other students sat in the chapel all day, passing into the north wing as recitations demanded. Only a few had rooms near enough to study in during recitation hours. The chapel was the large room below. It was furnished with common wood-bottomed chairs and three-legged, cherry desks; a very good pattern for those times. Both desks and chairs were firmly screwed to the floor by the aid of small iron plates. Modern school furniture had not yet been invented. The ladies had the south side of the room, the gentlemen the north. The whole upper story of the building was unfinished lumber rooms.

The school was a rather large "Select School," with a primary department attached. Its patronage was more extended than "Select Schools" commonly enjoyed—New York furnishing several pupils and Canada at least one. Few were planning for college. Am not certain that there was even one looking to such a course. The only class I can distinctly recall was a class in geometry with four members—Benjamin J. Hershey, John W. Horner, William B. Hazen, and Orris Clapp Atwater. It was a rather even class, so far as that study was concerned. No advance echoes of the guns of Fort McAlister foretold Hazen's distinction.

There were no literary societies. Probably most of the students had never heard of such things. Indeed there were no societies of any kind. There was some literary work and there were "public exercises" at the close of the term, but no literary enthusiasm. Literary interest had its real beginning early in the second year under the lead of Corydon E. Fuller, Garfield, and others. I put Fuller first for probably the original impulse was due to him. Garfield was only twenty, while Fuller was apparently much older and more experienced.

The behavior of the students was exceptionally good. Do not recall a single case of discipline or of public reproof.

Small as our company was and unnoticed by the busy world, it contained one future major-general of the coming Civil War, and the prospective wife of another, who was also to be "Mistress of the White House" and "First Lady of the Land." But there were no halos around their heads and nothing disturbed our perfect democratic equality.

Reminiscences by Alanson Wilcox For forty-six years Alanson Wilcox has been familiar with Hiram and is an honorable part of its history. The following are among the many of his bright reminiscences:

I first came to Hiram in June, 1855, the day after Commencement. Living in Medina county, thirty-five miles west of Hiram, I had been misinformed **First Coming to Hiram.** as to the date of that great day. I drove the distance in a carriage and arranged to attend the Institution the next year. There were giants in those days. Symonds Ryder was Bishop of the church and usually conducted the services. Perhaps the previous winter Isaac Errett held a meeting of days. Mr. **Isaac Errett's Great Meeting.** Ryder was anxious to have his son, Symonds, Jr., come into the church. The meeting had continued two weeks, with several additions in the first few days, but the last week no responses came to the gospel invitation. They decided to close the meeting.

Mr. Errett preached a sermon ending with an apostrophe to God, telling Him what he had done for the salvation of the people, and threw the responsibility on to the sinner to decide the mighty question of life or death. In the old meeting-house at Hiram was a double platform—one elevated for the preacher and a lower one for the elders. Mr. Errett, not expecting any to come forward for confession, did not leave the pulpit; Mr. Ryder was on the lower platform. The congregation rose to sing and, lo! many persons came from all parts of the house to confess their sins and the Christ. Some climbed over the seats in their anxiety to reach the platform. The singers were choked with emotion and could not sing, and there was weeping for joy in all parts of the house. Among those who responded to the gospel invitation was Symonds Ryder, Jr. In the excitement Bishop Ryder turned to Mr. Errett and, drawing both hands down over his face, his eyes streaming with tears, cried out: "Brother Errett, there is too much excitement here," and he was the most excited of them all.

I remember one time Mr. Ryder preached a sermon on "Breaking Steers," and at another time on the "Holy Kiss,"

Bishop Ryder's Sermon.

and when Zeb Rudolph's boarders went home they continued the discussion, and W. H. Prehm, from Illinois, suggested that the immediate application of the subject would be pleasant and stepped to one of Mr. Rudolph's daughters, and they both vigorously responded in giving the "Holy Kiss."

The first time I saw James A. Garfield was in the assembly room of the old meeting-house. He was visiting

First Sight of Garfield.

Hiram from Williams College. He was pointed out to me while the congregation was standing and singing. Mr. Garfield stood erect, his head leaning back and his face turned to heaven, and with great emphasis he joined with the others in singing—

"How firm a foundation, ye saints of the Lord,
Is laid for your faith in his excellent word."

Teacher Garfield was full of resources and did not always confine the class to the text-book. He utilized the

The Teacher Garfield. things that were occurring to illustrate a subject or a lesson. One day when he was hearing a class in Kames' Elements of Criticism, the stove-pipe came out of the chimney, and, while the janitor was putting it back into place, Mr. Garfield asked members of the class to express that act in various phrases. One said "put it in;" others, "crowd it in," "shove it in," "place it in," "adjust the pipe in its place," "cram it in," "drive it in," "place it back," and "cautiously proceed to place the pipe in its original position." In this way he added zest to the recitation and cultivated the discriminating powers and tastes of the members of the class.

Harvey W. Everest boarded at Zeb Rudolph's. His lady-love was Miss Sarah Harrison, and she boarded at C. L. P. Reno's. Being both student and teacher, he could call on his sweetheart often. While his **What Happened to H. W. Everest.** visits were above criticism, when he returned to the Rudolph mansion he tried not to disturb the household and guests; and would take off his shoes and ascend the stairs in stocking feet, noiseless as a cat after a mouse, to his sleeping apartment. The young American boarders had their funny natures stirred by this stealthy midnight coming; and so one night they got together all the tinware of the household and fastened it together at the head of the stairs and so connected it with a card, which was fastened to the door, that when it was opened the whole kit of tinware would, like an avalanche, tumble down stairs, making noise enough to wake every sleeper in the house. And so, though the course of true love ran smoothly, the way up stairs was obstructed and the sparking hero was ushered to his apartments with noise of many tin pans and amid the suppressed laughter of the household.

Once upon a time I sang in the Glee Club, and in one public entertainment I whistled the solo, "Listen to the Mocking Bird." I went out preaching a **Mr. Wilcox as a Singer and Poet and Preacher.** few times, and the first dollar I received for preaching was from the Mantua church, and with that I bought "The Christian System." One day I had to write an essay, and going to my boarding house at Mr. Rudolph's, I found them at the annual autumnal slaughter of swine, and I wrote a poem on "Killing Pigs."

Being a member of the Delphic Society, they sent me to Cleveland to select and purchase some kind of metal badge for the officers and members. No one in the society knew what was wanted for the emblem. I visited watchmakers and hardware stores and finally decided to take the society some silver stars and other ornaments used on horse bridles. I was as proud of my purchase as was Bellerophon when he carried the beautiful and ornamented bridle to catch the flying horse Pegasus. Henry M. James was a committee to take them back.

In those days the stream east of Hiram was larger than it is now, and a dam had been placed in it half way between the bridge and sugar camp. One Monday the gentlemen students were going bathing in the dam and there was an ambitious strife to see who would get in first. Then came the race and disrobing, and I was among the first to dive into the water. With head under water I swam across the pond. That was the only way I could swim. Then I dove, and was swimming under water to the shore on the opposite side, and, raising my head above the water, I found it deep —over my head. I could not swim and down I went—once—twice—three times, and the third time my feet touched bottom; and while all the acts of my life were passing in my mind, I thought if I could give a spring with my feet on the bottom and rise up out of the water and call my companions to help, I would be saved—and so I did. They formed a line of hands and drew me to the shore and onto the bank and rolled me over, and did the best they could to relieve me of the extra dose of Adam's ale which I had imbibed. I was several days in recovering from this calamity; and I think the old lady was half right at least who told her boy he must not go into the water till he had learned to swim.

I well remember the picnics when the Hiram Sunday-school turned out with one, two and four-horse rigs and

A Hiram Sunday School Picnic.

went to Nelson Ledges and returned by Garrettsville. I was selected as marshal. Holland Brown, father of Jessie Brown Pounds, furnished me with a white, high-headed, galloping saddle horse for the occasion. I was dressed in light colored clothes and wore a red sash. The horse was proud of himself and rider and galloped gaily up and down the line of the procession. The next Sunday I was to preach in Garrettsville, and some of the old dames doubted whether such a gay rider could be an acceptable Christian, and especially a preacher. But I lived through it.

The Walk Around the Cemetery Square.

One year there was a *fad* in the Institution on walking for health; and a score and more of students walked round the Raymond, Norton, Cemetery Square before breakfast. Charles P. Bowler and I performed this feat several times.

J. H. Rhodes had a large class in elocution and for deep breathing and exploding the vowel sounds the line would be formed on the campus and the whole

J. H. Rhodes' Class in Elocution.

welkin would ring with A—*a*—A up to OU—*ou*—OU. Some were reminded of the story Mr. Garfield told about the boys who were learning the Greek alphabet; they rushed out of the school room shouting, "Alpha-Beta-Gamma-Delta." An old lady passing along was frightened and ran into a house, declaring that the boys were going to kill her. When asked what the boys did, she declared that they ran out of the school house and after her, exclaiming: "After her," "beat her," "catch her," "jam her," "kill her." Poor soul! She mistook the alphabetic names for words of death.

Many Changes.

The old water ram that forced the spring near "Independence Hall" to the fountain on the campus has given place to the complete system of water works; the tallow candle to the electric light plant; the old "stone jug," where I taught school, to the village school house; the old college building to the new: the Methodist church house to the magnificent Y. M. C. A. building; and Dr. Trask and Dr. Squire for Dr. Page and Dr. Dyson.

"I cannot sing the old songs,
  I sung long years ago,
For heart and voice would fail me,
  And foolish tears would flow;
For by-gone hours come o'er my heart
  With each familiar strain.

"I cannot sing the old songs,
  For visions come again
Of golden years departed,
  And years of weary pain;
Perhaps, my earthly fetters broken
  And my spirit ever free,
My voice will know the old songs
  For all eternity."

ECLECTIC DAYS.

Long ways back, but I was there, yes, in 1851.

When the erysipelas epidemic raged in February, 1852, I went to Aurora for Lucy Baldwin, a young lady of whom there is kindest memory, and drove Alanson Baldwin's span of gray horses through a drifting snow storm, in bringing her to the bedside of Anna Hershey, at Mrs. Drake's. Anna died. The remains were taken north on a sleigh, to the Lake Shore railroad, thence to Williamsville, N. Y. The anxiety and distress at the time closed the school, but the chapel was quite full when the closing hour came. The valedictory was set over to me. Doubtless good as scores of such since, but none knew the effort it cost. Greatness is from occasion and surroundings, as well as brains. Of the students of that year Garfield had been one, but was away teaching during the winter.

Reminiscences by W. J. Ford.

The following memoir of Miss Anna C. Hershey, the first student to die at Hiram, by her sister, Mrs. Franc H. Rogers, of East Milton, Massachusetts, is a touching tribute to the memory of one of Hiram's earliest and noblest students:

Anna C. Hershey.

Anna C. Hershey and her sister Marie, of Williamsville, New York, were students at Hiram in the fall of 1851 and the winter of 1852. They were daughters of the saintly Benjamin Hershey, who, hearing the plea of the Disciples from the lips of Porter Thomas, John Henry and others, renounced Universalism and became an elder in the Christian church at Williamsville. After his death his widow, Mrs. Esther Hershey, continued the training of her children in the faith of their parents. Old established and well-equipped denominational schools were close at hand; but the then new school at Hiram was preferred, because it was to foster New Testament Christianity. Hiram was nearly two hundred miles away, and could be reached only by steamboat and stage. Anna was a very healthy girl, 21 years old, but in February she took a severe cold, from which she could not rally, and after a week of intense suffering, on February 12, 1852, her spirit took its flight. The next day they started with the body in a sleigh to carry it back to her widowed mother in Williamsville. Peter Hershey and Clark Ransom, students from Erie county, also Miss Ada Becket, of Canada, and Professor Norman Dunshee accompanied the bereaved sister Marie on the sad journey. Thus ended the career of one of Hiram's first and one of Hiram's brightest students—a young lady whose Christian character was no less marked than her mental endowment.

A Famous Dramatic Entertainment.

In the afternoon of Commencement Day, June 10, 1858, a colloquy formed a part of the program. Its title was "Orsini's Conspiracy," and the personæ colloquii were :

Louis Napoleon,	E. A. Ford
Pellissier, Grand Marshal,	M. F. Pratt
Billault, Prime Minister,	Amzi Atwater
Orsini,	H. C. White
Pierre,	B. H. Bostwick
Rudio,	C. B. Harris
Dr. Pironti,	H. S. Chamberlain
Montano,	O. N. Ferry
Castello,	R. L. Chapman
Sir John Grenville,	J. S. Dille
Baron Von Hamburg,	C. A. Bennett
Count Villier,	F. M. Green

(Orsini, Pierre, Rudio, Dr. Pironti, Montano, Castello — Conspirators.)

1st Citizen,	- - - - -	H. Woods
2d Citizen,	- - - - -	Sutton Newcomb
Empress Eugenie	- - - -	Electa V. Beecher
Madame Orsini,	- - - -	Rachel Shannon
Theressa Montano,	- - - -	Jennie Ferry
Felicia Orsini,	- - - - -	Hattie M. Drake

The exercises of the afternoon besides the colloquy consisted of the following parts:

1 LATIN SALUTATORY, - - - - - -
        T. H. Darrah, *Ebensburg, Pa.*
2 ORATION, - - - - Constitutional Reform
        Clark Braden, *Bazetta.*
3 ORATION, - - - - - Mythology
        H. D. Carlton, *Shalersville.*
4 ORATION . - - - - British India
        W. H. Turner, *Troy.*
5 ORATION - - - - The Crusades
        C. P. Bowler, *Auburn.*
6 GERMAN DIALOGUE - - - (From Schiller.)
        W. Schmickley, *Germany.* E. B. Monroe, *Mogadore.*
7 ORATION - - - - - The Inner Life
        W. L. Hayden, *Deerfield.*
8 ORATION - - - - King Philip
        P. C. Reed, *Auburn.*
9 ORATION - - - The Grammar of Nature
        A. Wilcox, *Hiram.*
10 VALEDICTORY - - - The Great Awakening
        O. C. Atwater, *Mantua Station.*

Of some of the characters in the play Mr. Ford has furnished a brief description:

Frank M. Green

Frank M. Green.   You know him. He was here early as 1853, and in 1858 took part in a play written by Miss Booth and Garfield, "The Conspiracy of Count De Orsini," which was brought on the stage in the big tent Commencement Day afternoon. Frank played against Hiram Chamberlain, and brandished his sword with great skill, cutting right and left, until we thought him fit to send to West Point; but he turned to a better calling. He grasped the "Sword of the Spirit," and became a famous preacher, clear of mind and heart, "rightly dividing the word of truth." In the missionary field, he swept the round of the States, and on from the sands of the South to Nova Scotia.

You will excuse me for saying that, ten years later than 1858, he was in about the best real performance I know of. With his wife attending, amid the June roses of Lubec in old Maine, he said the ceremony at the wedding of Mary E. Staples and W. J. Ford. It was one of his many feats of this kind, but good and lasting.

When his home county of Summit wanted a popular champion of the rights of the people, one who had convictions and would stand squarely by them, front face against the enemy and the trickery of politicians, they elected him, and he did splendid service in the Ohio legislature.

HIRAM S. CHAMBERLAIN

Hiram S. Chamberlain. In the play, made a desperate sabre stroke, his sword sweeping the wind on Frank's head, and the whizzing clip within an inch of his nose, in such terrifying swiftness that the shining blade flew from his hand and went crashing on the floor, before the excited crowd, to whom he was in dead earnest.

During the Civil War he entered the Union army and served with distinguished ability. After the war he remained in the South, where he yet lives. His home is at Chattanooga, Tennessee, and he is an honorable and honored citizen of his adopted state.

"Hi, old High." The boys all liked him, and would swing their hats and sing. He did not forget the Eclectic School days, and the play of 42 years ago, when he made a generous gift at the Jubilee of 1900.

ELECTA V. BEECHER

Electa V. Beecher. Was the Empress Eugenie in that play. She swept the stage in regal robes, and was the one admired in the eyes of ambitious youth, and envied by the girls. She married, and has been since the queen supreme in the home of George Miller in Freedom and Garrettsville, and has led on in the interests of good society.

George Miller and Mrs. Dr. Lee were students in 1851. George roomed first right hand door going into the basement.

ELIAS A. FORD

Elias A. Ford. Was Louis Napoleon, and had a military hat of the 1812 time, with red plume and white tipped feather. His part was played and kingdom won. How quick, from this acting on the stage, to the real. In the dread carnage of Stone River, his regiment, Forty-first Ohio, fought on the pivot of battle, facing all points of compass, the last day of December, 1862. He was last in command of Company B. A minnie ball passed through his right lung. Lying on a mattress in an army wagon, New Year's day, in a fearful race of four miles over the pike, from pursuit of Wheeler's cavalry, the blood jolted in clots from his wound, upon the mattress. The furious driver came to a blockade in the road, but sprang his horses in a cut up the bank, rounding the Pike curve, in the rear of the Fourth Michigan cavalry. The fire from their revolving rifles, when the pursuing rebels came round the road bend, dropped six men from their saddles. That jolting ride, and onward to Nashville, saved E. A.'s life. In twenty days he was writing from the hospital in regular correspondence to the Cleveland *Herald*. Being made brevet captain and honorably discharged, he went to railroading, and became one of the first passenger agents in this country, and is in the Pennsylvania service. His palace car has better style than Napoleon's militia hat and red feather of 1858, but he is plain E. A. F. all the same, and remembered the Eclectic in a Jubilee gift.

Of those who took the prominent parts of the play all are yet living.

Mary M. Buckingham. Mary M. Buckingham's name appears in the roll of students in the first year of the Eclectic Institute. Of her home and history the following are interesting particulars:

On the west side of the road, across the valley north from Hiram Hill was an orchard in 1851. It was on the farm bought by John Buckingham, and in it the first regular commencement exercises were held. On that occasion Emily Ford had on a red sash and marched the girls' column down the hill road. The second regular commencement was in the tree shade, at the northeast corner of the campus, and Garfield was Ahazuerus, and Lucretia, Esther. Mary saw all there was of these display days, and she knows as much town history and Eclectic story of student freaks and solid progress as any one now in this modern water fed and electric lighted town.

The closing century found her one of a quartette of ladies, Miss Marcia Henry, Mrs. —— Churchill and Mrs. W. J. Ford, in chapel on watch December 31st, 1900, and all of them read historic notes to a delighted town multitude.

Mary graduated at Oberlin, went to Kansas and married John L. Patterson, a good lawyer in Lawrence. She taught in the University and at other points in the State. Cheerful as a girl, she is lifting along her burdens in the most hopeful and helpful way, and is again teaching, now in the old Buckingham home at the foot of the hill. Of her scholars, there are two real Japanese girls, who are being educated for mission work, and she has pride in such bright students. She is matron of the "Ladies' History and Culture Class" in Hiram, and with steady dignity presides over and questions such a modern deliberative body, and considers it a high honor.

The career of Mormonism at Hiram was brief, but hot while it lasted. Symonds Ryder, who for a short time gave heed to its advocates and lived in the midst of the scenes he describes, says: "In the winter of 1831 Joseph Smith, with others, had an appointment in the south school house in Hiram. Such was the apparent piety, sincerity and humility of the speakers, that many of the hearers were greatly affected, and thought it impossible that such preachers should lie in wait to deceive. During the next spring and summer several converts were made, and their success seemed to indicate an immediate triumph in Hiram. But when they went to Missouri to lay the foundation of the splendid city of Zion, and also of the temple, they left their papers be-

The
Mormon Episode
at Hiram.

hind. This gave their new converts an opportunity to become acquainted with the internal arrangement of their church, which revealed to them the horrid fact that a plot was laid to take their property from them and place it under control of Joseph Smith, the prophet. This was too much for the Hiramites, and they left the Mormonites faster than they had ever joined them, and by fall the Mormon church in Hiram was a very lean concern. But some who had been dupes of this deception, determined not to let it pass with impunity; and, accordingly, a company was formed of citizens from Shalersville, Garrettsville, and Hiram in March, 1832, and proceeded to headquarters in the darkness of the night, and took Smith and Rigdon from their beds and tarred and feathered them both, and let them go. This had the desired effect, which was to get rid of them. They soon left for Kirtland. All who continued with the Mormons, and had any property, lost all; among whom was John Johnson, one of our most worthy men; also, Esquire Snow, of Mantua, who lost two or three thousand dollars." The letter from which this extract is taken was written to A. S. Hayden by Symonds Ryder, February 1, 1868.

In 1831 Mr. Ryder was informed that by special revelation he had been appointed and commissioned an elder of the Mormon church. "His commission came, and he found his name misspelled. Was the Holy Spirit so fallible as to fail even in orthography? Beginning with this challenge, his strong, incisive mind and honest heart were brought to the task of re-examining the ground on which he stood;" and soon the spell of enchantment was broken, and the delusion was ended.

Somewhat more in detail, Hartwell Ryder, son of Symonds Ryder, and now past his eightieth year, on the night of December 31, 1900, at a public meeting in Hiram, described the tarring and feathering of Rigdon and Smith: "Large numbers met in the Hinckley brick-yard at night. They organized, one party to go to Rigdon's house, and another to the Johnson house. The move was to be secret. Not a word was to be spoken. Rigdon was taken out, near to an oak tree, now standing on the south side of the road, and treated to a coat of tar and feathers. All that summer after, the boy Hartwell saw feathers on the ground. Where the Stevens house now stands was the Johnson house, and there the other party found Joe Smith in bed, in the west room, above the cellar story. They put him out from this loft, down into the hands of those outside. About the time this was done, at Rigdon's a young woman in another room had been wakened, and was striking a light to see what was going on. Perceiving there would be a revelation of the characters in this religious play, a tall man inside, imitating the voice of Elder Symonds Ryder, commanded that they be let out. The outsiders opened the door, and out they went, before the light of discovery came. It is but just to say that Ryder had nothing to do with this affair. Smith was taken about twenty rods south, and received his coat of tar and feathers. Thus ended the Mormon absurdity in Hiram in 1831-2. Some twelve or fifteen went off into the wilds of Missouri, and were, with the church, driven from there, and lost their property.

Hiram students were not less patriotic in the great war between the States, North and South, from 1861 to 1865, than those of other Institutions in northern Ohio. Of those who held high rank were Major General James A. Garfield and Brigadier General William B. Hazen, **Hiram Soldiers 1861-1865.** both of whom were among its earliest students. The larger part of the Hiram soldiery, however, belonged to the two literary societies, the Delphic and the Hesperian. The following is as nearly a complete and accurate list as could be obtained:

Soldiers from the Delphic Society. 1—*David D. Bard,* Capt. Co. I, 104th O. V. I. Mortally wounded in battle at Franklin, Tenn., Nov. 30, 1864.

2—*W. F. Bard,* Co. F, 45th O. V. I. Died in prison at Andersonville, Ga., March 25, 1864.

3—*Clifton A. Bennett,* Capt., 1st Regt. U. S. colored troops.

4—*Charles H. Bill,* Capt., Co. G, 2d O. V. cavalry. Mustered out with regiment at close of the war.

5—*Charles P. Bowler,* Co. C, 7th Regt. O. V. I. Killed in battle at Cedar Mountain, Va., Aug. 9, 1862.

6—*Jesse L. Bowell,* Co. D, 143d O. V. I. Mustered out with regiment. Deceased.

7—*D. W. Buckingham,* Co. F, 2d U. S. sharpshooters. Wounded at Gettysburgh, Pa, July 3 ,1863. Died in service Nov. 26, 1863.

8—*L. L. Campbell,* Lieut. Co. L, 2d O. V. I. Mustered out with regiment at close of war.

9—*G. W. Carson,* Co. A, 42d Regt. O. V. I. Mustered out with regiment at close of war.

10—*H. S. Chamberlain,* Lieut. Co. B, 2d O. V. C. Capt. and A. Q. M.

11—*W. P. Chamberlain,* Lieut. Co. A, 23d O. V. I. Mustered out with regiment.

12—*W. H. Clapp,* Lieut. Co. A, 42d O. V. I. Lieut. Col. 21st Ind. U. S. A.

13—*C. W. Clark,* Co. A, 42d O. V. I. Lieut. U. S. colored troops.

14—*Wallace Coburn,* Co. C, 7th O. V. I. Mortally wounded at Winchester, Pa., March 23, 1862.

15—*P. M. Cowles,* Co. A, 42d O. V. I. Mustered out with regiment at close.

16—*Frank A. Derthick,* Co. C, 150th O. V. I. Mustered out with regiment.

17—*A. R. Dewey,* Co. C, 150th O. V. I. Mustered out with regiment.

18—*O. E. Dewey,* Co. E, 177th O. V. I. Mustered out with regiment at close.

19—*Hiram Durkee,* Co. D, 23d O. V. I. Killed in battle at South Mountain, in Maryland, Sept. 14, 1862.

20—*E. H. Eggleston,* Capt. Co. M., Maj. 2d O. V. C. Wounded at Hanover C. H. in Virginia, May 30, and at Cedar Creek, Va., Oct. 19, 1864.

21—*J. C. Ellis,* Co. H., 150th O. V. I. Mustered out with regiment.

22—*D. D. Evans,* Co. E, 167th O. V. I. Mustered out with regiment.

23—*Parmenas C. Faunce,* Co. I, 6th O. V. C. Wounded at battle of Wilderness, Va., May 7, 1864. Disabled.

24—*E. A. Ford,* Lieut. Co. B, 41st O. V. I. Wounded at Stone River, Tenn., Dec. 31, 1862. Disabled.